TURNING TIDES

TURNING TIDES:
Caribbean Intersections in the Americas and Beyond

Heather Cateau and Milla Cozart Riggio
Editors

IAN RANDLE PUBLISHERS
Kingston • Miami

First published in Jamaica, 2019 by
Ian Randle Publishers
16 Herb McKenley Drive
Box 686
Kingston 6
www.ianrandlepublishers.com

©Heather Cateau and Milla Cozart Riggio
ISBN: 978-976-637-980-3

**Cataloguing-In-Publication Data available from the
National Library of Jamaica**

All rights reserved. While copyright in the selection and editorial material is vested in Heather Cateau and Milla Cozart Riggio, copyright in individual chapters belongs to their respective authors and no part of this publication may be reproduced, stored in a retrieval system or transmitted in any form or by any means electronic, photocopying, recording or otherwise, without the prior express permission of the publisher and author.

Cover photographs:
David Rudder and Beryl McBurnie provided by Banyan archive
Peter Minshall: photograph by Todd Gulick.
C.L.R. James: National Library of Jamaica
Dance of the Cloth: photograph by Charlotte Elias
The Red Chador Series: photograph by Masahiro Sugano
Amy and Marcus Garvey in Hartford: photograph by Pablo Delano

Book and Cover Design by Ian Randle Publishers
Printed and Bound in the United States of Ameica

TABLE OF CONTENTS

Foreword: Declaring the Conference Open » vii
    Earl Lovelace

Acknowledgements » ix

Introduction: Turning Tides – and Pages » xi
    Milla Cozart Riggio and Heather Cateau

Part I: Keynotes and Border Crossings

1. C.L.R. James and the Misunderstanding of American Civilization: The Containment of a Post-colonial Critique » 1
    H. Reuben Neptune

2. Connecticut-Caribbean Connections: A Focus on the British Caribbean from the 17th to the 21st Centuries » 22
    Heather Cateau

3. A New Mediterranean: The Caribbean in the Euro-American Imaginary » 36
    Gary Reger

4. Africa and the African Diaspora in the Curriculums of Central America's Caribbean Countries » 55
    Dario A. Euraque

Part II: Negotiating Cultural Identity – Gender, Religion and Ethnicity

5. Ramabai and Gainder, Gaiutra and Sujaria are Turning Tides: Great-grandmothers' and Great-granddaughters' Odysseys and Narratives of the *Kala Pani* » 73
    Judith Misrahi-Barak

6. Expressions of Feminist Forms in the Indo-Muslim Community of Trinidad » 88
    Halima-Sa'adia Kassim

7. Itinerant Caribbean Feminist Forms: Islamic Feminism in Trinidad and Tobago » 104
    Janet L. Bauer

8. In Praise of Excellent Ettie: Narrative Constructions of the Affective Impact of Caribbean Migrant Women's Work » 126
    Paula Morgan

Part III: Performing Cultural Identity – Carnival Arts and Music

9. It's not all Sequins and Bikinis? Power, Performance and Play in the Leeds and Trinidad Carnival » 145
   Emily Zobel Marshall

10. Rudder: International Chantuelle as In-zile » 165
    Louis Regis

11. The Current Calypso Music Scene in Trinidad and its Outlook: The Perspective of an International Follower of the Genre » 179
    Urs Berger

Part IV: Challenging Cultural Assumptions – The Research X-Change

Research X-Change Introduction » 193
Milla Cozart Riggio

12. Gender Without Borders Special Session: Research X-Change Workshop – LGBTQ Students and Communities » 195
    Brunhild Kring and Cheryl Greenberg

    Diversity, 'Perversity' and Anger » 209
    Gerard Hutchinson

13. Culture and Memory in the Caribbean » 211
    Nicole Alea, Katija Khan, Consuelo Pedro and Sarah A. Raskin

Part V: Culture in Action – The Artists Speak

14. The Museum of the Old Colony » 247
    Pablo Delano

15. A Proposal for 'performing Marcus and Amy' » 252
    Tony Hall

    'Marcus and Amy' in Hartford, Connecticut » 266
    Dario A. Euraque

16. Inside the People TV, Our Images, Our Stories, Money in the Bank » 269
    Christopher Laird

17. Artists Talk: Peter Minshall and Anida Yoeu Ali » 307
    Moderated by Christopher Cozier

Contributors » 327

Index » 337

Foreword:
Declaring the Conference Open

Delivered February 18, 2016

Earl Lovelace

The conference *Turning Tides* places all societies touched by the Caribbean sea and Atlantic ocean at the centre of Western Hemispheric discussions. And seeks to provoke wide-reaching and trans-disciplinary conversations about the concerns that intersect the cultures and societies bordered by the Atlantic Ocean and beyond. These conversations are important and can clarify for small poor societies and big rich ones what is happening in what we hope is still our world.

Some of us used to think of Globalization as a one way street, with finished goods and services, ideas, technologies, leisure activities, amusements flowing from the North to the South. And nothing flowing back. The other side to this traffic is people. Those who consume these emblems of Western success and wealth – tv, film, video and internet – want to get to the societies that produce them. They want to get to the promised land, and they do so to such a degree that they begin to change significantly the make-up of the country in which they were presumed to be guests.

All over Europe the previously colonized are now making their presence felt in the capitals of what used to be their mother countries. They do not just melt into this new world, they come with their cultural forms, their carnivals and dance hall, with their football boots and cricket bats and the place begins to change. London carnival attracts as many people as the whole population of Trinidad. New York and Toronto are big carnival scenes that tell the impact of these immigrants on the host countries.

What is the impact of this kind of cultural change on the different communities that make up America? What do these developments have to do with what appears to be a renewed racism, with immigration, with racial profiling? What do they have to do with what appears to be a new insularity and self-absorption in previous colonial capitals?

On the other hand, those who live in the previous colonies, consuming the culture and ideas and goods, feel ourselves living in a world over which we have no control. Those intellectuals living abroad now quite rightly question the idea of nation. They see it as an outmoded concept and see themselves as a nomadic people lifting their tents to wherever the grass is green. Where is home? What is home? And there are questions waiting for us to address – Federation – outstanding questions from colonialism that we are only articulating now: Amerindian slaughter, reparatory justice for Africans' unpaid labour in the enslavement era, Haiti.

The more closely we look at our condition today the more we feel the need for enlightened conversations. The world depends on us maintaining and applying the values that affirm what it is to be human. These conversations will become more productive if we have them as neighbours, with a responsibility to the place we share and with responsibility to the people we share it with.

It is an honour to declare this conference open.

Earl Lovelace with UWI Princpal Clement Sankat, Trinity President Joanne Berger-Sweeney and Keynote speaker Dr. H. Reuben (Harvey) Neptune, Conference opening, Feb. 18, 2016.
(Photograph by Pablo Delano. All Delano photographs used with permission).

Acknowledgements

This project was anchored by an organizing committee which had a core in Connecticut (CT) and one in St. Augustine. On the Trinidad side, we must say thanks to the former University of the West Indies (UWI) Principal Clement Sankat, the former Dean of Engineering and now Principal of the St. Augustine Campus Brian Copeland and Sharan Singh of the International Office. The St. Augustine Committee was headed by Dean Cateau and included Dr Armando Garcia, Dr Karen Sanderson-Cole, Dr Renée Figuera and Dr Krishna Seunarinesingh. We must also acknowledge the hard work of Megan Marshall, Ronald Francis and Melanie Pouchet, the Research Assistants in the Faculty of Humanities and Education whose job it was to pull the Conference together on the ground. Maria Gomez and the thoughtful staff of UWI's University Inn, as well as Gerard Ramsawak and Oda van der Heijden of the Pax Guest House, invaluably offered a 'home away from home' for our participants. Christopher Cozier and Sean Leonard of Alice Yard provided an alternative venue in Port of Spain. We also cannot forget the Trinity-in-Trinidad Study Away coordinators and staff Shamagne Bertrand, Florence Blizzard, Gregory Bertrand and Tony Hall, as well as Sunity Maharaj-Best of the Lloyd Best Institute of the West Indies, and our tireless Trinidad drivers led by Antony Andrews and Ivan LaRose. Raviji of the Hindu Prachar Kendra assisted with the cultural performances. These Trinis were joined by countless others – highlighted by the performers and artistes who gave freely of their time to showcase their culture: Brother Resistance, Felix Edinborough as Pierrot Grenade, the Ronald Alfred family of jab jabs, Ms. Poojaa Malhotra and her Hindu dancers, and many more.

On the Trinity side, we owe equal thanks to ex-President James Jones and former CFO Paul Mutone, who first conceived the idea of Trinity House with Principal Sankat and Sharan Singh of UWI, and President Joanne Berger-Sweeney, who made it a reality. The Trinity side of the Conference organizing Committee was headed by Professors

Dario Euraque and Pablo Delano, now co-Directors of Trinity's new Center for Caribbean Studies, and the Center's first Director Leslie Desmangles. The programme subcommittee included Professors Garth Myers, Davarian Baldwin, Stefanie Chambers, Pablo Delano, and Eric Galm, who helped to select the more than twenty Trinity professors who trekked from Hartford, CT, to join us at *Turning Tides*. Deans Sonia Cardenas and Melanie Stein provided the support that allowed Trinity faculty to make the journey. Pablo Delano was the official photographer of the Conference. Juan Carlos Euraque drove for us literally day and night. The backbone for this project was reinforced by Lisa Sapolis, who led our Study Away office during the time we developed the Trinity-in-Trinidad Program, along with Eleanor Emerson, then Acting Director of Study Away, and associate Zachary McInnes. Without History Department Administrative Assistant Gigi St. Peters, supported by English Department Admin Assistants Margaret Grasso and Christina Bolio, our Conference could not have happened.

Neither the Conference nor the book would have been possible without the financial underwriting from the Caribbean and the United States (US): in Trinidad and Tobago, from the Faculty of Humanities and Education of The University of the West Indies, the Tourism and Industrial Development Company of Trinidad and Tobago (TIDCO), and the Ministry of Sport; at Trinity College, particularly from the Offices of the President and Dean, the Department of History, the Allan K. Smith Endowment of the English Department, and the Center for Caribbean Studies. The Lloyd Best Institute of the West Indies (LBIWI) and the Faculty of Humanities and Education at UWI (St. Augustine) provided space and facilities for Professor Riggio during the final assembly of the text; Shamagne Bertrand assisted with final editing; Todd Gulick invaluably helped ensure the accuracy of both text and Minshall images in 'Artists Talk'; Sunity Marahaj-Best, Professsor John Agard and Marguerite Lucerne provided housing and, along with Gregory Bertrand, transport for Professor Riggio.

Our deepest appreciation goes to Ian Randle and his professional staff, who created this book. Cross-cultural projects create many challenges. One of the biggest for us was the language itself: how to mediate between British Caribbean and US English. Our solution was to use British spellings for many words, but to use 'z' instead of 's' for words for which these spellings represent cultural variants. The hybrid English that resulted is in itself an emblem of the integration of cultures which we hope this book represents.

Introduction:
Turning Tides – and Pages

Milla Cozart Riggio and Heather Cateau

What happens when we reposition our understanding of 'The Caribbean' and broaden our thinking beyond the traditional major players in the geo-political sphere?[1] Guided by this question, the University of the West Indies (St. Augustine Campus, Trinidad and Tobago) and Trinity College (Hartford, Connecticut, United States [US]) collaborated to produce *Turning Tides: Caribbean Intersections in the Americas and Beyond*. This international conference was held on The UWI St. Augustine Campus and at special venues in Port of Spain, Trinidad, between February 18–20, 2016. By placing all societies touched by the Caribbean Sea and Atlantic Ocean at the centre of Western Hemispheric discussions, *Turning Tides* took the concept of intersections seriously. It provided a forum for thinking beyond regions, across languages, and amongst the humanities, social sciences, and the natural sciences.

At the same time, UWI and Trinity College affirmed the relationship that had been bringing Trinity College students to Trinidad since 1998. Artistes and thinkers such as Tony Hall, Earl Lovelace, Hollis 'Chalkdust' Liverpool, Peter Minshall, André Tanker, Lloyd Best, Sunity Maharaj-Best, and Caribbean Nobel Prize winner Derek Walcott, among many others, had in their turn travelled to Trinity College to teach, direct, perform, talk, and enrich the Trinity College community. Trinidadian students have found a home in our Northern *Trini'ty* for the past twenty years. This rare academic, cultural, and artistic partnership has not only created a cross-Atlantic Trini family, but it also turns the tides, bringing the Americas together in a way we hoped to solidify with the Conference and its aftermath. To confirm and consolidate this partnership, UWI built a Trinity House for students and study abroad staff on The UWI, St. Augustine Campus. UWI Principal Clement Sankat and Trinity College President Joanne Berger-Sweeney inaugurated the House during *Turning Tides* (see illustration).

Trinity College President Joanne Berger-Sweeney and UWI Principal Clement Sankat dedicate Trinity House, Feb. 19, 2016.
(Photograph by Pablo Delano)

Designed to be inclusive, *Turning Tides* provoked wide-reaching and transdisciplinary conversations about the instabilities, changes, developments, perspectives and future trends of what we call the Grand Caribbean: all the regions, whether insular or mainland, that ring the Caribbean sea or are implicated in Caribbean culture, from New Orleans to Honduras, Costa Rica, and beyond. At the same time – and this book reflects a similar focus – the culture of Trinidad and Tobago itself, where the Conference was held, took centre stage. Of the 17 pieces in the book, well over half focus on Trinidad, although when possible within a larger diasporic, Caribbean, North American, and British (even Middle Eastern) range.

Our aim was to host a Conference with international academic presenters, but not to presume rigid barriers between artists, scholars, and activists. Iconic figures like Brother Resistance (Lutalo Masimbo) moderated sessions. In format the Conference included panels, individual papers, posters, roundtable discussions, performances, the premier exhibition of Pablo Delano's *Museum of the Old Colony,* and some alternative session formats. The aim was to take advantage of the unique performative culture of Trinidad and Tobago while engaging international movements across land, sea and culturescapes. The themes were broad in scope. We welcomed proposals that dealt with but were not limited to:

- First Peoples/Indigenous Peoples
- Colonialism, Imperialism and Capitalism
- Diasporic Societies and Transculturation
- Religions and Rituals
- Gender and Sexuality
- Ecosystems and Ecologies
- Technology and Innovation
- Carnival, Festivals and Heritage
- Sports and Sports Management
- Language, Culture and Social Media
- Governance, Economy and Development
- Representations in Film, Art and Media
- Development Challenges – Crime, Education, Migration

One thinks of 'turning tides' as a movement of sometimes raging sea waters that flow in a different, hopefully more favourable direction. Turning pages has something of the same connotation – 'turning the page' or, as we sometimes call it, 'turning over a new leaf', means beginning anew. It is with this sense of new beginnings that we at the University of the West Indies and Trinity College are now turning our tides into pages. The *Turning Tides* Conference lives in the memories of those of us who were privileged to attend it. *Turning Tides,* the book, will extend the life of this event by putting selected essays/presentations from the Conference into print. In keeping with the theme of our interaction, we offer you a book published in the Caribbean, by Ian Randle, a Jamaican publisher.

We cannot hope to induce the spirit of the Conference, or to capture the creative cacophony of events that brought us all together for three days in February, 2016. However, the pieces in this volume reflect the varied nature of the presentations made at the conference. The contributions range from artists' statements to peer-reviewed, culturally inflected chapters, and also peer-reviewed preliminary results of fresh collaborations. All essays have been revised and updated for publication (though 'Artists' Talk', Tony Hall's Marcus Garvey Proposal, and Christopher Laird's Banyan report have kept their original formats). This volume testifies both to the vibrancy of

Turning Tides, the Conference, and of the culture of Trinidad and Tobago within the context of the Grand Caribbean. It reflects the far-reaching interests of a large Caribbean multi-national university and a small New England college, in a region in the US whose connections with the West Indian Caribbean go back to the seventeenth century – and strengthens the nature of the interaction between them. It therefore could not be more fitting that the distinguished Trinidadian novelist Earl Lovelace opened the Conference – and by extension this book.

Part I: Keynotes and Border Crossings. The first of four essays in this section is the revised keynote address of the Conference, in which H. Reuben (Harvey) Neptune assesses 'C.L.R. James and the Misunderstanding of *American Civilisation*', James's posthumously published critique of US culture. Neptune corrects critical misunderstanding of James by tracing his 'interrogation of the totalitarian cultural politics in the Republic' within the context of President Donald Trump's emergence. From this perspective, American history and mythology radically altered when the colonial and post-colonial division morphed from 'New World' and 'Old World' to 'First', 'Second,' and 'Third Worlds.' Promoted to what Neptune calls 'gold medal' status and grouped with Europe, rather than its own hemisphere, the United States – as James perceived it – lost its bearings and its natural destiny as a post-colonial nation, laying the groundwork for the emergence of a pop culture totalitarian leader. In the only paper that was not initially presented at *Turning Tides*, Dean Heather Cateau has revised the Mead History Lecture she delivered at Trinity College: 'Connecticut – Caribbean Connections.' She examines a previously unstudied chapter in relationships between the British Caribbean and the US State of Connecticut from the seventeenth to the twenty-first centuries. Focusing on trade and maritime enslavement, Cateau also shines a new light on a history of exchanges beginning four hundred years ago that we were not even aware existed. In 'A New Mediterranean: The Caribbean in the Euro-American Imaginary,' Gary Reger, a classical historian by training, traces the widespread metaphor of the Caribbean as a 'new Mediterranean' through its complex history, concluding by reframing ways in which these two different 'sunny' regions were thought to function, both as dangerously seductive lures and as cathartic, healing regions. Dario A. Euraque – the Director of the Honduran Institute of Anthropology and History during the 2009 military coup in Honduras – concludes this first section by expanding the reach beyond the insular Caribbean to the sometimes forgotten Central American Caribbean. His detailed and insightful analysis of 'Africa and African Diasporas in the Curriculums of Central American Caribbean' compares the presence and absence of African elements in the curricula of countries throughout Central America (Costa Rica, El Salvador, Guatamala, Honduras, Nicaragua, and Panama).

Part II: Negotiating Cultural Identities: Religion, Gender, and Ethnicity. These four essays focus on gender definitions within the richly divergent ethnicities and religions of Trinidad and Tobago. In 'Ramabai and Gainder, Gaiutra and Sujaria are Turning Tides,' Judith Mizrahi-Barak deals with Hindu female narratives that evoke the crossing of the Kala Pani ('dark waters'), which brought indentured Indian workers in such numbers that, concentrated in Trinidad, they now marginally constitute the largest single ethnicity in the Republic of Trinidad and Tobago (35.43% compared to 34.22% for Afro-Trinidadians, as per 2011 census; see Central Statistical Office, T&T Government, 2012). Trinidadian Halima Sa'adia Kassim and US-based Janet Bauer, who has done extensive field work both in Trinidad and Iran, provide two different looks at the extraordinary women of the Muslim Diaspora in Trinidad and Tobago and elsewhere: Kassim's 'Expressions of feminist forms in the Indo-Muslim community of Trinidad' and Bauer's 'Itinerant Caribbean Feminist Forms: Islamic Feminism in Trinidad and Tobago.' Paula Morgan concludes this section with 'In Praise of Excellent Ettie,' an essay that highlights migrant women's work, both through literary analysis and personal reflection.

Part III: Performing Cultural Identities: Carnival Arts and Calypso. These three essays focus on culture and the arts. In 'It's Not All Sequins and Bikinis? Power, Performance, and Play in the Leeds and Trinidad Carnival,' Emily Marshall compares what is sometimes called the 'Mecca' of Caribbean carnivals (Trinidad) to the oldest continuous Caribbean carnival in Europe, the West Indian carnival of the English City of Leeds, which celebrated its 50 year carnival history in 2017. Louis Regis's 'David Rudder: International chantuelle as Inzile' defines David Rudder, now living in Toronto, as effectively an exile in his own country. In 'The Current Calypso Music in Trinidad and its Outlook,' calypso collector Urs Berger traces the fraught history of both legal and illegal distribution of calypsoes and outlines some options for making calypso music more widely available.

Part IV: Challenging Cultural Assumptions – The Research X-Change. This section turns the tides once more, this time in the direction of the future. Organized by Sunity Maharaj-Best and Milla Cozart Riggio, *The Research X-Change* was an experimental, workshop-based segment of the Conference. Conceptualized as a vehicle through which the Conference could create conversations between scholars, activists and practitioners from North America and the Caribbean, *The Research X-Change* was designed to explore new projects and possibilities, bringing together researchers and change agents who had not previously met. The half dozen sessions are represented here by two essays: Dr. Brunhild Kring of the New York University student health services co-ordinated a workshop that included Luke Sinnette, Lead Social Worker for 'Friends for Life' and Colin Robinson of the Trinidad and Tobago LGBTQI Advocacy group 'CAISO: Sex and Gender Justice,' along with scholars such as Professors Cheryl Greenberg and Donna Marcano (a Trinidadian) of Trinity College. This workshop produced a difficult but productive conversation focusing on LGBTQ issues from a multi-cultural perspective. Drs Kring and Greenberg distilled the essence of that conversation and enhanced it with further research in 'Genders without Borders: LGBTQ Students and Communities.' Dr Gerard Hutchinson of UWI adds a statement appended to this essay. And finally, Trinity Professor Sarah Raskin collaborated with UWI researchers Drs Nicole (Albada) Alea and Katija Khan, and with Consuelo Pedro, a Trinidadian who studied at Trinity College and is now working for her Doctor of Physical Therapy (DPT), to look at the way culture influences the processes of memory in 'Culture and Memory in the Caribbean.' All essays in Sections I – IV have been peer-reviewed.

Part V: Culture in Action – The Artists Speak. This section serves as a creative addendum that changes the tone of the book, as the presence of the artists creatively stirred the waters of the Conference. One of the highlights of the Conference was the opportunity for artists to 'speak' in their varied voices. Photographer Pablo Delano provides a brief peek at the virtual museum premiered in Port of Spain at Alice Yard during *Turning Tides*. Entitled *The Museum of the Old Colony,* this installation – which has now been shown throughout the Americas, from New York to Argentina, Connecticut,

Massachusetts, and the Caribbean – uses the name of a sticky sweet drink ('Old Colony') still served in Delano's native Puerto Rico to identify the unintended ('sticky sweet'?) self-referential satire of photographs taken in Colonial Puerto Rico. Tony Hall's **'performing Marcus and Amy'** offers a proposal for a popular theatre project rehabilitating Marcus Garvey, the Jamaican activist and would be king-maker, whose reach extended from Limon, Costa Rica, to North America with a programmatic intention of returning Africans to their homeland. In the manifestations of this project to date, Garvey and his two wives-collapsed-into-one-persona, both named Amy, reappear in their full splendor, as enacted by Trinidadian actors Michael Cherrie and Penelope Spencer. The Garveys, who first appeared under Tony Hall's direction in Port of Spain during carnival 2016, made a 'State visit' to Hartford, Connecticut, in December, 2017, sponsored by the newly established Center for Caribbean Studies under the auspices of President Berger-Sweeney of Trinity College. In 'Inside The People TV, Our Images, Our Stories, Money in the Bank' Christopher Laird, the Co-founder and Director of Banyan, which houses the largest archive of Caribbean cultural productions, interviews, and other materials, provides a rare overview of the fully-catalogued, climate-protected Banyan archive. This section ends with 'Artists Talk,' a lightly edited conversation between three widely celebrated, internationally acclaimed, unique artists: T&T artist masman Peter Minshall and Cambodian-American performing artist Anida Yoeu Ali, moderated by Trinidad artist Christopher Cozier, a co-founder of the Port of Spain artistic space called Alice Yard.

Envisioned more as a beginning than an ending, *Turning Tides* could not have happened without the cooperation of many who gave generously, both of their time and money from sometimes pressured budgets. We say thanks to our colleagues and supporters in both Trinidad and Connecticut. We are deeply indebted to Ian Randle who had the vision to undertake this publication and to his staff who have seen it through.

Milla Cozart Riggio	Heather Cateau
Trinity College	The University of the West Indies
March, 2018	

Note
1. The opening sentence and portions of the first five paragraphs of this Introduction were taken from the *Turning Tides* Call for Papers, as a way of imbedding that call into the fabric of this proceedings volume.

Part I: Keynotes and Border Crossings

CHAPTER 1
C.L.R. James and the Misunderstanding of American Civilization:
The Containment of a Post-colonial Critique

H. Reuben Neptune

...because it is very easy for the writing of a black man or a West Indian to be admired for the wrong reasons. Derek Walcott[1]

For most of the past two centuries, articulate observers from Latin America and the Caribbean did not regard the United States (US) as part of the enlightened world, at least not the 'world' identified with European nations like France or England or even Germany. Rather, the intelligentsia from *Nuestra America* apprehended the northern Republic far more humbly and familiarly. They saw it as a New World society struggling with 'civilization' in the prevailing Eurocentric sense of the term. To erudite commentators south of the Rio Grande, the Colossus of the North appeared – whatever its vast material might – to be faced with the hemisphere-wide predicament of establishing a sovereign imagination in the wake of modern European colonialism. In fact, when late nineteenth century Latin American *pensadores* drew on Shakespeare's *Tempest* to characterize the nation of Yankees, they cast it not as a culturally sophisticated Prospero, but as a brutish and utilitarian Caliban of a northern kind.[2] Not until the 1970s, over two decades into the Cold War, did thinkers in the rest of the Americas begin to fall for the fiction that Norteamericanos had been so historically privileged that they constituted a 'First World' exception to their 'Third World' continent.

In the light of this crucial yet largely neglected bit of history, the call at the Turning Tides conference to adopt a Pan-American perspective presented a welcome occasion to *turn the tide* against the Cold War world view by putting the US back in its proper hemispheric historical place.[3] The following discussion does so by recalling a Caribbean intellectual tradition of treating Yankees as ordinary 'Americans' in the shared continental sense rather than as representatives of the top tier of the three-world planet, gold medalists in the global games of human progress. It will name a few contributors to this tradition (like George Lamming and Derek Walcott), but the main focus, fittingly, will be on a brilliant writer born and buried just a few miles from the St. Augustine Campus of the University of the West Indies: C.L.R. James. In 1950, after a dozen years of improvised residence in the US, James completed an urgently written prospectus dealing with the culture and history of the Republic. The remarkably farsighted document, titled 'Notes on American Civilization,' was a mammoth proposal for a slim book that James, in fact, never began; consequently, the manuscript languished among his papers for decades. In 1982, though, it was rediscovered by Robert Hill and, a decade later, published with a new abbreviated title, *American Civilization* (1993).[4]

This text, unfortunately, has been the casualty of a profound and consequential misunderstanding. It has been read for the most part as a reflection of the author's intellectual romance with the US, as evidence that ' James basically loved America.'[5] *American Civilization*, according to most commentators, represented the product of a mind seduced and dazzled by its subject. James approached the Republic with the naive zeal of what Trinis call a *'never-see-come-see'*, they suggest.[6] Reviewers who cherish the author for his radical imagination find themselves particularly perplexed. For despite finding merits in *American Civilization*, they too have judged the study as lacking in James's characteristic critical rigour, even (mis)taking the work for a curious excursion into 'American exceptionalism'. Andrew Ross, for example, admits bewilderment that James could analyse the US with such 'quixotically cheery faith'.[7]

This prevailing view of James as too overwhelmed with admiration to produce a critically detached piece about the Republic is woefully false and, worse, perverse. For, in fact, *American Civilization* was not inspired by love and happiness; to the contrary, it was concerned with frustration and violence. Precocious if not prophetic, the manuscript amounted to an interrogation of the totalitarian cultural politics in the Republic. As James states in the introduction, 'I trace as carefully as I can the forces making for totalitarianism in modern American life, and I relate them very carefully to the degradation of human personality under Hitler and under Stalin' (38).

The objective here, though, is to do more than merely correct the historiographical record; a complementary and perhaps deeper task is to relate the misunderstanding of *American Civilization* to reviewers' larger failure to reckon with James's geopolitical imagination. Specifically, they have ignored his apprehension of the North American Republic as a former colony in the New World rather than as part of the First World (The latter, of course, would have been an anachronism, for 'Three Worlds' was not yet a 'thing' in 1950). James conceived of the US as an historical product of modern colonialism, derivative of and yet different from Europe. His frame, it might be said, calibanized the Yankees. Note James's words:

> From the first day of my stay in the US to the last I never made the mistake that so many otherwise intelligent Europeans made of trying to fit that country into European standards. Perhaps for one reason – because of my colonial background – I always saw it for what it was, and not for what I thought it ought to be. I took in my stride the cruelties and anomalies that shocked me and the immense vitality generosity and audacity of those strange people (13).

Once *American Civilization* is read from this geopolitical angle, from this post-colonial vantage point, the work becomes legible as entirely consistent with the intellectual radicalism for which James has become justly famous.

Indeed, the following discussion reinterprets James's text as an effort to decolonize historical knowledge about the 'origins of totalitarianism'. Whereas mid-twentieth century theorists privileged the European terrain (Hannah Arendt quickly comes to mind), he showed his originality by foregrounding North America.[8] Heavily informed by Alexis De Tocqueville, *American Civilization* argued that an unbridled and unreflective romance with Lockean ideas of 'free individuality' since colonial times had disposed people in the Republic toward a totalitarian solution of their frustrations. According to James, the majority of US citizens, labouring under corporate capitalism, had become so desperately despairing at their failure to realize the heroic dreams promised in the nationalist imagination that they were prepared to live vicariously through violently amoral political heroes. Evidence of this totalitarian potential could be found in the society's cultural fictions, James proposed. This explains his serious interest in the nineteenth-century novel *Moby Dick* with its Hitler-like protagonist and in twentieth-century films that supplied sadistic gangster heroes to satisfy the demands of a frustrated national audience. The business of popular culture further interested James because of its heavy investment in the production of 'stars' (Hollywood actors especially) as real-life heroes to be consumed by the admiring American masses. This manufacture of celebrity by the entertainment industrial complex was helping ultimately to condition the nation for a totalitarian leader, he warned.

In fact, a good way to capture the critical post-colonial significance of James's manuscript on the US is by way of an analogy with his earlier and now celebrated work on Haiti. Insofar as *Black Jacobins* has been hailed as an effort to decolonize Europe's revolutionary enlightenment by tracing its ironic connections with slavery, James's 1950 manuscript on the US deserves to be welcomed as an essay to decolonize Europe's liberal freedom by tracing its ironic connections with totalitarianism. A fundamentally unhappy illumination thus lay in this text. To be sure, James composed it with such bright intellectual energy that the dark ominous subject matter can easily disappear in a superficial reading. Yet to miss that his central concern was indigenous totalitarianism is a grave error. James, it turns out, formulated a critical problem uncannily appropriate for our times. Though he certainly had no way of predicting the 'human pseudo-event' that is President Donald Trump, it is almost impossible today to not read *American Civilization* as an advanced warning about a heroic style of cultural politics many now despairingly dub 'Trumpism'.[9]

Before exploring Caribbean thinkers' regard for the US as a New World post-colony, it is important to underline that their view was once a geopolitical given. It was only in the wake of World War II that the post-colonial status of the Republic became forgotten within Western intellectual circles. The key to this amnesia lies in a Cold War story, namely, the fiction of a three-world planet. Prior to the 1950s, the earth was generally presumed to be made up of 'two worlds': the old and the new. In this dyadic understanding, the US belonged to the 'New World', where, significantly, it shared historical temporality with other colonized communities across the continent (Argentina or Haiti, for example). However, with the Cold War invention of the three worlds schema, the North American Republic became relocated, or, better, promoted. It was advanced from the New to the First World.

Gone with this geopolitical promotion was the long established presumption of historical commensurability across the Americas, the old idea that US and Haiti belonged on the same hemispheric plane of history. North Americans, cast as part of the First World, became imagined as historically ahead of the rest of the continent, which was left behind in the lagging Third World. Historiographically speaking, the continent became de facto segregated and the Pan-American frame effectively obsolete. With the onset of the Cold War, it became inconceivable that the US was caught in the same historical predicament as the rest of the formerly colonized New World.

Yet decades into the Cold War, Caribbean thinkers refused to forget. As with early twentieth-century Latin American thinkers like Rodo and Dario, they continued to see the colossal Republic as a Caliban, simply writ very large. Recall in Haiti, for example, the apprehension of North Americans who militarily occupied the black Republic from 1915 to 1934. For local witnesses, the US citizens in their midst seemed like *'de grossier personnages'*, people who lacked refinement and any bearings of 'civilization', according to Michel Rolph Trouillot. These armed sojourners actually had the ironic effect of degrading the brand of whiteness in the eyes of Haitian elites, Trouillot observed (130). This sense of North Americans as embarrassing public embodiments of whiteness was also manifest in twentieth-century colonial Trinidad, where British and local white elites often found the conduct of US citizens intolerably denigrating. Evident in the 1930s when hundreds of white drillers moved to labour in the island's oil industry, this sentiment became conspicuous a decade later when thousands of soldiers and civilians arrived in wartime to build and fortify US bases on the colony (see Neptune 56–60, 161–172).

The dubious regard for the cultured claims of the US persisted among the Caribbean intelligentsia into the postwar period. George Lamming, the Barbados-born writer who worked and lived in Trinidad during the years of 'American occupation', registered this disrespect for the Republic's literary bona fides in his classic 1960 text, *The Pleasures of Exile*. When Lamming sought to explain his nonchalance about the book's critical reception – as opposed to its market success – in the Republic, he flatly admitted that 'American judgement did not impress me' (152). In fact, Lamming declared that insofar as the creative imagination was concerned, 'America does not even exist.' His text, remembered most for identifying the Caribbean with the cursed (and cursing) Shakespearean figure of Caliban, is also notable for its low estimation of the intellectual achievements of the Yankees. Just over a decade later, Derek Walcott, St Lucia-born Trinidad native, could be found articulating a similar a case that the US, as part of the Americas, was not to be confused with a culturally intimidating

Old World European power. In a 1974 essay Walcott stressed that Caribbean people shared time and space with the materially powerful Republic, clarifying from the start that: 'To us, in many ways, America is a young country' (4).

Yet no writer from the region put the US in its proper New World historical place with more critical depth, urgency and sophistication than C.L.R. James did in *American Civilization*, a work conceived in the wake of Europe's totalitarian atrocities and in light of the nation's assumption of ideological leadership for the West. Back in 1932, when he first left Trinidad for England, James had described the US in passing as 'dreadful' (117). Now, having been in the belly of the beast (as Marti might have said) and, more, having researched the entrails, the published historian and practising Marxist theoretician felt compelled and prepared to make a critical and substantive contribution to the field of American Studies.

The manuscript attests that James's dread of the US had not abated but, indeed, deepened. *American Civilization* amounted to a warning that a portentous hopelessness pervaded the society, that the nation faced a gravely violent and largely undiagnosed crisis rooted in its colonial past. Moved by an historical plot more ironic than tragic, the study projected the Republic as a former colony whose peculiarly passionate investment in the Eurocentric civilizing ideal of individual freedom had left it vulnerable to totalitarian rule. For the author, moreover, this North American post-colonial crisis contained lessons for the larger study of totalitarianism. James's introduction was explicit: 'I believe that the close study of the United States will explain most easily to the people of Western Europe why totalitarianism arises, the horrible degradation it represents, its terrible cost to society, the certainty of its overthrow' (38). Bafflingly, reviews of *American Civilization* have repressed this disturbing post-colonial critique, instead, misrepresenting the text as a curious celebration of the nation's democratic achievements, especially its entertainment industry.

The following discussion helps to correct the misunderstanding through three steps. First, it recounts James's basic argument that connects an historical crisis in the post-independence nationalist imagination to the vulnerability to totalitarianism in the contemporary US. The discussion then underlines his implicit post-colonial method, his conceptualization of the North American Republic as derivative of and yet deviant from Europe. Also noted here is the crucial informative role De Tocqueville played for James. The reinterpretation of *American Civilization* ends by honing in on the climactic chapter, 'Popular Arts and Modern Society.' The point here is to underline James's analysis as evidence not of a fondness of US mass culture but a horror of its manifest totalitarian politics.

American Civilization contained a terrifying historical critique. According to James, the 'free individuality' idealized in modern European liberalism made a uniquely deep and enduring impression on the patriotic imagination in the former British North American colonies. Indeed, this ideal of individualism maintained a remarkably romantic quality in the US up to the middle of the nineteenth century. By the century's end, though, a major transformation was underway, James argues. The emergence of corporate capital and, later on, the growth of the state bureaucracy increasingly frustrated and even crushed the quest for this 'free individuality'. If the struggle for happiness was once real, it became increasingly futile. Over the course of the twentieth century, he contends, despair and doubt overtook the Republic, so that by the New Deal era the nationalist project had arrived at an ominous phase of exhaustion. Hope in the idea of Americanism as heroic individualism had been lost. Poignantly, James judges this 'hopelessness' to be 'infinitely deeper than it was in Europe in the years preceding World War II' (30). He meant this comparison to be chilling, an alarm that conditions in the US had become ripe for a native answer to Hitler. The modern atrocity of totalitarianism had been hinted at in the Republic a century earlier in *Moby Dick*, James observed; now it was spectacularly displayed courtesy of the nation's 'entertainment' industry.

This devastating thesis appears throughout *American Civilization* with varying degrees of subtlety, intricacy and allusiveness. It is stated with particular clarity, though, at the end of chapter four ('Freedom Today'). As James turns to analyse the popular arts, he sums up the argument to that point:

> Upon a people bursting with energy, untroubled by Feudal remains or a feudal past soaked to the marrow in a tradition of individual freedom individual security, free association a tradition which is constantly held before them as the basis of their civilization, upon this people more than all others has been imposed a mechanized way of life at work mechanized forms of living a mechanized totality which from morning till night, week after week, day after day, crushed their very individuality

which tradition nourishes and the abundance of mass produced goods encourages. The average American is baffled by it, has always been. He cannot grasp the process by which a genuine democracy escapes him. With the crash of the economic system in 1929 and now the perpetual crisis of world war threatening world-wide destruction, all the tensions are arising, confusedly but remarkably to the surface. These tensions have been the driving force in the extraordinary scope and manifestations of what is loosely called in the US the entertainment industry (116; quotation verified as accurate).

Bearing this passage in mind, it is possible to take a brief tour of *American Civilization*. The work begins by establishing the particularly heroic historical character of liberal freedom in the US nationalist imagination. The opening chapter claims that the absence of feudal relations in North America encouraged the 'free individuality' theorized in European liberalism to be conducted with a particular uninhibitedness. In his own words: 'the ideas of European individualism thus find their clearest expression concretely in the US and very nearly their finest political expression' (41). The prevailing conditions in British North America made these colonies a perfect laboratory for testing liberal precepts, James argues. The result was the consolidation of a national consensus around a liberalism practised to the adventurous extreme. As he puts it, the 'real achievement' of the US nationalist imagination was the idea of 'the freedom, the energy, the heroic quality of the individual pursuing his daily vocation' (46).

American Civilization then affirms the enduring hold of this notion of 'free individuality' on the nationalist imagination by examining nineteenth-century US intellectual life. Though James promises to examine an array of figures within the intelligentsia in the projected book, he deals mostly with two writers, Walt Whitman and Herman Melville, and one activist, Wendell Phillips. Whitman matters to James insofar as the poet expresses the national ideal of romantic individualism. In fact, he mostly excoriates Whitman's corpus for evading the glaring issue of the growing gap between this ideal and reality in the US. Melville, by contrast, appears as a genius in *American Civilization* and serves virtually as James's intellectual muse. He hails Melville as the author of an effectively prophetic masterpiece, *Moby Dick*, 'the only serious study in fiction of the type which has reached its climax in the modern totalitarian dictator' (76). The protagonistic figure of Captain Ahab, according to James, brilliantly captured the vicious problems of heroic individualism and its totalitarian potential in the US. As he explains: 'The old heroic individualist America [Melville] knew; but he could see as artists see that the old individualism was breeding a new individualism, an individualism which would destroy society. The prototype of this was Ahab. The modern dictator whose prototype he is, is best exemplified by Adolf Hitler' (76). Finally, James briefly profiles Phillips, highlighting him as an historical exemplar of the potential function for intellectuals in the revolutionary challenge that had to come if the US was to avoid descent into totalitarian enslavement.

American Civilization, having established the vitality of the idea of heroic freedom in the Republic's nationalist tradition, then noted that the actual practice of 'free individuality' had been effectively destroyed by the emergence of big corporate capital by the late nineteenth century. This period marks a critical moment in the US past in James's analysis; it witnesses the emergence of a perverse 'new individualism' characterized by captains of industry willing to realize their dominating Ahab-esque roles. His discussion of this epochal transformation, it should be noted, involved a challenge to one of the giants in US historiography, Frederick Jackson Turner. While James credits Turner for having rightly recognized the 'complete break' that occurred in the post-Civil War Republic, he also chides the historian for wrongly relating it to the closing of the frontier. The key issue was a change not in nature, James counters, but in the scale of capitalist organization (101–103). *American Civilization* then explains that the wider public had become conscious of the disappearance of the old ideal of 'freedom'; 'The outstanding social fact of the US is that the population has gone a long way on the road to recognizing that freedom has been lost,' writes James (107). The romantic nationalist illusion about liberalism was no more. The expectation of 'free individuality' had been replaced by 'security', by the promises of the 'Welfare State', according to him.

The awareness of this loss of 'freedom' is decisive for James's argument. Here, for him, lies the key to the crisis that has made the US vulnerable to the totalitarian style of rule. The problem for the masses of workers in the Republic was not so much inadequate wages and vacation and so-called 'bread and butter' issues. Their troubles lay in the deeper realm of social psychology and cultural politics. Citizens despaired at being unable to imagine themselves as individuals heroically struggling for happiness – the promise of post-colonial US nationalism. What they actually experienced was, in his words, 'the endless frustration of being merely a cog in a great machine' (167). The result was masses of embittered Americans enraged at the absence of opportunities to express their personality in daily life and resentful enough to seek vicariously revengeful compensation in the violent action of other dominant heroic figures.

These citizens had not yet made this move to seek out a totalitarian leader, but, in their choices of entertainment, James saw dark forebodings. As he put it, 'by carefully observing the trends in modern popular art and the response of the people we can see the tendencies which exploded into the monstrous caricatures of human existence which appear under totalitarianism' (161). American audiences had demonstrated a preference, in James's view, for entertaining themselves with 'gangsters', personalities who defied the established order, who successfully 'cheat, lie, scheme, plot, are brutal, cruel, lustful, expressing their free individuality' (129). And through this choice of entertainment they had been culturally conditioning themselves for a totalitarian hero. This was the key thesis in *American Civilization*.

While James identifies this frustration and the desperate reaction to it with the vast majority of US citizens, he acknowledges populations that have endured the nation's general problems with a particular intensity and consequence. Namely, his study addresses 'Negroes, Women and The Intellectuals,' the title of the last substantive chapter. These groups face 'barriers' to participation in the political culture and thus help to illuminate larger national issues, according to James. Taking African-Americans as a 'sort of touchstone', *American Civilization* describes their condition as 'intolerable' and symptomatic of broader US failures (201). Not only have they been denied the basic liberal promise of America but efforts to ameliorate the situation of African-Americans have been 'demoralizing', according to James, because 'the greater the efforts made, the more terrible are the new forms in which the old social problems reappear' (206). His discussion of women in the US emphasizes a similar unbearable frustration. They were advanced a relatively decent amount of equality in theory, he argued, but faced a reality that was quite different. Women, in fact, had to put up with a society that demanded them to be 'submissive' and to accommodate men as 'dominant' (215). Finally, James deals with intellectuals, describing them, in a biting analysis, as the nation's most hopeless group. They had become anachronisms in the US, according to him, yet rather than recognize this and emancipate themselves from an obsolete category, intellectuals persisted in maintaining a barrier between themselves and the working masses. The result, James warns, is a frustrated isolation that renders them susceptible to joining totalitarian bureaucracies that help discipline workers into slavery (258).

American Civilization ends on a portentous note, warning of a violent struggle over totalitarianism coming at the heart of Western liberal democracy. With characteristic revolutionary faith, however, James forecasts that totalitarianism would be defeated ultimately. The US masses would become 'abolitionists' and 'wipe away the conditions of their own slavery', he writes (276). This belief would be received by some as utopian; James also anticipates, so he preempts a response: 'Utopia? It is possible that it is.... But I believe in the instinct of humanity to survive and that is the only way it can survive' (276). *American Civilization* was ominous but not pessimistic.

Essential to James's interpretive method, it must be appreciated, was apprehension of the US as a product of modern colonialism. For him, the North American Republic was best approached as a transplanted European society and its history best studied in light of the impression made by the powerful ideas and institutions that constituted Europe's 'civilization'. Note, for example, how James describes his opening chapter on 'Individuality'. It was 'an account of the development of economic forces, social relations and their specific expression in the US from 1776–1876,' he writes, then immediately adds: 'These are seen, however, in relation to developments in Europe and in relation to European commentators, in particular de Tocqueville' (40). The same point is reiterated when James states that 'an essential part of the method' involved in juxtaposing developments in the US with the European counterpart is that 'we have to see the interrelations between the European development' (41–42). In his mind, it was a given that the past of the North American Republic, like that of all other New World societies, was both derivative of and deviant from Europe's historical experience. *American Civilization*, in short, was informed by a frame that we today would label post-colonial.

In fact, the entire argument was built around the proposition of US liberalism as a perilously extravagant post-colonial brand. To begin with, James took for granted that the Republic inherited its ideas about 'free individuality' from the intellectual imagination of metropolitan Europe. Telling is the following passage: 'Ideologically, however, the European past hangs over the country. Jefferson is the product of Locke. The great pamphleteer of the revolution is a European, Tom Paine, the embodiment of the revolutionary consciousness of Europe' (40–41). Yet, for James, just as important as the obvious derivation of European ideas and institutions was their remarkably different expression in the New World colonial context. North American conditions, he emphasizes, were nothing like what prevailed in Europe where liberalism was thought out. Here, bourgeois individualism got its best start. In his words, 'Without the political and ideology relations of feudalism and a landed aristocracy which form the concreted milieu of the development of European culture,' the Republic, 'shows the ideal conditions for which Europe struggled so hard' (40). With this claim (and variations that appear across the opening chapter), James did not intend to celebrate US exceptionalism. Rather, he sought to emphasize just how deviant the development of liberalism in North America would appear from the historical perspective of metropolitan Europe.

In particular, *American Civilization* contended that in the 'ideal' situation offered by the British colonies, Europe's liberal notions of freedom and individuality took on a drastically new and romantic character. They became enchanting possibilities. Relative to Europe, according to James, the liberalism cultivated in the Republic was consensual, uninhibited and unreflective. This was the significance of the contrast he drew between the outburst of Jacksonian democracy in the US and the 'outpouring of such literary and philosophical genius' in Europe in the same time period (45). What Europeans could only debate and imagine, people in North America had an opportunity to experience more or less in actuality. As he put it, 'the brilliant European theory is counterposed to the American reality' (41). Whereas European thinkers (like Ricardo, Hegel and Fourier) were engaged in contentious and artistic speculations about freedom, US citizens were agreeing to settle the issue in practise and often through violence. With very little disagreement over the tenets of liberalism, no significant political thought was needed in the US, according to *American Civilization*, and little if any was produced. James is emphatic about the source of this intellectual failure in the Republic: '*The central reason is the absence of sharp social differentiation and conflict*' (42; italics mine). Much like contemporary 'consensus theorists' (Louis Hartz or Daniel Boorstin),

James was convinced that the post-colonial US was distinguished by a relatively easy and unthinking agreement around liberalism.

It is this liberal interpretation of the former British colony that accounts for James's deep indebtedness to *Democracy in America* (1835-38), the famous study by Alexis De Tocqueville. He acknowledges from inception the crucially informative role played by this French student of history and society. 'I propose to write an essay closer in spirit and aims of de Tocqueville than any of the writers who have followed him,' explains his introduction (31). De Tocqueville's text provided James the key guide to identifying the US brand of liberalism as distinctly hegemonic, even despotic and unrestrained. Telling are the passages that James lifts directly from *Democracy in America*; one ends with De Tocqueville observing that, 'I cannot explain my meaning better than by saying that the Americans show a sort of heroism in their manner of trading' (44). Later, he cites De Tocqueville's emphatic statement regarding the absence of genuine intellectual contest and antagonism in the Republic: 'In no country,...is there such lack of free and independent discussion' (48). In *Democracy in America*, James discovered the original outlines of the US nationalist imagination and, especially, the outsized and unquestioned, almost coercive role it gave to the liberal idea of the individual energetically in pursuit of commerce.

Finally, the post-colonial interpretation in *American Civilization* also draws on De Tocqueville in a largely unacknowledged but meaningful way. Like the author of *Democracy in America*, James judges the Republic as unaccomplished, insecure and dependent in the realm of aesthetic culture. De Tocqueville, it should be remembered, commented on the absence of indigenous artistic production in the former British colonies. Three decades into the nineteenth century, he observed, English literature, Shakespeare in particular, still held sway in the US. De Tocqueville, indeed, portrayed North Americans as a people who 'paint with colors borrowed from foreign mores' (804). James assumed a similarly dismissive view. He practically takes it for granted that, in the realm of the arts and the intellect, the Republic – as Lamming would later explicitly observe – simply did not yet exist. 'In this sphere of human life', James plainly declares, 'the mighty civilization of the US by universal agreement stands at the bottom of all great civilizations' (32). For him, in fact, it was a 'parallel without paradox', the amazing disparity between the 'vast accumulation of wealth and the tradition of liberty' in the North American Republic and its minimal contribution to the global 'history of culture'.

What the nation did generate on an unprecedented scale, according to *American Civilization*, was an 'entertainment' industry, one that was destined to manifest across the globe and help manage the imaginations of the masses everywhere. James, to be sure, was never convinced that the products of this big business of satisfying millions made for much memorable art; 'ephemeral vulgarities on a colossal scale' was his actual phrase for what the industry often produced – James sounding like his countryman V.S. Naipaul (36). Yet it was these very entertaining vulgarities that James studied seriously. The 'popular arts', in fact, constituted his primary evidence in making the case for the presence of totalitarian cultural politics in the US – James, in this respect, sounding less like Naipaul than Stuart Hall.[10]

The chapter titled 'Popular Arts and Modern Society' represents the crux of *American Civilization*. 'At every stage in a book there is reached a certain climax,' James opens, 'We approach it in the sketch for this chapter' (119). He then proceeded to analyse 'entertainment' in the contemporary US for its complicity in totalitarian hero-worship. Though a few pages discuss 'Some Positive Aspects in Popular Art' as well the 'Drama Of Greece' as a model of the culture that might be achieved in the US, the bulk of the chapter adopts an anthropological approach to analyse comic strips, radio shows, movies and middlebrow literature. James treats these forms as expressions of the desires and frustrations of 'the folk', which in the North American context would be 'the mass'. Taking seriously what many trivialized, he embraced 'entertainment' as 'social and psychological manifestations of the American life and character' (37). The text is clear:

> It is in men like David Selznick, Cecil De Mille and Henry Luce that we find the clearest ideological expression of the sentiments and deepest feelings of the American people and a great window on the future of America and the modern world (119).

James rationalized this method of treating entertainment as articulate artifacts of the mindset of 'the masses' by referencing the consumerist logic of the liberal capitalist market in the Republic. The producers of culture were interested above all in profits – neither propaganda nor poetry, he explained. They thus paid serious attention to the demands of the audience. For those producing entertainment, the imperative was to satisfy the masses, or to go out of business.

Hence, observes James, an 'enormous amount of energy, thought and intelligence are spent to probe and profit by this mass demand.' Entertainment was a liberal democratic business, he underlines; individuals were free to vote with their dollars; that was their right. As James puts it, 'the mass is not merely passive. It decides what it will see. It will pay to see that' (123). If audiences had no interest in a certain form of entertainment, the industry was not going to produce it. The converse was also true, according to him; 'huge and consistent success are [sic] an indication of mass demand' (123). In this way, James justified his treatment of the 'popular arts' as a medium for discovery of the 'deepest feelings of the masses' (123). In his view, the movies and detective stories that sold in the millions captured, however imperfectly, what moved the vast majority of American people, or, at least negatively, what held no appeal for them.

Entertainment, then, was an arena in which the typically inarticulate masses had acquired a registering voice. And since the Great Depression, according to James, the kinds of cultural fictions purchased by the vast majority of consumers in the US suggested something ominous. In his analysis, the sphere of popular entertainment betrayed a violent frustration with the state of affairs and, more, a readiness to resolve their issues vicariously through the entertainment of a totalitarian hero. Whether discussing Dick Tracy, or *Public Enemy* or the best-selling fiction of now forgotten African-American writer Frank Yerby, James underlines the emergence of a relatively new obsession with 'violence, sadism, cruelty, the release of aggression' in the contemporary US (122). The outstanding protagonists in the big grossing comics, and radio shows and movies and middlebrow literature, he argues, amounted to amoral primitivistic characters with more than a twist of misogyny in most cases. The new hero was embodied in what James brands the 'gangster-detective'. The two elements of this composite figure were only superficially opposed, he explains; both were united on a deeper level in their 'scorn for the police as the representative of official society' and their willingness to take matters into their own hands (124). Displaying a brutal disdain for the established order, the 'gangster-detective' was a man ready, in James's words, to 'break every accepted rule of society', a man 'who lives in a world of his own according to an ethics of his own' (125, 129).

The rise of this sadistic new hero culminates the argument in *American Civilization*. This novel fictional character is not accidental but indeed indexical, for James. The 'gangster-detective' reflects the exhaustion of the nationalist cultural politics fueled by the liberal idea of free individuality. In his own words:

> Nor is this gangster-private detective type at all accidental as a symbol of a frustrated population. The gangster did not fall from the sky nor does he represent Chicago and the underworld. He is the persistent symbol of the national past which now has no meaning – the past in which energy, determination, bravery were certain to get a man somewhere in the line of opportunity. Now the man on the assembly line, the farmer, know [sic] that they are there for life; and the gangster who displays all the old heroic qualities in the only way he can display them is the derisive symbol of the contrast between ideals and reality (126–7).

The 'gangster-detective', in short, appeared in fiction to do what the embittered and enraged masses of US citizens have found themselves incapable of doing in reality. In the form of 'entertainment', this hero provided vicarious compensation for the loss and frustration of free individuality in the Republic.

In this new fictional figure, in fact, James discerns the same simmering passion that possessed Ahab in *Moby Dick*. For him, the gangster-detective emerges as the tell-tale sign of the preparedness for totalitarian times in the post-colonial US. James makes all of this explicit in the very next paragraph.

> [T]he film, strip, radio-drama are [sic] a form of art which must satisfy the mass, the individual seeking individuality in a mechanized, socialized society, where his life is ordered and restricted at every turn, where there is no certainty of employment, far less of being able to rise by energy and ability or going West as in the old days. In such society the individual demands an esthetic compensation in the contemplation of free individuals who go out into the world and settle their problems by free activity and individualistic methods. In these perpetual isolated wars free individuals are pitted against free individuals, live grandly and boldly. What they want, they go for. Gangsters get what they want, trying it for a while, then are killed. In the end 'crime does not pay' but for an hour and a half highly skilled actors and a huge organization of production and distribution have given to many millions a sense of active living and in the bloodshed, the violence the freedom from restraint to allow pent up feelings free play, they have released the bitterness, hate, fear, and sadism which simmer just below the surface (127).

The nation's masses were now choosing to identify with the power expressed by violent heroic action, in short, with a totalitarian character. The gangster, according to James, has become the symbol of the democratic liberal freedom in the North American Republic. A century and a half after independence, the American people had become taken by/with the demonically adventurous figure of Melville's imagination.

James's analysis, it is crucial to note, is resolutely historical. The 'gangster-detective' had not always been the outstanding protagonist in scripts for entertainment in the US, he emphasizes. In fact, this type of hero had little impact before the 1930s, according to James. Comedy had seized a major part of the national imagination, with artists like Harold Lloyd, Mack Sennett and especially Charlie Chaplin turning in genius performances. With the Great Depression, however, things changed. Gone were the 'old days' when the national mood was 'happy, carefree and confident' (135). Despair and anxiety set in and rendered these comics uncongenial, writes James. This was his point in highlighting the change in the reception of the work of Charlie Chaplin before and after 1929: 'Chaplin in those days could laugh at the world and the world could laugh with him. But the Depression killed him as it killed all genuine creativity in the cinema' (134). Ever since the 1930s, according to *American Civilization*, film producers began 'vying with each other in bloodshed and violence, cruelty sadism and disregard for all established standards' (132).

Finally, and perhaps most suggestively for our own post-Great Recession present, is James's discussion of the 'domination of the star system' and its complicity with totalitarian cultural politics. According to him, a signal development in the entertainment industry – especially in film-making – since the Great Depression was the professional production and packaging of 'star' personalities. 'What has happened,' James explains, ' is that side by side with the representation of murder violence atrocity evil, the masses have fostered a system where a certain selected few individuals symbolize in their film existence *and their private and public existence* the revolt against general conditions' (142; italics in original). What interests him, though, is not the fact that these celebrities are fabricated, 'synthetic characters' produced by 'a vast army of journalists, mag writers publicity men etc.' (145). Rather, it is the symbolic roles these 'stars' play for the masses. James contends that through these 'stars', Americans 'live vicariously, see in them examples of that great individuality which is the dominant need of the vast mass today' (146). Celebrity, according to him, was now serving as a substitute, functioning to 'fill a psychological need of the vast masses of people who live limited lives' (146).

In fact, James's ultimate worry in *American Civilization* was the potential crossover of this manufactured symbolic heroism from entertainment to politics, where a fundamentally similar substitution defined totalitarianism. As he puts it, 'we have seen how, deprived of individuality, millions of modern citizens live vicariously, through identification with brilliant notably effective, famous or glamorous individuals. The totalitarian state, having crushed all freedom, carries this substitution to its last ultimate' (161). This feared translation of the 'star' into totalitarian leader had not yet happened in the Republic, but James saw it as a distinct possibility. Note his reference below to Father Coughlin,[11] a name synonymous with fascism in the interwar US:

> It is clear that in the modern mechanized collectivized world, with its building up on the one hand all sorts of possibilities and vistas for the individual personality, and on the other its confinement of the personality to a narrow routinized existence with the mechanical means, there arises the need to realize the thwarted possibilities or certain parts of them through some symbolic personality.... For a brief period Father Coughlin showed the political possibilities that slumber behind these manifestations of our time. Other countries have shown not only the possibilities but the realities (147).

In Father Coughlin, according to James, the specter had been raised. He glimpsed in this political figure evidence that the US masses, frustrated with their powerlessness to participate meaningfully in the nationalist project, were prepared to devote themselves loyally to a hero of the totalitarian mode. James is clear in the conclusion: 'the great mass of people no longer fear power. *They are ready to allocate today power to anyone who seems ready to do their bidding*' (263; italics mine).

Over six decades after its completion, *American Civilization* reads with a resonance that perhaps not even James could imagine. Today, a former reality-tv star, Donald J. Trump, has excited politics in the Republic with promises of restoring the national glory of great heroic free individuality. Trump's massively entertained and patriotic followership, many of whom are presented as frustrated and enraged, suggests the emergence of a constituency willing, in James's phrasing, to allocate power to him as the man ready 'to do their bidding'. How far Trump can go toward using these millions of supporters for a successful totalitarian takeover remains to be seen – James himself would have gambled against it. What is already doubtless, though, is the unfortunate absence of a critical challenge to 'Trumpism' that assumes the form of the humbling post-colonial approach taken in *American Civilization*. This missing line of oppositional critique, following James, would foreground nationalist presumptions of heroic liberalism and exceptional greatness as foundational to the perils facing the US.

Notes
1. 'A Tribute to C.L.R. James,' in Selwyn R. Cudjoe and William E. Cain, *C.L.R. James: His Intellectual Legacies*. (Amherst, MA: University of Massachusetts Press, 1995), 35.
2. I have in mind the writing of José Enrique Rodó and Ruben Dario. For more on Dario, see Carlos Juaregui. For a brief, recent historical account of the Caliban trope, see Peter Hulme.
3. This essay is a revised version of the keynote lecture given at the Turning Tides conference held at UWI, St. Augustine, 2016. It is part of larger book project addressed to 20th century US historiography.
4. C.L.R. James, *American Civilization*, (edited and introduced by Anna Grimshaw and Keith Hart with an Afterword by Robert A Hill (Cambridge, MA: Blackwell Publishers, 1993).
5. Paul Berman, 'The Romantic Revolutionary,' *The New Yorker* 72, (July 29, 1996): 68–73.
6. Part of the issue here is what academics might brand the 'the geopolitics of intellectual authority', or what simply could be called the struggle over the significance of place in deciding who is qualified to produce what kind of knowledge. The dominant interpretation of *American Civilization* makes it out to be the work of a Third World mind captivated by the First World modernity.
7. Ross 75–84. Ross is singled out because his brief discussion, despite its failure to figure out James' critical point, is actually one of the more penetrating. The misunderstanding of James's text began early: see the editorial introduction by Anna Grimshaw and Keith Hart. Robert Hill makes a valiant though ultimately unsuccessful effort to redeem the manuscript. See 'Literary Executor's Afterword' which appears at the end of *American Civilization*, pp.293–366. Bill Schwarz encourages the romantic reading of the text, describing the author as 'enthusing with the greatest passion about the democratic capacities of the civilization with which he had fallen in love.' (p.19) The romance is taken up literally by Joshua Jelly-Schapiro. For a fair sense of the established portrait of the 'American James', see Gair ed., in particular the essays by Eric Porter and Richard King. See also more recently, Enzo Traverso, esp. 166–174.
8. Hannah Arendt, *The Origins of Totalitarianism*. For contemplated connections between James and Arendt, see Richard King.

9. The term 'human pseudo-event' is taken from Daniel J. Boorstin, whose analysis of 'celebrity' shares much with James's in *American Civilization*; see Boorstin 45–76.
10. See, for example, Stuart Hall and Paddy Whannel, *The Popular Arts* (London, London Hutchinson Educational, 1964).
11. Charles Coughlin (1871–1979) was a Canadian-American Roman Catholic priest based in Michigan. One of the first public commentators to use radio to reach mass audiences, he was known for his virulent anti-Semitism and fascist leaning. He was forced off the air in 1939 (ed. Note).

Works Cited:

Arendt, Hannah. *The Origins of Totalitarianism*. New York: Harcourt Brace, 1951.

Bolton, Herbert E. 'The Epic of Greater America.' *American Historical Review* 383 (1933): 448–74.

Boorstin, Daniel J. *The Image: or, What Happened to the American Dream*. New York, NY: Atheneum, 1962.

Dario, Ruben. 'El Triunfo de Caliban.' *Revista Iberoamericana,* 1898.

Gair, Christopher, ed. *Beyond Boundaries: C.L.R. James and Postnational Studies*. London; Ann Arbor, MI: Pluto Press, 2006.

Grimshaw, Anna, and Keith Hart. 'American Civilization: An Introduction.' In C.L.R. James *American Civilization,* 2–25. Cambridge, MA: Blackwell, 1993.

Hall, Stuart, and Paddy Whannel. *The Popular Arts*. London: London Hutchinson Educational, 1964.

Hayes, Carlton J.H. 'The American Frontier: Frontier of What?' *American Historical Review* 51, no. 2 (1946): 199–216.

Hill, Robert. 'Literary Executor's Afterword.' In C.L.R. James *American Civilization*, edited by Anna Grimshaw and Keith Hart, 293–366. Cambridge, MA: Blackwell, 1993.

Hulme, Peter. 'Caliban: Roberto Fernandez Retamar's American Intelligence.' *Small Axe* 20, no. 3 (2016): 115–22.

James, C.L.R. *American Civilization,* edited and introduced by Anna Grimshaw and Keith Hart. With an Afterword by Robert A Hill. Cambridge, MA: Blackwell Press, 1993.

———. *Letters from London: Seven Essays By C.L.R. James,* edited by Nicholas Laughlin. Port of Spain, Trinidad: Prospect Press, 2003

Jelly-Schapiro, Joshua. 'C.L.R. James in America; or, the ballad of Nello and Connie.' *Transition* 104 (2011): 30–57.

Juaregui, Carlos. 'Caliban: icono del 98: a Proposito de un articulo de Ruben Dario.' *Balance de un Iberoamericana*, 184–85 (1998): 441–55.

King, Richard. 'C.L.R. James, Hannah Arendt and the Return of Politics in the Cold War.' In *Beyond Boundaries: C.L.R. James and Post National Studies,* edited by Christopher Gair. London; Ann Arbor, MI: Pluto Press, 2006.

Lamming, George. *Pleasures of Exile*. London: M. Joseph, 1960.
Neptune, Harvey. *Caliban and the Yankees: Trinidad and the US Occupation*. Chapel Hill, NC: University of North Carolina Press, 2007.
Porter, Eric. 'Summer of Hummer: C.L.R. James American Civilization and the (Necro) Political Crisis.' In *Beyond Boundaries: C.L.R. James and Post National Studies,* edited by Christopher Gair, 39–58. London; Ann Arbor, MI: Pluto Press, 2006.
Rodó, José Enrique. *Ariel*. Austin, TX: The University of Texas Press, 1988. First published in 1900.
Ross, Andrew. 'Civilization in One Country? The American James.' In *Rethinking C.L.R. James.*, edited by Grant Farred, 75–84. Oxford and London: Blackwell, 1996.
Schwarz, Bill. 'C.L.R. James' *American Civilization*.' *Atlantic Studies* 2, no. 1 (2005): 15–43.
Traverso, Enzo. *Left Wing Melancholia: Marxism, History and Memory*. New York, NY: Columbia University Press, 2016, esp. 166–74.
Trouillot, Michel-Rolph. *Haiti: State Against Nation: The Origins and Legacies of Duvalierism*. New York, NY: Monthly Review Press, 1990.
Walcott, Derek. 'The Caribbean: Culture or Mimicry,' *Journal of Interamerican Studies and World Affairs* 16, no. 1 (1974): 3–13.

CHAPTER 2

Connecticut-Caribbean Connections:
A Focus on the British Caribbean from the 17th to the 21st Centuries

Heather Cateau

Background

The St. Augustine Campus of the University of the West Indies (UWI) and Trinity College, in Hartford, Connecticut have been collaborating over the past twenty years in the areas of student and staff exchanges and collaborative research. For the past ten years, The UWI has cultivated a similar relationship with the University of Connecticut. These evolving relationships have prompted focus on not just contemporary but also historical connections. I first came across historical references connecting the British Caribbean to Connecticut in some of the plantation papers of British Caribbean estates that I had read. I knew, therefore, that there were clear links between the British Caribbean and Connecticut that began centuries ago. I was further surprised to discover that Connecticut had the third largest population of Caribbean people, being surpassed only by New York and Miami. Instinctively I felt that this was caused by a deeper explanation than mere proximity to New York. My next step would be to try and detail some of those links and to explore the possibility that both communities still possess characteristics today that were forged out of the circumstances of the seventeenth and eighteenth centuries. As I began to trace roots of the connectivity from a historical perspective, I felt as if I was planting a seed that kept growing. It began with trading connections between the two areas and ended with an exchange of not only goods but also people, ideas and culture which I contend had its roots in the seventeenth century. I became convinced that the British Caribbean and Connecticut are connected by a cultural matrix that grew out of the historical trading linkages that connected our two societies.

What connections can there be between islands in the Caribbean Sea and a land locked area in the United States (US)? My research just scratches the surface and my initial focus is on the British

Caribbean. However, it should be noted that even in this preliminary phase I have come across references to the French Caribbean as well as the Spanish Caribbean. This should not be surprising. In spite of attempts to limit trade within the British Empire, the Navigations Laws, like the Molasses Act of 1733, which governed trade between the British colonies at that point, could not be effectively enforced. Illegal trade was therefore rampant. Thus trading links in the seventeenth and eighteenth centuries were not as exclusive to the British North America colonies and the British Caribbean colonies as contemporary legislation suggested. Indeed the Caribbean was really a place where many of the borders we accept as normal today were imposed and ineffectively policed. Trinidad is an excellent example of a territory with strong linkages to Britain, France and Spain officially and unofficially. Therefore, at times French and Spanish territories are mentioned in the discussion; however, the focus is primarily on the British Caribbean.

The Economic Context

This research took me straight back to the person considered to be the founding father of Trinidad and Tobago – Dr Eric Williams, our first Prime Minister. Williams was a historian and, in fact, started his professional life as a professor at Howard University. He is most known for his path-breaking work in *Capitalism and Slavery*. The time he spent living and working in the US would have considerable influence on his scholarship. One of the themes that he develops in this book is that of the nature of the relationship between British colonies in North America and British colonies in the Caribbean. For Williams these were sister colonies that grew up together depending on each other and contributing to each other's development and economic prosperity (Williams 108–125).

The economic philosophy of the seventeenth century was that of mercantilism. This meant that colonies were established for the benefit of the mother country (Britain). Trade was, therefore, restricted in order to ensure that most of the profits from trade and commerce accrued at the centre and not in the periphery (Sheridan 40–41). Thus, monopoly was also the order of the day. This restricted the trading partners of British colonies to Britain or other British colonies. The other dimension of the economic philosophy that impacted on the relationship was the sugar frenzy that took hold of the islands. The colonies, developed for exploitation, became machines which produced sugar using the most brutal and intensive systems. Africans were enslaved to work on the plantations and land was exploited to produce as much sugar as possible. At the height of the sugar revolution there was so much money to be made that no land was left untouched, not even land earmarked for food production. The islands would use all their land to produce sugar, becoming dependent on external sources for food supplies (Milkofsky 3).

In Williams's words '...only the possession of the mainland colonies permitted this sugar monopoly of the West Indian soil' (110). 'To subsist,' wrote Abbe Raynal, 'it is necessary to cultivate a province in Europe' (Williams 110). Britain voluntarily abdicated this privilege as the lesser of two evils, to the mainland colonies. It was in this way that the North American colonies came to have a recognized place in the imperial economy, as purveyors of the supplies needed by the sugar planters and the enslaved population. The mixed husbandry of the Northern and Middle colonies supplemented the specialized agriculture of the West Indies (Milkofsky 5). Thus, this relationship between Connecticut and the Caribbean can be thought to have begun as early as the 1650s.

The Connecticut Context

The economic background has been set – Connecticut's location did the rest. Because of its location and proximity to a navigable river, Connecticut became a vital port for the shipment of items to and from the Caribbean. The first recorded venture I have found dates to 1649. Merchants from Wethersfield and Hartford invested in the building of a small vessel, The *Tryall*. As the name implied, the intention was to make a trial run establishing trading links with Barbados. The *Tryall* sailed from Connecticut with food stuff, lumber and other supplies (Milkofsky 3). As time went on the trading relationships grew and were strengthened particularly with Barbados and St. Kitts (Milkofsky 3).

A specialized trade soon developed connecting British North America and the British Caribbean. It is important to note that there were two dimensions to the trade and that it did not only involve the larger ports we tend to focus on. Large vessels serviced Boston, New York, Philadelphia, Norfolk and Charlestown. However, these larger vessels relied on smaller vessels for supplies. The smaller size of these vessels allowed for speed and efficiency (Milkofsky 5). The larger vessels usually made one transatlantic trip a year but the smaller vessels made multiple trips, in some cases as many as 14 a year (Lang and Cabot). These vessels connected America's major seaport towns with their second-tier ports. Connecticut's coasters were indeed very active in this area (Grasso, 19).

Within this second group there were also smaller vessels that serviced the needs of the Caribbean colonies directly. These ships averaged 70 feet in length (Lang and Cabot) but could be as large as 150 feet on deck (Milkofsky 4). Inventories indicate that the ships from Connecticut were often crowded with livestock and other supplies. If we use our imaginations we can understand why previous writers have described them as unglamorous and notoriously unsteady. These vessels were therefore aptly referred to as horse jockeys (Lang and Cabot). However, these authors also suggest that both numerically and economically they were just as important a part of maritime history as their more prestigious sisters. They further note that though 'less romantic', these vessels provided every bit as much 'risk and adventure'.

A system soon evolved. Ship captains worked with several merchants. Two trips were usually made, one after fall harvest and one in spring. The average length of a voyage was two to five weeks. However, there could be much variation because of the weather, the difficulty of sourcing supplies, problems with the reliability of local contacts and intermittent warfare. The voyage usually involved stops at several islands. In some cases larger three mast ships were used, but smaller ships were preferred. Larger vessels were slower and took weeks to load (Milkofsky 4). The peoples of Connecticut and the British Caribbean were no strangers. In the islands themselves people from Connecticut had agents, family members and friends. They ensured that the cargo was disposed of as quickly as possible (Milkofsky 3–4).

These voyages were important in themselves but just as important as the profits to be made was the nature of the trade. Foods supplies were exchanged for sugar, rum and molasses (Milkofsky 4). In the case of the British Caribbean the latter two were the most important. They already had a market for their sugar. However, rum and molasses were considered waste products and were of no real value to them. Even so, this trade allowed them to purchase vitally needed food (salted fish and herrings) for themselves, but even more importantly for the enslaved populations, as well as lumber and staves (for buildings and the very hogsheads to ship their sugar with), with waste products (Milkofsky 4).

This substantially increased the profitability of the plantations.

In the case of North America, the British Caribbean provided a significant outlet beyond their shores for their supplies (Milkofsky 5). New York could not have provided such a market. However, the backward and forward linkages were just as important. Work was created in Connecticut for saw mills, ship builders, ship yard workers, sail and rope makers and, of course, farmers. With the income earned, they in turn were able to purchase British products like cloth, tools and other domestic goods (Milkofsky 4). This in yet another turn enhanced the profits made by Britain. Distilling was also a very important industry. Joel Lang describes rum and gin pouring from distilleries in New London and Hartford. Rum was needed for the fisheries, the fur trade, for naval rations and was a vital part of the cargo on slave ships (Milkofsky 5). As we develop the linkages, the circle becomes wider and wider. The connection with the British Caribbean must have been indirectly extended to seamen, carpenters, painters, tradesmen, artisans, common agents and to development of services such as insurance and dock facilities.

Middletown Custom House Records reveal an active trade between 1790 and 1809 from the Connecticut River Valley to the Caribbean. St Kitts and Barbados were the most popular ports of call. There were also several ships that went to Haiti and Jamaica (Farrow et al. 3–44). Ships included the *Polly and Betsey*, the *Matilda*, and the *James* (Milkofsky 2–4). On October 25, 1795, the manifest of the cargo on the *Polly and Betsey* included: barrels of salted beef and pork, shad, pickled codfish, cheese, butter, beans, potatoes, corn, onions and apples. There were also barrels, staves, hoops, lumber, shingles and oak planks. We can also add live animals – 314 geese, 40 turkeys, 5 hogs and 200 sheep (Milkofsky 4).

There were ships that also carried cattle. Connecticut was a leader in the export of livestock, meat and dairy, cheese, butter, grain, flour, onions, tobacco and lumber (Lang and Cabot). Joel Lang notes that

> ...early in the colonial period much of Connecticut's produce was shipped out of Rhode Island and Massachusetts. But after the revolution, Connecticut came to dominate the West India trade more directly. In some years, more than half its exports went to French islands, especially the one known as Santo Domingo, then the leading sugar producer in the West Indies (Farrow et al. 3–44).

MANIFEST of the cargo on board the *Brig. Polly & Betsey* *Benjamin Gleason* master, destined to *Jamaica* Port of Middletown, *Oct. 21, 1795*

Brands.	Number, Kind and Quality of Articles.
A. Hall	One hundred fifteen lb. Beef
	Three lb. Pork
J. Gaylord	Thirteen lb. Woodfish pickled
	Two lb. Suet
	4041 lb. Cheese
	622 lb. Butter
	3 lb. Beans
	294 bus. Potatoes
	116 bus. Corn
	2000 bunches Onions
	8.2.0.0 Red Oak Staves
	3.4.0.0 Hoops
	220 hoop poles
	7194 feet boards
	170 shook heads
	334 feet oak plank
	314 Geese
	40 Turkies
	5 Hogs
	200 Sheep
	20 water kegs

A master of a vessel is not to receive on board for exportation to a foreign port, any beef, pork, flour, fish, put up for exportation; butter or lard, not duly branded according to law.

I solemnly swear, to the best of my knowledge and belief, to the truth of the above manifest, and that the articles therein mentioned, which are subject to inspection, have been duly inspected; and branded according to law. *So help me GOD.*

Middletown Oct. 21, 1795 — *Benj.n Gleason* Master.

Manifest of Cargo on board Brigatine Polly & Bestey, October 21, 1795
Source: Connecticut River Museum

In 1731, according to the Connecticut Governor at the time, Joseph Talcott, there were 44 trading vessels on record. However, the number of vessels had quadrupled and the tonnage increased 20 fold by the 1770s (Lang and Cabot).

In time there were over 300 vessels (Lang and Cabot). Approximately 100 vessels departed from shipyards in New London, New Haven, Norwich, Middletown and Hartford in 1784 alone (Lang and Cabot). Bernard Bailyn believed that by 1770 many New Englanders may have been experiencing the highest standard of living the world had ever seen (Farrow et al. 3–44). He continues that fortunes made in the West Indian trade would support the industrial and financial revolutions which were to follow. Eric Williams develops this theme extensively in *Capitalism and Slavery* (Farrow et al. 3–44; Williams 210). It will take another project to calculate the full extent and scope of this trading relationship. This task is further complicated by the number of territories involved as well as the difficulty of verifying official and unofficial figures and the further complication of a thriving illegal trade. However, data from the British Naval Office can provide a vivid picture of the nature and extent of the trade. Table 2.1 provides the recorded trade from North America to Jamaica from 1768 to 1774 and Table 2.2 provides a listing of the goods exported from Jamaica to North America during this period. Together the tables give us a clear understanding of the wide range of goods involved as well as the quantities and the number of vessels involved. When we bear in mind that this is the officially recorded trade figures for one British colony, it is clear the full dimensions of the trade have the potential to be quite large. Thus the impact on most societies must have also been considerable.

Table 2.1 (a): An Account of All Imports into Jamaica, from America, for Seven Years; Taken from the Books of the Naval Office:

From Jan. 1 to December 31.	Brls. of Flour	Brls. of Bread	Kegs of Biscuits	Brls. of Rice	Hnds. of Fish	Brls. of Fish	Brls. of Beef & Pork	Brls. of Oil	Brls. Pitch, Tar, & Turpentine	Staves and Shingles	Feet of Lumber
1768	22.620	7,822	2,258	4,211.5	2,149	2,980	4,781	387	1,564	8,311,069	3,168,539
1769	28.749	10,175	2,468	4,862.5	3,340	8,028	5,894	863	2,527	8,879,810	4,273,894
1770	37.442	11,203.5	4,527	15,475	1,607	9,228	5,225	698	1,561	6,918,202	3,406,598
1771	27.103	9,152	3,858	5,744	2,414	9,673	3,630	368	2,005	6,405,282	3,368,570
1772	19.637	9,952	5,208	3,084	2,587	12,575	3,505	616	1,881	12,398,282	4,031,105
1773	30.815	9,430	5,111	5,219	4,152	12,801	2,811.5	780	1,995	13,980,641	5,245,562
1774	23.610	7,532	4,638	6,898	2,733	12,179	9,152	480	1,131	11,752,000	4,181,

Table 2.1 (b)

From Jan. 1 to December 31	Bunches of Onions	Wood-hoops	Hogshd. Shakes	Horses & Cattle	Bushels of Salt	Tons Iron	Casks of Hams	Firkins of Butter	Boxes soap & Spermaceti Candles	Bushels of Corn, Pease, Etc.	Vessels
1768	13,808	11,800	595	135	-	-	-	38	1,832	55,475.5	197
1769	32,668	2,237	12,000	1,149	-	-	-	53	385	38,853	249
1770	36,220	28,925	2,051	536	-	-	-	303	2,026	37,753	287
1771	19,350	107,150	2,203	548	-	-	-	301	2,217	37,120	264
1772	10,710	118,975	2,231	263	-	-	-	200	2,292	24,870	281
1773	41,600	168,230	3,234	648	-	-	-	497	2,761	42,315	323
1774	36,643	70,700	-	499	9,160	50	411	400	1,215	52,470	299

N. B. There are no entries in the books, from the out-ports, in 1768.
Source: Colonial Office Papers, Jamaica. C. o. 140/60, fol. 43.

Table 2.2: An Account of all the Sugar, Rum, Coffee, and Molasses, Exported from Jamaica to America, for Seven Years; Taken from Books of the Naval Office:

		Hnds of Sugar	Puncheons of Rum	Casks or Bags of Coffee	Casks of Molasses	No. of Vessels
From Jan to Dec	1768	902	1,039	589	626	84
	1769	1,407	4,443	971	2,265	140
	1770	1,958	4,513	1,223	1,021	170
	1771	1,421	2,545	1,030	938	141
	1772	1,513	4,294	1,331	753	143
	1773	1,513	7,438	1,001	1,003	184
	1774	1,811	8,660	2,816	902	

Source: Colonial Office Papers, Jamaica, C. O. 140/69, fol. 43.

Thus the profits from sugar and the slave trade touched many people and places – even in Connecticut. The British Caribbean and Connecticut were not only connected through trade, but also through the enslavement system. African enslavement touched all of us both directly and indirectly. Enslaved persons from the British Caribbean even took up residence eventually in Connecticut (Milkofsky 5). It is easier to follow the trail of sugar, rum, and molasses, their most important products (Milkofsky 5), but Brenda Milkofsky believes that most of the 5,000 enslaved persons in Connecticut at the time of the Revolutionary war came there through trade with the Caribbean (Milkofsky 5). The extent of this connection needs to be more thoroughly researched, but it is clear that enslavement must have contributed to the commercial economy. There were also farms in Connecticut that depended on enslaved labour (Milkofsky 6). The extent and nature of enslavement in Connecticut have been explored by writers like Jennifer Frank in *Beyond Complicity-The Forgotten Story of Connecticut's Slave Ships* (http://www. courant. com/courant-250/moments-in-history/hc-250-beyond-complicity-story-gallery-20140604-storygallery. html) and Joel Lang in *Salem-The Plantation Next Door* (www. courant. com/news/special-reports/hc-plantation.artsep29-). There is much more work that needs to done in this area. However, we do know that although the numbers were much smaller than in the Caribbean, elements of the enslavement culture must have been parallel. In fact, as in other societies that were connected to the colonial and enslavement systems,

Connecticut newspapers followed the events of the Haitian revolution in 1791 very closely (Farrow et al. 3–44).

However, in spite of these connections, the single most influential connection between Connecticut and the Caribbean was far more intangible. We share the culture of maritime communities - these are ties that bind and shape our communities in ways we do not fully understand. The sea – and in the case of Connecticut the river - were important to the development of both communities. This in turn shaped societies that had much in common. Our societies were shaped not just by what was traded and how much money was made, but the fact that trade brings with it a different ontology, a different way of seeing the world. It connects people in ways not thought of, it breathes a spirit of adventure, it engenders a culture of great degrees of acceptance and tends to foster resilience and resistance. This in turn tends to lead to a challenge of the statuesque. Both our societies can be described as having porous boundaries. What flowed across those boundaries were not only sugar, rum, molasses, food and lumber, but also individuals, ideas and aesthetics, creating what Bolster describes as a culture characterized by hybridity (*Black Jacks* 42).

We can start with the very issue of enslavement. The Caribbean economy dictated that maritime enslavement would be central to its very existence. Enslaved seamen lived qualitatively different lives from those on land (Cateau 1–3). Legislators could not control either their movement or the nature of their interaction as they would have liked. One could well imagine that from the seventeenth to the nineteenth century blacks worked on all kinds of vessels that plied the route between Connecticut and the British Caribbean. Free blacks, runaway enslaved persons and enslaved seamen who had the consent of their 'owners' gravitated towards trading vessels. They worked as sailors, stewards and cooks (Cateau 5–8). Wages were much higher and there was far more independence (Cateau 10–12). There was also a greater chance of eventually becoming free.

In historical documents, accounts and stories we meet several people who used the maritime activities to advance their quest for freedom. One of them is an enslaved person: Venture Smith. His story begins with him being sold as a child to a slave owner on Fishers Island, New York. However, he was able to secure freedom for himself and his family. In the 1770s he worked on a whaler, and eventually became a landowner in Haddam, Connecticut (Bolster 'To Feel...' 1181). This success was due in great part to his small-boat freighting ventures. Nor was Venture Smith the only enslaved person to use the sea to advance. During the Revolution many black men served as privateers on ships in the Continental Navy. The Connecticut and Massachusetts state navies were known for enlisting all the black sailors they could recruit (Bolster 'To Feel...' 1174)). In the north particularly, such service could sometimes lead to freedom. This was the path to freedom used by Prince, an enslaved mariner from Lyme, Connecticut, who was able to use his privateering proceeds to secure freedom from his master, Captain Joseph Mather. He was freed in 1779 (Bolster *Black Jacks* 11).

According to Marcus Rediker, maritime culture produced 'egalitarian impulses' which while by no means colour blind or prejudice free often confounded the racial etiquette of the time (Rediker 286). Racial boundaries did exist, but they were often altered in the contexts of the institutions, the practical realities of the ship and what I call the culture of the sea. Enslaved persons came to constitute two to three per cent of the population in Connecticut in the mid to late eighteenth century, but they frequently lived in clustered maritime towns (Bernard Bailyn in Farrow et al. 3–44). Thus maritime enslavement shaped the local black society until the American Revolution while free black seafaring shaped it afterwards. I contend that this maritime culture also fostered and advanced Connecticut and British Caribbean connections.

This culture was shared by other persons connected to the sea and must have shaped the entire community to some extent. There would have also been ship captains who resided in Connecticut and the Caribbean. Captain Nathaniel Howard always brought home items from his visits to other places and his wife sold them from her store (Howard 78). John Smith of Middletown, Connecticut was a sea captain whose voyages took him to Martinique, Antigua and Trinidad. He was connected with several vessels including the *Mehitabel*, the *Lucy*, the *Rising Sun* and the *Almena* (John Smith and Phelps family papers, 1752-1904, Connecticut Historical Society, CHS). There is also the example of the Farringtons who moved from Connecticut to establish a trading business in Trinidad. Unfortunately both died there (Martha Williams incoming correspondence, 1784–1793, CHS). Excerpts from *Chronicles of a Connecticut Farm* written in 1905 (by Mary Perkins) describing dinner in the 'happy years' after the revolution related stories of '...stores of ham and huge cheeses, casks of West Indian rum, brandy, and all sorts of West Indian preserves...' (Farrow et al. 3–44).

Thus, both people and goods were moving between the Caribbean and Connecticut. However, in many senses it was more than this – it was a shared space. Caribbean people owned property in Connecticut and other areas and North Americans owned plantations in the islands. The Gedney Clarkes of Salem owned extensive plantations in Barbados and Guiana. Their son became Surveyor General of Customs in Barbados, member of the House of Assembly and, subsequently, the Council (Williams 112). North Americans soon discovered the value of the Caribbean sunshine. Planters in the islands in turn headed to North America to restore health concerns that they felt were being compounded by the heat of the tropical climate. The climate in North America was more similar to what they were accustomed to in Britain. It is also said that 'West Indian heiresses' were as valued in North America as they were in Britain (Williams 112). Not surprisingly, in both the British Caribbean and Connecticut a very wealthy class was created from the trade.

Horace Hayden, the Father of the Dental Profession, in his youth made several voyages to the West Indies and engaged in businesses in the West Indies, Connecticut and New York (Howard 278–279). Joshua Leffingwell of Hartford, Connecticut organized his life so that he could enjoy spending the winter in a warm climate in the early nineteenth century. He was an architect and builder in Hartford, and he and his brother John built a number of buildings including the Hartford Bank, Center Church and the Old State House. It would surprise many to know that he also constructed houses, disassembled them and shipped them to Trinidad. He then spent the winter months in the sunny, warm Caribbean climate where he could assemble the houses. There are several references to this in his diary and in account books (Joshua Leffingwell Diary and Account Book, 1805–1808, MS 73124, CHS). This was clearly not an isolated incident, but a way of life. We should not assume that he was alone. The two societies seem to have interacted and shared a common space on many levels from the eighteenth well into the nineteenth century and even before.

It should not be too surprising, therefore, that when labour was needed after the Second World War, tobacco farmers looked to the Caribbean for assistance. Beginning in 1947, thousands of Jamaicans and Puerto Ricans came to Connecticut (Glasser 26–31). Their impact is still felt today. Such connections have continued into the twenty-first century. In our contemporary time the University of Connecticut is leading a multi-phased investigation in Tobago to find and study the remains of 16 vessels that were sunk in a fierce battle in Scarborough in 1677. Ironically, this archaeological discovery promises to yield much historical information about shipbuilding and maritime culture. Thus the fact that we are maritime communities whether through the river or the sea is still bringing us together. The team began working in 2012 (nauticalarch. org/projects/all/central_america_caribbean/the rockybay project).

Another sign that our communities are connected comes from the fact that Credit Unions in Connecticut and Trinidad have been in partnership since 2001 and working on several projects involving leadership training and youth development (WOCCU International Partnership Blog January 11, 2015 15:27). Seen in this light, the fact that in 1998 Trinity College developed the Trinity-in-Trinidad Program to explore Caribbean Civilization seems a natural progression. For four months students are immersed in carnival, parang, Rameela and true 'Trini' culture. However, the rich, diverse, unique multi-ethnic culture of Trinidad and Tobago is built on a foundation that was partly shared by Connecticut. I have seen students become immersed in our culture so much so that last year one student played in the National Panorama competition.[1] Perhaps our connection may be ultimately based on shared historical experiences. The politics, art, history, religion, food, music, environment and indeed the very ethos of our two communities have evolved from a maritime culture which facilitated the movement of peoples of all colours and economic groups, but most importantly it facilitated the sharing of ideas and ideologies, and created a new sense of space and facilitated the growth of freedom in many senses (economic and non-economic). In our maritime communities borders are not barriers and there is no border that is insurmountable. There is room for further study both in the Caribbean and in Connecticut. I have just scratched the surface.

Notes
1. Indeed, throughout the years, Trinity students have been in the Soca Monarch finals (The Celtic Connection 2004), performed in Dimanche Gras; they have performed with the Malick Folk Performance Group, organized ceremonies at the Hindu Prachar Kendra, and participated in other ways in Trinidad's many-faceted society and culture. Rachel Platten, whose 'Fight Song' catapulted her to the top of the US music charts a few years ago, was a student in Trinidad of Andé Tanker; she also participated in Soca Monarch performances, 2004. (ed. Note).

Works Cited
'Beyond Complicity – The Forgotten Story of Connecticut's Slave Ships.' Courant.com. http://www.courant.com/courant-250/moments-in-history/hc-250-beyond-complicity-story-gallery-20140604-storygallery.
Bolster, Jeffrey. *Black Jacks: African American Seamen in the Age of Sail.* Cambridge, MA: Harvard University Press, 1997.
———. '"To Feel Like a Man": Black Seamen in the Northern States, 1800–1860.' *The Journal of American History*, 76, no. 4 (March 1990): 1,173–199.
Browne, Kim. *Measuring America: Your Guide to Caribbean Population Statistics.* U. S. Census Bureau.
Cateau, Heather. 'Independence in Enslavement: Bringing Enslaved Seamen to Light.' In *In the Fires of Hope Vol 2.*, edited by Debbie McCollin, 1–16. Kingston, Jamaica: Ian Randle Publishers, 2016.
Connecticut River Museum Archival Records. www.ctrivermuseum.org/customhouse-records/
Farrow, Anne, Joel Lang, and Jennifer Frank. 'Complicity: How Connecticut Chained Itself to Slavery.' *Northeast Magazine,* September 2002, Chapter 1.
Glasser, Ruth. 'Tobacco Valley: Puerto Rican Farm Workers in Connecticut.' *Connecticut Explored* (Fall 2002): 26–31.
Grasso, Christopher. *A Speaking Aristocracy: Transforming Public Discourse in Eighteenth Century Connecticut.* Chapel Hill, NC: University of North Carolina Press, 2012.
Howard, Daniel. *A New History of Old Windsor, Connecticut.* Windsor Locks, CT: The Journal Press, 1935.
John Smith and Phelps family papers, 1752–1904. Harford, CT: Connecticut Historical Society.
Joshua Leffingwell Papers, Harford, CT: Connecticut Historical Society.
Martha Williams incoming correspondence, 1784–1793. Harford, CT: Connecticut Historical Society.
Lang, Joel and James Cabot. 'Horse Jockeys in the West India Trade.' *The Hartford Courant,* no. 250, Moments in History. Hartford. September 29, 2002.
Lang, Joel in *Salem-The Plantation Next Door.* http://www.courant.com/news/special-reports/hc-plantation.artsep.
Milkofsky, Brenda. 'Connecticut and the West Indies: Sugar Spurs Trans-Atlantic Trade.' 7 Jan 2016. http://www. connecticuthistory.org.
Pierpont Fuller, Grace. 'An Introduction to the History of Connecticut as a Manufacturing State.' MA Thesis. Smith College Studies in History, edited by John Spencer Bassett and Sidney Bradshaw Fay, 1915.
Rediker, Marcus. *Between the Devil and the Deep Blue Sea: Merchant Seamen, Pirates and the Anglo-American Maritime World 1700–1750.* Cambridge, MA: Cambridge University Press, 1989.
Sheridan, Richard. *Sugar and Slavery.* Caribbean Universities Press, 1974.
Williams, Eric. *Capitalism and Slavery.* Chapel Hill, NC: University of North Carolina Press, 1944.
WOCCU International Partnership Blog, January 11, 2015.

CHAPTER 3

A New Mediterranean: The Caribbean in the Euro-American Imaginary

Gary Reger

European explorers who, starting with Columbus, came into the Caribbean world soon realized that the Caribbean forms an enclosed sea. Buttressed by the Gulf of Mexico, land rings it to the north, west, and south; and to the east, the Antilles demarcates its boundary against the open Atlantic. At the end of the eighteenth century the German polymath Alexander von Humboldt, who travelled to South America and the Caribbean between 1799 and 1804 and reported his observations in his multi-volume *Personal Narrative of Travels to the Equinocitial Regions of the New Continent, During the Years 1799–1804*, may have been the first explicitly to call the Caribbean an 'American Mediterranean'.[1] This notion became a theme for many non-Caribbean observers, especially from the United States (US), in the nineteenth and twentieth centuries.

My exploration of the two worlds of the Mediterranean and the Caribbean rests on a substructure of intellectual engagements with history, geography, race, and economics. While it is impossible, in the scope of a short essay, to examine in detail all the complex strands of this tapestry, it seems important at least to trace their lines. First comes landscape, because the ways in which people view the landscapes (and seascapes) of the Mediterranean and Caribbean worlds inform emotional, intellectual, and social reactions to them. As an example that intersects with both of our seas, consider the emotional responses evoked by islands for many Euro-American observers, from Lawrence Durrell, whose *islomania* – one of the 'diseases as yet unclassified by medical science' – encapsulates his own mental relation to the islands of the Mediterranean, to professional geographer David Lowenthal's lyrical appreciation of the special charms islands have for him, even though he is perfectly aware of the rose-coloured glasses through which we may view these often impoverished and exploited landscapes (Durrell 15; Lowenthal 'Islands').

This emotional connection inflected upper-middle class notions about islands as tourist destinations. In this imaginary, islands are magical, different, special. On the other hand, both the Mediterranean and Caribbean worlds include territories that are not insular and have long histories of colonialism, racism, and exploitation by Euro-American centres of power (both political and economic) that have clashed with demands by local inhabitants for self-determination, freedom, and respect. These histories intersect with the imaginary of the Mediterranean-Caribbean analogy.

This exploitative relationship, however, does not tell the whole story of the Mediterranean and Caribbean worlds and their experiences in the twentieth century. The largely tourist imaginary traced in its emergence from Humboldt's geographic analogy sits on the thin threshold where visitor meets islander in an often highly mediated and artificial intersection. It misses, or only tangentially connects with, efforts by islanders to shape their own destiny, to economic drivers unrelated to tourism, or to the social and political conflicts that all societies are subject to. The optic through which I compare the Mediterranean-Caribbean worlds is hardly the only, or even a privileged, one.

This essay focuses on *ideas* about the Caribbean and Mediterranean. The great diversity of these seas – geographically, historically, socially, culturally – tends to be erased in the notions outsiders have about them. Thus, while I am aware of the mistake of treating them as if they were simple unities, the questions I am asking here compel me to ignore the extraordinary diversity to concentrate on ideas about these seas that are in fact simplistic and distorted. In doing so, I hope to show also some of the hazards in approaching either region in this way. Misunderstanding abounds, not least in the misleading analogy of the Caribbean as an 'American Mediterranean' whose history I am seeking to trace. I remark here and there on certain aspects of the problematics, without any claim to comprehensiveness.

The Mediterranean Caribbean of Alexander von Humboldt

As Humboldt (vol. 6, 801) states bluntly, 'the Caribbean Sea is like the basin of the Mediterranean'. Writing of 'the state of Capitania-General of Caraccas', he remarks that it is 'bathed by the Little Caribbean Sea, a sort of mediterranean' (vol. 3, 428; note the lower-case 'm'). A discussion of earthquakes in the Caribbean basin leads him quickly into a long digression in which he makes explicit the similarities he sees between the two:

> [F]or we MUST not forget, that, notwithstanding the distance which separates these countries, the low grounds of Louisiana, and the coasts of Venezuela and Cumana, belong to the same basin, that of the Gulf of Mexico. This *Mediterranean Sea, with several outlets,* runs from the south-east to the north-west; and an ancient prolongation of it seems to be found in those vast plains.... When we consider geologically *the basin of the Caribbean sea, and of the Gulf of Mexico*...[m]ore than two thirds of this basin are covered with water.

For Humboldt the Antilles form a 'Mediterranean Archipelago', dominated by volcanoes and extending in a 'great arch...from Paria to the coast of Florida' by which they 'close this interior sea on the eastern side....'[2] The analogy's sloppiness is hard to ignore: there is no 'Mediterranean Archipelago' (the closest one gets are the islands of the Aegean, often so treated from antiquity to the present day, but they do not make an arch and enclose nothing) and the Mediterranean is not bounded by a chain of islands on any side but by mainland masses. Indeed, closer examination of the geography and geology of the two seas would deeply undermine the comparison. A largely limestone substrate underlies much of the Mediterranean basin; mountains, some quite high, encircle parts of it, the results of tectonic uplift. Several Caribbean islands are volcanic, and the climate is mostly tropical wet savanna, while the Mediterranean is steppe, either hot or cold (in the Köppen-Geiger classification: see Peel et al.). And of course much of the Caribbean is exposed to hurricanes; no such storms arise in the Mediterranean.

Humboldt really does not mean to say the seas are somehow the same thing in different places; rather, he draws on analogies as a heuristic device to render familiar to his European readers exotic phenomena and topographies:[3] to 'domesticate' a foreign landscape or a place by evoking its resemblance to something familiarly Mediterranean. Thus, when he discusses the boiling springs of the island of Guadeloupe, he evokes the bubbling hot springs of the Bay of Naples (and those of Palma Island in the Canaries); in another passage he compares the palms of Cariaco to the 'chamaerops' of Mediterranean shores or provides his readers with an easy conceptualization of Haiti as 'an island more than three times as big as Sicily, in the middle of the Mediterranean of the West Indies'. Perhaps most vividly – and romantically – he brings home a long description of how the noonday silences of the Caribbean world, under terrific heat, are broken by the 'many voices' of insects and lizards

> ...proclaiming to us that all nature breathes; and that, under a thousand different forms, life is diffused throughout the cracked and dusty soil, as well as in the bosom of the waters, and in the air that circulates around us. The sensations, which I here recalled to mind, are not unknown to those, who, without having advanced to the equator, have visited Italy, Spain, or Egypt. The contrast of motion and silence, that aspect of nature at once calm and animated, strikes the imagination of the traveller, when he enters the basin of the Mediterranean, within the zone of olives, dwarf palms, and date trees.[4]

Humboldt's other interest in the analogy derives from his theory that civilization originally emerged on the Mediterranean coasts. Susan Gillman quotes a telling heading from his last book *Cosmos*, published in English in 1850 and 1858, which encapsulates his view: 'The Mediterranean considered as the starting point for the representation of the relations which have laid the foundations of the gradual extension of the idea of the cosmos' (510, quoting Humboldt, *Cosmos* vol. 1, 119). But he had already formulated this view in his *Personal Narrative*, when he asserts that '[t]he existence of the Mediterranean has been closely connected with the first dawn of human culture among the nations of the west.'[5]

This idea clearly extended in Humboldt's judgment to some Spanish possessions. In comparison to some of the regions visited, there are, he asserts,

> more accurate notions of the political relations of countries, and more enlarged views on the state of colonies and their mother countries, at the Havannah and Caraccas. The numerous communications with commercial Europe, with that sea of the West Indies, which we have described as a mediterranean [sic] with many outlets, have had a powerful influence on the progress of society in the island of Cuba, and in the five provinces of Venezuela. Civilization has in no other part of Spanish America assumed a more European physiognomy (vol. 3, 472).

The 'Mediterraneanness' of this Caribbean world, with Atlantic outlets that create communication links with Europe, is precisely what allowed the flow of European culture west. It was indeed for Humboldt the Mediterranean that served as the cradle of civilization and the 'Mediterraneanness' of the Caribbean that allowed European civilization to flourish there.

Despite Humboldt and his followers, the thinness of the argument connecting these two regions is remarkable. Later observers took up the analogy, but often viewed it through a more explicitly critical lens. For example, the French geographer Élisée Reclus, who published a universal geography in the late nineteenth century, admitted freely that this so-called 'Mediterranean' of the New World, which, like the Mediterranean of the eastern hemisphere, 'is divided into secondary basins…in other respects presents little resemblance to that great inland sea' (1). For anyone who scans the 'American Mediterranean' literature produced in the late nineteenth and early twentieth century, and later scholarly use of the term, the weaknesses of the analogy are unmistakable; indeed, it seems at times that scholarship has adopted the expression as a clever trope for the Caribbean. Matthew Pratt Guterl's fascinating account of Southern slave owners' schizophrenic relations with the Caribbean world is called *American Mediterranean*, but nowhere in the book does he explore the origins or value of or problems with this designation.[6] Likewise in *Struggle for the American Mediterranean*, a study of US and European conflict over the Caribbean and Gulf of Mexico world, Lester D. Langley accepts the analogy but never really explores its content or meaning, beyond the ways it was used as a convenient shorthand. He notes simply that 'The term was popularized in the protectorate era of the early twentieth century, when Americans looked naturally upon themselves as the carriers of civilization to backward peoples,' citing Stephen Bonsal's 1912 *American Mediterranean* as his only reference (x). And indeed, neither Bonsal's book nor Ober's *Our West Indian Neighbors* (1904), whose titles prominently display the phrase,[7] have much to say to enlighten readers about the actual parallels or analogies that may have governed the application of 'Mediterranean' to the Caribbean; Ober never actually uses the word 'Mediterranean' anywhere in his book after a brief mention at the beginning.

There is another intellectual problem that bedevils the analogy. Gillman argues that for Humboldt the Mediterranean as a 'reference point…is paradoxically not static' (512–13). This is perhaps not quite right, as Humboldt's use of the Mediterranean analogy seems to me to depend on the Mediterranean as a 'static' term of comparison. But Gilman's observation does reflect the fact that the Mediterranean was no more conceptually fixed than the Caribbean, for even as Humboldt was peppering his massive *Personal Narrative* with Mediterranean comparisons, the Mediterranean was changing as geographic and conceptualized space.

In Florence Deprest's study of changing geographic ideas about 'the Mediterranean' in three 'universal geographies' published between 1829 and 1934, the governing view of the Mediterranean in the earlier nineteenth century was as a space of separation: the sea divided Europe from Africa. Potent in this view was also the notion that the Mediterranean served to separate civilization from barbarism. In this analysis the south, especially, had degenerated under Islamic rule; a North Africa that had flourished under the Romans was transformed into a wasteland under the Arabs. This view of the Mediterranean, expressed in the universal geography of V.A. Malte-Brun, was congruent with Humboldt's own ideas about the Mediterranean world as the origin of civilization: 'It is,' he wrote, 'from the African shores that the old Egyptian colonies brought to barbarian (*sauvage*) Europe the first germs of civilization. Today Africa is the last part of the ancient world that awaits from the hand of the Europeans the salutary yoke of legislation and culture.'[8]

This 'Mediterranean', not a unified geographic – let alone social or cultural or historical – space, seems to me to be the Mediterranean that governs Humboldt's comparisons with the Caribbean. That is to say, although Humboldt occupies an important position in the history of the conceptualization of the Caribbean as an 'American Mediterranean', his notions are embedded in a view of both seas that was changing rapidly across the nineteenth and earlier twentieth centuries. We can see this transformation clearly in the work on the Mediterranean by Élisée Reclus (1876), for whom the Mediterranean was no longer a divider but a uniter. It became, in Deprest's words, a 'world space…based on the expansion of networks of commerce and navigation.' Indeed, Reclus urged that 'the uncertain currents [*flots*] of the Mediterranean have had on historical development an importance more considerable than the land on which men lived' (Deprest 80). This, I suggest, is a reconceptualization of the Mediterranean that spilled over also into thinking about the Caribbean as an 'American Mediterranean'. It too served to link rather than divide.

But it must be said that Humboldt anticipated this too.

> The shore of Columbia is more varied, and its spacious gulfs, such as that of Paria, Cariaco, Maracaybo, and Darien, were at the time of the first discovery better peopled than the rest, and

> facilitated the interchange of productions. That shore possesses an incalculable advantage in being washed by the Caribbean sea, a kind of inland sea with several outlets, and the only one pertaining to the New Continent. This basin, the different shores of which belong to the United States, the republic of Columbia, Mexico, and some maritime powers of Europe, gives rise to a peculiar system of trade, exclusively American. The south-east of Asia, with its neighbouring Archipelago, and above all, the state of the Mediterranean in the time of the Phenician and Greek colonies, have proved the happy influence of the nearness of opposite coasts which have not the same productions, and are inhabited by nations of different races, on commercial industry and intellectual cultivation. The importance of the inland sea of the Antilles, bounded by Venezuela on the south, will be still augmented by the progressive increase of population on the banks of the Mississippi; for that river, the Rio del Norte and the Magdalena, are the only great navigable streams which it receives. The depth of the American rivers, their immense branches, and the use of steam boats, every where facilitated by the proximity of forests, compensate to a certain extent the obstacles arising from the uniform line of the coasts, and the general configuration of the continent, in the promotion of industry and civilization.[9]

The prophecy of extraordinary development Humboldt lays out here looks to the interconnections – the 'connectivity' – of trade, natural resources, and access that endow his Caribbean with perhaps even more bountiful opportunities than the old Mediterranean.

At this point one might wonder whether there is anything more here than an antiquarian exploration of an analogy that has collapsed under the weight of its own inappropriateness. Humboldt's invocation of the Mediterranean to evoke aspects of the less-familiar Caribbean for his readers may have served a useful heuristic purpose in the early nineteenth century, but the different physical conditions of the two regions and developmental directions they have taken may make it seem obvious that there is little for us to glean from it today. I would like to suggest, however, that the notion of the Caribbean as an 'American Mediterranean' enjoyed a kind of shadowy afterlife that can be seen in particular in two spheres: first, in the role of major dominant urban centres facing the seas – which appealed, in the case of the Caribbean, notably to Southern slave-holders – and the emergence of the two regions as tourist destinations.

The Urban Worlds of New Orleans and Alexandria

In his study of Southern slaveholders' ante- and post-bellum relations with the Caribbean world, Guterl assembles a composite description of New Orleans from an 1857 book on Cuba by James Phillippo:

> New Orleans quite simply looked like many other port towns and cities in the Caribbean. James Phillippo, for one, noted that the "general air and *tout ensemble*" of the Crescent City brought forth "a confused remembrance of some of the best Spanish and French West India towns". Phillippo could not help, moreover, but focus on "the varied character of the inhabitants", from the 'Southern Planter' to the "unpolished Irishman" to "Chinamen", but most especially including the local slave population, "exhibiting almost every variety of shade of colour, from the jet black through all conceivable transitions to white almost as pure as that of Europeans". This topsy-turvy, mixed up society was most obviously marked by endless 'peculiarities': "No city in the world," he concluded, "presents greater contrasts of national manners and languages."[10]

In thinking about the Caribbean as an 'American Mediterranean', what strikes me here is the echo, from other and completely different works, of the character of later nineteenth- and earlier twentieth-century Alexandria in Egypt. This great Mediterranean port city emerged from a backwater, supporting barely 20,000 inhabitants when Napoleon invaded Egypt in 1798, to one of the largest, richest, and most cosmopolitan cities of the Mediterranean world by the end of the nineteenth century. The dynamic ruler of Egypt between 1805 and 1848, Muhammad 'Ali Pasha, chose Alexandria as his opening to the West. It was a city to which he attracted a polyglot population of Italians, Greeks, and various western Europeans, where Arabic was heard in the slums and streets but Greek, French, and English in the salons. Most importantly it was a bustling centre of commerce that rested most especially on the export of Egyptian cotton.[11] Ironically, it was the American Civil War, with the blockade of Southern exports, which opened the window for Egypt to wrest the European cotton market from Southern slave suppliers. (In a deeper irony, perhaps, the very best variety of cotton, Sea Island cotton, grown on the barrier islands off the coasts of the Carolinas and Georgia, seems to have derived from an Egyptian variety apparently first bred in a garden in Cairo).[12]

This urbanized, pulsating, diverse Caribbean-Mediterranean, infused with commercial values, thriving on the production, sale, and transportation of commodities – including, most egregiously, the human goods of the New Orleans slave markets – was inhabited by a highly diverse and often racially and ethnically oppressed population. It stands in marked contrast to both the topographic and geographic vision of Humboldt's analogies and the idealized, if not to say whitewashed, tourist destination that both seas became (or were becoming). As we segue into a discussion of the transfiguration of the Caribbean into a different kind of 'American Mediterranean' – the construction of a tourist model based in part on an analogous transformation of the Mediterranean and the imaginary of Southern California as another 'American Mediterranean'[13] – it is important to bear in mind this radically opposing way of seeing the two seas as analogous.

It is a bit of a puzzle why the idea of the Caribbean as an American Mediterranean appealed to Southern slave-owners. We do not generally think of the Mediterranean as a slave-holding space, although in fact it was. Plantation slavery, especially to raise sugarcane, arose in the Mediterranean (notably on Cyprus) long before it took hold in the South. Throughout the nineteenth century much of the Mediterranean littoral was under Ottoman control, and the Ottoman state strongly resisted northern European efforts to be forced to abolish slavery. Slavery persisted in French Algeria long after the metropole outlawed it in the colonies in 1848. Muhammad 'Ali recruited his army largely from slaves captured in what is today's Sudan, following a long-standing Ottoman practice.[14] This slavery link is speculative, for I have not encountered any explicit references to Mediterranean slavery in my readings about the appeal to Southerners of the Caribbean as a space where slavery persisted after 1865 in Brazil, Cuba, and Puerto Rico or where abolition (in their view) led to disaster (especially in Haiti), and I offer this merely as an observation; perhaps, indeed, as Guterl suggests in passing (16), the real appeal may have derived from Southerners' admiration of the Greek and Roman Mediterranean, which they certainly did see as a font for justifications of their own commitment to slavery (see Winterer). There may, however, be another element working here, one that also fed into the matter of tourism: that is the reconfiguration of both spaces as places appropriate for northerners, both European and American, to holiday.

Refashioning the Mediterranean

The Mediterranean had long been a tourist attraction for a certain class of educated, sophisticated northern Europeans, for whom the Grand Tour, originally focused on Italy, was *de rigeur*.[15] Americans like Samuel Clemens, Henry James, and William Dean Howells emulated their European counterparts, and indeed in the 1920s the Riviera drew wealthy (and not so wealthy) American bohemians seeking sun and sex. F. Scott Fitzgerald's 1934 *Tender Is the Night* takes them for its subject. One major appeal to northerners of the Mediterranean (aside from its climate) was the notion that you could be 'freer' there; for some, like a Norman Douglas or André Gide, this meant the ability to indulge sexual desires forbidden at home (that they were forbidden also in the south did not seem so much to matter).

To configure the Caribbean as an American Mediterranean tourist destination, however, required facing some problems. Chief among these were climate, health, and race, all three of which were deeply interconnected in nineteenth and twentieth century thinking about geographic space. The change in sensibilities about health first affected the Mediterranean.[16] While many early commentators had seen the hot south as dangerous for white man's health, 'disease ridden, morally degrading, and even deadly' (Carey 129), the later eighteenth and earlier nineteenth centuries saw a 'Mediterranean turn', as sun and sea became reconfigured from dangerous heat to revivifying, regenerating warmth. For northern Europeans – especially the British – the later nineteenth-century Mediterranean came to be constructed as a space of health, in particular around the pervasive problem of 'consumption' (tuberculosis – TB). Theories of causation for TB before the advent of the germ theory focused on environmental and dispositional propositions. The enclosed spaces of factories or stress, ennui, and overwork, acting on biological and psychological predispositions, could bring on the telltale cough. Doctors came to recommend the Mediterranean climate not for some direct atmospheric effect on consumptives, but rather the complex interactions of warmth, open air, relaxation, escape from daily stress, and other factors (see Pemble 84–96).

An analogous change overcame a pre-existing supposition of the unhealthiness of the tropical Caribbean. Mark Carey has traced out the factors that drove this change. Medical thinkers in the nineteenth century began to argue that mountains, the presence of regular winds, agriculture, economic development and 'civilization' all marked out spaces as 'healthy', and observers of the Caribbean world noted that these features appeared there, in the hills and mountains of Jamaica or the breezes that swept Barbados. Thus notions that the tropical climate of the Caribbean was dangerous eroded. These ideas were, of course, deeply imbricated with race: the view that black Africans thrived in hot tropical climates that enervated whites was, of course, a driving factor in the slave trade that brought so many Africans to the Caribbean in the first place.

As the Mediterranean was reconfigured as a safe and healthy space for white northern Europeans, this turn served in part to combat the trope that the Caribbean was 'tropical' and therefore unsuited for 'white men'. See, for instance, Stephan Bonsal's insistence, in 1912, about the weather:

> It would be thought that such a vast body of tepid waters...would raise the temperature in this region of the torrid zone so high as to render the islands uninhabitable. There are, however, the counteracting influences of the atmospheric currents, and of altitude, by which most fortunately the action of the Gulf Stream is neutralised and the surrounding lands of the isthmian region and the islands are made suitable for the settlement of white men (7).

American settlers in Cuba, Bonsal assures us, 'are thrifty, hard-working, and honest, and...stand active open-air work better than any other men of the white race'. The '[l]azy Creoles', of course, resent them. Bonsal stresses that racial antagonism in Cuba is due to the behaviour of the 'Negroes', who, he says, organize themselves into criminal gangs.[17] Yet even as Bonsal was writing, the US was experiencing revved-up anxiety caused precisely by perceptions about the olive races of the Mediterranean, who were immigrating in greater and greater numbers: Italians, Sicilians, Greeks. In 1861–1870 immigrants from southern Europe amounted to only 0.9 per cent of total immigration; by 1901–1910, that figure had exploded to 26.3 per cent (Giordano; figures from Osterhammel 156). There is considerable historical irony in the promotion of the Caribbean as an American Mediterranean in travel literature at the very moment that American cities like New York were teeming with southern European immigrants whose cultural practices and racial identity offended and frightened many whites.

Feeding such concerns was a long-standing association between dark skin and sexual immorality. Lurid tales of callow Southern boys drawn into lusty, wayward, and ultimately disastrous liaisons with dark-skinned mulattoes were a staple of popular literature in later nineteenth and early twentieth century America. Thomas Dixon's *The Sins of the Father* (1912) was only the most infamous of the genre. The French medical writer J.J. Virey had warned in 1819 that in black women 'voluptuousness [excites] a degree of lascivity unknown in our climate, for their sexual urges are much more developed than those of whites'. Heat, too, provoked sexual exuberance according to much thinking, both medical and popular, of the same period. So the southlands of the Mediterranean, like also the tropical islands of the Caribbean, carried a charge of danger for whites – unless and until, of course, pleasure elbowed aside other aims as the goal of travel (J.J. Virey 196, quoted in Littlewood 194–97). Here again, indeed, we encounter another irony, for in part, and for at least some travellers, it was *precisely* the promise of sexual laxity that shaped Mediterranean, and so also Caribbean, appeal. The pleasures a Norman Douglas sought in his Italian 'crocodiles' (the boys who were the target of his pederasty) find their echo in the salacious evocations of Creole women in a book like Lafcadio Hearn's *Two Years in the French West Indies* (1890; see also Gentles-Peart).

Finally, there is the problem of slavery and agriculture. As Matthew Pratt Guterl has recently argued, Southern American slave-owners, planters, and opponents generally of abolition saw the Caribbean as their own Mediterranean, yoked together on multiple parameters. Economically – and, inextricably, socially – they saw the Caribbean world as a proof-test of enslavement as a system for successful cultivation of tropical commodities like sugar and cotton.[18] Where abolition prevailed, disaster followed; Haiti was, of course, their *bête noire*,[19] but Jamaica, which they also saw as a failed experiment, drew their criticisms. Cuba, still committed to slavery after the Civil War, was argued to demonstrate the continued need for enslaved labour to cultivate these crops. The areas that persisted as slave-holding bastions in the Caribbean, like Brazil, attracted disaffected southerners, some of whom moved permanently in hopes of transplanting their slave-driven monoculture to the Caribbean world. These figures continued to regard the hot tropics as deleterious for whites and so economically exploitable only by use of enslaved Africans (Carey 138).

A Mediterraneanized Paradise[20]

'Those who want to turn their backs on civilisation', observes Ian Littlewood in his survey of sex and travel,

> are sometimes drawn to the harsher places of the earth – the desert, the mountains, the heart of the jungle – but these are destinations for the ascetic; they have more to do with curbing desire than fulfilling it. Rebels in the cause of personal liberty have usually preferred the enticements of the tropical island, and the image that attracts them has remained more or less unchanged for a couple of centuries (144).

Ian Strachen, writing on tourism in the Anglophone Caribbean, offers a slightly different take:

> At various periods in the past five hundred years, paradise has been associated with notions of the primitive, innocence, savagery, and a lack of civilization, as well as of ignorance, nakedness, health and happiness, isolation from the rest of the world and humanity, timelessness, nature's beauty and abundance, life without labor, human beings' absolute freedom and domination over nature as God's stewards on Earth, and connections of paradise with concepts of wild pleasure, perpetual sunshine, and leisure (Strachan 5).

Both observers, however, are certainly looking through different facets of the same phenomenon: the reconfiguration, seen through North American eyes (and indeed also northern European), of the Caribbean as a prime tourist destination, offering the same seductions as the Mediterranean. In the later twentieth century, the Caribbean and the Mediterranean converge most explicitly. In this confection the two spaces are seen as tourist destinations, constricted by the elision of all the other ways these spaces work, especially the social, economic, and environmental problems that bedevil them. They are linked, in a shadow world, to the very tourist machinery that depends on and relentlessly promotes sun, surf, sea, sand, sex, and a sort of domesticated exoticism. Both seas proffer an abundance of islands and seashores, replete with big resorts or boutique hotels, staffed by exotic – but not *too* exotic – 'natives' who speak excellent, though locally accented, English, and whose lives away from the liminality of sea and sand are artfully concealed. The wealthy northerners who form much of the clientele may be greeted with smiles but mocked behind their backs or openly resented. The Mediterranean remains, it seems, the most touristed destination on the planet (though problems of drawing boundaries and collecting data render the claim at least slightly slippery),[21] but the Caribbean has almost equal appeal, and, for Americans, the advantages of proximity and, now, greater perceived safety, unless overwhelmed by fear of Zika.

Some final reflections

In this essay, I have tried to draw together some of the strands that make up the notion of an 'American Mediterranean'. The actual, physical Mediterranean served for Europeans as a ground for the pursuit of not only health but also explicitly sensual and personal pleasure liberated from confining northern European mores. Intertwined with these pursuits was always anxiety about race, marked both in changing ideas about the 'healthiness' for whites of hot, tropical climates and the persistent notion that dark skin and hot climates provoked sexual libertinism. The analogy was loose but persistent; exploration of the use of the comparison by Alexander von Humboldt tells us much about the lability of the idea and the ways in which his work did, and did not, contribute to later applications of the term.

It is perhaps appropriate to end by reiterating the warnings with which I began. The optic through which I have viewed and analysed the Mediterranean-Caribbean trope is neither complete nor exhaustive. There remain many other ways to consider these two worlds, alike in some respects, different in others. In particular, the touristic position that I explore in the latter part of the essay, by its nature, avoids engaging the very urgent problem of agency. The tourist may, too often, not even see the point to Gayatri Chakravorty Spivak's question, 'Can the subaltern speak?', let alone offer an answer. But, I suggest, the absence of an answer, indeed the obliviousness to the question, carries its own urgency. We live in a world in which tourism has become, for better or worse, the institution through which many upper-middle class people (and not just Euro-Americans) interact with their 'hosts' when they travel. (In terms of the Mediterranean and Caribbean, one thinks immediately of the huge tourist ships that now ply both seas.) Questions of authenticity of experience may bedevil the traveller, but that yearning for the 'real' may not include a desire to peek beyond the threshold to examine the complexities of life on a Grenada. It is useful to be reminded of the structures of touristic experience, seen here through the reconfiguration of Humboldt's old analogy. Again, I cannot claim here any comprehensiveness; this topic is immense, with a long and complex history.[22] I only hope that this tentative and very incomplete foray into a big and wide-ranging question may offer a useful, though small, contribution to an ongoing discussion that bears not only on academic matters of intellectual history but on the real-life experiences of the islanders who inhabit that lands of the Mediterranean and Caribbean Seas.

Notes

1. On Humboldt and the 'American Mediterranean', see now Gillman, to whom I am deeply indebted; see also Wulf 51–108 and Taglioni. The University of Chicago Press has announced a project to translate the whole of his work into English: see http://press.uchicago.edu/ucp/books/series/HUMBENG.html (accessed February 5, 2016). I use the seven-volume English translation of von Humboldt and Aimé Bonpland's *Personal Narrative of Travels to the Equinoctial Regions of the New Continent During the Years 1799 to 1804* by Helen Maria Williams published in 1818, checked, when possible, against the French original.
2. Humboldt and Bonpland vol. 4, 8–10, 36–38; see also vol. 5, 863–64.
3. So more generally Wulf 51: 'Humboldt compared everything he saw with what he had previously observed and learned in Europe.'
4. Humboldt and Bonpland vol. 3, 200 n., 200–201; vol. 6, 113; see also vol. 6, 551, and vol. 1, 46–47; vol. 4, 505–506. *Chamaerops humilis* is the European fan palm. See also his analogy between Mediterranean and Caribbean 'electric torpedoes' (eels): vol. 4, 345 with n., and his calling the 'Caribees' the Bedouin of Guyana (vol. 5, 500). Several of the passages cited below are also quoted and studied by Gillman 509–12, who notes (at 510) Humboldt's use of '*the* Mediterranean' (her emphasis) as his '*point d'appui*' (511).
5. Humboldt and Bonpland vol. 6, 184; vol. 5, 499–500. I have modified the standard translation of Helen Maria Williams to correspond better with the French; she rendered *la Méditerranée* as 'our Mediterranean' and *la culture humaine* as 'human cultivation.' Gillman 511, quoting both the translation and the original, remarks only on the discrepancy between 'the' and 'our'.
6. All I have noticed is this: 'The title of this book is derived from a reading of the sources, but it also owes something to a very different work of history,' that is, Langley; Guterl 193 n. 6.
7. The full title of Ober's book is *Our West Indian Neighbors: The Islands of the Caribbean Sea, "America's Mediterranean": Their Picturesque Features, Fascinating History, and Attractions for the Traveler, Nature-lover, Settler and Pleasure-seeker*.
8. Deprest 75 and 92, treating K. Malte-Brun's *Précis de la géographie universelle* of 1810–1829, revised by his son in 1851–1854; *L'Europe méridionale* by Élisée Reclus of 1876; and M. Sorre and J. Sion's *Méditerranée. Péninsules méditerranéennes* of 1934. In the notion of the

sea as divider one hears echoes in Henri Pirenne's famous thesis, now refuted, that with the Islamic conquest of North Africa what had been a single unifying sea became instead a barrier. On the trope of North African degeneration under Arab rule, see especially Davis. Deprest 79, for the quotation from Malte-Brun (my translation).

9. Humboldt and Bonpland vol. 6, 183–84, 208, on trade in flour.
10. Guterl 2008, 31, quoting James Phillippo, *The United States and Cuba* (London: Pewtress 1857), 303 and 306 (*non vidi*). Guterl continues in sentences I have not quoted to excerpt a number of other authors of about the same date.
11. See the fundamental, exhaustive study of Ilbert 1996. For Muhammad 'Ali, see Fahmy 1998; on his imperial ambitions, Ibrahim 1998, 198–210. The Alexandrian poet C.P. Cavafy (1863–1933) owed his English education – so effective that he spoke his native Greek with an English accent all his life – to his family's business in the cotton trade.
12. See Porcher and Fick 2010 (reprint of the 2005 edition published by the Charleston Museum), 89–100. For the impact of the Civil War, Becket 2014, 242–73, 293–94, 297–99.
13. As an aside, it may be worth recalling that early boosters of California configured the state, especially its southern part, as a 'Mediterranean', a comparison that rested in part on an analogous climate and geology (both good for grapes), as Karl Offen has reminded me. This matter would require far more space to be explored properly than I have in this essay (see Remondino, for example, and Starr).
14. Ottoman slavery, Toledano 1983; persisting slavery in French Algeria, Brower 2009, 141–96; Muhammad 'Ali's army, Helal 2011.
15. Gaztambide-Géigel shows how late the usage spread; he gives 1898 as the date at which the Caribbean became a 'Mediterranean' (137), but this requires a narrower optic than I have adopted here.
16. A thorough treatment of the whole congeries can be found in Pemble, and see Gordon; both discuss the problem of health and the Mediterranean, which was viewed earlier as dangerous. Littlewood 204–208, on Americans on the Riviera.
17. Bonsal 21–22, 41; in Jamaica, he asserts, the blacks are doing better than elsewhere due to the 'guidance of intelligent and sympathetic white men' (59). Bonsal sprinkles comments about whites and blacks through the hundreds of pages of his book.
18. Becket 88–97 on the emergence of a slave-driven cotton culture in the Caribbean; May for Southerners' attraction to the Caribbean as a slaveowners' paradise.
19. Ober 154: 'As God made it, Haiti is a dream of delight; as the black man has defiled it, no white person can live there and be content.' One could expand indefinitely examples of this kind of judgment.
20. Carrie Gibson entitles her chapter on Caribbean tourism 'Invented Paradise' (338).

21. Gordon 203, relying on data from the World Tourism Organization, which publishes annually a *Compendium of Tourism Statistics*.
22. See McCannell, *The Tourist* and especially *The Ethics of Sightseeing*. For a good case study of the interaction of tourist and host in a once-remote Chinese town, see Notar. I am very grateful to the organizers of the Turning Tides Conference, where a very different version of this essay was first floated, for their invitation, to everyone at the University of the West Indies for their hospitality, and especially to Gordon Rohlehr for his many incisive comments. I only regret that I could not take more of them into account. Heather Cateau and Milla Riggio provided very helpful comments and suggestions which considerably improved this paper. Karl Offen's comments identified several places I needed to think more clearly, and I have tried my best to incorporate, or at least acknowledge, his suggestions. All remaining problems should be credited to my account alone.

Works Cited:

Becket, Sven. *Empire of Cotton: A Global History*. New York, NY: Alfred A. Knopf, 2014.

Bonsal, Stephen. *The American Mediterranean*. New York, NY: Moffat, Yard, 1912.

Bower, Benjamin Claude. *A Desert Named Peace: The Violence of France's Empire in the Algerian Sahara, 1844–1902*. New York, NY: Columbia University Press, 2009.

Carey, Mark. 'Inventing Caribbean Climates: How Science, Medicine, and Tourism Changed Tropical Weather from Deadly to Healthy.' *Osiris* 26 (2011): 129–141.

Daly, M. W., ed. *The Cambridge History of Egypt. Volume Two: Modern Egypt from 1517 to the End of the Twentieth Century*. Cambridge, MA: Cambridge University Press, 1998.

Davis, Diana K. *Resurrecting the Granary of Rome: Environmental History and French Colonial Expansion in North Africa*. Columbus, OH: Ohio University Press, 2007.

Deprest, Florence. 'Méditerranée. L'invention géographique de la Méditerranée. Eléments de reflexion.' *L'espace géographique* 31 (2002): 73–93.

Durrell, Lawrence. *Prospero's Cell and Reflections on a Marine Venus*. New York, NY: E. P. Dutton, 1962.

Fahmy, Khaled. 'The Era of Muhammad 'Ali Pasha, 1805–1848.' In *The Cambridge History of Egypt. Volume Two: Modern Egypt from 1517 to the End of the Twentieth Century*, edited by M.W. Daly, 139–179. Cambridge, MA: Cambridge University Press, 1998.

Gaztambide-Géigel, Antonio. 'The Invention of the Caribbean in the 20th Century (The Definitions of the Caribbean as an Historical and Methodological Problem).' *Social and Economic Studies* 53 (2004): 127–57.

Gentles-Peart, Kamille. *Romance with Voluptousness: Women and Thick Bodies in the United States.* Lincoln, NE: University of Nebraska Press, 2016.

Gibson, Carrie. *Empire's Crossroads. A History of the Caribbean from Columbus to the Present Day.* London: Macmillan, 2014.

Gillman, Susan. 'Humboldt's American Mediterranean.' *American Quarterly* 66 (2014): 505–28.

Giordano, Paolo. 'Italian Immigration in the State of Louisiana. Its Causes, Effects, and Results.' *Italian Americana* 5 (1979): 160–177.

Gordon, Bertram M. 'The Mediterranean as a Tourist Destination from Classical Antiquity to Club Me.' *Mediterranean Studies* 12 (2003): 203–26.

Guterl, Matthew Pratt. *American Mediterranean. Southern Slaveholders in an Age of Emancipation.* Cambridge, MA: Harvard University Press, 2008.

Hearn, Lafcadio. *Two Years in the French West Indies.* New York, NY: Interlink Books, 2001. Originally published in 1890.

Helal, Emad Ahmed. 'Muhammad 'Ali's First Army: The Experiment in Building an Entirely Slave Army.' In *Race and Slavery in the Middle East. Histories of Trans-Saharan Africans in Nineteenth-Century Egypt, Sudan, and the Ottoman Mediterranean*, edited by Terence Walz and Kenneth M. Cuno, 17–43. Cairo: American University in Cairo Press, 2011.

Humboldt, Alexander von. *Cosmos. A Sketch of the Physical Description of the Universe*, translated by Elise C. Orté. 2 vols. New York, NY: Harper & Bros, 1850 and 1858.

Humboldt, Alexander von, and Aimé Bonpland. *Personal Narrative of Travels to the Equinoctial Regions of the New Continent, during the Years 1799–1804*, 7 vols., translated by Helen Maria Williams. London: H. G. Bohn, 1852–1853.

Ibrahim, Hassan Ahmed. 'The Egyptian Empire, 1805–1885.' In *The Cambridge History of Egypt. Volume Two: Modern Egypt from 1517 to the End of the Twentieth Century*, edited by M.W. Daly, 198–216. Cambridge, MA: Cambridge University Press, 1998.

Ilbert, Robert. *Alexandrie 1830–1930. Histoire d'une communauté citadine.* 2 vols. Cairo: Institut français d'archéologie orientale, 1996.

Langley, Lester D. *The Struggle for the American Mediterranean. United States-European Rivalry in the Gulf-Caribbean, 1776–1904.* Athens, GA: University of Georgia Press, 1976.

Littlewood, Ian. *Sultry Climates. Travel and Sex.* Cambridge, MA: Harvard University Press, 2001.

Lowenthal, David. 'Islands, Lovers, and Others.' *Geographical Review* 97 (2007): 202–29.

———. 'Living with and Looking at Landscape.' *Landscape Research* 35 (2007): 637–59.

MacCannell, Dean. *The Ethics of Sightseeing.* Berkeley, CA: University of California Press, 2011.

———. *The Tourist. A New Theory of the Leisure Class. With a New Introduction.* Berkeley, CA: University of California Press, 2013.

May, Robert E. *The Southern Dream of a Caribbean Empire, 1854–1861.* Gainesville, FL: University Press of Florida, 2002.

Notar, Beth E. 'Producing Cosmopolitanism at the Borderlands: Lonely Planeteers and 'Local' Cosmopolitans in Southwest China.' *Anthropological Quarterly* 81 (2008): 615–50.

Ober, Frederick. *Our West Indian Neighbors: The Islands of the Caribbean Sea, 'America's Mediterranean.' Their Picturesque Features, Fascinating History, and Attractions for the Traveler, Nature-Lover, Settler and Pleasure-Seeker.* New York, NY: J. Pott & Co., 1904.

Osterhammel, Jürgen. *The Transformation of the World. A Global History of the Nineteenth Century*, translated by Patrick Camiller. Princeton, NJ: Princeton University Press, 2014.

Peel, M. C., B. L. Finlayson, and T. A. McMahon. 'Updated World Map of the Köppen-Geiger Climate Classification.' *Hydrology and Earth System Sciences* 11 (2007): 1,633–644.

Pemble, John. *The Mediterranean Passion. Victorians and Edwardians in the South.* Oxford: Clarendon Press, 1987.

Porcher, Richard Dwight, and Sarah Fick. *The Story of Sea Island Cotton.* Layton: Gibbs Smith, 2010.

Reclus, Élisée. *The Earth and its Inhabitants: The Universal Geography, vol. III. Mexico, Central America, West Indies*, edited by A.H. Keane. J.S. Virtue & Co., Limited, n.d.

Remondino, Peter Charles. *The Mediterranean Shores of America: Southern California: Its Climatic, Physical, and Meteorological Conditions.* Philadelphia, PA: F. A. Davis Co., 1892.

Spivak, Gayatri Chakravorty. 'Can the Subaltern Speak?' In *Marxism and the Interpretation of Culture*, edited by C. Nelson and L. Grossberg, 271–313. Basingstoke: Macmillan Education, 1988.

Starr, Kevin. *Americans and the California Dream, 1850–1914.* New York, NY: Oxford University Press, 1973.

Strachan, Ian G. *Paradise and Plantation. Tourism and Culture in the Anglophone Caribbean.* Charlottesville, VA: University of Virginia Press, 2002.

Taglioni, François. 'Les méditerrannées eurafricaine et américaine: Essai de comparaison.' In *Mare Nostrum. Dynamiques et mutations géopolitiques de la Méditerranée*, edited by André-Louis Sanguin, 73–88. Paris: Éditions l'Harmattan, 2000.

Toledano, Ehud R. *The Ottoman Slave Trade and its Abolition, 1840–1890.* Princeton, NJ: Princeton University Press, 1983.

Winterer, Caroline. *The Culture of Classicism. Ancient Greece and Rome in American Intellectual Life, 1780–1910.* Baltimore, MD: Johns Hopkins University Press, 2004.

Wulf, Andrea. *The Invention of Nature. Alexander von Humboldt's New World.* New York, NY: Alfred A. Knopf, 2015.

CHAPTER 4

Africa and the African Diaspora in the Curriculums of Central America's Caribbean Countries

Dario A. Euraque

I. Introduction

During the last 15 years, the historiography of Central America has registered new contributions to the study of colonialism, and the presence and ethno-history of Africans in this region.[1] This has been especially the case in Costa Rica and Panama, followed by Honduras, Nicaragua, Guatemala, and lastly El Salvador, although it is unclear what explains this shift. In the case of Costa Rica, it probably stems from the overall much more advanced historical training at the university levels than elsewhere in Central America. In the case of Panama this might be explained by the greater influence of Panamanian black political culture in the society at large than elsewhere in Central America, perhaps with the exception of Honduras.

Some of the most interesting studies have articulated their arguments and problematics with questions and debates associated with the literature on the African Diaspora in the Americas in general and with the older traditions of studying slavery in the region, including comparative perspectives on the United States (US) and the Island Caribbean, particularly the Spanish speaking areas. This discussion addresses the following question: To what extent have the new research and publications on the historiography of the African Diaspora in Central America affected the ways that school curricula present the history of the Afro-descendant populations in the countries of the region with colonial nexus to the Island Caribbean?

The presence of people of African descent in Central America dates to the arrival in the region of the Spanish conquistadors in the first decades of the sixteenth century. Today that fact is discussed in a new, innovative historiography. This historiography registers the presence and evolution of mixed-race peoples of African descent in either cultural or phenotypical terms. The official racial and ethnic categories deployed in colonial and post-colonial Central America left ample testimony of the legacies of the history of the African Diaspora in this region. These racial and ethnic classifications included *negros, mulatos, pardos, zambos, morenos, negros caribes* and *negros ingleses*, and they illustrate subtleties in the Afro-descendant miscegenation that occurred in Central America. During the last 15 years a new historiography registers this critical dimension of the colonial and post-colonial history of the region.[2]

Two questions are pertinent in this context: To what extent has this new academic historiography affected what children in primary and secondary schools in Central America learn about African history and the African Diaspora? Secondly, to what degree have states and governments in Central America been interested in integrating this new historiography in their national educational curricula?

This essay addresses these questions. It originates with research that the author carried out on behalf of UNESCO on these issues between October and December 2009. The contract required the team I led to diagnose the teaching materials and curriculum on the subject of African history and the African Diaspora as discussed in the new historiography. The study was based on a broad range of materials: official curriculum, social science and literature text books, and civic calendars used in the different countries of Central America. The Currículos Nacionales Básicos (CNBs), or Basic National Curriculums (BNCs) for 2005 to 2008 are a major source of data.

II. General Aspects of African and African Diaspora History in Central America

As noted, today the African origins of many Central American countries dating back to the arrival of the Spaniards themselves in the first decades of the sixteenth century are widely acknowledged among academics. These origins are often linked to the African Diaspora, via the trans-Atlantic slave trade between 1500 and the 1870s, and later to the nature of the West Indian migrations to the region to work in Caribbean agro-export economies after the 1870s, as railroad workers and plantation labourers.

In this general context, nonetheless, colonial 'blackness' in Central America is recognized to have differed substantially from the picture we have of the African Diaspora elsewhere in the Americas. The most recent and innovative scholarship in Central America on these topics challenges the African Diaspora historiography dominant in the Americas, which focuses on Brazil, the US, and other regions in the Caribbean, whose history of African slavery was linked to the plantations organized to produce for world markets, particularly in sugar.

For example, according to Gudmundson and Wolfe, Hacienda San Jeronimo in Guatemala, which in the latter eighteenth century 'was home to the largest single group of slaves in Central America', with 600+ slaves, 'along with permanent and temporary Indian and mixed race workers', represented the extreme exception when characterizing the material context of 'black and blackness' in this region (153). Rather, more typical throughout rural and urban Central America was 'the multiethnic environment of Hacienda San Jeronimo', with much, much smaller concentrations of slaves and with many slaves often classified as *mulatos* and/or *pardos*. This is what is most important for scholars who want to compare the Central American case with the more familiar canonical cases of the Latin American and Caribbean historiography: Brazil, Cuba, Jamaica, Puerto Rico, Colombia, etc.

The imagined post-colonial 'black' worlds of Central America were often reduced, as in the case of Guatemala, to the West Indian migrations in Puerto Barrios and Livingston, tiny urban areas facing the Caribbean Sea; the same was true for Costa Rica and Honduras, littoral areas which since the colonial period were often known collectively as 'la costa', and where bananas were cultivated by the US foreign companies and exported to the US. In this narrative, in Costa Rica, blackness was narrowed to the Caribbean Province of Limon, headquarters to the United Fruit Company. In Honduras, colonial blackness and the colonial African Diaspora were erased, and only the Garifuna who arrived on its Caribbean coast, exiled from St. Vincent in 1797, were acknowledged (see Euraque and Martinez 2016). The erasure of Honduras's colonial blackness by the end of the nineteenth century included eliminating the very important contributions of African slavery in the construction of the mid-eighteenth-century Fort San Fernando de Omoa, on the Caribbean coast of Honduras. During the transition to the twentieth century, liberal nation-state builders even erased the remnants of the use of mulattos as a census category and more. Between the 1950s and 1970s, special attention was given to the history mostly of the Garifuna, today Central America's largest and most visible Afro-descendant population resident beyond the region, especially, in the US, in New York City, Los Angeles, and New Orleans.

Table 4.1: Basic National Curriculums of Central America (Concepts registered in the BNCs per country for Social Sciences, Civics and Spanish)

	Colonialism	Indígenas	Cultural Groups	Ethnicity	Black	Mestizaje	Race	Africa	Slavery
El Salvador	8	2	2	2	1	0	2	1	0
Guatemala	3	4	6	2	0	3	0	0	0
Honduras	4	3	7	3	0	0	1	1	0
Nicaragua	9	17	5	0	1	5	0	0	0
Panamá	7	6	4	2	3	1	0	2	0
Costa Rica	10	6	2	1	3	2	0	1	2
Totals	41	38	26	10	8	11	3	5	2

Dario A. Euraque & Yesenia Martinez, *The African Diaspora in the Educational Programs of Central America* (New Jersey: Africa World Press 2016, 7)

The perspective presented is that the BNCs generally focus on the relationship between the past and cultural and ethnic groups during the Spanish colonial period. Colonial processes involving other European powers are rarely mentioned, and when they are, it is in very superficial ways. Costa Rica and Panama are exceptions to this pattern.

The numbers per columns and totals register the number of pages on which each concept or word appears as available in the BNCs for each country (Table 4.1). These figures do not include the Social Science BNCs for Panama or the BNCs for Civics for Panama in the eighth, ninth and eleventh grades. Finally, these figures do not include the BNCs for the first and second grade for Nicaragua. We lack the number of total pages of all studies as a whole.

The history of Spanish colonialism is conceptualized as remote and as having only a fragile connection with the nineteenth and twentieth centuries and contemporary Central America. The complicated relationships between British and French colonialism in the Caribbean do not appear in the official textbooks and the BNCs, nor do they cover connections with Central America during the nineteenth and twentieth century, and their relationship with the African Diaspora. Second, and following from the first, when the colonial past is mentioned and cultural groups are addressed, 'indigenous groups' are identified as 'our ancestors' or 'as the first peoples'. Moreover, the indigenous societies most often discussed were 'state societies' or proto-states. Emphasis is given to indigenous groups that mastered urban life and monumental architecture like the Maya in Honduras and Guatemala or Mesoamerican cultures in general. This is problematic because current archaeological and historical research shows that most indigenous peoples in Central America before Spanish colonialism did not live in states that produced such monuments and were not urban dwellers.

Third, the racial-ethnic miscegenation that began with Spanish colonialism, known generally as *mestizaje* or *ladinización*, appears in Central American BNCs as having occurred between indigenous state-societies and presumably white Spaniards. References to an Afro-descendant presence and its varied specificities were excluded. Panama is the exception and to a lesser extent so is Nicaragua. To a degree this is a function of how Spanish colonialism, and colonialism in general in the Americas, is conceptualized. It almost always excludes slavery as a subsystem of trans-Atlantic colonialism. Therefore, the status of the slaves as active historical subjects in Central America's past is completely marginalized in the region's BNCs.

This curricular vacuum is also reflected in the absence of blacks and blackness in the civic calendars and celebrations authorized by Central American states. Again, Afro-descendant history and heritage are missing from the celebrations and national holidays registered in the official primary and secondary school calendars in the region with the exceptions of Honduras and Panama and to a lesser degree Costa Rica. The same results are evident when we generated an inventory of the official commemorations of the indigenous past. The general proposition remains that the subject of indigenous peoples is associated with a remote past, a colonial past, neutralized by a homogenous *mestizaje* or *ladinización* that was especially profound in the case of Nicaragua. The exception is in Honduras, where the Lencan warrior Lempira is celebrated; the Honduran currency was named after him in 1926.

There is a specific problem with references to the African Diaspora in the BNCs. Rarely if ever is the continent of 'Africa' mentioned. Thus, there are no references to any particular African country as a source of peoples of African descent in Central America. Not only is the notion of 'Afro-descendant' absent in the BNCs, but also only rarely do the following words appear in the BNCs or its text books: *negro* or *negra*. Rarely does the word *mulato* or *mulata* make it into these materials with the exception of Costa Rican texts. Finally, rarely is there a discussion of even the complicated racial and ethnic categorization system known as *castas*, which was extensive and amply evident in Central American colonial documents.

These omissions are in part associated with the history of academic social science thinking in Central America after World War II. Anthropological or even sociological approaches were rarely used in writing on the racial and ethnic legacies of colonialism. All the countries in Central America followed the lead of UNESCO social science initiatives in the immediate post-World War II period. They removed racial and ethnic classifications from official census data, and hence removed their potential effect on school curricular programmes. More importantly, the omissions are no doubt linked to the history of *mestizaje* or *ladinización* in Central America, that is, to the particular ideology of racial miscegenation assumed by all Central American states after the 1870s. That ideology erased or minimized blackness from the official imagination and was embedded at all levels of education. Of course, indigenousness was embedded almost as completely (see Arias).

III. Analysis of the BNCs by Country

El Salvador

In the Salvadoran BNCs, cultural groups – and certainly not those with an Afro-descendant history – are not mentioned between the first and sixth grades. Between the seventh and eleventh grades, several units of the Salvadoran BNCs introduce themes and conceptual components that have a vocabulary of cultural diversity, race and ethnicity. In the ninth grade, 'the ethnic factor as a source of exclusion and conflict' is mentioned, but unfortunately it is without a global framework and is unconnected to El Salvador's history. African slavery in Central America and the presence of Afro-descendants in El Salvador are not recorded in its colonial or post-colonial history. Emphasis is placed not on colonialism but upon immediate and contemporary history, particularly upon armed conflicts and subsequent peace agreements, again with no reference to ethnicity or race.

Guatemala

In the Guatemalan BNCs, the need to cultivate competence in 'citizen formation' is identified with regard to 'pride with respect for one's family, social and cultural group'. The development of this competence runs through all grades. In the third grade, this emphasis is reaffirmed when a 'Social and Natural Environment' competence is taught. This is when one 'coexists in a supportive, respectful, and tolerant manner in spaces where gender, ethnic and social class diversity is shared'. This competence also requires 'respect for the rights of all cultural or ethnic groups'. At the same time, students get homework assignments to 'identify groups that now live in Guatemala and Central America: Mayas, Garifunas, Xincas and Ladinos'.

The omission of Afro-descendant history is overwhelming, even if there is some appreciation of ethnic identities. Statements in the Guatemala BNCs about Spanish colonialism do not include recognition of slavery, the importance of black men and women or even mention of the African continent in a cultural sense. Then, in the fifth grade the 'assessment of the recommendations of the Peace Accords for overcoming racism, sexism and ethnocentrism' against blacks suddenly appears. This attention disregards Spanish colonialism, black culture and the small Afro-Caribbean and Garifuna presence in Guatemala itself. But ironically, racism against indigenous people is recognized, probably a bow to the influence of the important Pan-Mayan movement that emerged in Guatemala in the 1990s.

Honduras

The Honduran BNCs do not include the concepts of slavery or blackness. The study of 'Africa' refers only to its political division and its geography. The word 'Garifuna' appears only once in the Honduran BNCs. This is an enormous gap given the fact that since the arrival of their ancestors in 1797, after British imperial authorities exiled them from the island of St. Vincent to Honduras, this Afro-indigenous descendant group has been historically recognized in official documents throughout Honduran history. The only association we found with African heritage in the Honduran BNCs is in a second grade homework assignment in an unit called 'Social Organization and Home Activities'. In Honduras, as in the cases of El Salvador and Guatemala, the role assigned to 'cultural groups' in the BNCs is always associated with indigenous groups, and it is to these groups that 'ethnicity' is attributed. The Honduran colonial system lacked any acknowledgement or discussion of blacks and African slavery. The texts used in different school levels in Honduras also lack documentation and presentation of academic historiography. Despite Garifuna leadership, even today there is no national holiday that celebrates Joseph Satuye, the Garifuna leader who resisted English colonialism in St. Vincent in the Lesser Antilles. He is celebrated in the iconography of Garifuna intellectuals as a hero of their resistance in Honduras, elsewhere in Central America, and often in US urban centres.

Nicaragua

As noted, the Nicaraguan BNCs prove Sergio Ramirez's argument in *El Tambor Olvidado* (The Forgotten Drum) that 'the mutilation of our history when removing its African component is astonishing.... The race championed is the mestizo Indo-Spanish race, more indigenous than Hispanic.' Ramirez goes on to say that miscegenation means: 'blackness is still intolerable. It is not discussed' (10; translation mine). The Nicaraguan BNCs provide evidence supporting Ramirez's claims. The BNCs and the list of Nicaraguan national holidays associate Africanness and blackness almost exclusively with the colonial struggles in the Atlantic and Caribbean zone of the Autonomous and Miskito regions of the country.

In fact, by the 1970s, Nicaraguan intellectuals and the state had sanctioned a national imagination bereft of blackness, and indigenous identity had been reduced to their resistance against the Spaniards during the colonial period, but having simultaneously largely excluded the living Miskitos, Sutiabas and others. This situation actually originated much earlier in the context of Nicaragua's own version of *mestizaje* or *ladinización*. The triumph of a silent indigeneity within a homogenous *mestizaje* achieved preeminence in the 1920s and 1930s in the context of the formidable coffee economy that consolidated at that time, as Jeff L. Gould argued in pioneering work long ago (see Gould).

Juliet Hooker more recently segmented the 'official mestizaje' process in Nicaragua in the twentieth century into three periods: 'vanguardismo, Sandinismo, and...mestizo multiculturalism'. 'These emerged in the 1930s, 1960s, and 1990s respectively in Nicaragua.' In this process, blackness lost out, even when the Sandinista Revolution triumphed in 1979. Indeed, even when Nicaragua in 1987 became 'one of the first Latin American countries to adopt multicultural citizenship reforms that assigned special collective rights to *costeños*, the black and indigenous inhabitants of its Atlantic Coast region', these progressive macro legislative initiatives did not translate into rethought primary and secondary school curricular change during the subsequent two decades (all quotations 14).

According to Margarita Vannini, Director of the Institute of History of Nicaragua and Central America, 'the theme of African heritage is rather invisible in textbooks and school programmes. We have tried to introduce the concept of multiculturalism, but when dealing with this issue, people always identify it with the Caribbean Coast of Nicaragua.'

Panama

The Afro-descendant presence in the Panamanian BNCs was clearly evident in the 'Content' and corresponding homework assignments. This was particularly the case in middle level Social Sciences, and in particular, in the unit on 'History of Panama' for the eleventh grade. I believe that the clear distinction of Panama in comparison with El Salvador, Guatemala and Honduras is due to Panamanians' appreciation of the Afro-Caribbean migration to and from their country and the role these migrants played in the construction of the canal across the isthmus (Table 4.2). In one of the BNCs, under the 'Content' of 'Historical Events of the Peoples' section for the fifth grade, the need to address the 'cultural contributions of Afro-colonial and Afro-Caribbean blacks' is forcefully stated.

Michael R. Conniff has estimated that between 1850 and 1950 some 400,000 people of African descent went to and through Central America. Of those who remained, most made homes in Panama and Costa Rica. Lesser numbers settled in Honduras, and even smaller numbers in Guatemala and Nicaragua (Table 4.2). Most left Jamaica, and Barbados, and the great majority immigrated between the 1880s and the late 1910s. It is important to mention that during this period West Indians migrated to Cuba and the US in almost equal numbers as suggested in Table 4.2. Between 1919 and 1920, some 50,000 Jamaicans travelled to Cuba, and between 1901 and 1924, slightly over 100,000 West Indians made it to the US, mostly to urban centres like New York. Many of these were Jamaicans, and many, like Marcus Garvey, ended up in New York after contract and non-contract labour stints in Costa Rica and/or Panama.

Table 4.2: West Indian Presence in Central America, 1850s–1940s

Decades	Panamá	Costa Rica	Honduras
1850s	5,000	–	–
1870s	–	–	200–300
1880s	50,000	2,000	1,000
1910s	150,000	43,000	4,500
1920s	40–50,000	33,000	4,000
1940s	90–100,000	15,000	4,000

Source: Darío A. Euraque, 'The Historiography of the West Indian Diaspora in Central America viewed from Honduras'. Paper presented at the University of the West Indies, Mona Campus, Kingston, Jamaica, 21 February, 2002, 3.

Costa Rica

Ironically, Afro-Caribbean migration to Costa Rica between the 1880s and the 1930s and the social and political activism of the 1950s, 1960s, and 1970s, today amply documented, did not produce the same impact in the Costa Rican BNCs as it did in Panama (See Fernandez). The Afro-Caribbean differentiation within the general Afro-descendant colonial legacy is not recorded in the Costa Rican BNCs. In the Costa Rican BNCs general patterns for the rest of Central America predominate, with certain nuances in format and presentation. The conceptualization of the relationship between the conquest and miscegenation generated during the Spanish colonial period is not enriched with the colonial Afro-Caribbean legacy. This is despite the fact that the historiography about Costa Rica has recently benefitted from important contributions about colonial slavery and the African Diaspora, particularly in the work of Rina Cáceres.

The most distinctive aspect of all the Costa Rican BNCs is the particular manner in which the role of October 12 is redefined as an event and a national holiday. The results are pedagogic homework assignments suggested in the different school years in Costa Rica. For example, according to the BNCs of Costa Rica, October 12 – the former 'Discovery' or 'Columbus Day':

> ...should become the special occasion to call for a reassessment of the Spanish language, given that this is the most significant product of the Conquest. It should be emphasized that language is what best expresses the soul of a people without forgetting that one thing is the Spanish spoken in Spain and another is the Spanish spoken in Costa Rica. However, this cannot ignore the

legitimate right of the indigenous and Afro-descendant groups to express themselves in their own languages; thus, it is the obligation of the educational system to extol the plural-cultural character of our country.

The great upsurge in migration during the 1910s began to diminish in the 1920s and virtually collapsed in the 1930s during the Depression. After World War II, the West Indian presence in Panama, Costa Rica, and Honduras did not benefit from renewed immigration from Jamaica and Barbados; they actually struggled to maintain communities that had been consolidated in the 1910s and early 1920s. In the 1950s, the West Indian communities, mostly from Jamaica, had declined precipitously in Honduras. By the early 1960s, West Indian immigration shifted to Great Britain. From 1951 to 1961, 230,000 to 280,000 West Indians migrated to the industrial centres in England. West Indian immigration to the US increased again in the 1940s with a programme of rural contract labour modeled on one existing for Mexicans. By 1945, this programme had brought almost 40,000 Jamaicans, Barbadians, St. Lucians and British Hondurans to work in the US. After the 1980s, a new boom in West Indian migration to the Northeast of the US supplemented the older migrations, especially those who had settled in New York. The Jamaican-born population in the US in 1980 of about 196,000 had doubled by 1990.

Briefly, how has the existing historiography about the West Indian Diaspora treated immigration and the communities that settled in Panama, Costa Rica and Honduras? First, the immigration of peoples from Jamaica, Barbados and other islands is generally approached in terms of their migrant labour status and not connected to the history of slavery and colonialism. A particular focus of these studies is the racial tensions between West Indians and the 'others' already living in the regions, especially the mestizo/Hispanic 'others'. Second, this general perspective usually locates West Indian migrant labour in two scenarios: The first context includes the construction of infrastructure projects and their maintenance, especially railroads, as well as ports and of course the massive Panama Canal. The second context for studying West Indians as migrant labourers has been as agricultural workers in export agriculture, especially sugar and bananas.

Few studies have attempted detailed social histories of the West Indian Diaspora as complicated, changing communities divided along class lines and articulated with the complexities of gender issues.

Panama's West Indian communities in the 1980s received some attention along these lines, culminating in the work of Michael L. Conniff. For the Costa Rican case, important studies detail the social histories of the West Indian communities there, mainly in the work of Ronald Harpelle, Avi Chomsky, Carmen Murillo and Lara Putnam. Putnam's work is especially path-breaking because she systematically engages connections between gender and race, connections explored not only between West Indian women and Hispanic-Indian populations. But this work was equally important in analyzing how West Indian men have related to West Indian women in the context of adaptation and struggle.

The historical migration of Afro-Caribbean peoples to the Central American region should pose challenges to interpretation of 'colonialism' and post-colonialism in Panama, Honduras, and Costa Rica; however, it is reflected only in the BNCs of Panama. What really catches the eye in the Panamanian BNCs is the obvious seriousness with which Afro-descendant peoples are treated in the content and that this respect does not exclude other cultural groups – indigenous groups, Europeans, and in this latter case, distinctions between Anglo-Saxons, Hispanics, and others. In the case of Panama, the relationship between conquest, colonization, and miscegenation not only records a complexity within the country, but it is reiterated equally when Panama is related to the rest of the region and the continent. Panama is the only country in Central America where December 2 is officially recognized as 'International Day of the Abolition of Slavery.' Also unique is the fact that according to the Decree of May 30, 2000, this day [May 30] of each year was declared a 'Civic and Memorial Day of Black Ethnicity.'

An informed observer of the politics of social movements in Panama and Costa Rica offers the following context that is very relevant to explaining the advances in the Panamanian BNCs. According to Robert Sierakowski, 'Just as the Universal Negro Improvement Association (UNIA) and Marcus Garvey's work and agitation had rippled through Central America's Caribbean coast during the 1910s and 20s, the impact of the US Civil Rights movement and the figure of Martin Luther King Jr. would inspire many in the coastal regions to more openly demand social justice. With many Afro-Panamanians and Afro-Costa Ricans studying in and travelling and migrating to the US, the demands of those years echoed back through new organizations and activist groups. Laws banning racial discrimination were passed by Panama in 1956 and Costa Rica in 1960 and 1968. Likewise, with the later rise of the Black Power movement in the US, there was a turn towards a more militant form of ethnic politics among some of the youth. Similarly, the diverse indigenous groups ringing the coast also played a part in the emergence of the international indigenous rights movement in the 1970s, organizing for land rights, cultural autonomy, and an end to marginalization and discrimination' (9–10).

IV. Conclusion

About fifteen years ago, Dr. Ronald Soto Quiroz, from Costa Rica, published an important essay entitled 'Disappeared from the Nation: Indigenous Peoples in the Construction of Costa Rican National Identity, 1851–1942.' The essay analysed the ways in which indigenous people were presented and discussed in Costa Rica's school textbooks between the mid-nineteenth century and the first forty years of the twentieth century. Soto Quiroz argued that the intellectuals who generated those textbooks mostly used the indigenous past to legitimize a national Costa Rican community based on a homogenous conception of a White race.

Moreover, wrote Soto Quiroz, 'the geography and history curriculums used in official public education did little more than contribute to a particular commitment to a homogenous race when they emphasized the division and classification of human beings by their physical characteristics, origin, language, religion, occupation and civilization of the said race' (31). If in Costa Rica's BNCs, indigenous peoples disappeared as historical subjects from curricular programmes and school textbooks, we could expect that more or less the same development would happen elsewhere in Central America. However, in those countries that enjoyed an important indigenous demographic presence, including Guatemala, and El Salvador, and in Honduras to a lesser extent, the disappearance of indigenous historical agency was a more complicated process and continued well into the twentieth century.

Today the BNCs of Central America do not remove the indigenous peoples from the colonial and post–colonial past, nor are they removed from the process of racial, ethnic and cultural miscegenation (*mestizaje*), especially when it comes to their role as labour. In contemporary Central America, the indigenous past is accorded an important place in the region's educational systems and curriculums. It is always within a version of the Indo-Hispanic matrix for each country, as I have briefly summarized in this essay. It is also amply documented in the historiography that we have reviewed. However, the history of Afro-descendant people today in general in Central American official curricula and school textbooks remains minimal. That is despite advances in the new historiography on the presence of African peoples and the African Diaspora in Central America. Subtle exceptions to this general proposition are registered in the available documentation for Panama and Costa Rica, and to a lesser extent for Honduras. These exceptions, nonetheless, focus primarily on the Spanish colonial period, without relating this process with the region's connection to French and British colonialism. In general, the place of slavery and the trans-Atlantic slave trade in the history of colonialism and post-colonialism are marginalized, including the legacies resulting from Afro-Caribbean migrations of the late nineteenth and early twentieth century in the labour history of the Caribbean.

Notes
1. This essay draws freely from Dario A. Euraque & Yesenia Martinez, *The African Diaspora in the Educational Programs of Central America* (New Jersey: Africa World Press, 2016). See also Dario A. Euraque, 'Political Economy, Race, and National Identity in Central America, 1500–2000,' in *Oxford Research Encyclopedia of Latin American History* (Oxford University Press, forthcoming).
2. Much of the literature is reviewed in David Díaz Arias 2005 and Euraque, forthcoming.

Works Cited:
Arias, David Diaz. 'Entre La Guerra de Castas y La Latinización. La Imagen del Indígena en la Centroamérica Liberal, 1870–1944.' *Revista de Estudios Sociales*, Bogotá, Colombia, no. 26 (April 2007), 58–72.
———. 'La Invención de las Naciones en Centroamérica, 1821–1950.' *Boletín*, AFEHC, Asociación para el Fomento de los Estudios en Centroamérica, No. 19 (Diciembre 2005). http:.//ress.afehc.apinc.org/articulos2/fi chiers/portada_afech_articulos14.pdf.
Chomsky, Avi. *West Indian Workers and the United Fruit Company in Costa Rica, 1870–1940*. Baton Rouge, LA: Louisiana University Press, 1996.
Conniff, Michael. *Black Labor on a White Canal: Panama, 1904–1981*. Pittsburgh, PA: University of Pittsburgh Press, 1985.
Euraque, Dario and Yesenia Martinez. *The African Diaspora in the Educational Programs of Central America*. New Jersey: Africa World Press, 2016.

Euraque, Dario A. 'The Historiography of the West Indian Diaspora in Central America viewed from Honduras.' Presentation, University of the West Indies, Mona Campus, Kingston, Jamaica, February 21, 2002.

———. 'La Diáspora Africana en Honduras: Entre la esclavitud colonial y la modernidad del Protagonismo Garífuna.' In *Del Olvido a la Memoria, Vol. I, Africanos y Afromestizos en la Historia Colonial de Centroamerica*, edited by Rina Caceras Gomaz, 37–56. San José, Costa Rica: Oficina Regional de la UNESCO, 2008.

———. 'Political Economy, Race and National Identity in Central America, 1500–2000.' In *Oxford Research Encyclopedia of Latin American History*. Oxford: Oxford University Press, forthcoming. doi:10.1093/acrefore/9780199366439.013.521.

Fernandez, Reina Rosario. *Identidades de la población de origen jamaiquino en el Caribe costarricense (segunda mitad del siglo XX)*. Santo Domingo: Cocolo Editorial, 2016.

Gould, Jeff L. *To Die in This Way: Nicaraguan Indians and the Myth of Mestizaje, 1880–1965*. Durham, NC: Duke University Press, 1998.

Gudmundson, Lowell and Justine Wolfe, Editors, *Blacks & Blackness in Central America: Between Race and Place*. Durham, NC: Duke University Press, 2010.

Harpelle, Ronald L. *The West Indians of Costa Rica: Race, Class, and the Integration of an Ethnic Minority*. Montreal: McGill-Queen's University Press, 2001.

Hooker, Juliet, '"Beloved Enemies": Race and Official Mestizo Nationalism in Nicaragua.' *Latin American Research Review* 40, no. 3 (2005): 14–39.

Murillo Chaverri, Carmen. 'Vaivén de arraigos y desarraigos: identidad afrocaribeña en Costa Rica, 1870–1940.' *Revista de Historia*, Costa Rica, núm. 39 (Jan.–Jun., 1999): 187–206.

Putnam, Lara. *The Company They Kept: Migrants and the Politics of Gender in Caribbean Costa Rica, 1870–1960*. Chapel Hill, NC: University of North Carolina Press, 2002.

Ramirez, Sergio. *Tambor Olvidado*. Managua, Nicaragua: Editorial Aguilar, 2007.

Sierakowski, Robert. 'Central America's Caribbean Coast: Politics and Ethnicity.' *Oxford Research Encyclopedia, Latin American History* (September 2016). http://latinamericanhistory.oxfordre.com/. Accessed June 13, 2017.

Soto Quiroz, Ronald. 'Después de la nación: los indígenas en la construcción de la identidad nacional costarricense, 1851–1942.' *Ciencias Sociales* 82, (December 1998): 31–53.

Part II: Negotiating Cultural Identity – Gender, Religion and Ethnicity

CHAPTER 5

Ramabai and Gainder, Gaiutra and Sujaria are Turning Tides: Great-grandmothers' and Great-granddaughters' Odysseys and Narratives of the *Kala Pani*

Judith Misrahi-Barak

'What happens when we reposition our understanding of "The Caribbean" and broaden our thinking beyond the traditional major players in the geo-political sphere? *Turning Tides* is an international conference that takes "intersections" seriously by placing all societies touched by the Caribbean Sea and Atlantic Ocean at the centre of Western Hemispheric discussions' and provides 'wide–reaching and transdisciplinary conversations about the instabilities, changes, developments, perspectives and future trends which intersect the cultures and societies bordered by the Atlantic Ocean and beyond' (*Turning Tides Call for papers*). The call for contributions out of which this volume has emerged gives me the frame I need to bypass the traditional vertical and national power relations between the former colonizing 'centre' and the former colonized 'margins', focus on the intersections between the Black Atlantic and the Indian Ocean, and examine how fluid, multidirectional, transnational and cross-cultural interactions are articulated through fictional and non-fictional narratives.

Since this article will be looking into the intersections between India and the Caribbean (and more precisely Trinidad and Tobago, and British Guiana/Guyana), I need to refer briefly to the frame set up in *Minor Transnationalism*, where Shu-mei Shih and Françoise Lionnet define the transnational space as 'a space of exchange and participation wherever processes of hybridization occur and where it is still possible for cultures to be produced and performed without necessary mediation by the center' (5). These 'minor-to-minor networks that circumvent the major altogether' (8) are a development of the horizontal relations delineated by Deleuze and Guattari through the image of the rhizome,[1] and by Edouard Glissant through theories of *Relation*. A relational perspective that would be transnational or, more precisely, *transcolonial*, is one of the most interesting developments in post-colonial studies, one that was urgently needed.

Quite obviously, because unequal relations between dominant culture and dominated culture do not belong to the past only, one can hope that an emphasis on the cultural intersections between two formerly colonized regions, such as India and the Caribbean, will reinforce strategies of knowledge and empowerment. From the standpoint of our twenty-first century, examining the work of two contemporary writers such as Ramabai Espinet and Gaiutra Bahadur, and looking into the different ways they have researched their personal and collective crossing of the *kala pani*, should help us understand the role and function of narrative in such research. Since Espinet writes poetry and fiction while Bahadur writes non-fiction, I want to consider the issue of the genre that is chosen for the narrative, fiction or non-fiction, and the impact of such a choice.

Let us set the stage for readers who may not be familiar with the nineteenth-century migrations from India to the Caribbean, and remind those who are. Large scale migration out of India began with indentured labourers in the 1830s when hundreds of thousands of Indians, both voluntarily and involuntarily, left the subcontinent and crossed the *kala pani* (literally, in Hindi, 'black water', the 'forbidden' sea between India and the Americas) to work in the sugar colonies as *bound coolies*, not only in the British Empire but also in the French and Dutch colonies. These migrants were responding to the need for labour on the plantations after African enslavement was legally abolished in 1834 and fully terminated in 1838. Many were taken to Fiji and Mauritius, as well as Guadeloupe and Martinique. Almost one and a half million indentured immigrants went to the British, Dutch and French Caribbean.[2] Indians were also recruited later in the nineteenth and early twentieth centuries to work in South and East Africa on the railways and in other industries. Most went mainly to Kenya, Uganda and Tanzania.

It is difficult to imagine the scope of these migrations, and how they were organized. However, the archives in Kolkata, Port of Spain and London do provide material that allows us to imagine what these migrations must have been like, dispensing a host of direct and indirect details about each stage of the journey. Starvation, chronic debt, domestic violence, caste oppression and other such factors pushed the hopeful emigrants away from their villages. They came by train from remote places in Bihar, Bengal, Uttar Pradesh, until they were recruited (and sometimes kidnapped or lured onto the ships heading to the Caribbean, Mauritius, or Fiji) by the *arkatis*, the recruiters working for the British, finally reaching Calcutta.³ They had to communicate through interpreters and translators, and submit to the selection tests to see if they were fit for work in the sugar colonies. Their emigration passes stated their name, sex, approximate age, marks of identification, village of origin, next of kin if any, their caste, and the ship they were boarding as well as the exact date of departure. Whether they all knew if they were boarding for Mauritius, Fiji, or the West Indies is not entirely certain. However, looking at the river Hoogly, picturing in one's mind's eye the Garden Reach depots, and seeing what is left of the dockyards in Kidderpore [Khidirpur] certainly feed the imagination.⁴

Some three months were required to cross the *kala pani*, the black waters of the Indian Ocean and the Atlantic. It was long enough for all castes to mix and mingle on the ship, upper caste and lower caste, from Brahmins to Shudras to Untouchables. This intermingling was so pervasive that one of the scholars doing extensive work on indentureship and the crossing of the *kala pani*, Brinsley Samaroo, has coined the phrases 'Brahmin by birth', or 'Brahmin by boat':

> Men and women from the villages of Uttar Pradesh and Bihar, looking around in the receiving depot and seeing no one who could attest to their true origins, gave themselves new names which indicated the upward direction which they now wished to pursue. They were now *Singh* (lion), *Sher* (tiger), *Raj Kumari* (princess), *Maha Raj* (Great King) or *Maha Bir* (Great Warrior). There were now many new Brahmins by boat rather than by birth (20).

Borders and boundaries were crossed, identities reshuffled and reinvented. Only a minority made the crossing back to India at the end of their five-year contracts. Multiple reasons can be mentioned. At the end of the nineteenth century indentured labourers often had to pay for their passage back to India but they could not afford it.⁵ In addition, five years is a long enough period to settle down and start raising a family. Further, once they had become acclimatized to a society where caste did not exist, or at least not with the same implications, it was difficult to adjust to India again, and the returnees were often rejected by their communities. In Metiabruz, not far from Garden Reach, there was even an area where returned emigrants were stationed, waiting for the ships from the Caribbean and hoping to re-indenture themselves. Repatriation occurred until the 1950s, a time when India was already finding it extremely difficult to manage the flows of post-Partition migrants.⁶ As Samaroo notes, 'this loss of caste meant rejection and social ostracism upon return, causing many to opt for *tapuha* (island) status rather than *Maha Bharat* (Great India) ascription' (20).

The descendants of these early migrants now constitute a substantial and fascinatingly diverse diaspora. Many writers and scholars have explored the perception of the ancestral space, the manifold representations of 'Mother India', its place in the imagination of the descendants of indentured labourers, and its impact on the way contemporary identities have been shaped. Stories have become deliberately constructed narratives of a homeland one does not even remember and sometimes has no first-hand knowledge of. New sovereign identities that have developed horizontally and not vertically are now accommodated in fluid and multiple ways.[7]

Indo-Caribbean literature per se did not emerge in Trinidad and Tobago, and Guyana before the 1960s and 1970s in the independence period even if one can trace pioneers as early as the late nineteenth and early twentieth centuries and then again in the 1940s.[8] But unlike the Afro-Caribbean novels that in the 1990s emulated the original slave narratives from the eighteenth and nineteenth centuries and the African-American neo-slave narratives from the 1960s, there was no such process with the Indo-Caribbean narratives.[9] No original first-hand, fully-fledged accounts were written between the 1830s and 1917 during the time of indentureship. There were letters written to journals and local newspapers, but they did not have the same scope as the original eighteenth-century Atlantic slave narratives.[10] Oral testimonies given by the indentured servants themselves or by their descendants were only much later transcribed and archived.[11]

Indo-Caribbean writers in the latter part of the twentieth century took up fiction to try and give their voices back to the voiceless descendants of indentured labourers, sometimes getting their inspiration directly from the memories of the people who had been indentured servants one or two generations before. A few fiction writers are particularly representative of this early period: for Trinidad and Tobago, V.S. Naipaul (*A House for Mr Biswas* 1961), Harold Sonny Ladoo (*No Pain Like This Body* 1972) and Ismith Khan (*The Jumbie Bird*, also in 1961). For Guyana, one should also mention Peter Kempadoo (*Guyana Boy* 1960) and Raj Kumari Singh ('I Am a Coolie' 1973).

It is only fairly recently, in the past thirty years perhaps, that Indo-Caribbean literature began to catch up with African-Caribbean literature that had tended to be in the foreground and contributed to having the Caribbean defined through its Black Atlantic connection rather than its Indoceanic one. Among the next generation of Indo-Caribbean writers, many names are now well known, such as Cyril Dabydeen, David Dabydeen, Mahadai Das, Ramabai Espinet, Arnold Itwaru, Shani Mootoo, Sam Selvon and Ryhaan Shah, among others. Gaiutra Bahadur entered the stage as a journalist and a non-fiction writer recently.

I would now like to bring together Espinet's novel *The Swinging Bridge* (*SB*) and Bahadur's book *Coolie Woman: The Odyssey of Indenture* (*CW*) to illustrate why it is fruitful to read these two fiction and non-fiction narratives together. The tension between the two approaches is palpable: Bahadur's is directed towards reading the familial and communal, personal and collective archives, journeying back to Guyana and to India, and finding a path back to her family as descendants of indentured labourers; Espinet shapes a novel out of the scraps and pieces of information and historical knowledge that her Indo-Trinidadian family has (or has not) passed on. Both have the same fascination for what has been archived, or has been left unarchived and for what has to be re-constructed with the help of historical and intuitive imagination.

In *SB*, there is a clear split in the narrative between the fictional level and the historical references that form the backdrop to the novel.[12] On the fictional level, Mona, whose ancestors came to Trinidad and Tobago from India at the time of indentureship, lives in Canada. She may take after her creator Ramabai, but she is not Ramabai. Mona is a film director, forced back to her native Trinidad and Tobago by her brother, Kello, who has also settled in Canada and is dying of AIDS. He asks her to be his proxy in a deal over the land that he wants to bring back into the family before he dies, to correct what veered off course when their father sold their land in order to move to San Fernando, Trinidad's second city, in the south of the island. Mona accepts his request to act as his proxy because he is her 'second self'[13] and also because she has not settled her own score with their father, Da-Da, whose patriarchal, sexist and violent behaviour has marred her childhood and teenagerhood. In her adulthood, however, her father has 'let go' (81), and the story is now hers.

The narrative is the story of her reclaiming. The upcoming death of the brother brings about a reluctant revisiting of the past, individual and collective, and, more importantly, brings about the repossession of the present. Her temporary return to Trinidad and Tobago enables her to open a new space of reconnection. Through the untold stories of her ancestors, through the homage paid to the women in her family who migrated from India to the Caribbean in the nineteenth century, and through the unearthing of personal and family archives, Mona reconstructs herself. To do so, she needs the figure of her great-grandmother, Gainder, the epitome of the Indian free woman and one whose untold story Mona tries to reconstruct at last. This enables her to also tell her own.[14]

The split between the fictional narrative and the documented history is materialized in the structure of the novel and through the different fonts that are used. At the beginning of each of the three parts of the novel, the readers are offered passages in italics that remind them of the crossing of the *kala pani* within the context of both the collective and the personal, familial narrative. The first part 'Borrowed Time' opens up through a kind of double-entrance lock, a passage in italics mentioning the train from Benares to Calcutta (Kolkata), the *Garden Reach* depot where indentured immigrants were registered, and *The Artist* sailing to Trinidad in 1879. All this leads to the last and transitional sentence, 'My foremothers, my own great-grandmother Gainder, crossing the unknown of the *kala pani*, the black waters that lie between India and the Caribbean' (4). The second part 'Manahambre Road,' when Mona goes back and forth between Canada and Trinidad, also opens through another passage in italics, focusing more precisely on Gainder on the ship, and how she was sexually harassed by a sailor, and rescued by Jeevan, one of the *jahaji bhai* ('brotherhood of the boat'). The third part 'Caroni Dub,' entirely set in Trinidad, opens with even more details about Gainder, the thirteen-year old girl who has escaped an unwanted marriage through indentureship, and marries Joshua, a Trinidad-born Christian convert who will ask her never to sing or dance in public again.

SB implements a highly specific narrative structure, based on an original treatment of time in its relationship to space, a kind of diasporic *space-time*, if I can paraphrase Deleuze's notion of 'espace-temps'. Space appears to be expansible – the Indian subcontinent has prolonged itself into the Caribbean, which in turn has opened up towards Canada. On the contrary, time seems to be shrinking – with Kello dying, 'so little of it was left' (199). However, time also becomes an expandable material since Mona stretches its contours by going back to the immediate past as well as further back, to her childhood and to her ancestors' history.

Both time and space acquire a new flexibility. An instance of this is how the tempo of the narrative accelerates or decelerates according to its diegetic needs. Indeed, the reader follows the development of the narrative through the swift and fluid alternation between *story*-time (the chronological axis that events would have followed if they had been taking place in real life, i.e. Mona in Toronto and Montreal, involved in a film project) and *text*-time (the events as they are organized in the text by the writer, i.e. the passages in italics about the history of the *kala pani*; the childhood memories that are projected onto Mona's psyche and onto the page; all the pauses, ellipses, analepses and prolepses in the text).

Story-time and *text*-time clash with, or brush past, each other, more or less smoothly. The pace of the novel is that of the trains taking Mona back and forth between Montreal where she lives and Toronto where her brother Kello is dying, as well as the movement that takes her from Canada to Trinidad and back. But the movements in space are duplicated by the movements in time, through mind and memory, and such movements endow the novel with its energy and fluidity, while enabling Mona to repossess her present.

Repossession is also at the heart of Bahadur's *CW* even if the format and structure of the narrative appear to be widely different from Espinet's *SB*. Casting a glance at the endnotes and the bibliography at the end of the book, one sees how heavily Bahadur has relied on the archives and the density of the archival work she has managed to perform for the book. It is very impressive, and this is often what is mentioned first in the published reviews of the book. Her search for documents and archives has taken her from the India Office Records of the British Library in London, to the National Archives of the UK in Kew, to the Oral and Pictorial Records in the Alma Jordan Library at the University of the West Indies, St. Augustine Campus, to the New York Public Library, to the Rajkumari Singh Centre in New York, and of course to the Public Record Office in Georgetown, Guyana.

So, it could appear that the search is dominated by archival work bent on retrieving as much information as possible about the indentured labourers. It is, and yet, it is not. Bahadur certainly wants to understand and decrypt the past of her ancestors but it is always with the purpose of understanding her fellow Guyanese's, and her own, present. Key sentences can be found at different places in her narrative:

> I tried to imagine the alternate reality in which I had never migrated, and the Cumberland house still stood, and I grew into a Guyanese woman, pure and simple, no hyphens. Through that looking-glass, who would I be? Who might I have become, and where would I fit, in a society that offered not wholeness but dismemberment – still – for some women? I merely had to come to terms with the fact that I couldn't reclaim the past. But these women had met an opposite and far worse fate: they had failed to escape history (194).

What is so compelling in Bahadur's narrative is the avowed fascination for the search itself, much more than for any objective results. It is the fascination for what she calls 'an ongoing exercise in speculation' (173), a speculation into 'the gaps' and what 'the records do not say' (150). The drive is just as much towards speculation and imagination as towards making the archives speak: 'Like so much else that's important, it can only be imagined' (78). She speculates so much that she wonders whether it is okay: 'Is it wrong of me to speculate like this?' (66). She shows how much speculation and imagination go hand in hand, and cannot be separated, just like the personal and the collective. This speculation actually provides her book with its backbone and energy.

This rather unusual and non-traditional approach prompts the unique structure and organization of the book. Several elements have to be underscored. The first one is that, even if one wanted to, it would be impossible to separate the personal exploration from the historical investigation, the family pursuit from the US to Guyana to India, from the archival research. One often thinks one is reading about indentured labourers, boarding the ships, or working in the fields, but then suddenly, round the corner of a sentence, here is a very personal mention of Sujaria, the admired great-grandmother whose tracks Gaiutra has been following for years. Among the many instances that could have been quoted on this, here is one that refers to the death rate:

> During the most catastrophic years of the coolie trade, between 1854 and 1864, the death rate on ships to Guiana was 8.54 percent, equal to that on slave ships in the final decades of the eighteenth century. But *by the time my great-grandmother sailed*, the mortality rate on most indenture ships had fallen to between 1 and 2 percent (62, my emphasis).

The second element to be foregrounded is the variety of rhetorics used throughout the volume: the dominating trope appears to be the *quaesitio*, a series of rhetorical questions to which no definite answer is expected. Again, the following excerpt is a case in point, but by no means an isolated instance:

> In the beginning there was a boat. Having emerged from its belly, as survivors, the indentured Indians could no longer be who they had been. Like the slaves before them, they were an entirely new people, forged by suffering, created through destruction. In this sense above all else, theirs was a middle passage.
>
> How do I even begin to situate my great-grandmother in this odyssey? If I draw an imaginary line from moment to moment on the ships, from glimpse to glimpse of women aboard, will her shape emerge, constellation-like? Could the wrong shape emerge, if I connect the wrong moments to each other? How do I know which are right? Will her constellation give off light? (63).

Later, speculating about her grand-father being born on board:

> How was it that my grandfather, also premature, escaped this oblivion? Fully a third of the infants born on his ship died before it docked. What saved him? And what if he hadn't survived? Would my Sujaria have shared a fate, as well as a name, with the other Soujharia? (64).

On the following page a whole paragraph simply lists questions over fifteen lines.

The third element I want to underline, which is linked to the re-imagining of history, is the way Bahadur uses her findings and transforms them. She re-imagines, reconstructs and rewrites the historical elements, giving them a new narrative shape, as if she, Bahadur, was re-telling the indentured labourers' stories, remodelling their tongues to pass the stories on better. Anthropologists and sociologists have worked on colonial archives and correspondence, surgeons' log books, medical reports, letters to the editors of local newspapers and journals. Some texts, or a re-transcription of descendants' oral interviews, have been published. Bahadur chooses still another, totally cross-generic, method. She mingles fiction and non-fiction to reinforce the power of narrative and the force of the imagination. She uses literary devices in order to fine tune her discourse, constantly reformulating her questions. Modal verbs, for instance, and verb tenses are always used in meaningful ways, to intensify the narrative, giving it a sense of real, often recurrent action, even though it is projected into imagination. See the use of 'would', for instance:

> The night before *The Main* pulled into Georgetown, Crompton [the second mate] would descend into the hold of the ship. In the twilight of the lanterns, meant to expose exactly this kind of trespass, the *sirdhar* on watch would see him browsing the women's section. Crompton would search, without success, for someone (54).

Sometimes the present tense fulfills the same function: 'I imagine evening on Plantation Enmore: the drunken, sticky scent of scorched cane spikes the air. The fields have been set on fire, and ash from the singed leaves settles on everything' (105).

And sometimes it is a direct address to the reader that is meant to capture the imagination:

> Remember Maharani, the child widow who ran away after spilling milk, the woman who sounded so thrilled to be alone? When she arrived at her plantation, every unattached woman went off with a man – but not Maharani. She managed to resist until her indenture was almost over (85).

Bahadur continues the story, reconstructing it in her own words, simply adding an endnote that states:

> This story is reconstructed from: Maharani and her daughter Mahadaye Ramsewak, interviews by Patricia Mohammed, 1990, tape 33, OP62, Oral and Pictorial Records Programme, Alma Jordan Library, UWI, St. Augustine, Trinidad, as well as Maharani, interview by Noor Kumar Mahabir, *The Still Cry*, Trinidad: Calaloux Publications, 1988, pp. 79–88 (footnote 47; 227).

Many other examples could be given. Out of correspondences, petitions, hearings and trial transcripts, Bahadur reconstructs life stories, parallel to Sujaria's, of all those women whose actual names she reveals and prints: Baby, Eliza Jones, Kishuny, Maharani, Laungee, and so many others.

If Espinet has chosen to create one fictional, solid character, the film director Mona, Bahadur has chosen to re-create the myriad lives of indentured women. Both writers focus on narrative and feed on stories. What Bahadur says when she visits her long-lost Indian family in Bihar is probably what drives Espinet too:

> I have never felt anything but pride in my great-grandmother, for her honest if menial toil and for her bravery in crossing borders. My Bihari fourth cousins thought I might covet their land. I did

covet something, to be honest. The riches I was after were stories: theirs, my great-grandmother's, my own. Call it a quest for identity, or an exploration for narrative gold. Even use the awful word 'roots'. It may be clichéd, but it's raw and nervy and real nonetheless. Many Indo-Caribbeans I know suffer from a kind of phantom leg syndrome. Dismembered from our imaginary homeland, we have felt the absence of the severed limb of India for generations. And if that meant I had to bend at the waist, like an obedient great-granddaughter seeking blessings, then I would have to do so, suspending doubt (176).

Espinet's way of 'suspending doubt' is also to build stories, or *a* story, Mona's story, implicating her in a fictional quest for junctures to overcome ruptures. If Bahadur reconstructs stories from archival documents, Espinet fictionalizes the process in a more obvious way but have we not seen that Bahadur also introduces fiction in her historical examination? In both cases the structure of the narrative lends meaning to the complex constitution of a specific space-time that Espinet and Bahadur both belong to in the Diaspora.

In both books, the elements that empower the narrative, and the self that produces it, to take shape and jell may be slightly different. But only ever so slightly. The presence of the visual and auditory image may be specific to *The Swinging Bridge*, through film and music (European 'rhapsody', African-American jazz, and Caribbean calypso).[15] But the mingling of fiction and non-fiction and the activation of voice define both *CW* and *SB*. Whether authorial or narratorial, voice is what provides both narratives with their unity and strength. It can be the myriad unheard voices of indentured women Bahadur makes us listen to, giving each one of their names, or the recreation by Espinet of the character of Baboonie, a half-crazy, beggar woman who used to come to Mona's family house in Trinidad for work. Gainder and Sujaria were both coolie women of Brahmin origin. Baboonie is the dark shadow of their flamboyant selves, she could have been one of the women mentioned by Bahadur, and her voice should be heard here too. Mona remembers Baboonie, and how she would listen to the sounds that used to come from her shack:

> As I listened, I realized that the sound was a voice, singing with the rain yet high above rain and river at the same time, the notes discordant but clear, beating out a rhythm that I recognized. It was the rise and fall of women singing Ramayana at kathas. The words were in Hindi and I knew only a few of them – dhuniya, popo, beti, kala pani. And there were others that I heard night after night and will never forget, their harshness ripping through

earth and water and tearing up the air around me so that even breathing became fearful – kangaal, parishan, triskaar, thokna, parishan, parishan, parishan...pani, pani. The voice rose and fell in harmony with rain and river and wetness, pani, pani, pani... the whole world grieving in unison, crying tears into the river that flowed inches from my head, threatening to carry me in its rushing waters down to the sea, the sea near the belly of the map of Trinidad, just near the part where the mouth of the Serpent opens, swallowing me into the rain of everything the jaw of night had opened up and revealed while Baboonie fought off intruders upon her body with curses and threats and words sung from the holy books, while bundles and bundles of rags walked upright in the early morning, following the strong men of the village as they walked with proud brushing cutlasses, lashed with cloth by wives and daughters, walking to work, walking to do task work, to earn the dollars that made homes and families and life. Dreaming of voices, high and sweet, singing in the rain of grass and fields and butterflies, of playing and laughing and dancing in the forest, freer than the water making its wayward journey to the sea, singing the wetness and dislodging stones from the hard hearts, the hard sinews of strong men, singing...(112–13).

If crossing the *kala pani* meant a radical severance, this excerpt deliberately goes the other way, reconstructing the unending music of words and flow of images. It weaves again, in recollection, the web of Indian life and suffering, but also the sheer energy and resilience that come out of it. A single uninterrupted sentence (from 'And there were others that I heard'), impossible to cut into, impossible to stop. Both books are true homages to the women who crossed the *kala pani* and their *jahaji bahins* ('sisterhood of the boat'). One can hear Mona's and Gaiutra's own beat through the echoes of their ancestors' voices, painstakingly reconstituted and made to resound again through history and imagination woven together. Both of them have 'connected the dots' (Espinet 293) and taken on 'the back-breaking work of re-invention' (Espinet 303).

Bringing together *The Swinging Bridge* and *Coolie Woman* against the backdrop of the history of the *kala pani* has enabled a better understanding of the complex network of geographical and historical intersections, from the perspective of generational and generic crossings, and of the need to resort to both fiction and non-fiction, one feeding on the other and *vice versa*. These narratives of two women writers who retrace the steps of their ancestors intersect in so many ways, reconstructing and reimagining the *translations* Gainder and Sujaria have performed from their native India to their adopted

Trinidad and British Guiana. Neither of them selects fiction or non-fiction as an exclusive method of writing. Even if one can easily identify the novel and the essay, both writers mingle fiction and non-fiction to reinforce the power of narrative and the force of the imagination in reconstructing historical events that are so complex and multiple in their complexity. It is the only way to ensure a better understanding of the present.

Notes

1. This continuously growing horizontal underground stem has become an image of multiplicity, fluid metamorphosis, and development away from the colonial centre. Contrary to a genealogy that would come from a unique root that develops vertically, the rhizome connects multiple roots horizontally. See Deleuze and Guattari, and also Glissant.
2. See Vertovec. Vertovec recapitulates on different sources and offers a very useful cumulative table that gives the detailed numbers of Indian immigrants per country, over the different periods of indentureship (167).
3. Calcutta (Kalkota) was the main port of emigration for indentureship candidates. It remained the British capital of India until 1911, when it was considered that Delhi would be less vulnerable. Six years later, in 1917, indentureship was declared illegal, at least officially.
4. I want to express my sincere thanks to Gautam Chakraborty, Port Security Adviser at Kidderpore, Kolkata, who took time on his busy schedule to show me around the dockyards and the Memorial to the Indian indentured labourers, erected in 2011. The book to which he contributed contains a couple of enlightening chapters dedicated to the nineteenth century Indo-Caribbean migrations. See Majumdar and Chakraborty.
5. The Introduction to Dabydeen, Jonathan Morley, Brinsley Samaroo, Amar Wahab and Brigid Wells reminds us of all the differences in the repatriation schemes. As soon as the 1870s the planters tried to devise ways to convince indentured labourers at the end of their contract period to commute their right to a return passage into money or land (XLIX). After 1895 they simply had to contribute to their own fare if they wished to repatriate.
6. The Introduction to *The First Crossing, being the Diary of Theophilus Richmond* devotes several well documented and moving pages to the repatriation schemes of the 1950s (XLVII–LXI). As indicated in this Introduction, the *M. V. Resurgent* sailed from Georgetown harbour on September 4, 1955. It was carrying the last 235 repatriates to Calcutta (XLVII).

7. See the work done by Crispin Bates, Marina Carter, David Dabydeen and Brinsley Samaroo, Vijay Mishra, Jeremy Poynting, Rajesh Rai, Peter Reeves, Hugh Tinker, Peter Van der Veer, among other scholars. See also Christian & Misrahi-Barak, eds.
8. See *Lutchmee and Dilloo*, by Edward Jenkins (1877); *Those That Be in Bondage: A Tale of Indian Indenture and Sunlit Western Waters*, by A. R. F. Webber (1917); *Gurudeva and Other Indian Tales* by Seepersad Naipaul (1943).
9. See, for instance, such slavery novels as *The Longest Memory* or *Feeding the Ghosts* by Fred D'Aguiar, *The Harlot's Progress* by David Dabydeen, *The Book of Negroes* by Lawrence Hill, *Cambridge* or *Crossing the River* by Caryl Phillips. In the francophone sphere one can think of *L'Esclave vieil homme et le molosse* by Patrick Chamoiseau, *Moi, Tituba, sorcière noire de Salem* by Maryse Condé. All these novels, published between the late 1980s and the 2010s, respond to the dual tradition of the original slave narratives from the eighteenth – nineteenth centuries and to that of the neo-slave narratives written by African-American writers from the 1960s–1980s. For more details about this revisiting, see Misrahi-Barak 2014.
10. See the work that has been done by Clem Seecharan on Bechu, for instance.
11. See the anthropological work that has been done by Kumar Mahabir, Patricia Mohammed or Peggy Mohan in transcribing some of the interviews they conducted in bhojpuri, the language the indentured labourers had brought with them from Bihar and Uttar Pradesh.
12. This article furthers two previous articles I published on Ramabai Espinet's work: 'Ruptures and Junctures' 2013; and also: 'Rifts and Riffs' 2014.
13. Ramabai Espinet, *The Swinging Bridge* (Toronto: HarperCollins, 2003), 51. Further page references have been inserted in the main text.
14. Espinet also carries out this process of 'rehabilitation' through her academic work. One may refer to articles such as 'The Invisible Woman in West Indian Fiction.'
15. See Misrahi-Barak 'Rifts and Riffs, Roots and Routes in Ramabai Espinet's *The Swinging Bridge*' where this idea is developed.

Works cited:
Bahadur, Gaiutra. *Coolie Woman – The Odyssey of Indenture*. London: Hurst and Company, 2013.
Carter, Marina. *Voices from Indenture: Experiences of Indian Migrants in the British Empire*. London & New York: Leicester University Press, 1996.
Carter, Marina, and Khal Torabully. *Coolitude, an Anthology of the Indian Labour Diaspora*. London: Anthem Press, 2002.

Christian, Rita and Judith Misrahi-Barak, eds. *India and the Diasporic Imagination.* Series *PoCoPages,* Collection 'Horizons anglophones.' Montpellier: Presses Universitaires de la Méditerranée, 201.

Dabydeen, David & Brinsley Samaroo, eds. *India in the Caribbean.* London: Hansib Publishing, 1987.

Dabydeen, David. *Across the Dark Waters: Ethnicity and Indian Identity in the Caribbean.* London: Macmillan Caribbean, 1996.

Dabydeen, David, Jonathan Morley, Brinsley Samaroo, Amar Wahab and Brigid Wells, eds. *The First Crossing, Being the Diary of Theophilus Richmond, Ship's Surgeon aboard the Hesperus, 1837–38.* Coventry: The Derek Walcott Press, 2007.

Deleuze, Gilles, and Félix Guattari. *Mille Plateaux.* Paris: Les Editions de Minuit, 1980.

Espinet, Ramabai. *The Swinging Bridge.* Toronto: Harper Collins, 2003.

———. 'The Invisible Woman in West Indian Fiction.' In *The Routledge Reader in Caribbean Literature,* edited by Sarah Lawson Welsh & Alison Donnell, 425–30. London: Routledge, 1996.

Glissant, Edouard. *Introduction à une poétique du divers.* Paris: Gallimard, 1996.

Mahabir, Kumar. *The Still Cry. Personal Accounts of East Indians in Trinidad and Tobago during Indentureship 1845–1917.* Tacarigua, Trinidad and Ithaca, New York: Calaloux Publications, 1985.

Majumdar, Anindo I.A.S. and Gautam Chakraborti, eds. *Calcutta Port – Ageless Annals.* Kolkata: Kolkata Port Trust, 2010.

Misrahi-Barak, Judith. 'Ruptures and Junctures: Reinventing and Repossessing the Diasporic Self in Ramabai Espinet's *The Swinging Bridge.*' In *Repenser la diversité: le sujet diasporique,* edited by Corinne Duboin, 127–39. St Denis de la Réunion: Océans Editions, 2013.

———. 'Post-*Beloved* Writing: Review, Revitalize, Recalculate.' *Black Studies Papers* 1, no. 1 (2014): *Slavery Revisited*; 37–55. http://elib.suub.uni-bremen.de/edocs/00103775-1.pdf.

———. 'Rifts and Riffs, Roots and Routes in Ramabai Espinet's *The Swinging Bridge.*' In *Tracing the New Indian Diaspora,* edited by Om Dwivedi, 235–251. Amsterdam: Rodopi / Cross Cultures, 2014.

Samaroo, Brinsley. 'Chinese and Indian Coolie Voyages to the Caribbean.' *Journal of Caribbean Studies,* 14, nos. 1 & 2 (2000): 3–24.

Shih, Shu-mei, and Françoise Lionnet, eds. *Minor Transnationalism.* Durham, NC and London: Duke University Press, 2005.

Vertovec, Steven. 'Indo-Caribbean Experience in Britain: Overlooked, Miscategorized, Misunderstood.' In *Inside Babylon: The Caribbean Diaspora in Britain,* edited by Winston James and Clive Harris, 165–78. London & New York: Verso, 1993.

CHAPTER 6

Expressions of Feminist Forms in the Indo-Muslim Community of Trinidad

Halima-Sa'adia Kassim

Using secondary sources and conversational narratives, this essay looks at micro-level configurations of feminist forms in the Indo-Muslim community of Trinidad and Tobago. Historical and contemporary examples of Muslim women's presence/absence in the religious public sphere are examined. The discussion builds on the premise that the Muslim community, though a minority, is heterogeneous, and the consciousness and practice of Islam are nuanced. It concludes that Muslim females have not only been beneficiaries of a changing social and technological order and that community social spaces reinforce certain cultural beliefs, practices and attitudes, but also that Muslim women draw together the strands of their religious identity and politics to own their choices and express their empowerment within the sub- and wider community. One may ask: How is feminism configured and expressed within the Muslim community? Indeed, is Islamic or Muslim feminism even possible within a westernized/secular society?

Muslim Population in Trinidad and Tobago

Muslims constitute five per cent of the population (or 65,705) according to data from the 2011 Population and Housing Census (PHC), with 34,892 persons recorded as males and 30,813 as females (PHC 2011). The Muslim population comprises *inter alia* Africans, [East] Indians, and Syrian-Lebanese. For the purpose of this paper, the focus is on [East] Indian Muslims or Indo-Muslims.

Within Islam, there are two sects – Sunnis and Shias (Shi'ites). In Trinidad and Tobago, as worldwide, the Sunnis comprise the majority and adherents are mainly of the Hanafi school, one of the four schools of Islamic jurisprudence. There are also followers of the Deobandi and Salafi and Wahabi movements. Sufis are also present in small numbers and the Ahmaddiyas, generally considered an unorthodox movement by Sunni Muslims, are also present in Trinidad.

Reconstruction of the Community

The [East] Indian Muslims are primarily descendants of indentured labourers who arrived from India during the eighteenth and nineteenth centuries and were mainly Sunni. By the late 1800s, the Indo-Muslims had articulated the framework for their existence based on core values set out in the *Qur'an* and the *Hadith* (a report of statements or actions of Prophet Muhammad (u.w.b.p),[1] or of his tacit approval or criticism of something said or done in his presence). They built symbols (*masjids*), accepted heroes like Prophet Muhammad (u.w.b.p.) who served as a model of behaviour and established rituals manifested through the Islamic greeting of salaams and social and religious ceremonies (Kassim 2015, 227). This reconstructed Islam was based predominantly on the memory of the migrants, oral tradition and interactions with the Hindu community. In the words of Patricia Mohammed (2015, 298) the Muslim migrants 'practiced Islam that was syncretized with aspects of Hindu culture'. It was infused with cultural artefacts and traditional practices. In discussing Islamic iconography in Trinidad, Mohammed (2015, 302) notes that Islam has a 'muted aesthetic presence' in comparison to the iconography of other religions; for example, mosques are less decorated than most temples and/or churches.

Migration, settlement and religion impact the constructions of gender and gender relations. While 'hierarchies of caste and practices of patriarchy' (Chatterjee 218) were challenged during the period of indenture, there was the reassertion of patriarchal values post-indenture. A new cultural identity premised on what was perceived as notions of the ideal Indian woman based on classical Indian culture and patriarchy was forged (Chatterjee 218). Further, Mohammed (2002, 168) asserted that Christianity and Islam influenced the development of notions of femininity and masculinity among the Indo-Muslims.

The reconstruction of the Muslim community in Trinidad can be broadly categorized into four periods: 1890s to 1930s (general religious and cultural reconstitution with supporting institutions), 1930s to 1960s (religious institutional building and consolidation), 1960s to 2000 (focus on cultural citizenship), and 2000 to present (contention with globalization and modernity). To assess the extent of women's autonomy and self-determination would require evaluation of all four periods, but this analysis will focus on selected incidents from the 1930s to the present.

Antecedents in Indo-Muslim Women's Voices

Two concepts – *purdah* and *fitna* – that emerged during the late indenture and post-indenture periods imposed behavioural codes (*qa'ida*) related to dress and boundaries in male/female interactions that amounted to a gender ideology (implicit or explicit) within the Muslim community, which remains relevant today in the religious public spaces. It instituted social placement based on gender and asserted the androcentric culture of the 'new' society. The cultural and religious reconstitution that came with the shift from indentureship to peasant cultivation and the establishment of village settlements led to women simultaneously being idealized and having a low status in everyday life (Gross 64–65).

In discussing the transmission of gender ideology as embedded in folk and religious songs, Mohammed noted that 'with the loss of patriarchal control in Trinidad there emerges the other side of duality which characterizes women' and 'their "untamed nature"...which men must vigilantly keep in check' (2002, 153). This 'untamed nature' of females coincides with the Islamic concept of *fitna* where the woman is the embodiment of beauty and enchantment, temptation and disorder. *Fitna* results through the collapse of spatial boundaries that suggests the absence of *purdah*. In exploring the concepts of Indo-Caribbean femininity, Mohammed also spoke to the concept of *fitna*, which she saw as 'implicitly employed by both the colonial authorities and the male patriarchy in reference to Islamic women to control their sexuality and display of seductive femininity' (2012, 13).

Within the Muslim community, there was the (re)introduction of *purdah* (seclusion/segregation), which regulated the extent of interactions and movements of women. The wearing of the *orhni* (a long scarf worn across both shoulders and around the head), which is generally associated with modesty and was often used when one was in the public arena, is an example of *purdah*. Mohammed stated that the wearing of the *orhni* 'symbolizes aspects of femininity expected of an Indian woman – keeping one's body covered and unexposed. By shrouding the head and obscuring visage, women symbolically displayed acceptance of the norm that they should be shielded from the watchful eyes of men' (2002, 136).

Muslim women were not allowed to attend the masjids for *namaaz* or for the prayers (also known as *salaah*) that commemorated sacred occasions like *jum'aah* (Friday prayers), *'Id-ul-'Adha* (Feast of Sacrifice),

'Id-ul-Fitr (Feast of Breaking the Fast) and *tarawih* (extra nightly prayers during the month of *Ramadan*). This absence of the women in the religious domain changed circa 1928 when they joined the *'Id-ul-'Adha* prayers at the Haji Gokool Mosque in St. James; however, there was no intermingling between the sexes as a screen was erected dividing the men from the women (*East Indian Weekly* 1928:06:02). In other words, although women were present in the *masjids* for the special *namaaz, purdah* was observed.

What exactly precipitated this change is unclear. Mohammed alluded to the influence of visiting missionaries with their different doctrines together with the position of women in a new host society, which together meant that the norms regarding Islamic practices became more flexible than the doctrine that was preached or stated in the Holy Books (1993, 148). Several *hadith* compiled by Al-Bukhari and Sahih Muslim encouraged women to attend prayers at the mosques.[2] The Muslim community was beginning to adopt the *Sunnah* (a body of established customs and beliefs that make up a tradition) and shed some of the restrictive gender practices, at least in relation to mosque attendance.

Perhaps the most profound change in the social visibility of Muslim women in the religious public sphere was in the 1930s with the return of Moulvi Ameer Ali from Lahore, India (now in Pakistan) as a religious scholar. Undoubtedly, having been influenced by the liberal ideology associated with his alma mater, Ahmadiyya Anjuman Ishaat-I-Islam, Ali offered fuller citizenship, participation rights and social visibility to Indo-Muslim women locally. It would be recalled that the 1930s to the 1950s was a period of Muslim religious institutional building and consolidation. To that end, he encouraged the members of the Tackveeyatul Islamia Association (TIA: Society for the Strength of Islam) – of which he was *Mufti* (a legal expert who is empowered to give rulings on religious matters) – to allow their female relatives to join the organization and attend religious lectures and activities of said body. This earned him the wrath of the more traditional Muslims of the colony, who continued to emphasize *purdah* 'as a safeguard against the present wave of immorality and careless abandon' (Kassim 1999, 139). This reduction of *purdah* was not contrary to the practices of Sunni Islam. Knowledge, Islamic or secular, is seen as important to the development of *taqwa* (God consciousness) and gives the individual a greater opportunity to contribute to the development of the community.

By supporting women's movement into the public sphere, Ali was providing them with such an opportunity. Women during the time of the Prophet Muhammad (u.w.b.p.) and the Caliphate used to venture their opinions on subjects relating to Islamic *Shari'ah* (law) and *fiqh* (jurisprudence), as exemplified by Ayesha, the wife of the Prophet. Neither was it uncommon for Muslim women to speak among a mixed audience, voicing a concern or making an inquiry during the time of the Prophet. Thus, Muslim women's entry into the public sphere as instigated by Ameer Ali was not *bid'a* (innovation), but a continuity of ancient practices.

This institutional-sponsored empowerment of Muslim women saw females moving into the public religious space during the period between 1933 and 1939, particularly in San Fernando (Trinidad's second city, in the southwest) and speaking out on issues specific to Islam as well as the wider community, e.g. socialism, education, economy, empowerment and equality, political representation, etc. In the lectures on empowerment and equality, the women spoke out against male attitudes towards women, particularly in relation to oppression of females and the system of *purdah*. They made calls for the personal rights of women, including fair and just upholding of the Islamic perspective of *quiwama* (maintenance and protection). Women became advocates for altering their social invisibility and inferiority. There were also exhortations to look back to the actions of the wives and daughters of the Prophet Muhammad (u.w.b.p.), for example, Khadija, Ayesha and Fatimah, and of magnates and sovereigns who endowed colleges and universities in the fifth and seventh centuries in the East.[3]

This call to consider the antecedents was used as a tactic to encourage females not to accept their social invisibility and inferiority, because Islam is rich with examples of women who were active in public life. In an attempt to counter the ignorance and provide 'social and religious reformations', there were calls in March 1936 for 'ladies' clubs, societies, magazines and reading rooms…[to be established to support the] Social, Cultural, Political and Educational advancement of Muslim ladies' (Kassim 1999, 139, 143–144). By September 1936, a Muslim female body was founded as a branch of the TIA for moral, social and intellectual improvement of its members. Females also participated in debates from 1936 to 1939 covering subjects such as the economy of the island – cocoa and oil, the influence of the pulpit and press on civilization, the arming of nations, cinema, library, marriage, home-lessons, travelling, male-female social equality and women accessing seats on the Municipal Council as part of female only teams or mixed teams (Kassim 1999, 146–57).

These activities took place against the backdrop of labour strikes and riots, and agitation and advocacy by the Indian community for the establishment of their own denominational schools and recognition of their marriages, among other grievances. Several factors contributed to making women socially visible. These included education (access to primary school education and possibly secondary schooling), a growing middle class (particularly, commercial and property owning, and religious leaders) and the mixed ethnicity of San Fernando and its environs, which allowed new ideas and a loosening of conservative practices. Added to this mix was the presence of a religious leader with liberal ideas.

Contestation for Space – Indo-Muslim Women

Community social spaces reinforce certain cultural beliefs and attitudes and the mosque, a community space, not only reinforces an Islamic identity, but also transmits messages that support the retention and performativity of patriarchy and can lead to gender disparity and conflict. There are clearly defined spaces in the Sunni *masjids* (mosques) that ensure *purdah* for *namaaz*. Women's access to a *masjid* is defined by separate entrances to prevent intermingling of the sexes, imposing *purdah* from the point of entry and reinforcing a cultural bias of women as temptations to men. It thus shifts focus from piety and purity of the practitioners. Various *Qur'anic* verses were used to justify this claim.[4] Sometimes it is a screen, a curtain or balustrades that demarcate the spaces for men and women.

This prescribed sexual separation and segregationist approach to mosque attendance is based upon *Shari'ah*-based legalist orthodox discourse (Buisson 101).[5] The socially constructed, gendered space defined by barriers is connected to definition of gender roles and is also premised on the concept of *fitna* wherein social relations are defined disproportionately by sexuality. The *Qur'an* is equally clear that women and men are supporters and contributors to establishing the Muslim community by upholding *inter alia* core Islamic beliefs (articles of faith) and practices (five pillars of Islam)[6] and have equality in worship or piety and the concept of accountability.

Women fought to reclaim spaces within the *masjids* from the 1970s, which was a period that saw the influence of Arabization of Islam, globally and in Trinidad. The Jama Masjid in Port of Spain was a site of contestation around 1974/1975 when the Tablighi movement emerged with the arrival of a *Hafiz* (a person who knows the Qur'an by heart) from Gujurat, India. The *imam* (priest) was then Moulvi Ishmael Adam, also from India, who provided an opening for the *Hafiz*. The mosque had two prayer Halls – the men's hall on the southern side and the women's on the northern side running east to west. It should be noted that while the Tablighi believe women can go to mosque, they prefer that women instead engage in readings or *taleem* in the privacy of someone's home. That belief led to a slow encroachment on the women's space and the shifting of the barriers, which imposed *purdah* on the adherents. Given that there was a large women's prayer section and an active 'Ladies Association' at the mosque, the women opposed this development. Despite the help of the young son of Zoonnahar Mohammed, a member of the *jamaat* and of the Ladies Association, Asad Mohammed recalls the final result was a reduced space for women and the introduction of the curtain as the new *purdah* measure. Also, a decision to construct living quarters for the *Hafiz* at the same location led to incursions in the hall where the women held functions. Again, the women unsuccessfully objected. A similar incident occurred at the Nur-e-Islam *masjid* around 1978 involving the shifting of the partition, thereby decreasing the prayer area allocated to females.[7] It is argued that the contestation to preserve space in the *masjids* is seen as an example of 'feminist commitments…to navigate the terrain between being critical of sexist interpretations of Islam and patriarchy in their religious communities' (Shaikh 155).

The events of the 1970s at Jama and Nur-e-Islam *masjid* did not take place in a vacuum; they occurred against the backdrop of preparations for the First World Conference on Women in Mexico (1975) and the international decade for women. Locally, there was the establishment of the National Commission on the Status for Women (1974) on which Zenobia Mohammed was the Muslim representative.

The preservation and use of prayer space in the mosques by women continue to be a challenge leading some women to raise their voice against the perceived injustice and/or document their experience. On 'Id-ul-Fitr 2007 (October 13), Rose Mohammed objected to the sudden appearance and placement of barriers to separate the males and females at the TML Mosque in St. Joseph, which is a manifestation of *purdah* in the prayer area (Reddock 2015, 237, 242; Kassim 2012, 8). Reddock (2015, 235–236) noted this practice at a community mosque (San Juan) and recorded Nabbie's experience of having to use the separate entrance at the *masjid* as a young girl. The same obtains at many *masjids* throughout the country currently. Nabbie's experience is no different from females attending Islamic knowledge classes at Darul Uloom (Cunupia) in or around 1989/1990 who were told that their male relatives or husbands should not enter the compound to drop or collect them because a sense of modesty and *purdah* must be preserved. Kassim (2016, 162–63) also recorded her experience of being removed from the programme that celebrated the life of Haji Rukhnudeen, a pioneer of Islam, at the Tunapuna *masjid*. The objection by the *imam* and other senior members were related to a female addressing a mixed audience, which they saw as ill-advised based on the *Sunnah*.

Is There a Place for Feminism Among Muslims?

I draw upon the understanding of Islamic feminism from Shaikh (148), a South African feminist scholar, who sees feminism as a crucial awareness in women of their subordination in society and engagement in activities to transform gender power relations so as to create a society based on the principles of gender justice, human equality, and freedom from structures of oppression.[8] The Muslim community is heterogeneous and Muslim women are also representative of the heterogeneity of their community. They have integrated their faith commitments and participation into their lives to different extents. It is possible for women to simultaneously see themselves as feminist and as religious and to see their religion as empowering. By looking at women's religious commitments and their engagements with their socio-religious environment (Islamic and Western), one sees women's agency critically as being nuanced, stretched and reconfigured. In that way, feminist notions of agency as predominantly active and resisting are subverted and expanded to include continuity, stasis and stability (Höel 80).

In the 1930s when females participated in the religious public fora and again, in the second decade of the twenty-first century, the women who participated publically within Muslim-controlled spaces demonstrated that they were not without autonomy. They seized the opportunity provided by a male religious leader and demonstrated that men's power and women's power can be understood in terms of the reciprocity of influence that prevails in interactive situations. This demonstrated that segregation of men and women need not necessarily imply restriction of women or their subordination (Kader 85–86). It was a clear example of gender negotiations as conceptualized by Mohammed (1993), which took place in the developing heterogeneous Indo-Muslim community. However, the women recognized the gender constraints present in the masculinist/hetrosexist space in which they operated and thus, wore the *orhni* as a marker of *modesty* and morality (Göle 465). They questioned the concepts of *purdah, fitna* and *qa'ida* and called for the liberation and emancipation of Muslim women. Nevertheless, many of the issues they raised were concerns of a developing middle class with little appeal to the lower class of Muslim women in an economy that was suffering from a worldwide depression in which the working class experienced low wages and unemployment with deteriorating living standards and lack of adequate (or in most cases any) representation. In what Adrienne Rich describes as 'politics of location', the women who found their voices were essentially responding to their own social reality (213).

These women did not couch their ideas and actions as feminist; instead they situated themselves within an Islamic discourse to legitimize their ideas. Nevertheless, these women had some level of awareness of the gender differentials within the community and had the 'capacity to put this cause at the centre of their lives' (Delmar 16). They were, as I have argued elsewhere, 'in the process of developing a collective consciousness which would produce a new faculty and process of valuation' (Kassim 1999, 210).

In Shaikh's 2003 definition of Islamic feminism, the fundamental components of belief and one's relationship with *Allah* (God) and the five pillars of Islam and the six articles of faith are upheld. Further, within Islam the concept of justice is seen as a supreme virtue and, as such, creates a state of equilibrium in the distribution of rights and duties (IslamReligion.com). It may be posited that this concept of justice is not only aligned to fairness, but also accountability (or *khilafah* which refers to every person, female or male, being accountable for their actions in this world). Blending this notion of religious epistemology and Islamic value system means Muslim women see feminism as a tool that allows them to question their faith position, critique aspects of it and to do so in a way that allows women and men to enjoy a more worthwhile participation in their community.

Both Yasmin, a twenty-plus year old Sunni *hijabi* (woman who wears a *hijab*/headscarf), and Farida Mohammed, a member of the Ahmadi movement in her fifties, noted that Islam provides women and men with a core set of rights.[9] However, 'people do not know how to interpret *Qur'an* and *Hadith*' (Kassim 2011, 11:29). Farida Mohammed noted that 'all the leaders of the Ahmadi movement, who are men... have stood up for women and women's rights...according to Islam' (2013, 04:30). These females explicitly acknowledge Islamic critical texts as the basis for theological equality and the upholding of rights according to Islam.

Feminism also frames its debates in terms of choice, which is seen as an indicator of female emancipation. However, religion or the practice of it by women may be a choice by some women who do not see it as a form of oppression but as a source of power and comfort. Saba Mahmood in her study of Islamist women in Cairo effectively saw the obedience within the faith and to *Allah* not as obedience to men or patriarchal systems but to a transcendental power (cited in Salem np). It may be argued that the realities of women in Islam are nuanced, complex and polymorphous: dependent not only on intersectionalities of ethnicity, class, age, education, etc., but also on the extent of one's faith commitments and consciousness.

Feminist activities are supported by several tools to improve the social conditions and justice afforded to Muslim women or promote women's issues in the religious public sphere. Borrowing from Margot Badran, Shaikh (157) noted that there exists a typology of feminist activism. These include various types of feminist writing from scholarship to fiction; everyday activism, including initiatives in social services, education, and professions; and organized movement activism, including political and even confrontational movements for women's emancipation.

Using that typology, we see within the Muslim community examples of feminist activism. One of the key Muslim organizations, the Anjuman Sunnat-ul-Jamaat Association (ASJA), already has a Ladies' arm which engages in social services. There is also a National Muslim Women's Association that engages in social services and education. Zoonnahar Mohammed, Nafeesa Mohammed and Rose Mohammed all challenged the reduced spaces for females in the community hall or the prayer halls of the *masjids*. For Muslim women who have developed an 'alternative way of understanding and approaching gender relations in Islam' (Shaikh 156), their experience of gender discrimination and conflict in the public sphere is expressed through feminist writing. Rose Mohammed (2009), Sarah Nabbie (2012) and Halima Kassim (2016) documented their own experiences as Muslim women in Muslim settings in popular non-fiction or scholarly works. These women were working out the terms of their public participation and as Hosein (2015, 255, 264) noted, women's negotiation with associational governance is a gendered struggle with both women and men defining appropriate gender roles and spaces. Within these religious defined spaces, there is 'controlled emancipation' and idealized gender notions. Hosein (2015, 263–64), who examined the non-participation of Muslim women in the executive elections of a religious body, stated that 'ideals of patriarchal leadership…are based on interpretations of respectable gender roles in Islam but also on larger non-Islamic and national gender ideologies' (263–64).

Rose Mohammed has suggested that there are 'many bright and intelligent young Muslim females [who] must be willing to raise their voices and not be subject to the authority of the *imama* (priests)'. She also suggested that they need to think critically and engage fully with the tenets of the faith and counter some of these 'silly ideas' (quoted in Kassim 2013, 5). For that to happen would require moving beyond current delivery of social services, knowledge and awareness. There is a need not only for a critical mass of religiously educated females,[10] but also the development of a tradition of *ijitihad* (independent reasoning) that contests the interpretations of the sacred texts, *Qur'an* and *Hadith*, and also decentres the domain of interpretation from the male *ulema*. This would be similar to the way Salem contextualized Islamic feminism as a 'field that can be broadly defined as an attempt to exercise power over knowledge production and meaning making within Islam' and activism.

As such, what exists now is a feminism that is essentially 'an amorphous set of ideas and practices' (Mohammed 2003, 25) where females process, construct and understand their lived realities within a confined space and come to some level of awareness of difference. Although as females they are 'subjected to relations of power [they] create space within those relations for the exercise of agency' (Salem).

Conclusion

This paper has provided examples of feminist activity within the Muslim community expressed at the level of the individual, highlighting that Muslim females exercised agency in the public religious sphere from the 1930s. It juxtaposed this feminist commitment with the concepts of *fitna* and *purdah* that remain dominant in the community. By 'conceptualising religion as a positionality' it provided a useful way for 'doing research that does not a priori reject the experiences of religious women as patriarchal' (Salem). It is important to uncover historical incidents like those spoken about above via personal narratives (or others referenced through *khutbah* or sermon) that demonstrate the way in which spatial allocation in public religious spheres is used to manage the exercise of (relative) power and agency in post-independence Trinidad, where there was a focus on cultural citizenship as the Muslim community contended with the increasing influences of globalization and modernity.

Religious spaces are not only conservative but tend to be patriarchal, and women's religious lives and expressions are dominated by 'a pattern of exclusion and participation' (Gross 15). Muslim women, particularly those with a feminist consciousness, function in two public spheres – Muslim and Western – and as such, they have to be aware 'of sexist interpretations of Islam and patriarchy in their religious communities' and that of the wider community. This dual notion of critical consciousness 'is an acceptance of the assumption that Islam and women's rights belong to essentially different domains and that Muslim women bring them together strategically as "an act of radical subversion"' (Shaikh 155). This expression of feminist consciousness exhibited by Sarah Nabbie (Bamboo Masjid), Zoonnahar Mohammed (Jama *masjid*, Port of Spain), Nafeesa Mohammed (Nur-e-Islam Masjid, San Juan) and Rose Mohammed (Jinnah Memorial Masjid, St Joseph) and others emerged from their faith, commitment and knowledge.

To scale-up feminist activities would mean that there must a critical mass that have voice and influence to articulate their ideas of empowerment and emancipation for women to claim mosque spaces and assert meaningful participation in administrative activities of the *masjid*s and participation in public religious activities. An organized feminist movement would also have to contend with the problematics of *fitna* and *purdah,* the lack of a tradition of local *ijitihad* and the strains of fundamentalism. Given the high anti-Muslim sentiments globally, it is unclear if Muslim women in Trinidad would consolidate and become more conservative or if there would be action to liberalize the interactions and use and preservation of space at the *masjid*.

Notes

1. Islamic tradition dictates that 'upon whom be peace (u.w.b.p)' follow the utterance and text of Prophet Muhammad's name.
2. A *hadith* by Bukhari, a compiler of *hadith*, encouraged females to attend the 'Id congregation and hear the preaching of Islam. In another *hadith*, Muslim, a compiler of *hadith*, recorded that the Prophet said 'Do not stop the women from going to the mosques at night.' It is also recorded by Muslim that 'The best rows for men are the front ones, and the worst rows are the last ones. And the best rows for women are the last ones, and the worst are the front ones.'
3. TG 1936:03:12.14. Rahamut in this section of her address makes reference to Cairo, the daughter of Mameluke Sultan Malik who established an educational institution; the daughter of Malik Asraph known as Khartoon who erected a college at Damascus and Sheikha Shudha who in the fifth century Hegua lectured publicly at the cathedral mosque in Baghdad on rhetoric and poetry. Sheikha Sudha, according to Rahamut, was known as Fakh-un-Nisa, The Glory of Women. Khadija was the Prophet Muhammad's first wife, mother of his daughter Fatimah, the mother of the twins Hasan and Hussein, whose martrydom is the central event separating the Shias from the Sunnis today. Ayesha was another of Muhammad's wives, often said to be his favorite.
4. The verses used in this claim are 24.31 and 33.53.
5. According to Abu Dawud, a compiler of *hadith*, in the case of *salaah* where women aspired to go to the *masjid*, the Prophet (S.A.) advised them in the following manner, 'it is better for a woman to offer her salaah in her bedroom than in the living room and it is better for her to offer her salaah in the living room than in her courtyard' (Abu Dawud). It has also been narrated that Umm Humaid Sa'idiyya (R.A) once said to the Prophet (S.A), 'O Prophet of Allah, I desire to offer prayers under your leadership.' The Holy Prophet (S.A) said, 'I know that, but your offering the prayer in the corner is better than your offering it in your private room and your offering it in your private room is better than offering it in your courtyard and your offering it in your courtyard is better than offering it in the neighbouring mosque' (Reported by Ahmad and Tabarani). See Darul Uloom Trinidad and Tobago, on intermingling and free mixing between muslim men and womem. (May 21, 2012, http://www.darululoomtt.net/intermingling-free-mixing-muslim-men-women/).
6. The five pillars of Islam refer to basic and mandatory acts that govern a Muslim's life namely; (i) Shahada (declaration of faith); ii) Salaah (prayer); (iii) Zakaat (obligatory charity); (iv) Sawm or fasting during the month of Ramadan; and (v) Hajj (pilgrimage to Mecca). The six articles of faith are: (i) belief in Allah (God); (ii) belief in His Angels; (iii) belief in His Books; (iv) belief in His Messengers; (v) belief in the Last Day; and (vi) belief in divine destiny.

7. This incident has been documented by Reddock in her discussion of Muslim women in Trinidad and their struggle to reclaim space in mosques (see 232–36).
8. Shaikh defined Islamic feminism as a discourse that 'addresses questions of human wholeness from the perspective of a foundational God-human relationship that roots the process and goals of individual, societal, and political life in the attainment of a right relationship with God. Questions of justice, freedom, and equality, therefore, are always situated and valued vis-à-vis a larger framework for understanding the nature of reality' (cited by Shaikh 2012, 22).
9. There are several verses in the Qur'an that speak to gender equality and relations – some speak to the equality of the males and females (see 4.32, 5.41, 9.71, 24.2, and 33.35) while others focus on the complementarity of the sexes and/or gender (see 4.34).
10. There are special Islamic schools, Haji Rukhnudeen Institute of Islamic Studies and the Darul Uloom Institute, or special classes for women, but they tend towards passive learning behaviours (surface learning) rather than deep learning or an approach that supports *ijitihad* (independent reasoning). It is seen as independent or original interpretation of problems not precisely covered by the *Qur'an* and *Hadith*). Darul Uloom offers the following programmes/courses: *Aadhilah* (Islamic knowledge), Hafiz (one who memorises the Qur'an), *Faadhilah* (Associate degree in Islamic Studies), and Diploma in Islamic Studies.

Works Cited

Andersson, Annika. *Honor Killings – the Survival of Patriarchy in Different Societies*. Diss. U of Lund, 2003. Web. Apr.–May 2016.

Buisson, Johanna. 'Gender Segregation in Islam Protection or Destruction?' *KUFA REVIEW* 2, no. 1 (Winter 2013): 99–122. Web. Apr.–May 2016.

Chatterjee, Sumita. 'Communitarian Identities and the Private Sphere: A Gender Dialogue Amongst Indo-Trinidadians (1845–1917).' In *Community, Empire and Migration. South Asians in Diaspora,* edited by C. Bates, 206–223. London: Palgrave Macmillan, 2001.

Delmar, Roslind. 'What is Feminism?' In *What is Feminism?*, edited by Juliet Mitchell and Ann Oakley, 8–33. Oxford: Blackwell Publishers, 1989.

Göle, Nilüfer. *The Forbidden Modern: Civilization and Veiling*. Ann Arbor, MI: University of Michigan Press, 1996.

Government of Trinidad and Tobago. Trinidad and Tobago 2011 Population and Housing Census Demographic Report. Ministry of Planning and Sustainable Development Central Statistical Office. 2012.

Gross, Rita. *Beyond Androcentrism*. Missoula, MT: Scholars Press, 1977.

Höel, Nina. 'Feminism and Religion and the Politics of Location: Situating Islamic Feminism in South Africa.' *Journal of Gender and Religion in Africa* 19, no. 2 (2013): 73–89. Web. Apr.–May 2016.

Hosein, Gabrielle. 'Democracy, Gender and Indo-Muslim Modernity.' In *Islam and the Americas*, edited by Aisha Khan, 249–68. Gainesville, FL: University Press of Florida, 2015.

IslamReligion.com. *The Religion of Islam.* Web. Mar.–Apr. 2016.

Kader, Soha Abdel. 'The Role Of Women In The History of Arab States.' In *Retrieving Women's History: Changing Perceptions of the Role of Women in Politics and Society*, edited by S. Jay Kleinberg, 79–98. Oxford and New York: Berg Publishers, 1988.

Kassim, Halima-Sa'adia. 'Forming Islamic Religious Identity among Trinidadians in the Age of Social Networks.' In *Crescent Over Another Horizon: Islam in Latin America, the Caribbean, and Latino USA*, edited by María del Mar Logroño-Narbona, Paulo G. Pinto, and John Tofik Karam, 225–54. Austin, TX: University of Texas Press, 2015.

———. 'Identity and Acculturation of Trinidad Muslims. An Exploration of Contemporary Practices.' In *Indentured Muslims in the Diaspora: Identity and Belonging of Minority Groups in Plural Societies*, edited by Maurits S. Hassankhan, Goolam Vahed, Lomarsh Roopnarine, 141–80. Delhi: Manohar Publishers, 2016.

———. Personal interview with Farida Mohammed, April 30, 2013.

———. Personal interview with Yasmin, November 29, 2011.

———. 'The Depths of Rose, "A Wind that Rose": A Woman called Feroza Rose Mohammed.' *Caribbean Review of Gender Studies*, no. 6, (2012): 1–16. Web.

———. *Education, Community Organisations and Gender Among Indo-Muslims of Trinidad, 1917–1962*. PhD Diss., University of the West Indies, 1999.

Mohammed, Feroza Rose. *Speak Out: Perspectives of a Muslim woman from the Caribbean*. Caroni: Lexicon Trinidad Limited, 2009.

Mohammed, Patricia. 'Island Currents, Global Aesthetics: Islamic iconography.' In *Islam and the Americas*, edited by Aisha Khan, 295–326. Gainesville, FL: University Press of Florida, 2015.

———. 'Changing Symbols of Indo-Caribbean Femininity.' *Caribbean Review of Gender Studies*, no. 6, (2012): 1–16. Web.

———. 'Like sugar in coffee: third wave feminism and the Caribbean.' *Social and Economic Studies* 52, no. 3: (2003) 5–30.

———. *Gender negotiations among Indians in Trinidad 1917–1947*. England and The Hague: Palgrave Macmillan and Institute of Social Studies, 2002.

———. *A Social History of Post Migrant Indians in Trinidad from 1917 to 1946. A Gender Perspective*. PhD Diss., The Hague, Netherlands: Institute of Social Sciences, 1993.

Nabbie, Sarah. 'What If Khadijah Did Not Work and Aisha Did Not Speak? Reflections of a Young Indo-Trinidadian Muslim Woman.' *Caribbean Review of Gender Studies*, no. 6, (2012): 1–6. Web.

Reddock, Rhoda. '"Up Against a Wall": Muslim Women's Struggle to Reclaim Masjid Space in Trinidad and Tobago.' In *Islam and the Americas*, edited by Aisha Khan, 217–48. Gainesville, FL: University Press of Florida, 2015.

Rich, Adrienne. 'Notes towards a politics of location.' In *Blood, Bread, and Poetry: Selected Prose 1979–1985,* edited by Adrienne Rich, 210–31. New York: Norton and Company, 1994.

Salem, Sara. 'Feminist Critique and Islamic Feminism: The Question of Intersectionality.' *The Postcolonialist* 1, no 1 (2013). Web. Mar.–Apr. 2016.

Shaikh, Sa'diyya. *Sufi Narratives of Intimacy: Ibn'Arabī, Gender, and Sexuality.* Chapel Hill, NC: The University of North Carolina Press, 2012.

———. 'Transforming Feminisms: Islam, Women and Gender Justice.' In *Progressive Muslims: On Justice, Gender and Pluralism,* edited by Omid Safi, 147–62. Oxford: Oneworld Publications, 2003. Web. Apr.–May 2016.

CHAPTER 7

Itinerant Caribbean Feminist Forms: Islamic Feminism in Trinidad and Tobago

Janet L. Bauer

Feminist Tides in the Global Caribbean: The Caribbean Meets Islamic Feminism[1]

The term 'itinerant feminisms' suggests innovation, improvization, and creativity in adapting to new circumstances. To the extent these forms emerge from movement, travel, and circulation that generate encounters and 'mixing', such feminisms are amplified by the conditions of migration and diaspora that have produced the polycultural landscapes of Caribbean feminisms, as well as of Caribbean Islam. The allusion to 'mobility' at once captures the global circulation of both feminist and Islamic knowledge and practices. The frictions of encounters emerging in such interstitial places produce a creolization (adaptation or accommodations) that Stuart Hall (2017) argues invites inquiry, comparison, and resistance to existing authority and spatial order, and necessitates the recognition of imbrication or complex entanglements of elements of these forms (see Hafez 2011).

In other words, the Caribbean is a place where global 'feminist' and 'Islamic' currents intersect locally with the potential for generating conceptual and methodological innovations about difference and relations of power in feminist thinking.[2] To further interrogate the contributions of Caribbean feminism in rethinking and destabilizing western-dominated feminist approaches, I will make use of ethnographic research I have conducted since 2002[3] on Trinbagonian[4] Muslim women's active engagement with what I call 'Heritage Islam', by which I mean an intentional effort to define oneself within what one perceives to be ancestral traditions of Islam. I argue that itinerant forms of feminism that emerge out of mobility, imbrication and creolization create indigenous feminisms in Trinidad and Tobago, re-articulating some challenges in contemporary feminist theory – particularly those involving relationships of difference (race, class, and generation).

However, central to understanding the contributions of Trinbagonian Muslim women's activism to the feminist conversation are the global circuits of Islamic knowledge, debates about creolization in Islam, and changes in women's religious authority. As in other Muslim Diasporas, travelling missionaries (see Kassim 2002), texts and electronic media in Trinidad and Tobago have brought new ideas about 'correct' Islamic practice – including expectations for women's roles and behaviour, contributing to the creation of major Trinbagonian Muslim organizations with particular ethno-racial compositions. Today this revitalization is represented by the conservative (some would say puritanical or wahabi) Tablighi or Deobandi missionary movement originating in South Asia and reflected in the rising importance of the Darul Uloom Institute (and to a lesser extent, other madrassas or Muslim schools). Darul Uloom propagates standardization of textual interpretations (and arguably the wearing of *niqab* or full face veil and plural marriage) as well as decreolizing Islam of influences considered nonIslamic. As one of the main sites for engaging Heritage Islam, Darul Uloom training has made pious knowledge (paradoxically) a basis for Muslim women's changing leadership roles and for changing relationships among Muslim women from racially diverse jamaats (Muslim associations and mosques) of Afro-, Indo- and Latino Trinbagonians.

Searching for Islamic Feminisms: The 'Middle East' comes to Trinidad and Tobago

What does it mean to be a good Muslim woman under ever-changing global and local ideas about what this entails? Muslim women everywhere must reckon with stereotypes about who they are at a time when there is both increasing Islamophobia and increasing pressure for 'halalization' (conforming to standardized notions of what is acceptable in Islamic tradition). Exploring Islamic heritage can provide ways of positioning self and community in the new climate of Islamophobia. Although being a Muslim feminist can range from conforming closely to specific Islamic teachings to being 'inspired' by Islamic principles to achieve women's full participation in society (see Karam 1997), I focus on women, as individuals and groups, whose activism is consciously located within the framework of Islam. These Muslim women in Trinidad and Tobago are 'intentional' about perfecting their knowledge of Islam and deploying it in their lives to benefit women, seeing themselves as ambassadors of an Islamic way of life. Such women are serious about conveying that they feel liberated through their engagement with their religious faith (frequently through listserve and other internet posts to support one another). Their activism is a kind of *dawa* (education or social service to others) – whether a woman sees it as feminist or not (and most women I interviewed did not readily apply the label 'Islamic Feminist' to their activities without detailed rationalization).

In refashioning identities, 'making space' and debating women's roles along new lines, Trinbagonian Muslim women often reference the Middle East as an historical source of authentic Islamic practice, on the one hand, and as a contemporary example of women's cultural oppression, on the other, drawing them further into global debates about women's rights in Islam. Middle Eastern styles of modest clothing are one point of reference, including the *niqab* or complete *hijab* with face veil worn by numerous Darul Uloom-affiliated women. However, like Western feminists, they often essentialize the complexities of women's activism or Islamic feminism in Muslim-majority countries like Iran, as Aminah (an older Indo-Trinidadian Muslim woman leader) did upon learning that I had conducted research in Iran, when she explained that Muslim women in Trinidad lived in a modern society (Bauer 2009). By 'modern' she meant, they were not 'backward' like Iranian women, who endured oppressive restrictions.

While debating Islamic Feminism, some Western feminists are accused of 'romanticizing' the idea that Islam could be used to challenge patriarchy (Moghissi 1999; Mojab 2001) with others suggesting that feminists (Western and Muslim) ignore the opportunities that Heritage Islamic activism offers (Abu-Lughod 2002; Zine 2006). Muslim women like Omaima Abu-Bakr believe that 'with a bit of re-interpretation of classic texts, Islam and feminism can work hand-in-hand'; others are not so sure (Adams 2015).

In her search for 'Islamic Feminism' from the Middle East to Central Asia and the United States (US), ethnographer Elizabeth Fernea (1997) accentuated the diversity of Muslim women's activism. But, while early twentieth century feminists saw little conflict between their activism and their faith (Badran 1996), contemporary Muslim women have found many of their traditional practices that gave them status in their community (like healing ceremonies) are now considered by male Imams to be un-Islamic (Masquelier 2009), sometimes attributed to creolization. Practising piety or learning to read Arabic provides new access to social standing in the community (Brink and Mencher 1996).

Thus, women are studying Islamic theology and law in order to enhance their positions in communal and public life (Pang 1996; Afkhami 1997; Schulz 2008; Bano and Kalmbach 2011; Mahmood 2011; Hafez 2011; Brink and Mencher 1996; Kuenkler and Fazaeli 2012). From West Africa to Egypt, and Iran to China, Malaysia, and Indonesia, women's access to Koranic literacy and their attempts to, as Cooke (2001) and Hafez (2011) suggest, 'claim Islam as their own' has had an indelible impact on women and their communities, especially in Muslim-majority countries where many cultural traditions are entwined in Islamic practice. Sometimes, access to Islamic education also opens up opportunities to challenge the standing of cultural traditions, as seen in the arguments Malay and Indonesian women are making about *figh* (man-made jurisprudence) versus *sunna* (the example of the Prophet) and to support cultural practices that do not conflict with *sunna* (Basruddin 2016; Rinaldo 2013; Van Doorn-Harder 2006).

These debates have sometimes required women's rights activists to confront their exclusion of women because of class, ethnicity, or lack of membership in the 'sorority' of those working to confront patriarchal practices (cf. Bauer 1993, 1994; Paidar 1997, on Iran). The emergence of Islamic (or more Muslim-centred) feminism for some (especially working class or non-elite women) provides a language of rights by which to challenge social as well as state-supported patriarchy, although others have been dubious about effecting change within religious patriarchy where male scholars are the ultimate arbitrators of Islamic behaviour. In the meantime, the post-Islamic turn toward adopting the language of rights has set Islamic and secular feminists on a path of 'convergences' of sorts, producing more dialogue in movements for gender equity (Fazaeli 2006).

Islamic Feminism and its Discontents in Trinidad and Tobago: Multiple Muslim Publics and the Cultural Debates

Having freedom of movement, choice in dress, or greater voice in securing even the basic rights afforded by Islam but perhaps denied in social practice (like choice of spouse and control over one's own resources) may be central to women's struggles 'for equality' in many Muslim-majority societies today (see Milani 2011). However, these may not be the key concerns of Muslim feminists in Muslim-minority diaspora contexts that afford broad civil rights.

Among an older generation of Trinbagonian Muslim women, leaders are women like the (uncovered) wife of a former politician, who works across sectarian boundaries. Refusing to call herself 'a Muslim woman', she lives her life as an example of what a good Muslim in a multicultural society should be. This philosophy brings her ironically close to Darul Uloom-trained women who also see themselves as 'ambassadors' for a different kind of Muslim woman, defined in terms of a very specific set of approved behaviours.

Right now Trinbagonian women who adopt an Islamic framework for their community activism explain that Islam provides them with a full set of rights and liberties, achieved through adherence to prescriptive rules for Islamic living. These women also assume an active role in discussing how to accommodate Islamic text and *sunna* to local circumstances (in private individual study and in public venues of classes and meetings); as in Indonesia and Malaysia, they produce lively lectures, questioning whether cultural habits contradict good Islamic practice. For example, while they are told in (Tablighi-influenced) study groups and classes that they should live modestly and travel with a mahram (a family member), they explain that this is not practical in a 'Western context' where they are driving their own cars and working in businesses with men (Bauer 2017). Simple modesty, balance and consideration will do in these cases, they say. As for the choice of covering, one Latina Muslimeh (trained as a lawyer) told me freedom was 'the right to keep my body private' by wearing the *hijab* (and for one period in her life, the *niqab*), which liberated her from the male gaze (Bauer 2017).

Debates over defining 'authenticity' in Islamic practice often focus on implementing women's God-given rights, eliminating cultural remnants from the practice of Islam, or decreolizing Islam. With its complex of schools, courses and students, Darul Uloom Institute (a controversial arbiter of religious knowledge) is a nexus for the shifting community debates about authenticity in Islam. The teachers it trains are becoming a primary source of religious instruction across diverse Muslim organizations. As elsewhere, women find that their bodies become the site of 'contestation', where community practice and well-being are defined through behaviours like correct *hijab* and refraining from singing *qaseeda*s (poetry about the Prophet Muhammad or women of his family) at community or women's events.

In almost every *jamaat*, I have heard of the problem of 'the Arab-centric or Indian-centric culture' of Islam in Trinidad and Tobago. The oppression of women, as one TML[5] woman told me, originates from Arab culture, not from Islam. Others feel that too much Indian culture (like the *oorney* as Islamic covering) is distracting people from real Islamic practices. An older generation of traditional women leaders is comfortable with incorporating many local cultural traditions into their practice – women like Rose Mohammed who declared her love for wearing (Indian) saris and publicly challenged the influence of Deobandi thinking on Muslim women (Bauer 2006). After I spoke on Muslim women reformers' use of *ijtihad* or interpretation at a TML Ladies Group in 2007, one member announced that Muslims need only follow the Koran to facilitate women's interests. Then privately she told me that the Koran would not really protect women if their husbands abused them. The Darul Uloom-trained Aneesa (below), however, insisted that earlier (male) jurisprudents, who developed the body of Islamic *fiqh* (jurisprudence), rendered opinions that must be observed, insisting that a good Muslim husband would not abuse his privileges in protecting women.

Disrupting the Landscape: the Case of the Dueling Women's Groups

The growing contestation around de-creolizing Islam is reflected in competing women's organizations at one of the mosques in San Juan outside of Port of Spain, Trinidad. Here the controversy has extended to a struggle over use of (physical) space as well as over the pursuit of 'authentic' Islam. The San Juan neighbourhood is undergoing demographic change reflected in a mosque where for various reasons (like residential and employment patterns) *jumah* or Friday prayers and *eid* services are becoming more racially diverse. The traditional 'Ladies Organization' (as I am calling them) focuses on charity and community work and represents the founding and (mostly Indo-Trinidadian) traditional, elite families.[6] Challenging them is a more recent group I will call the 'Sisters Association',[7] led by women whose authority and status are bolstered by their religious training at Islamic schools like Darul Uloom and who engage in the *dawa* of teaching 'correct' knowledge to others.

The Ladies Organization call themselves traditionalists and justify certain practices – like women's singing *qaseeda*s – within legacy traditions approved by previous missionary sheiks, while the Sisters Association views these practices as unacceptable innovations (*bida*). The mosque conflict demonstrates some resistance to Deobandi-influenced revival as well as emerging, barely articulated issues of race relations. With greater racial diversity across jamaats and the emergence of non-elite, Darul Uloom-educated women teachers, the influence of older, traditional Indo-Trinidadian women leaders like Haleema (and Aminah) is being destabilized.

In 2007, Haleema, a founding member of the Ladies Organization and some of the other members, began to complain about the emergence of the Sisters Association guided by younger women, such as Aneesa, who wore *niqab*. Haleema, in a headscarf tucked behind her ears, told me, 'These others are squatters and poachers.' Aneesa, who did not complete university but who is articulate and well-respected and has studied extensively at Darul Uloom, represents the increasing number of women from less religiously prominent families or unaffiliated, increasingly Afro-Trinidadian or mixed jamaats being certified through Darul Uloom.

Haleema suggested the new members are coming to the mosque for material reasons.

> They come in and see these beautiful facilities and just take charge.... Where did this other women's group come from – all over I guess...some got married in this area – some of them are multiple wives. We don't subscribe to that. All things that were rejected by other countries, they bring it here and impose it upon poor Muslim women.... Their ideology or thinking is not what we're used to.... He [the new Imam] let these women... start up their own women's group. [We] had encouraged them to participate in our activities but they didn't want to.

After the creation of the Sisters Association, the Ladies Organization still met in the mosque, but there was so much conflict that they now meet in a nearby residence owned by one of the members.
Haleema continues,

> My mother and aunt brought us up – to help out the community, be useful to our community. This new [women's] group pays themselves for volunteer work. We don't believe in that – we do real volunteer work.... We are the independent ladies, not under a committee or the new Imam.

When she describes the new classroom buildings that are part of the mosque expansion, she mentions that

> The Darul Uloom have been going around the country and getting a foothold in all the *masjid*s, most of which belong to ASJA.[8] Wherever they see a weak link...they come and spread their tentacles. They condemn us for what we practice. We invite some of them [for *maulid* functions] but we stand for a function – when we do then they go outside. Their practices are different.[9]

The historical stature of Haleema's Indo-Trinidadian family in the community provides little weight in a mosque now led by someone affiliated with Darul Uloom. 'They've put a wall up in front of our faces,' she says. 'They've said that there has to be a barrier between men and woman. I've been to Mecca – and there you have to be in *purdah* but here in San Juan in this day and age, can you believe they put up this barrier so that men are separated from women? We can't join in with those people.... At our [Ladies Organization] functions, the mosque barriers are removed and men and women move around freely together.' Complaining about the restriction in space, she asks:

> Why do we want to be locked up like in a cell. I don't like that. There is like a harem. They want the ladies to cover up head to toe in *niqab* with only their eyes showing. I'm a Trini, I'm a Muslim, I read the Koran and I practice what I read.... On *eid* day they give the women the inside part and the men go into the carpark. Who are you fooling? You can't fool God. For *Jumah* – we have to go to this confined space but on *eid* when all these people come, they think women have the whole of the inside but it's not true during the year...you can't fool God. What these men are doing it is not right. The mosque pretends they care about ladies but they don't.

However, Aneesa, a member of the Sisters Association who studied at the Darul Uloom Institute and has taught a variety of classes for women at the mosque, would disagree. Aneesa was confident when she explained women's place in this mosque. She invited us to attend the Sisters' Association events which we did on the occasion of a women's programme that included the celebration of an *hafiza* (one who had memorized the entire Koran) and a lecture on women's rights in Islam, which emphasized what they referred to as those 'other women's rights' – that is, the right to be obedient and loyal wives and mothers. Their vision is to be 'a dynamic Islamic association addressing the diverse needs of women', and their mission is 'to attract all sisters towards the *deen* [religion] of Allah by empowering them through education, participation and support, thereby creating an enlightened woman and forging a stronger family unit.'

During Aneesa's advanced class on *hadith* (based on the examples of the life of the Prophet Muhammad), this respected young mother reminded us of the beauty of Islamic knowledge and the need for women to be covered head to toe (because of the beguiling nature of women's ankles and to be closer to God), mirroring the messages given through her Darul Uloom training and visiting lecturers on the Islamic Broadcasting Network programmes. While her lesson that day was about the need for clarity in what is allowed and not allowed, Aneesa asserted a woman's right to adapt some aspects of Islamic learning to her own circumstances. Women can assume some public roles like speaking about Islam and, depending upon their education, offer *tafsir* (authoritative interpretations and textual commentary), although their main responsibilities should always be to their children, for whom they have a duty to be educated in order to raise and nurture them well.

Determining 'authentic Islamic knowledge' is a contested endeavour – more complicated than just embracing or relinquishing cultural traditions or seeking more 'authentic' textual interpretations. The cultural wars over creolization were brought into focus by Haleema's daughter in one event at the mosque several years later. In 2014 at a mixed gender event sponsored by the Ladies Organization to celebrate the Prophet's birthday, she publically declared the appropriateness of maintaining these religio-cultural traditions. Muslims needed emotion, she explained, and their devotional place in the Indo-Trinidadian Muslim landscape gave them the right to sing *qaseeda*s. She argued that visiting sheiks had authorized certain practices and rendered them appropriately Islamic. The new (and Darul Uloom-sanctioned) practices, she argued, were in fact the 'unIslamic' (*bida*) influences of Arab cultural traditions and salafism or fundamentalism and not authentic Islam.

And what of Aneesa? The Sisters Association has devolved into a group of women with particular interests in the mosque, no longer offering planned programmes and events. But Aneesa still teaches and one of her 'assistants' in organizing activities in the mosque is Afro-Trinidadian. As she grapples with balancing what is theologically required with what might suit her particular social context, she also engages the language of rights, just as Haleema and her daughter are also rethinking their engagement with the Sisters' Association. Aneesa elaborates that a woman has the right to ask her future husband to guarantee certain provisions – like a room of her own to get away from it all, as Aneesa admits she savours moments when she can slip away from her children and read theological texts. Women should not answer proposals too quickly because they must think about their own futures when making decisions about marriage. She may be facing what Hidayatullah described as 'the much feared question of whether it is possible for Muslim feminist exegesis of the Qur'an to survive the conclusion that our demands for gender justice may not cohere fully with the Qur'an....These paths may help us continue to read the Qur'an as Muslims and as feminists dynamically even if we come to inhabit those positions in ways that we could never have imagined' (2014, 195).

The day that Haleema's daughter delivered her public address, in contrast to several years earlier, she was wearing her *hijab* drawn more tightly around her head. This is consistent with something Haleema told me the next year when I visited her in the renovated mosque – that the two groups of women were getting along better, even though the women's section was now more permanently separated from the men's: 'we have to learn to live together,' she said. The mosque was refurbished and the women were seeking to accommodate each other, demonstrating the convergence of interests perhaps that Hafez says reflects an imbrication or entwining of roots (like the common stereotypes about Islam in the world) but not of similitude (2011).

Increasingly the leadership roles developed by an earlier generation of Muslim women like Aminah and Haleema, whose activism once crossed religious boundaries, are being transformed by a more diverse set of women like Aneesa from less influential families, classes or racial backgrounds. Seeking to promote an essentialized Islamist womanhood, albeit within the racially diverse *umma* (or wider Muslim community), their authority and (personal, communal and sometimes economic) status are bolstered by certification in Islamic knowledge. Initially many of the students of Darul Uloom-trained teachers that I met were Indo-Trinidadian but increasingly include Afro- and Latina-Trinbagonian converts, reverts, and 'born-Muslims'[10] who attended or sent their children to Darul Uloom classes. Increasingly, groups of diverse women (and youth) have begun to question the Deobandi perspectives. Especially among younger Muslim men and women (of 'nonelite' or nontraditional backgrounds), the new access to religious learning has provoked questions that may take debates about rights, 'practical' accommodations, and race relations in new directions.

Bayat's (2007) concept of a 'nonmovement' might suggest that the diffuse array of Muslim women activists, both *individuals in groups* (as in the current Sisters Association or individual women studying in

Aneesa's classes) and *formalized groups* (like the Ladies Organization) seeking empowerment, constitute an Islamic women's constituency moving toward accommodating others. The question is whether in the polycultural context of Trinidad, they can move toward a 'creole feminism' that entails cross feminist collaborations and addresses the challenges of race and gender in both Islam and feminism.

Islam and Feminism at Play in the Caribbean: Creole Feminism and Indigenous Sovereignty

The term 'play' stresses the fluidity and creativity in Islamic feminism's adaptation to diasporic conditions. Despite the push to 'de-creolize' and essentialize Trinbagonian Islam, Bulliet (1995), Khan (2004), Geertz (1957), el-Zein (1977) and others have established that creolization was a key process through which Islam emerged 'in place' adapting – historically and especially in diaspora – to local conditions. The model of 'creolization/decreolization' (as opposed to syncretism or hybridity) both underscores the dynamic innovation in the processes of change and also retains a role for agency in a 'glocal' context (Korom 196).[11] Mahdavi has suggested that post-Islamic struggles – i.e. to merge 'faith and freedoms, religiosity and rights' as described by Bayat, like periodic Islamic missions to Trinidad, reflect the historical cycles of reform and change, narrowing and opening up, through which creolization exerts itself to accommodate local contexts. In the case of Trinidad this includes encounters and relationships with non-Muslim communities (Bayat 2005; Mahdavi 2011; el-Zein 1977).

Trinbagonian attempts to re-engage Heritage Islam at this moment may not seem to be accommodating its message to the local conditions, as feminist ideas, human rights, and Islamic revivalism have done in the past (cf. Merry 2006; Eickelman and Anderson 1999), although women are beginning to examine their rights within Islam in the multicultural context of Trinidad and Tobago. In an earlier era of Muslim women's activism, Trinbagonian Muslim women maintained relationships across (not always racially diverse) faith and associational lines through personal and professional networks as well as kin relationships. The Islamic Academy and the National Muslim Women's Organization are two venues where Muslim women used to come together. Now, as the relationship between Haleema's daughter and Aneesa demonstrates, feminists or women's activists are experiencing the 'ebbs and flows' of convergence (on rights and freedoms) across *jamaat*s or women's groups, evolving around common concerns and shared cultural histories.

The efforts of younger activists to collaborate across boundaries, as an earlier generation did, may be recapturing some of the social intimacy (of intermarriage, daily interaction, and cooperation) that historically characterized sectarian relations in multicultural Trinidad, while engaging the challenges of race and gender difference more fully than their elders. This can be seen, for example, in the willingness of Aisha, an Afro-Trinidadian from the Islamic Resource Society, to publicly debate women's presence. Aisha, who is active in a variety of community organizations, appeared (in *hijab*) on the television programme *Cultural Experiences* a few years ago to discuss an HIV/AIDS awareness programme. Subsequently a chat thread appeared on a Trini Muslim listserve under the banner, 'Should Muslim Women Appear on Television,' claiming that it was inappropriate for Muslim women to speak on television 'or any other public forum'.[12] Aisha was willing to challenge this view that 'women's place' is in the home.

A week earlier, young women in *niqab* held a Maktubaan Nissa Seminar[13] in Cunupia to engage a race/age inclusive group of women from a wide variety of *jamaat*s in embracing 'true' Islamic womanhood. The program incorporated youthful enthusiasm and technology of light, colour, and sound in powerpoint displays, video presentations, and Sufi-inspired poetry about finding true love – in the example of the Prophet Muhammad. The poster read: 'True Love, Meet the Perfect Man, the Ideal Man, The Man of all Men, the Beloved of the Beloved, Come fall in love with the best of men, The Prophet Mohammed.'[14] These young women were weaving validation from gender-supportive Islamic traditions into an already existing legal tradition of support for certain rights for women.[15] While largely in line with Darul Uloom teachings, the workshop provided women a space to debate and discuss these topics.

For younger women as with Muslim youth elsewhere, Islamic piety also provides a way of creating independence from family through an identity inscribed in the global modern. In Trinidad, some youth are challenging the 'incorrect Islam' of their parents and grandparents or connecting to their parents' tradition in their own ways. Perhaps this partly explains the popularity of the Revival of the Umma (ROU), a co-ed movement that describes itself as 'an attempt to bridge the gap between the youth of today, and the learned elders of yesterday.'[16] The

ROU has held several annual community-wide conferences in Trinidad, one of the first featuring Mufti Menk, a charismatic, globally recognized religious authority among youth, who reminds women they must wear *hijab*. The ROU attracts a racially diverse group of members from many *jamaat*s and is organized around community outreach among Muslims and non-Muslims. Although the women members wear *hijab*, they are accused of 'gender-mixing' since male and female participants work together – for example in preparing meals for the soup kitchen. One young man readily offered that he had learned much from Salima, one of the female members, on how male and females may live and work together modestly and respectfully, by being responsible for their own behaviour toward one another.

Salima's roots in an Ahmaddiyya Muslim community (considered nonconformist and, by some, non-Muslim) speak to the imbrication of Muslims from different *jamaat*s, as youth intentionally engage Heritage Islam in enhancing women's rights. Many youth we interviewed lamented the lack of dialogue across *jamaat*s (particularly racially segregated ones) in this small country, while ROU members repeatedly reminded me that they have Afro- as well as Indo-Trinidadian youth members. In a broader sense, Muslim youth of different ethno-national heritages (like Nadia married to a Hindu and living in a Hindu neighbourhood and Aisha, a convert, whose family is primarily Pentacostal) point out that their shared experiences with other religious communities provide a basis for dialogue. These stories confirm the disruptive potential of race, class, and gender diversity to contest power structures and destabilize traditional modes of women's leadership, although it remains unclear whether women or youth can or will confront religious patriarchy (cf. Bauer 1996).

Tolerating Creolization: The Potential of a Creole Feminism

Such intersections across communities reflect the 'rhizomatic nature' of women's activism in Muslim Trinidad, pointing to shared, albeit nascent, recognition of the challenges of race and gender differences across the *umma*. Historical legacies of accommodating global influences to local circumstances may make the Islamic feminist 'nonmovement' here an example of 'creole feminism'. Caribbean-based feminist sovereignty in Trinidad and Tobago may have been momentarily challenged by Muslim women's re-engagement with 'heritage Islam' (and especially the influence of Deobandi thinking), yet the activism among a younger generation and the examples of some of the elder generation suggest some movement again toward convergence of distinct yet imbricated forms of feminism. In many ways their engagement exposes underlying tensions/uneasiness in Islamic and feminist ideals and realities. Given Islam's emphasis on the equality among believers (among men and women, in the tradition of the Prophet Muhammad; see Mernissi 1996), perhaps more than other women in the Caribbean, Muslim women stand at the centre of debates about race, class, gender, and culture in global perspective.

'Feminism' in this text includes organized and individual efforts to further the agency of women; 'Muslim Feminism' includes such activities undertaken within a variously defined Islamic framework. Here 'creole feminism' does not imply a fixed identity but a process of emerging, imbricated, global/local feminist forms that recognize contextual factors and different subjectivities, which themselves become indigenous through histories of shared experience. Such feminism, by definition 'multicultural', may stimulate reflective thinking about the power relationships among its parts (Hosein and Outar 2016).

Historical intersections of peoples, cultures, and colonial structures have produced Trinidadian feminism and Trinidadian Islam as 'creole' forms, perhaps best described by Hafez's use of the 'rhizome' metaphor,[17] which captures fluid subjects in time and space who share imprecise connections and embraces fluidities, frictions, and differences that might transform existing relations of power and of feminism (anticipated by Reddock 2007). In the context of multicultural Trinidad, where multiplex traditions of familial and communal interaction create a certain degree of comfort, accepting a creole Muslim feminism means accepting (not dismissing) tensions that arise from differences and retaining multiple subjectivities that render purity of form uninteresting and unproductive.

Competing Islamic feminisms in Trinidad and Tobago as elsewhere (cf. Fazaeli 2006 on Iran) illustrate points of intersection among these Islamic feminisms as well as among women's groups across religious and other differences. Feminist creolization, rather than offering only fragmented collision, affords possibilities of 'indigenous feminist sovereignty' (that is, a multicultural, cross-group collaboration). Trinidadian Muslim feminisms point to the authenticity of 'creole feminisms', rejecting the illusion of sovereignty as some kind of purity.

Bayat's notion of nonmovements suggests that unity in national feminist movements is also an unproductive model. Decentralized (non-essentialized or nonunified) movements (cooperation among differences) provide more potential for challenging structures of power (Bayat 2007).

The question remains to what *extent* can indigenous creole feminism be constructed to encompass the complexities of cross-group, multi-faith, secular/religious women activists whose differences include race and class in Trinidad? Could this serve as a model for a transnational feminism along the lines envisioned by Alexander and Mohanty?

Conclusion: The Caribbean Accents in Feminist Futures

Accepting creole feminism as a reservoir of creative 'indigeneity', we can return more confidently to the question of whether we can rewrite (Western, liberal) narratives of transnational feminism to challenge inequitable (race and class) hierarchies of power. Besides recuperating forgotten activists, as feminists elsewhere (including the Middle East and South Asia) have done, women working in the Caribbean have challenged thinking about subjectivity and relationships among feminists of the global north and south.[18] Muslim women's activism in Trinidad and Tobago brings us back to early modernity projects (and racialized thinking), which as Lowe suggests, emerged historically out of the confluence of labour/cultures imported from all corners of the globe to the Caribbean (2015). Can 'universality in diversity' (Yuval-Davis 1993) or intersecting conditions (creolized forms and rhizomatic nonmovements) produce a race/class inclusive, indigenous (here Creole) national feminism (as alluded to by Hosein) and provide a model for cross-national feminist collaborations?

Returning to itinerancy, we see many missed opportunities, despite many feminist proposals, to counter the 'misrecognition of the other' – as Basruddin points to in the failure of the 'Global North feminists [to learn] from Global South activists to decolonize feminism'. The case of Islamic feminisms as a creolized form in Trinidad suggests the possibility of building on rhizomatic similarities[19] (the recognition of which may counter the neoliberal focus on the individual) and episodic (historical) convergences, to achieve democratic feminist futures through transforming relationships among culturally and historically diverse feminist groups (see Hafez 2011; Jawayardena 1995; Alexander and Mohanty 1997).

The potential embodied in the shared histories of creolization converges with the many transnational feminist theoretical attempts to wrestle with the challenges of inequities in feminist power relations through dialogue and reflexivity (cf. Moghadam 2005, 2012; Tripp 2006; Yuval-Davis 1993; Dussel 2000; Romany 1994; Gunning 1997; Hosein and Outar 2016). Bridging the gaps of inequality in feminist encounters involves first of all respecting differences, not 'homogenizing' women or feminist groups (Yuval-Davis 1993), but seeing them as 'multiple subjects' (Hafez 2011; Hurtado 2005). It also necessitates recognizing both our connectedness and independence from each other. In Gunning's framework that includes understanding the other's history as well as one's own, the intersection of those histories (and relations of power) and the way 'the other' sees you as well as themselves – described by Alexander and Mohanty as 'historical, relational and comparative' approaches for achieving democratic feminist futures (Gunning 1997; Yuval-Davis 1993; Alexander and Mohanty 1997).

This approach requires overcoming misrecognition to acknowledge the hierarchies of power in Western liberal modernity and feminism (as expressed in Bourdieu 1984). It respects local and 'indigenous feminist sovereignties' while acknowledging the possibilities of building on historical imbrication in local and global connections, as noted for the nineteenth century in the work of Jayawardena (1995) and articulated more recently by Hosein and Outar in their work on pan-Caribbean Indian feminist thought, defined as 'theorizing of the intersection of Indianness, Caribbeanness, gender, and feminism', taking into account global historical connections and addressing perceptions of the Indo-Caribbean woman dominance in feminist conversation (Hosein and Outar 3–4).

Achieving democratic feminist futures requires debating current (race and gender) inequalities in the context of complicated and imbricated histories. One point of intersection is provided by the adoption of 'rights language', as in the case of Islamic Feminism in Trinidad and Tobago and in Basarudin's example of Musawah, a globally-connected Malaysian Muslim women's activist organization which 'advocates a fundamental understanding of Islam grounded in equality and justice and stitches it with human rights principles to allow for a more contextualized application'. (2016, 223). While it may not dramatically transform the structural and material factors that have set these conditions of difference in motion, the lessons of creolization as well as self-reflexivity may point us in the direction of reconceptualizing 'transnational feminism'. As seen in the example of Islamic Feminisms in Trinidad and Tobago, a creolized and somewhat momentarily resurgent form, 'democratic feminist futures' will involve accepting spatial and temporal flows and reversals, as well as persistent differences of form, in the movement toward more egalitarian transnational or transversal feminisms.

Notes

1. I would like to thank the organizers of the Turning Tides conference for giving me the opportunity to think about my work in more provocative ways.
2. Secor (2017) suggests 'mobility' can both 'enable and subvert the oppression of subaltern subjects' (221).
3. Since 2002, I have conducted ethnographic research (participant observation and interviews) among women in diverse Muslim communities across Trinidad and Tobago, often in collaboration with my colleague, Naima Mohammed. My research in Trinidad is part of my broader comparative project on women in different Muslim diasporic locations, in Iran, Turkey, Germany, Canada and the United States.
4. Trinbagonian designates the joint Republic of Trinidad and Tobago and/or its people and will be used throughout this essay. (ed. note)
5. The Trinidad Muslim League (TML) is one of the several Sunni Muslim 'umbrella organizations' with which *jamaat*s (or Muslim societies or associations) can affiliate around shared history and theology.
6. We have been interviewing women at the El Soccoro Mosque since 2006. See also mention of work with the traditional leaders of the mosque in Kassim's reference to her and Reddock's interviews with a woman leader at this mosque.
7. Here I am using shortened versions of the organization names as well as pseudonyms for our interviewees. We have conducted interviews across every major *jamaat* from 2002 to the present.
8. The mosque in San Juan was originally affiliated with the Tackveeyatul Islamic Association (TIA). The Anjuman Sunnat-ul-Jamaat Association (ASJA) is another umbrella affiliation.
9. In their 50th Anniversary Booklet, the Ladies Organization establishes that it 'continues to uphold the traditional Sunni Ahle Sunnat ul *Jamaat* practices such as Moulood, Tazeem, three days and forty days readings, Neeaz and other customs and practices sanctioned by Maulana Ansari, Maulana Abdul Aleem Siddiqui, Haji Rooknuddin Meah, Imam Gulam, Hosein and other learned and revered Scholars of Islam' – all circulating missionaries from Trinidad's past (2008, 28).
10. Many Afro-Trinidadian Muslim adults are converts or reverts as African Muslim slave laborers were not permitted to maintain Muslim traditions,

unlike Indo-Trinidadian indentured labor. 'Revert' acknowledges both the possibility that one's Afro-Trinidadian ancestors were Muslim and the view that everyone is born a Muslim – whether aware of it or not.

11. See Korom's discussion of Hosay controversy in Trinidad with the arrival of foreign protestors (2003).
12. 'We in Trinidad as Muslims have always encouraged our women to wear the *Hijab*…yes…Can any truly pious woman feel completely comfortable with her face being broadcast live to a million people all over Trinidad? Of course not.' [Found in conversation on MuslimTrini.com 2009.]
13. Some of the young women organizers participate in the Rashadi Foundation, a nonprofit 'under the patronage' of a graduate of Darul Uloom in India.
14. This is an accepted alternative spelling of the Prophet's name, which is always a transliteration.
15. See Deeb and Harb (2013) on Lebanese youth; Rinaldo (2013) and Van Doorn Harder (2006) for Indonesia; and Basrudin (2016) on Malaysia.
16. http://revivaloftheummah.com/sample-page/.
17. See also Judith Misrahi-Barak's essay in this volume for another discussion that uses this concept of the 'rhizome' (ed. note).
18. On recuperating women's activism in the Middle East, North Africa, and South Asia, see Mernissi (1996); Jayawardena (1985; 1995); Milani (2002); Bauer (1993). See also Caribbean feminist work on subjectivities (Hurtado 2005; Wekker 2006; and Mohammed 1998); on the importance of race and class differences (Reddock 2007; 2014); and conceptualizing creolization (a much contested form in the Caribbean) as indigeneity (Alexander, nd; Misri et al. 2006; Mohammed 1988).
19. The notion of 'rhizomatic' accentuates imbricated 'processes' (with multiple loci of power) rather than fixed 'essences' and allows us to consider how women 'narrate their selfhood and…embody discourses that blur the boundaries of the religious and the secular' (Hafez 2011, 18–19).

Works Cited:

Abu-Lughod, Lila. 'Do Muslim Women Really Need Saving? Anthropological Reflections on Cultural Relativism and its Others.' *American Anthropologist* 104, no. 3 (2002): 783–90.

Adams, Kimberly. 'Women scholars in Egypt reflect on the intersection of Islam and feminism; Interview.' https://www.pri.org/stories/2015-05-20/women-scholars-egypt-reflect-intersection-islam-and-feminism (May 20, 2015).

Afkhami, Mahnaz. 'Claiming Our Rights: A Manual for Women's Human Rights Education in Muslim Societies.' In *Muslim Women and the Politics of Participation: Implementing the Beijing Platform*, edited by Mahnaz Afkhami and Ernestine Friedl, 109–120. Syracuse, NY: Syracuse University Press, 1997.

Alexander, Jacqui M. 'Interivew with M. Jacqui Alexander.' *Women and Gender Studies Institute.* http://wgsi.utoronto.ca/research/faculty-projects/interview-with-m-jacquie-alexander. nd.

Alexander, J., and C. Mohanty. 'Introduction. Genealogies, Legacies, Movements.' In F*eminist Genealogies, Colonial Legacies and Democratic Futures*, edited by Alexander and Mohanty, xiii-xlii. New York, NY Routledge, 1997.

Badran, Margot. *Feminists, Islam, and Nation.* Princeton, NJ: Princeton University Press, 1996.

Bano, M. and H. Kalmbach, eds. *Women, Leadership, and Mosques: Changes in Contemporary Islamic Authority.* Leiden: Brill, 2011.

Basarudin, Azza. *Humanizing the Sacred. Sisters in Islam and the Struggle for Gender Justice in Malaysia.* Seattle, WA: University of Washington Press, 2016.

Bauer, Janet. 2005–2017. Ethnographic Interviews with Trinbagonian Muslim women and men referred to by pseudonyms in the text.

———. 'Reviving Gender, Reclaiming Islam: The Roles of Women in Trinidadian *Jamaat*s.' Paper Prepared for Conference on Muslim Women Leaders. Oxford University, Oct. 16–17, 2009.

———. 'Conclusion. The Mixed Blessings of Women's Fundamentalisms: Democratic Impulses in a Patriarchal World.' In *Mixed-Blessings: Gender and Religious Fundamentalism Cross-Culturally*, edited by Judy Brink and Joan Mencher, 221–56. New York: Routledge, 1996.

———. 'Conversations on Women's Rights Among Iranian Political Exiles: Implications for the Community-Self Debate in Feminism.' *Critique* (Spring 1994): 1–12.

———. 'Ma'ssoum's Tale: The Personal and Political Transformations of a Young Iranian Feminist.' *Feminist Studies* 19, no. 3 (1993) 519–48.

Bayat, Asef. 'Women's Non-Movement. What it means to be a Woman Activist in Iran.' *Comparative Studies of South Asia, Africa and the Middle East* 27, no. 1 (2007): 160–72.

———. 'What is Post-Islamism? *ISIM Newsletter*, 16, 5 (Autumn 2005).

Bourdieu, Pierre. *Distinction: A Social Critique of the Judgment of Taste.* New York, NY: Routledge, 1984.

Brink, Judy, and Joan Mencher, eds. *Mixed-Blessings: Gender and Religious Fundamentalism Cross-Culturally.* New York: Routledge, 1996.

Bulliet, Richard. *Islam: The View from the Edge.* New York: Columbia University Press, 1995.

Cooke, Miriam. *Women Claim Islam: Creating Islamic Feminism Through Literature.* New York: Routledge, 2001.

Deeb, Lara, and Mona Harb. *Leisurely Islam: Negotiating Geography and Morality in Shi'ite South Beirut.* Princeton: Princeton University Press, 2013.

Dussel, Enrique. 'Europe, Modernity, and Eurocentrism.' *Nepantia: Views from the South* 1 no. 3 (2000): 465–78.

Eickelman, Dale F., and Jon W. Anderson. *New media in the Muslim World: The Emerging Public Sphere*. Bloomington, IN: Indiana University Press, 1999.

El-Zein, Abdul Hamid. 'Beyond Ideology and Theolog: The Search for the Anthropology of Islam.' *Annual Review of Anthropology* 6 (1977): 217–54.

Fazaeli, Roja. 'Contemporary Iranian Feminism: Identity, Rights, and Interpretations.' Paper presented at the AMSS 35th Annual Conference. Hartford, CT, October 27–29, 2006.

Fernea, Elizabeth. *In Search of Islamic Feminism: One Woman's Global Journey*. New York, NY: Doubleday, 1997.

Geertz, Clifford. 'Ritual and Social Change. A Javanese Example.' *American Anthropologist* 59, no. 1 (1957): 32–54.

Gunning, I. 'Arrogant Perception, World Traveling and Multicultural Feminism: The Case of Female Genital Surgeries.' In *Critical Race Feminism*, edited by Wing, 352–59. New York, NY: New York University 1997.

Hafez, Sherine. *An Islam of Her own. Reconsidering Religion and Secularism in Women's Islamic Movements*. New York, NY: New York University Press, 2011.

Hall, Stuart, and Bill Schwarz. *Familiar Stranger: A Life Between Two Islands*. London: Lane Allen/Penguin, 2017.

Hidayatullah, Aysha A. *Feminist Edges of The Koran*. Oxford: Oxford University Press, 2014.

Hosein, Gabrielle, and Lisa Outar. 'Introduction. Interrogating an Indo-Caribbean Feminist Epistemology.' In *Indo-Caribbean Feminist Thought. Genealogies, Theories, Enactments*, edited by Gabrielle Hosein and Lisa Outar, 1–20. New York, NY: Palgrave-MacMillan, 2016.

Hurtado, Aida. 'Multiple Subjectivities: Chicanas and Cultural Citizenship.' In *Women and Citizenship*, edited by Marilyn Friedman, 111–29. Oxford: Oxford University Press, 2005.

Jayawardena, Kumari. *Feminism and Nationalism in the Third World*. London: Zed Press, 1985.

———. *The White Woman's Other Burden: Western Women and South Asia During British Rule*. New York, NY: Routledge Press, 1995.

Karam, Azza M. 'Women, Islamisms, and the State. Dynamics of Power and Contemporary Feminisms in Egypt.' In *Muslim Women and the Politics of Participation*, edited by Mahnaz Afkhami and Ernestine Friedl, 18–38. Syracuse, NY: Syracuse University Press, 1997.

Kassim, Halima. 'The Muslim Community Active Agents in their Acculturation: Gender and Education.' Port of Spain: Unpublished manuscript, 2002.

Khan, Aisha. *Callaloo Nation: Metaphors of Race and Religious Identity among South Asians in Trinidad*. Durham, NC: Duke University Press, 2004.

Korom, Frank. *Hosay Trinidad. Muharram Peformaces in an Indo-Caribbean Diaspora*. Philadelphia: University of Pennsylvania Press, 2003.

Kuenkler, Mirjam, and Roya Fazaeli. 'The Life of Two Mujtahidahs: Female Religious Authority in 20th Century Iran.' In *Women, Leadership, and*

Mosques: Changes In Contemporary Islamic Authority, edited by Masooda Bano and Hilary Kalmbach, 127–60. Leiden: Brill, 2011.

Lowe, Lisa. *The Intimacies of Four Continents*. Durham, NC: Duke University Press, 2015.

Mahdavi, Mojtaba. 'Post Islamist Trends in Post-Revolutionary Iran.' *Comparative Studies of South Asia, Africa and the Middle East* 31, no. 1 (2011): 94–109.

Mahmood, Saba. *Politics of Piety: The Islamic Revival and the Feminist Subject*. Princeton, NJ: Princeton University Press, 2011.

Masquelier, Adeline. *Women and Islamic Revival in a West African Town*. Bloomington, IN: Indiana University Press, 2009.

Mernissi, Fatima. *Women's Rebellion and Islamic Memory*. London: Zed Press, 1996.

Merry, Sally Engle. *Human Rights and Gender Violence: Translating International Law into Local Justice*. Chicago, IL: University of Chicago Press, 2006.

Milani, Farzaneh. *Words not Swords: Iranian Women Writers and the Freedom of Movement*. Syracuse, NY: Syracuse University Press, 2011.

Milani, Farzaneh. *Veils and Words: The Emerging Voices of Iranian Women Writers*. Syracuse, NY: Syracuse University Press, 2002.

Misir, Prem, Michael Banton and others. *Cultural Identity and Creolization in National Unity: The Multiethnic Caribbean*. Lanham, MD: University Press of America, 2006.

Moghadam, Valentine. *Globalization and Social Movements:. Islam, Feminism, and the Social Justice Movement*. Lanham, MD: Rowman and Littlefield, 2012.

———. *Globalizing Women: Transnational Feminist Networks*. Baltimore, MD: The Johns Hopkins University Press, 2005.

Moghissi, Haideh. *Feminism and Islamic Fundamentalism: The Limits of Post Modern Analysis*. London: Zed Press, 1999.

Mojab, Shahrzad. 'Theorizing the Politics of "Islamic Feminism".' *Feminist Review* 69 (2001): 124–146.

Mohammed, Patricia. 'Toward Indigenous Feminist Theorizing in the Caribbean.' *Feminist Review* 59 (1998): 6–33.

———. 'The Creolisation of Indian women in Trinidad.' In *Trinidad and Tobago; The Independence Experience: 1962–1987*, edited by Selwyn Ryan, 381–97. St. Augustine, Trinidad: University of the West Indies, Sir Arthur Lewis Institute of Social and Economic Research, 1988.

Paidar, Parvin. *Women and the Political Process in Twentieth-Century Iran*. Cambridge: Cambridge University Press, 1997.

Pang, Keng-Feng. 'Islamic "Fundamentalism" and Female Empowerment Among the Muslims of Hainan Island, People's Republic of China.' In *Mixed Blessings: Gender and Fundamentalism*, edited by Judy Brink and Joan Mencher, 41–58. New York, NY: Routledge. 1997.

Reddock, Rhoda. 'Radical Caribbean Social Thought, Race, Class Identity and the Post Colonial Nation.' *Current Sociology Monograph* 62 no. 4 (2014): 493–511.

———. 'Diversity, Difference and Caribbean Feminism: the Challenge of Anti-Racism.' *Caribbean Review of Gender Studies* 1 (2007).

Rinaldo, Rachel. *Mobilizing Piety. Islam and Feminism in Indonesia.* Oxford: Oxford University Press, 2013.

Romany, Celina. 'State Responsibility Goes Private: A Feminist Critique of the Public/Private Distinctions in International Human Rights Law.' In *Human Rights of Women*, edited by Rebecca Cook, 85–115. Philadelphia, PA: University of Pennsylvania Press, 1994.

Schulz, Dorothea. *Muslims and New Media in West Africa: Pathways to God.* Bloomington, IN: Indiana University Press, 2011.

Secor, Anna. 'Gender, Sexuality, and Mobility.' *Journal of Middle East Women's Studies* 13, no. 2, (2017): 219–21.

Tripp, Aili Mari. 'Challenges in Transnational Feminist Mobilization.' In *Global Feminism: Transnational Women's Activism, Organizing and Human Rights*, edited by Myra Marx Ferree and Aili Mari Tripp, 296–312. New York, NY: New York University, 2006.

Van Doorn-Harder, Pieternella. *Women Shaping Islam: Reading the Qur'an in Indonesia.* Urbana, IL: University of Illinois Press, 2006.

Wekker, Gloria. *The Politics of Passion: Women's Sexual Culture in the Afro-Surinamese Diaspora.* New York, NY: Columbia University Press, 2006.

Yuval-Davis, Nira. 'Women and Coalition Politics.' In *Making Connections: Women's Studies, Women's Movements,Women's Lives*, edited by Mary Kennedy, Cathy Lubelska, and Val Walsh, 3–10. London: Taylor and Francis, 1993.

Zine, Jsmine. 'Between Orientalism and Fundamentalism: The Politics of Muslim Women's Feminist Engagement.' *Muslim World Journal of Human Rights* 3, no. 1 (2006): 1–22.

CHAPTER 8

In Praise of Excellent Ettie: Narrative Constructions of the Affective Impact of Caribbean Migrant Women's Work

Paula Morgan

Caribbean female migrant workers have for generations negotiated the unstable and perilous interface of national, ethnic, class and gender boundaries. Located at the confluence of transnational labour flows and domestic power relations, their work has been pivotal to the economic sustenance of families and communities in their natal land. On the other hand, their mass migrations have been implicated in a range of social ills on the islands, ranging from loss of familial cohesion and coherence, to child shifting, abuse, and gang violence. Migration has been a fundamental coping strategy for Caribbean people – male and female. However, given the prevailing assumption that childcare is fundamentally a female task, the perception is that it is women who leave their children in the care of the extended family, in order to seek work and to send resources back through remittances. Much has been written about the devastating psychological impact of this strategy on children left behind. (Bakker Elings-Pels and Reis 2009; Dillon and Walsh 2012). Some are abandoned. Others are sustained on material objects shipped in barrels, delivered with the often empty promise of reunion with parents when things get better.

The focus of this enquiry is not on the children left behind, but on the women who migrate. This reading applies methods of literary and discourse analysis to constructions of the affective impact of Caribbean female migratory women's work in fictional and real-life narratives. The primary material is drawn from three sources. The first is Paule Marshall's representation in *Brown Girl Brownstones* (1959) of a significant moment in Caribbean American relations when the armies of Caribbean illegal and legal migrants swarmed to Brooklyn New York in the 1930s carrying families, hopes, dreams and aspirations into toxic racist environments. Their arrival in the wake of waves of ethnic white migrants is expressed in metaphors of defilement that belie their capacity to assimilate and move on from the common starting point.

Collectively they crave access to the brownstones on the margins of respectable housing areas: 'And as they left, the West Indians slowly edged their way in. Like a dark sea nudging its way onto a white beach and staining the sand, they came' (4).

Fierce negotiations of rights and terms of belonging unfold in the domestic sphere, in the homes of the white women where migrant household workers deliver domestic services.[1] Marshall's work bears comparison with Jamaica Kincaid's *Lucy* (1990), titled after its self-centred protagonist, who is obsessed with her own visceral reactions to her ontological positioning as servant, when she becomes an au pair to a kindly, well-meaning, liberal, Manhattan couple. These fictional representations will be compared with a contemporary real life narrative of a former primary school teacher who, in response to financial hardship generated by her husband's retirement and subsequent illness, opted for illegal immigration and care work for a season. The analyses of these three narratives focus on their continuities and discontinuities in relation to self-construction and transnational domestic labour relations.

By tracing specific, common themes, the paper examines these sources for insights into the correlation between the economic value ascribed to migrant women's lives as labourers and the imputation of social and cultural worth. It reads the ontological weight of this location and its impact on self-fashioning. It argues that the affective and corporeal dimensions of the experiences of Caribbean female migrant labourers are embedded in complex networks of social relations both in the Caribbean and in the metropole. Their acquiescence and/or resistance to their commodity value are inscribed viscerally on their bodies, influence their emotional and mental stability and stand to be variously transferred intergenerationally based on the gender of their offspring.

Migrant workers, and particularly those who migrate to work in the homes of metropolitan women in caregiving functions as domestics, au pairs or nannies, and geriatric care givers, occupy a problematic psycho-social location. The reality is that despite the numerous gains of the contemporary women's movement and the greater impulse towards cross gender sharing of household tasks, the primary domestic responsibilities remain on women. This is even more applicable within the framework of increasing privatization of social services. With enhanced access to education, lucrative careers and professional positions, metropolitan women increasingly employ migrant women

– legal or illegal – to carry the burden of repetitious, unsatisfying, domestic work.[2] There is an affective dimension of this work even when the task is to care for things. A clean orderly home enhances domestic atmospheres and focuses its energies and, by extension, grounds the physical and emotional well-being of its occupants. Where this involves care for the children and for the elderly, these low-waged caregivers are paid not simply to render physical services, but also to carry the emotional burdens of generously dispensing displays of warmth and love characteristic of their island cultures and upbringing, to emotionally needy children and elders who exist within more emotionally measured and restrained social environments.[3]

Caribbean domestic workers circulate in the transcultural zone which evolved in the aftermath of empire, that zone of habitations which Homi Bhabha characterizes as pierced through with the cry of the unhomely, when the broader workings of historical forces impinge on the domestic sphere to generate alienation and unbelonging. According to Encarnacion Gutierrez-Rodriguez in her study of Latino migrant domestic workers in Western Europe: 'the local face of the gendered and racialized division of work of the modern/colonial world system becomes a tangible and immediate reality in private households...the legacies of a colonial order, reactivated through racial and gendered segregation in the labour market and dehumanizing migration policies, are felt on an individual level and mobilized in our everyday encounters' (3). These workers consequently carry in their bodies and their psyches creative though discombobulating confluences of cultures, aspirations and values. Their lived realities of asymmetrical power relations are inscribed in mindsets and postures reflective of knowing one's place. The home as workplace becomes a transcultural contact zone where persons from divergent classes, ethnicities, nations and cultures mingle in private and intimate spaces. Here they are constrained to negotiate desires and aspirations, joys and sorrows. They are drawn together by necessity. The domestic stands in need of finances and is hamstrung by obligation; the employer stands in need of goods and services necessary to support positionalities and assumptions of entitlement. The exchange, based on these reciprocal needs, may be undergirded by deeply held convictions, commonly shared by service purchasers and service providers alike, that domestic servitude 'serves' the impoverished, while the weathly have rights to services necessary to sustain a privileged lifestyle.

The focus of this analysis is on affects. Gutierrez-Rodriguez argues that affects evolve within the dynamics and in the ambivalent movements emerging out of material social conditions; in other words, affects emerge out of concrete historical and geopolitical contexts:

> While they emanate from the dynamics of our energies, impulses, sensations and encounters, affects also carry residues of meaning. They are haunted by past intensities not always spelled out and conceived in the present. Immediate expressions and transmissions of affects may indeed revive repressed sensations, experiences of pain or joy. Although not explicitly expressed as such, they are temporal and spatial constellations of certain times, intricately impressed in legacies of the past and itineraries of the present/future (5).

Affective criticism traces the impact of transactions and relational encounters on feelings and encounters which in turn elicit often involuntary, deep-rooted bodily reactions. For Afro-Caribbean domestic workers, their race functions as an inescapable social marker of their ontological positioning as domestic workers, often in a manner that conflates the dynamics of enforced historical and voluntary contemporary labour migrations.

Both fictional narratives emphasize the impact of racialized embodiment on the sense of self; in other words, they examine what it means for migrant women who work in close confines with privileged white mistresses to inhabit the 'castles of their skins'.[4] Marshall speaks of the humiliation and denigration of the armies of domestics who congregated at corners in the hope that white mistresses would come along to select them for a day's work:

> It was always the mother and the others, for they were alike – those watchful, wrathful women whose eyes seared and searched and laid bare, whose tongues lashed the world in unremitting distrust. Each morning they took the train to Flatbush and Sheepshead Bay to scrub floors. The lucky ones had their steady madams while the others wandered those neat blocks or waited on corners - each with her apron and working shoes in a bag under her arm until someone offered her a day's work. Sometimes the white children on their way to school laughed at their blackness and shouted "nigger," but the Barbadian women sucked their teeth, dismissing them. Their only thought was of the "few raw-mout' pennies" at the end of the day which would eventually "buy house" (11).

The brown skin that the migrants inhabit becomes an extension of the major motif of the novel – the acquisition of the brownstone as a material possession that lends safety, security and belonging within a context of broader societal denigration and belittlement. For the older generation, it speaks to their portion of the American dream that anyone, notwithstanding class, colour and birthplace, can enter America and work themselves upwards to wealth, affirmation and social standing, and thereby alleviate grief at loss of natal land, and feel good about who they are and affirmed at what they have become.

What then is the intergenerational impact of such a psychosocial location? A fundamental hope in the heart of migrants is intergenerational mobility within the host society. Towards this end, they would suffer many an ignominy so that their children would find themselves accepted in the beloved new land. Indeed this is in itself a source of intergenerational conflict, as mothers particularly seek to maneuver their children into selective acculturation and prosperous professions so as to protect them from the harshness of poverty and denigration within the metropolitan environment.

Cross racial and cross generational conflict over the issue of upward mobility is at the centre of climactic incident, which is filtered through multiple layers of displacement. This pivotal encounter occurs between the white mistress and the progeny of the quintessential 'Excellent Ettie'[5] as iconic of the army of West Indian domestics. The catalyst is a theatre production in which the child of immigrants takes the spotlight in a life cycle dance and successfully displaces the children of their mistresses. It unfolds as a disciplinary act to cut down to size a black girl drunk with her first public triumph, in the wake of a superb public performance. When Selina dances, she releases healing energies as a profound sacred act, sacrificially and generously offering herself like a communion wafer, imparting an empowering positive flow of life force as a member of the generic family of man. Its positive affect is externalized in the transformation of the entire dance troop into a colour-neutral mass collectivity – a single thrashing amalgam of arms and legs.

The racist, jealous and angry parent individualizes and isolates Selina, extracting her from the warm collectivity of the youthful dance troupe to better transfix her into geopolitical strictures of the migrant domestic and to inject her with negative energies of hatred, marginalization and dispossession. The battleground is established in the affective domain before a single word is uttered. Hostilities and negative energies are transmitted from porous white to black body through touch: 'She took Selina's hand between hers, patting it, and Selina could feel her whiteness – it was in the very texture of her skin. A faint uneasiness stirred and was forgotten...' (285). Hers is an act of spatiotemporal recreation intended to take Selina back into 'her place' and entrench her in the location of quintessential icon Excellent Ettie, born for servitude and grateful recipient of charities of her white benefactress.

The incident, focalized through Selina's perspective on the encounter, causes the youth to 'recognize' her friend, fellow dancer and communicant, as the hateful, unknown, white girl whose hand-me-downs she had been forced to wear. And Selina's awareness that she is being made to bear the affective burden of her mother and other mothers in the interface with their white employers, as well as the hostile parent's jealousy, fury, frustration at intergenerational loss of white supremacy, is insufficient to protect her.

The affective impact goes beyond deflating the sense of empowerment, potentiality, competence of the triumphant youth and reinstating dependency, inferiority and denigration. The life changing onslaught functions on a visceral level to open wellsprings of collective woundedness and trauma. Looking at herself through the woman's eyes, Selina saw 'the full meaning of her black skin':

> And knowing was like dying – like being posed on the rim of time when the heart's simple rhythm is syncopated and then silenced and the blood chills and congeals, when a pall passes in a dark wind over the eyes. In that instant of death, false and fleeting though it was, she was beyond hurt. And then, as swiftly terror flared behind her eyes, terror that somehow, in some way, this woman, the frightened girl at the door, those dancing down the hall, even Rachel, all, everywhere, sought to rob her of her substance and her self. The thrust of hate at that moment was strong enough to sweep the world and consume them. What had brought her to this place? to this shattering knowledge? And obscurely she knew: the part of her which had long hated her for her blackness and thus begrudged her for each small success like the one tonight... (289).

The encounter, which alludes to Joseph Conrad's classical novel of imperialism, *Heart of Darkness,* becomes a traumatizing catalyst which repositions Selina as a trapped beast in an urban jungle forced into a Kurtzian encounter with the horror of blackness. The affect opens up a play of mirrors. The Western male's excursion on a failed civilizing mission into the African heartland only to encounter the horror of his own internal savagery and defilement is aligned in a complex symbolic crossover with the second generation female migrant's revelation as she peers into the depth and dreadfulness of her own rebellion, sexual impropriety, sneaking, lying, shamming, dissembling. Her adversary has imposed a psychosocial burden upon her as a symbolical repository of blackness, which a glance at her own heart nauseatingly reveals. The nauseating glance at her own heart condition is the unwelcome outcome of her adversary's imposition of a burdensome psychosocial location upon her as a symbolic repository of blackness.

Selina's triumph in the great leveler of the shared human life cycle from birth to death speaks to the quest through artistry rather than through the acquisition of material commodities, for a colour neutral basis for acceptance. The young girl's bid to carve a place of equality and honour which transcends race, as a human within a generic family of man, parallels her mother's quest for a house, which externalizes her worth and self-fashioning based on hard work, thrift and individual accomplishment. Marshall critiques the promise to migrants of finding a home within an equitable social order, reflecting in its place their disenfranchisement from their portion of the American dream.

Whereas the migrants of *Brown Girl, Brownstones* deal with overt racist cruelty, decades later Kinkaid's *Lucy* (1990) deals viciously with a vacuous liberalism in a manner that unmasks its subtle complicities with racism, and deflates and stuns her employers into silence. *Lucy* deals with a teenager's travel to metropolitan American as a caretaker for a wealthy, kindly, American couple. The text affords a view of the dynamic interplay between a self-identified feminist of the second wave movement in the United States (US) who undertakes to welcome and train a youthful third world sister, whose access into her Manhattan home is generated by vast inequities of wealth, privilege and the empowerment of racialized embodiment. Within the close domestic confines, Lucy minutely observes and invariably reacts to the way in which ideologies, nationality, race and class and gender are constituted within attitudes, orientations, and domestic practices of her hosts. The scenario can be read as testing notions of global sisterhood offered by the Western feminist movement, within the intimate domestic environment as grounds for the interplay of transnational migration, racialized embodiment and female to female labour and cultural relations.

As a young female migrant, Lucy leaves her home and takes upon herself the mantle of a servant. Yet, armed with an aggressive individualism and self-assertiveness, Lucy as transnational worker negotiates the domestic space bristling with resistance to any attempt to colonize her inner being into servitude. Much of the strength of her offensives is rooted in her acute sensitivity to the power of the affective domain. Her entrance into the metropolitan world constitutes an epistemological and ontological onslaught. The migrant worker enters the social and physical environment laden with individually and collectively generated dreams, hopes and aspirations. She encounters the built and natural environments through the filters of a new arrivant from a small place. Such a move is expected to satisfy suppressed longings, substantiate dreams of belonging, and lend substance and significance to the one who has 'arrived'. Lucy counters this impulse by deliberately dismantling 'fixtures of fantasy', opting to turn an incisive eye on worn buildings, ideologically implicated daffodils, and counterintuitive cold and inhospitable suns (3–4). She simultaneously flirts with and disrupts the 'Excellent Ettie' positionality. She theatrically adopts the black nanny/surrogate mother role to one of the children under her care, while rejecting the proffered positions of servitude in multiple other ways.

Lucy deals systematically with the onslaught of displacement by refusing to be drawn into alienating meaning systems. The well-meaning couple's insistence that she has not made herself at home, hence she remains a 'poor visitor', is greeted by a disclosure that refuses to allow them to deny complicity in transnational labour systems that fixate her as servant and them as masters. Instead, to foreground the ever-present potential for dependency of the live-in help to tip over into sexual exploitation, she counters by recounting a dream in which she is naked and being chased on a yellow road by the blond Lewis with his blond wife Mariah looking on, signaling her complicity with his pursuit. This dream resonates with her childhood dream of being chased by bunches of yellow daffodils representing the assimilating impulse of colonial and neocolonial forces which would seek to reduce her vibrant, diverse and colourful world to a uniform yellow. By reversing the immigrant/native perspective, Lucy undermines her employer's ascendancy and power of naming, and positions her encounter with them within the broader framework of geopolitical labour migrations.

This is significant given the strength and persistence of Lucy's own pursuit of autonomy through a sexual adventurism that she enacts as subject in rebellion against both the hidey hidey puritanical respectability of her Caribbean upbringing and her objectification as an exoticized target of desire. She similarly rejects her lover Paul when he representationally ossifies her in a photograph: 'standing naked over a boiling pot of food. I was naked from the waist up: a piece of cloth wrapped around me. Covered from the waist down' (155). Rejecting the conflation of cook and sexual object, a desirable exotic like Paul Gauguin's Polynesian beauties, Lucy determines: 'That was the moment he got the idea that he possessed me in a certain way, and that was the moment I grew tired of him' (155). Her aim is not simply to assert an alternative meaning system based on how she feels about her psychosocial positioning as domestic labour, but to constrain her employers and her lover to feel, to map and to confront the cartographies and trajectories of their privilege and their imprisoning stereotypes.

Her task then is to unmask their gentle impulses to entrap her in their evasive meaning systems and to constrain them to perceive, understand and experience the affects of their master servant relationship, on her terms. In the process, she also rejects assimilation to metropolitan norms and perspectives and challenges Mariah, the naïve white feminist who wants her young protégé to see and love her golden world, even while it is collapsing around her. Mariah, whose best friend steals her husband and her life, under Lucy's knowing and watchful eyes, while she dances through daffodils in blissful ignorance, is a gullible innocent compared to Lucy who has been trained in the stringent and terrible school of Caribbean gender relations.

The final section of this paper deals with the real-life narrative of a former primary school teacher in Trinidad who retired from her job at age 36 because of the demands of mothering nine children, only to find herself facing desperate straits when her husband and primary breadwinner of the home contracted a stroke a decade later. Elaine Bonaparte (name changed) recounts visiting her mother in Boston in the late 1990s for a rest from the arduous care of her large family and sick husband and spontaneously deciding to stay when a job came up which would enable her to contribute to her family's dire financial needs. At the time of the interview, which I conducted in Valsayn, Trinidad in May 2016, Elaine was a pleasant, chatty, upbeat woman of 67 years who was suffering from glaucoma induced by diabetes and was experiencing challenges moving about on her own due to failing vision.

The analysis probes the interview for affective themes, interrogates the point of access into the lived experiences and highlights correlations between this real-life narrative and the fictional texts. The major themes which emerge are explored as heuristic devices to demonstrate the manner in which the speaker reflectively, decades later, makes meaning of her experiences of migration and care work. As indicated by Van Manen, 'The thematic meanings of human experience are self-constituted. They reflect the ways that we tend to make sense of life as human beings – as human beings who are embedded within certain linguistic, historical and cultural contexts. That is why we can say that human meanings are discovered but also self-disclosing, constructed by us but also constructed of us' (99).

THEME: Impact of migration on interpersonal relations within the family

Elaine indicated that she came to the point of migration in the first instance as an act of care extended by her mother who wanted to assist her in the family crisis. It is telling that after mention of this action of kindness – sending a ticket so that she would come to Boston and thereafter inviting her to stay with her while she worked –, the mother is never overtly mentioned again. Instead there is a series of indirect statements which speak to Elaine's culture shock at the impact of migration. It was apparent, though not overtly stated, that the mother, despite her invitation and sponsorship of an airline ticket, breached Elaine's expectations by not extending the hospitality and generosity that are seen as normative within Caribbean culture. The mother's capacity to meet these expectations may arguably have been strained by the requirements to extend such courtesies to multiple visiting family members.

THEME: Differential treatment by white and black employers

Elaine Bonaparte claimed that her greatest challenges during the three years in which she did care work in the US came from the poor treatment she received at the hand of her black employers:

> What is unfortunate I found that most white people (lowered voice and eyes avoiding direct contact) treated the black caregivers better than black people did...ok (speaking slowly) one of the things I felt was that the white people were middle income, upper income people. They wanted a service...they were prepared to pay for it. And I guess the ones I worked with were not racial. They were glad to have you. You were good to them

and they responded with kindness. The black ones, however, were not necessarily that high up the income ladder and so they would watch every cent. And they would...ha...it was crazy...like food stuff and things like that they would look to see if you were eating, whereas the others would say 'Come sit have something to eat with us.' They would be looking to see...I now would normally carry my stuff but still you know there was that...you could feel it...so it was not as comfortable as working in the white homes (Bonaparte, Morgan Interview).

Elaine claims that she never encountered direct racism from whites; indeed they treated her in a gracious and generous manner. She surmised that this might have been because the majority were relatively well-off and prepared to pay for a service which she delivered cheerfully and generously. In turn, she indicated that the whites treated her fairly, paid promptly and made her feel welcome. The black employers, however, were not as pleasant and kind. Concluding that they might have been less well-off, she indicates that they tended to be less generous, friendly and welcoming.

THEME: Guilt and frustration at enjoying benefits in the United States while her children were experiencing lack at home

Elaine was in a far more beneficial position than many impoverished Caribbean women whose husbands and household breadwinners are suddenly incapacitated, precisely because she was able to benefit from employment in the metropolis, access to plentiful and affordable food and the capacity to alleviate her family's lot through remittances. Yet, she suffered from guilt.

> Another thing that was hard – an emotional one this time – was going to the grocery. When I went to the grocery in those days, things were extremely reasonable. And so I could go with let's say $50 I could buy whatever to take to the house. And I would think of the children home. And I would think how much I could have here...what are they having...because I knew the cost of living home. Ah...and that hurt. So at times even eating was painful. You understand what I mean (Bonaparte, Morgan Interview).

The economic inequities which she sought to overcome by migrating to capture better wages for her labour did not alleviate the pain of the inequities she bore in her body. The discrepancy between her ability to enjoy good, plentiful food, while her children faced a deficient and inadequate supply was manifested in guilt and discomfort while shopping. The stress and tension manifest in the visceral sensation of physical pain while eating.

THEME: Emotional and physical toll of caregiving

Elaine Bonaparte's greatest strength and vulnerability appear to be in the affective domain. This is what made her an excellent caregiver and this is what made her vulnerable to how she was treated. She testified to after-effects of a particularly challenging winter time job with a family of three elderly Caucasian sisters, in their 70s and 80s who lived in a cold hilly forested area called Forest Hills. Her task was to care for the sister who had suffered a stroke.

> ...And they would want the best for their sister obviously but they wouldn't stop to think what is was costing the person so they would say things like 'Elaine, could you take Betty for a walk.' Ah...taking Betty for a walk meant (speaking slowly) bundling Betty, putting her on the wheel chair and taking her down Forest Hills in winter...So that there is snow on the hills...you are pushing a wheel chair. You have to be very careful.... You are not pushing the wheel chair, you are going down but you are pulling it back to you because you don't want anything going wrong. So you get down the hill you take her around and then you come back upon the other side so now you are pushing this wheel chair up hill in the snow (Bonaparte, Morgan Interview).

The narrative begins as a first person account and shifts to the second person 'you' and even the third person 'they wouldn't stop to think about what it was costing 'the person'. These narrative choices all function as distancing devices. Arguably this distancing is in response to the pain and distress which the recounting evokes. The scenario unfolds in the telling as a series of actions that one is witnessing from a distance. Elaine explains very systematically and in minute detail how an apparently simple, straightforward and reasonable directive to a caregiver translates into a series of costly and arduous action. 'Taking Betty for a walk' means responsibility, risk, physical strain, cold, discomfort, distress – and at the deeper and more visceral level – it also means a series of bodily reactions to the requirements of servitude and range of long lasting physical effects:

> ...and I think that I remember when I had just come back to Trinidad I used to feel as if there was water lodged inside my foot. I think it was my body thawing out or responding. It actually felt like water in my feet and my fingers...up to now that hurt. I think that took a toll on my body more than anything else (Bonaparte, Morgan Interview).

Exposure to the strain and physical discomfort survives in her memory over a decade later as a sense of being water logged or more precisely feeling as if there were bubbles of water under her feet. The dampness, cold, lack of appreciation, and non-belonging become an alien force which invades her extremities and remains lodged in her hands and feet long after she returns to the warm Caribbean environment:

> I: So you are saying that they didn't regard what it cost you?
>
> Elaine: I don't think they were even aware because sometimes I would come back up and I would try to stay out long with her and I would come back up after say about half an hour out there in the snow and they would say 'Oh you'll are back. Betty, would you like to go again?' That kind of stuff (head nodding and voice lowered)...that was hard (Bonaparte, Morgan Interview).

Elaine reacts to being attentive to the need of the person in her care – that is taking regard of the personhood, vulnerability, and emotional needs of the patient. She is careful of the perspective and emotional stance of her employers, in this case a trio of elderly ladies, while describing their disregard of her personhood and the price she pays to extend a duty of care to them. This water loggedness is the affect that remains within her body, not simply as in individual sensorial reaction to cold but as an interiorized, visceral affect of unequal, racialized, historical and geopolitical power relations – being treated as inferior, exploited, taken for granted and unworthy of note. Ironically, although this event survives in her recounting as the most arduous and costly employment scenario, with negative impacts which linger in her body until today, it does not interfere with her perception that her Caucasian employers treated her better than her African-American ones.

What conclusions can one gather from these divergent scenarios? Creative writers have carefully charted transnational interface between worlds, cultures and ideologies. Female authors, themselves first or second generation migrants to the US, privilege in their fiction white on black racism – subtle or blatant, overt or tacit. The way Elaine Bonaparte chooses to order her narrative about this significant period of her life points to another disturbing dynamic – strained, if not adversarial relations between Caribbean migrant employees and African-American employers as a source of stress and discord. The perceived unwillingness to share, though ascribed to differential income levels, may arguably have been based on the caregiver's idealistic expectations of commonality and camaraderie determined by shared cultural and ethnic connections.

Significantly all three narratives dealt with the affective impact of transnational migration relations on the family. Mother–daughter conflict and differential expectations of the pathways the daughters should take to secure wealth, value and self-worth are central to both fictional narratives. In the personal narrative, the contention with the mother is implied rather than stated. Unwillingness to openly share is perceived as violation of the duty of care that persons owe each other within the family. Elaine Bonaparte, while praising her father's sister for her generosity states obliquely in relation to another relative: 'People say come and stay by me and when you get there, people are hiding food. When they come to your home, you bring yours openly and put in the refrigerator for all to use.'

In the more recent scenario, evoked in *Lucy*, the gains of the global women's movement are in no small manner responsible for the democratization of the right to press the financially needy sister/other into the servitude necessary to sustain privileged lifestyles. This analysis briefly examines the manner in which Caribbean female domestic workers trouble the waters as they negotiate the transcultural zone which evolved in the aftermath of empire. The fictional narratives point to intergenerational mobility over time and emerging power to manipulate material circumstances intended to benefit those who exercise mastery. The home and the dynamics of female-female interactions become a microcosm of global power dynamics released by the imperial encounter whose energies and affects are still circulating, evoking compliance or resistance. The eventual release of Marshall's protagonist to make her way back to the islands in search of moorings and the effective resistance of Kincaid's protagonist to the requirements of servitude happily signal a substantial shift in affect and self-fashioning of Excellent Ettie. The personal narrative shifts the focus away from the black/white, Caribbean/metropolitan binaries in the dynamics and affective impact of transnational domestic service.

Notes

1. Paule Marshall, a child of Barbadian immigrants to Brooklyn, saw this wave of migration as a significant historical moment as generating a unique away of life which needed to be documented before the era passed.
2. The same dynamic applies within the Caribbean, where the capacity of professional women to succeed at their demanding careers and jobs is predicated on the existence of a pool of low paid, lower strata domestic servants who attend to their childrearing and other domestic responsibilities.
3. This contemporary scenario echoes the dynamics of plantation society in which slave women and their mistresses formed strong though ambivalent affective ties as the enslaved provided domestic services, nurturing and caring, alongside models of socialization and caring for infants and children under their care. Jean Rhys' *Wide Sargasso Sea* and fictionalized autobiography *Smile Please* explore the intense emotional bond between the neglected child of the house and the black caregiver – Christophine/Meta. In both cases the black nurse and surrogate mother is credited with imparting to the child ontological well-being and epistemological moorings.
4. This concept is drawn from George Lamming's critique of ways of knowing and stereotyping which are based on externalities. He contends that the human spirit is endued with sovereignty of imagination. He stresses therefore the unknowability, inviolability and dominion of the human who resides in the castle of his skin.
5. The term 'Excellent Ettie' is based on the racist and reductionist description of the 'excellent' West Indian domestic servant named Ettie in the climactic incident of Paule Marshall's *Brown Girl, Brownstones*. This disciplinary tale is told to reposition the triumphant young dancer from centre stage to the margins, as a child of immigrants. (See Marshall 285–92; first mention of Ettie 287).

Works Cited

Bakker, Caroline, Martina Elings-Pels and Michele Reis. *The Impact of Migration on Children in the Caribbean* UNICEF Office for Barbados and Eastern Caribbean Paper No 4, August 2009. https://www.unicef.org/easterncaribbean/Impact_of_Migration_Paper.pdf.

Bhabha, Homi. *The Location of Culture*. London: Routledge, 1994.

Bonaparte, Elaine. Interview with Paula Morgan. Conducted at Valsayn Trinidad, May 2016.

Dillon, Mona and Christine A. Walsh. 'Left Behind: The Experiences of Children of the Caribbean Whose Parents Have Migrated.' *Journal of Comparative Family Studies* 43, no. 6 (November – December 2012): 871–902.

Gutierrez-Rodriguez, Encarnacion. *Migration, Domestic Work and Affect: A Decolonial Approach on Value and the Feminization of Labor*. New York and London: Routledge, 2010.

Kincaid, Jamaica. *Lucy.* 1991. London and Basingstoke: Picador, 1994.
Lamming, George. *In the Castle of my Skin.* London: Michael Joseph, 1953.
Marshall, Paule. *Brown Girl, Brownstones.* 1959. New York, NY: The Feminist Press, 1981. First Published in 1959.
Rhys, Jean. *Wide Sargasso Sea.* London: Penguin, 2000. First published in 1966.
——. *Smile Please: An Unfinished Autobiograpy.* London: A Deutsch, 1979.
Van Manen, Max. *Researching Lived Experience: Human Science for an Action Sensitive Pedagogy.* New York, NY: State University of New York Press. 1990.

Part III: Performing Cultural Identity – Carnival Arts and Music

We dedicate *Section III: Performing Cultural Identity – Carnival Arts and Music* to the memory of our fellow contributor, Dr Louis Regis (January 4, 1952–December 10, 2018), who died before the book was released. He will be remembered for his deep and genuine love for Trinidad and Tobago's culture, especially calypso music. His mastery pervaded all aspects of his teaching and research. As rigorous as he was passionate, he helped change the ways culture is integrated into the education system particularly at the secondary and tertiary levels. His calm disposition was matched by a deep insight that touched us all. We have lost a maestro of our culture. We consider it an honour to have one of his last contributions in this volume.

CHAPTER 9
It's not all Sequins and Bikinis? Power, Performance and Play in the Leeds and Trinidad Carnival

Emily Zobel Marshall

Trinidad Carnival 2013. Photograph by Max Farrar

This article examines the tensions between power, performance and play within the Caribbean carnival in Trinidad, whose carnival traditions have spread across the African Diaspora, and Leeds in Northern England, home to the longest-running Caribbean carnival in Europe.[1] One of the main criticisms aimed at contemporary Caribbean carnivals is that they no longer seek to challenge the power of the establishment but have become a spectacle of the body and a celebration of capitalist consumerism. This article asks if contemporary Caribbean carnival in Trinidad and Leeds are indeed all about sequins and bikinis, a vanity show that satisfies the tourist and male gaze, or if at the heart of carnival we still find a uniquely subversive performance aimed at overturning unjust, hierarchical systems of power.

Discourses of Carnivalesque Power

Traditional Caribbean cultural forms have been shaped by their ability to provide a psychological outlet for Caribbean people both on the plantations and during the post-emancipation period. Yet the Caribbean carnival has had, and still does have, an ambivalent relationship to power. Russian literary theorist Mikhail Bakhtin's idea of the 'carnivalesque', which focuses on carnivals in the hierarchical Middle Ages in Europe and Russia, still dominates carnival scholarship and analysis of the Caribbean carnival despite clear issues regarding the relevance of its applicability. Bakhtin's theories unfortunately give us little insight into the transformative effects of playing mas on the individual. The application of the theory of the carnivalesque to Caribbean carnival does not offer the researcher a lens through which to scrutinize the psychological transformations that Caribbean carnival engenders in a racialized post-colonial society. Those who play 'mas' [masquerade] in Caribbean carnivals reenact rituals of enslavement and liberation as a way of dealing with both the traumas of the past and the inequalities of the present. Traditional mas characters such as the Midnight Robber, Moko Jumbie, Blue Devils, Baby Doll, Dame Lorraine, Jab Molassie and Jab-Jab all perform roles in carnival that speak to the horrors of enslavement and often provide a visual or verbal commentary on contemporary injustices. Any meaningful analysis of the playing of this type mas needs to move beyond a Bakhtinian framework of analysis.

However, despite the various limitations of Bakhtinian theory in the examination of Caribbean carnival, the carnivals of the Middle Ages clearly functioned in many similar ways to those in the Caribbean. As Bakhtin famously explains, during the Middle Ages, the carnival played a key role in the lives of ordinary people as it gave them a chance to thwart strict social rules and turn officialdom (the authority of the church and the feudal system) on its head through role-reversal, parody, song, dance and laughter. Bakhtin describes the phenomenon of carnival as an ambivalent spectacle of rebirth and renewal that involves both actor and spectator in a parody of authoritarian structures. He writes: 'carnival brings together, unifies, weds and combines the sacred with the profane, the lofty with the low, the great with the insignificant, the wise with the stupid' (123). Allowances were made in Russian and European societies for these parodies of the powerful as long as they were performed through *humour*. As Bakhtin states 'much was permitted in the form of laughter that was impermissible in serious form' (127).

Akin to the carnival of the Middle Ages, carnival in the Caribbean has been utilized as a coping mechanism for people living in rigid hierarchical societies, and similarly to the Russian and European poor in the Middle Ages, the enslaved in the Caribbean celebrated the temporary reversal of oppressive structures. As cultural anthropologist Victor Turner explains, carnivals and other types of rituals have always been 'used for mocking, critiquing, detaching the group from sober, normal, indicative orderings, and subverting the grammars of their arrangements' (236). However, as contemporary critic Richard Schechner argues, although aspects of Bakhtin's ideas are applicable to an analysis of the Caribbean carnival, especially the Trinidadian carnival in its early form, the Caribbean is now a postcolonial democracy, not a feudal society in the Middle Ages or a site of enslavement and colonial rule. Schechner, therefore, wonders against which oppressive forces the contemporary carnival is now staged. The Caribbean carnival, he explains, may be a 'temporary relief from the authority (if not oppression and downright tyranny) imposed in the name of "democracy", but it is better described as a cultural form which simultaneously *critiques* official culture and *supports* it' (4).

Caribbean carnival is clearly a practice of resistance to the status quo through political engagement and the mockery of hierarchical power structures, but it is also a highly contradictory form; in providing a medium for people to 'let off steam' in a loosely controlled way, the carnival prevents civil unrest and aids the restoration of law and order. For Richard Schechner, there is a creative ongoing tension between a 'top-down and bottom-up movement' in Trinidadian carnival, which is a celebration in which European Christian traditions collide with Asian and African cultural forms:

> Carnival's deepest springs are the tensions between top-down (Euro-Christian pre-Lenten permitted carnival) and bottom-up (Afro-South-Asian never-ending cosmos at play) playing. The top-down predictable structured set of events is always on the verge of collapsing into bottom up chaotic unending creativity (10).

Caribbean carnival is therefore a hybrid form which critiques and supports officialdom, as it is an event full of the threat of the breakdown of structure – of violence, rioting and chaos – but it remains a threat and is not an open revolt or revolution. Much like the European carnivals in the Middle Ages in Bakhtin's analysis, by testing the boundaries and structures of a culturally hybrid contemporary society, the carnival simultaneously questions *and* reaffirms the social orders that govern it. Yet as this article will delineate, while Caribbean carnival at home and abroad is still highly politicized, in the twenty-first century cities of both Leeds and Port of Spain the oppressive forces against which carnival is now pitted are not so clearly defined, understood or delineated as they were during the eras of enslavement, colonialism, and, in the first three decades of UK carnival, periods of heightened racism, intolerance and social unrest.

'Scandalous Debauchery': The Roots of Caribbean Carnival

As well as strong West African and Indian cultural influences, Caribbean carnival has roots in the Catholic carnival traditions of Europe in the Middle Ages. This was a time of bacchanalian fun and excess before following the strict dietary and behavioural rules imposed by the period of Lent. In Trinidad, fearing the effects of the turmoil leading up to the 1789 French Revolution, French planters from the Caribbean islands of Haiti, Guadeloupe and Martinique accepted the invitation by the Spanish government in Trinidad to migrate to the island with their enslaved workers. The invitation was issued to all Catholic planters during the 1780s, and those that took up the offer brought with them to Trinidad their slaves, customs and cultural practices. The upper and middle classes held masked balls to celebrate carnival in which they often mimicked and ridiculed the behaviour and dress of the lower classes and the enslaved. The tradition took root and continued to be celebrated under the British, who captured the island in 1797 (Riggio 2004). As Caribbean carnival scholar Hollis Urban Liverpool explains in his examination of the historical roots of Trinidad carnival:

> French planters brought to Trinidad a legacy of Carnivals. In Romans, a town located southeast of Lyons, as early as 1560, there was an annual Mardi Gras parade. Long before 1560, however, Christians in France celebrated the pre-Lenten season

with pagan excesses climaxing on Mardi Gras with parades and mock trials of effigies (26).

Enslaved Africans, banned from the French Trinidadian balls, held their own celebrations drawing from their African traditions and, in a defiant role-reversal, mocked their master's behaviour and dress. After emancipation in 1838, the newly liberated merged these celebrations with a ritual known as *Cannes Brulées* (Canboulay) based on the re-enactment of putting out fires in the cane fields (a task slaves were often called upon to carry out), which was in part an act of resistance and in part a harvest ritual (Riggio 2004, 42). The ritual re-enactment, like so many carnival cultural forms, was seemingly contradictory and celebrated the extinguishing *and* starting of cane field fires. As Liverpool notes, the enslaved did at times deliberately set fires to the canes and as such their *Cannes Brulées* ritual was in part an act of passive resistance whereby they 're-enacted the event and laughed at the losses of their master' (31). As Historian Donald Wood notes, 'French-Speaking slaves before Emancipation [...] celebrated 'Canboulay' (Cannes Brulees), a torchlight procession to commemorate one of the few excitements of the plantation, a fire in the canefields' (243).

Stick fighting, or Calinda, commonly practised during Canboulay, was a martial arts style dance that originated in West Africa, full of the potential of real violence. Canboulay celebrations, which took place two days before Ash Wednesday (the first day of Lent), became, in a sense, a counter narrative to the Europeans' balls. The celebrations grew and spread throughout the post-emancipation period and evolved into major street celebrations with singing, drumming and lighted torches. Canboulay was predictably disapproved of by British and French Creoles, and struggles ensued as efforts were made to stop the street processions. In the play 'What's Good for the Gander, is Good for the Goose,' published in the newspaper *The Trinidad Spectator* (Feb 14, 1847) by a French Creole, the character Mr Cafarman, a merchant from the Port of Spain, reflects the 'sentiments of his class' in his attitude to carnival:

> You tell me those are rational beings with human faces who indulge themselves in such scandalous debauchery? Do you know anything more absurd than these disgusting Masquerades of the most backward times? More stupid than this [Trinidad] carnival? (Quoted in Cudjoe 96).

The attempts made by the British administration to prevent the Canboulay revelers' annual street celebration in Port of Spain led to the Canboulay riots in 1881 (Riggio 2004, 51). Over time, however, Canboulay metamorphosed into the wild and raucous *Jamette* street carnival, named 'Jamette' because those involved were thought by the upper classes to be below the 'diameter' of respectability (Liverpool 27).

Throughout the twentieth century, and in particular after independence from Great Britain in 1962, carnival grew to become one of the markers of Trinidadian identity and a huge national celebration. Nowadays, Trinidad carnival is deeply entwined with the social and cultural fabric of Trinidadian life. In his novel *Carnival* (2006), Trinidadian author Robert Antoni captures the sense of momentous anticipation – which he imagines even affects both natural and meteorological systems – before carnival begins on the island. Although Trinidad is too far south from the Gulf Stream to be threatened often by actual hurricanes, he explains, the island is hit once a year by a 'human hurricane':

> On this West Indian Island we board up once a year for a human hurricane. In the cool air you could feel the lull before the storm. The sudden stillness. Yet in the apparent vacuum you felt an electrical charge. Foreboding: some catastrophic, atmospheric event was about to take place. Even the birds were quiet. They knew. The potcakes up in the surrounding hills. An eerie silence (147).

Play with Serious Intent

Today Trinidadian carnival preparations can, for some, last a full year from the previous Ash Wednesday, but the official carnival season begins on Three Kings Day (twelfth night) and culminates in celebrations in Port of Spain with Dimanche Gras, when the king, queen and Calypso monarch are usually chosen,[2] as well as street processions on the Sunday, Monday, and Tuesday before Ash Wednesday. It is a celebration of hybridity, cross-cultural fusions, contradictions and creativity – a playing out of the horrors of an oppressive history through a celebration of a dynamic contemporary mix of African, European, Amerindian and South Asian cultural forms.

Trinidadian playwright and theatre-carnival practitioner Tony Hall explains that Trinidad is a country that has always been bold enough to create new things. Like a phoenix rising from the ashes of destruction, beauty is created on the island out of adversity. Hall highlights the resilience and creativity of Trinidadian culture by explaining how, against the historical backdrop of the banning of drums on the plantations in the nineteenth century, newly urbanized Trinidadians in the mid-twentieth century forged steel pans from the oil drums abandoned by the oil industry. Hall describes the Trinidadian carnival as 'a moving mural of people' (Hall Interview with Marshall 2006). Each different section is full of contrast and conflict; there is a visual story expressed through movement, colour, shape and sound.

The performance of contemporary carnival in Port of Spain and Leeds clearly still retains elements of political satire involving parody and mockery of the establishment and the use of carnival as a platform to bring attention to key political and social issues. In particular, this takes place in calypso songs, the playing of traditional mas and band costumes and placards designed to challenge and protest against social inequalities and political corruption. In Trinidad carnival 2017 the legendary 76-year-old calypso star Calypso Rose released a hit song entitled 'Leave Me Alone.' Quickly dubbed one of the first feminist calypso songs by the international press, the lyrics warn men to leave women alone on the road and to let them 'free up' and party without being groped or pestered:

> *Boy doh touch me*
> *Like you going crazy*
> *Men go behind*
> *Let me jump up in the band*
> *I don't want nobody*
> *To come and stop me*
> *Leave me let me free up*
> *Meh self and jump up*
>
> (Calypso Rose 'Leave Me Alone' 2017)

The song drew attention to recent sexual attacks on women during carnival season, a culture of 'victim blaming' amongst some Trinidadian politicians and officials in the wake of sexual assaults and the long-standing problem of domestic violence on the island. Following the horrific unsolved murder of a young female Japanese steel pan musician during carnival 2016, who, according to the *The Washington Post*, was found strangled and wearing a yellow bikini, the former mayor of Port of Spain, Raymond Tim Kee, was reported to have argued that the 'vulgarity and lewdness' of women on the road during carnival was partly to blame for crimes against them (Powers). Trinidadian carnival costume designer Anya Ayoung-Chee responded to Calypso Rose's song and the issues highlighted by it by partnering with local artists and activists to design t-shirts, worn by hundreds of Trinidad carnival goers in 2017, emblazoned with the phrases 'Leave Me Alone' – and the Trinidadian English version – 'Leave She Alone.' Ayoung-Chee also argues that women out on the streets in large numbers during carnival is an act of political activism in itself; 'coming out in the streets in the tens of thousands, owning your space, owning your freedom [...] what is that besides activism?' (Powers *The Washington Post* Feb 26, 2017).

While calypso has long been a platform for political lampooning, where powerful politicians of the day are mocked and the misconduct of the powerful is exposed, political satire also takes place in the carnival procession. A strong political vein runs through some of the mas performances in Leeds West Indian Carnival and the troupe 'Harrison Bundey,' sponsored by a Chapeltown law firm that specializes in personal legal matters including criminal, family, child-care, immigration and inquests into deaths in custody, consistently takes a strong political message on the road. Troupe themes include 'Free Dem – Close Guantanamo' (2008), during which members of the troupe were stopped from entering the park as they were deemed 'too political' by the authorities, 'Shame on You BP' (2010), in the wake of the Gulf oil spill, 'Blud ah go Run - Save the NHS' (the UK's famous National Health Service) (2012), which received a great reception from the crowd and 'World Soca Soccer – Love Football, hate FIFA' (2014), aimed at exposing FIFA corruption (Farrar, G).

At the heart of Caribbean carnival there is always play, but this is play with very serious intentions. Play challenges society's rules on a deep and unpredictable level; it opens up possibilities for change and can bring about the reversal of power structures. Play destabilizes power with its random, unstructured quality. Whether found in storytelling, carnival, a calypso, the theatre (a play), or in the school playground, play involves mimicking, masking, disguise, tricking and role-reversal. There are elements of play in all Caribbean carnival traditions, such as steel pan, calypso, traditional mas characters and calinda, yet within this type of play we find elements of repressed violence and anger born of a history of oppression and enslavement.

Harrison Bundey Troupe, 'Obama Say, BP Have Fe Pay!' Barak Obama in LWIC, 2010

Photograph by Max Farrar

Harrison-Bundey Troupe, 'Blud a Go Run': Save the NHS' in LWIC (2011)

Photograph by Max Farrar

In Trinidad carnival, the screaming blue devils who leap toward unsuspecting onlookers covered in blue paint, draped in heavy chains, shaking their limbs and spitting blood and breathing fire from their mouths – with hands outstretched for payment – speak to the desire to become feared and omnipotent, to play up to 'devilish' stereotypes of blackness harboured by whites and to demand reparations or repayment for the damage done to the island and its people. Bakhtin writes that the spectacle of fire at carnival is 'deeply ambivalent' as fire 'simultaneously destroys and renews the world' (126). If their aim is to reshape the social and political landscape, the fire-breathing blue devils must first destroy everything in their paths. As Milla Riggio and Rawle Gibbons explain in their analysis of the Trinidadian carnival devil mas in *Festive Devils of the Americas* (2015), the Blue Devil 'transgresses, subverts and reverses order and respectability with his intoxicating sense of freedom' (203). Their mas or play, they argue, is mischievous and celebratory – but also has a long-lasting power that goes beyond the moment of carnival:

> Both fear and threat are nuanced by the playful sense of mischief of all the festive devils, even though what they are playing out has a potency beyond the festival itself (218).

However, a fascinating paradox lies at the centre of the Trinidadian carnival, which is also mirrored in the carnival traditions of Leeds in England; although often perceived as a celebration of the thwarting of the norms and the transcendence of governing forces, a code of conduct governs each part of the proceedings, especially the main procession. Carnival mas bands normally have a king and queen and carnival sections are often held together by security guards holding ropes to keep the section intact and band members safe from the interference of interlopers – although crowd members sometimes still manage to infiltrate the bands. In Trinidad, mas players must buy their official, expensive mas costumes well in advance of carnival and each band performs in front of a panel of judges at several judging venues throughout the city – a moment when the band must be at its most orderly and structured. These more structured processions contrast with the J'Ouvert celebrations, a much more tangible expression of liberation. 'J'Ouvert' is from the French *jour ouvert* ('open day' or 'breaking of the dawn'), which again is also practised during Leeds West Indian carnival.

In Leeds, J'Ouvert revelers take to the streets, sometimes in their pyjamas, at dawn in the streets of Chapeltown, the heart of the city's Caribbean community. In Trinidad, J'Ouvert (jouvay) is even more immersive – carnival goers cover themselves in mud, paint or grease and dance together on the streets of Port of Spain to greet the sunrise. While jouvay does not offer a complete antithesis to the more organized structures of the main processions (there are still jouvay costumes to buy and security guards in the bands and performance venues to pass through), it does offer a counter narrative to the beads and bikini style masquerade.

In many ways, jouvay, which in Trinidad is also called 'dirty mas' in contrast to the 'pretty mas' which takes place in the daytime processions on carnival Monday and Tuesday, is a ritual symbolic of renewal, regeneration and rebirth, a process of transformation in which participants transcend their individuality and become a human 'mas'. With their bodies and faces covered in thick paint or mud, pressed up against the bodies of others, they become unrecognizable. This brings participants a freedom from certain acceptable norms of behaviour and the rampant individualism of consumer society; collectively, as they greet the sunrise, they are invited to enter a liminal zone. The term liminal is derived from the Latin word 'limen' meaning 'threshold' and can be described as a 'betwixt and between' space on the threshold between boundaries or binary constructions: a space in which perceptions or conditions blend and transformation occurs. As Victor Turner explains:

> [Liminality is]...in tribal ritual, a time outside time in which it is often permitted to play with the factors of sociocultural experience, to disengage what is mundanely connected, what, outside liminality, people may even believe to be naturally and intrinsically connected, and to join the disarticulated parts in novel, even improbable ways (286).

The liminal, according to Turner, is a distortion of the ordinary that allows one to play with 'cultural construction' and fill 'the liminal scene with dragons, monsters, caricatures, fantasies made up of elements of everyday experience torn out of context' (236). As they enter the liminal zone, jouvay revellers are in a sense reborn – as they become at one within the 'mas', they can let go of their former identities and understand their everyday experiences of life in new and unpredictable ways. Tony Hall describes jouvay as a ritual to the sunrise which involves a process of awakening symbolic of the struggles and history of the Trinidadian people. He explains; 'blacks awoke out of slavery, they manifested and emancipated themselves; it was a jouvay process' (Interviews with Hunte & Marshall 2006). The young protagonist of Antoni's novel *Carnival* (2006) experiences this sense of collective transcendence as the sun rises in Port of Spain during jouvay, albeit a fleeting one. Covered 'head to toe in every imaginable nastiness' he sees the 'indistinguishable' 'solid mass of humanity' on the road as harnessing the power to shape the future:

> This – I told myself, I proclaimed it every year, every jouvert morning – this could save the world.
>
> Standing in the middle of mainstage, my head thrown back, staring up at the blinding sun (159).

St Lucian poet Derek Walcott also encapsulates the importance of 'sunrise ritual' in the Caribbean in his Nobel lecture, yet for him the sunrise offers more than a fleeting glimpse at a better future but acts as a metaphor for the 'self-defining' phase of Caribbean culture itself:

> There is a force of exultation, a celebration of luck, when a writer finds himself a witness to the early morning of a culture that is defining itself, branch by branch, leaf by leaf, in that self-defining dawn, which is why, especially at the edge of the sea, it is good to make a ritual of the sunrise.

Blue devils on J'Ouvert Morning in Leeds, 2007
Photograph by Guy Farrar

Carnival, Capitalism and Commercialization in Leeds and Port of Spain

Despite the many freedoms and insights the ritual of jouvay offers at both a psychological and societal level, since independence Trinidadian carnival has become increasingly commercialized. There are now enormous bands and expensive costumes, unaffordable to many. Today carnival is a tourist attraction and a cultural product, attended by officials, endorsed and sponsored by the establishment and steeped in consumerism. There may be a danger of carnival becoming a hierarchy in which only the rich elite can afford the intricate costumes, with costume prices starting at around $500 US, many of which are bought by revelers and then thrown away as soon as carnival is over, resulting in mountains of rubbish and waste that have triggered projects aimed at recycling carnival materials (see Kempadoo-Miller 'Mango Sustainable Carnival Arts Project' 2011).

As theatre carnival practitioner Colin Prescod points out, capitalism could spiral the carnival 'out of the control of the people'. Rhian Kempadoo-Miller, Leeds West Indian Carnival designer, observes that Trinidad carnival is a unique cross-cultural fusion in which participants are not divided along ethnic lines, but because of the expensive costumes and 'pay to play' ethos, by income and class. One of the key founders of Leeds West Indian Carnival, Arthur France, describes a constant struggle to strike a balance between securing commercial sponsorship and funding for the event and keeping the traditional elements of Leeds carnival alive. However, the commercialization of carnival has not affected the much smaller-scale Leeds carnival to the same extent as in Trinidad; troupe members are often encouraged to input into the design and the making of costumes, which are in the main homemade, and only asked to pay a relatively small contribution to cover the costs of materials; for example, in 2017 the Harrison Bundey troupe charged £10 to £20 per costume.

In Britain, Caribbean-influenced carnivals have played a key role in the formation of black British identity. Furthermore, just as the Trinidadian carnival was a vehicle for protest against colonial oppression, they are mediums through which British racism was challenged and opposed. Founding member Arthur France, born in St Kitts, explains that the Caribbean carnival was established in Britain as a means of 'taking the heat out of the racial strife of the day' (quoted in Connor & Farrar 2004, 268). As Leeds-based scholar Max Farrar and the late Geraldine Connor, director of *Carnival Messiah* (1999), argue:

> Carnival in the UK understands that the anti-human negativity of racism is effectively challenged by the embodied, human performance of art - an art which has been created 'by the people and for the people' which occupies and transforms public space (268).

Carnival Committee, 1974; Vince Wilkinson, Hughbon Condor, Hebrew Rawlins, Arthur France, Kathleen Brown, George Archibold.

Photograph by Max Farrar

Leeds West Indian carnival is a much smaller event than Trinidad carnival, attracting around 150,000 people every year. Established in 1967, it is able to lay claim to being the first Caribbean street carnival in Europe run by Caribbean people. The London-based Notting hill carnival, initially founded in 1959 by Claudia Jones, was an indoor event until 1966 and only run by British Caribbeans from 1970 onwards. Leeds West Indian Carnival has enjoyed a very good relationship with Leeds City Council and other civic institutions, but has remained firmly in the control of the Carnival committee, a dedicated group of local people, predominantly 'elders' of Caribbean origin, who have shaped the carnival since its beginnings. The only year that there was serious trouble at Leeds carnival, in 1990 when two people were shot during carnival celebrations, is referred to by the carnival committee as its 'Annus Horribilus'. Every other year carnival has been celebrated peacefully and joyfully (Farrar, M. 2001, 3).

Arthur France readily describes the struggles he faced in convincing people to start the Leeds West Indian Carnival in 1967. He had to buy whole chickens from Otley market, pluck feathers for carnival outfits and transform local houses into 'mas camps'. France and his supporters begged and borrowed costume materials and galvanized the support of the police and Leeds City Council (Interview with Farrar). On August bank holiday 1967 the sound of steel pan filled the air and the first Caribbean carnival in Europe was ready to take to the streets. France states that he 'decided it would be run by West Indians, full stop. We're always labeled as not being capable of running things. We've proved them wrong.' The success of France and his cofounders in creating such a popular and long-lasting Caribbean-led carnival in Leeds based on these principles is a profound example of the success of an autonomous black struggle for recognition, respect and space in the British cultural sphere.

Emily Zobel Marshall (far left) and other troupe members in 'Unstitch the Rich,' Harrison Bundey Troupe 2013, LWIC
Photograph by Tina Have Lauesen-Day

Skin Mas: It's not all Sequins and Bikini's?

The main criticism leveled at contemporary Caribbean carnival, both at home and in the Diaspora, is that there are too many bikinis and too much flesh – in particular female flesh – on display. Women, Trinidadian post-carnival media headlines have screamed over the past two decades, have taken over carnival, and are flaunting themselves wantonly on the streets, playing mas with bacchanalian energy and putting their sexuality on show in vulgar displays of lewd dancing and skimpy costumes. For example, in an article entitled 'Women just as culpable for demeaning themselves' in the *Trinidad Guardian* (February 1, 2015), Catholic spokesman Vernon Khelawan asks:

> What is the message women send to the younger people, including their own children? It is acceptable to parade on the streets on Carnival days wearing only bikinis and sometimes a bra with only beads and feathers for cover, prancing and gyrating and so many times making sure that the TV cameras pick up the contortions through which they put their bodies?

However, critic Anna Kasafi Perkins argues that Caribbean women have 'subverted and continue to subvert' negative interpretations of the female body, in particular those found in the Christian traditions of Lent which, she argues 'devalue the physical being and oftentimes view it as a site of sinfulness and temptation' (373). Again, there is a clear tension here between Christian religious traditions and African cultural retentions, which influences the dances, mas characters and music of carnival. Perkins agues that carnivalesque performances in contemporary carnival by women 'revalues bodies, especially colonized female bodies' (361). In Trinidad, she continues, the negative responses to what is now called 'skin mas', due to the amount of skin on display, is in fact a knee-jerk reaction by men to female empowerment; they succumb to a growing sense of panic as women are 'taking over Mas, setting the pace and no longer being content to remain in the shadows playing adjunct to men' (368). In this sense, the mas of sequins and bikinis is in fact a progressive one, one which celebrates the female body in public through bodily transgressions and assaults conservative notions of a woman's 'proper place', notions often grounded in traditional Christian faith. In *Women in Mas* (1998), a special issue magazine with dedicated articles examining the controversy around the behaviour of women in Trinidad carnival, Peter Ray Blood points out:

> Some women argue that men play mas 365 days of the year, and women need 2 days to release the tension from the experience of abuse (growing numbers), harassment, unemployment, oppression and exploitation in many forms (39).

During slavery the black female body was the site of violence, ownership and reproduction. Today, daughters, mothers and grandmothers dancing wildly on the streets in revealing clothing directly challenge the construction of the black female body as property, a symbol of Christian virtue or as mother and child-bearer. Through their so-called transgressive acts, they reclaim the agency of their 'disciplined and devalued bodies' (Perkins 371). As Gabrielle Hosein, Head of the Institute for Gender and Development Studies at the University of the West Indies, argues, the bikini and beads masquerade should not be seen as undermining or counter to feminist political activism:

> It's the largest movement of women in Trinidad and Tobago seeking autonomy and self-determination around their sexuality and their bodies, in opposition to a particular kind of respectability politics…purely for the joy and pleasure they experience […]. One can see those goals as highly political in our world today.

(Hosein quoted in Powers *The Washington Post* Feb 26, 2017).

Conclusion

Carnival is multifaceted and replete with opposing forces, and this spectacle simultaneously reinforces some of the patriarchal stereotypes women wish to critique – it gives strength to the image of the overtly sexualized woman on display for the male gaze (Perkins 369). Indeed, carnival will always hold up a 'magic mirror' to humanity, which, according to Turner, will provide a 'reflexive meta-commentary on society and history' (166). Carnival reflects and refracts hierarchies of oppressive power within a society and both emphasizes and reduces the tensions and paradoxes within a community – and as such carnival will always remain a profoundly ambivalent, complex and contradictory cultural form.

In a patriarchal society, carnival will continue to provide a site for emancipatory acts by women, whilst simultaneously highlighting the limitations of their emancipation – a paradoxical tension that lies at the heart of Caribbean carnival. This tension is also reflected in the increasing commercialzation of carnival, which ensures its financial viability, and its anti-establishment underbelly that seeks to speak to the needs of the ordinary people living in unjust societies. Yet at the core of carnival is play with serious intent; the seemingly playful performances that carnival engenders continue to give voice to the desire to break free from the devastating effects of institutionalized racism, sexism, class prejudice and political corruption located in contemporary societies across the African Diaspora.

Burlesque Troup Leeds West Indian Carnival 2015

Photograph by Max Farrar

Notes

1. For more information on Leeds West Indian Carnival see: Connor, G & Farrar, M. (2004) 'Carnival in Leeds and London: Making New Black British Subjectivities,' in 'A Short History of the Leeds West Indian Carnival 1967–2000,' ed. Riggio, M. (2004) and Farrar, M. (2001), 259–69 [Accessed 5 May 2014]. <http://maxfarrar.org.uk/docs/CarnivalHistoryWYAS.pdf >
2. In 2017, the Carnival King and Queen had been chosen earlier with only the winners appearing during Dimanche Gras. The Calypso Monarch final competition was still held on Sunday night. In 2018, the King and Queen finals reverted to the Sunday night Dimanche Gras show.

Works Cited

Antoni, R. *Carnival*. New York, NY: Grove Press, 2006.
Bakhtin, Mikhail. *Problems of Dostoevsky's Poetics* in *Theory and History of Literature, Volume 8*, edited and translated by Caryl Emerson. Minneapolis, MN: University of Minnesota Press, 1984.
Baptiste, O. Publisher's Note. 'Women in 'Mas.' *Trinidad Express* Special Publication, Thursday, October 21, 1988.
Blood, P.R. 'Is Being Boss All? Women in "Mas".' *Trinidad Express* Special Publication, Thursday, October 21, 1988: 33.
Burton, R. *Afro-Creole: Power, Opposition and Play in the Caribbean*. London: Cornel University Press, 1997.
Campbell, A. *Staging Mas Project Document*. Unpublished Document. Leeds: The Arts Council, 2006.
Cohen, A. *Masquerade Politics: Explorations in the Structure of Urban Cultural Movements*. California: University of California Press, 1993.
Connor, Geraldine. Speech at 'Staging Mas' Seminar, Leeds Metropolitan University, Leeds, November, 2006.
Connor, Geraldine, and Max Farrar. 'Carnival in Leeds and London: Making New Black British Subjectivities.' In *Carnival: Culture in Action – The Trinidad Experience*, edited by Milla Cozart Riggio, 259–69. London and New York: Routledge, 2004.
Farrar, Guy. 'Harrison Bundey Troupe Themes.' Email to Emily Zobel Marshall, September, 2015.
Farrar, Max. 'A Short History of the Leeds West Indian Carnival 1967–2000.' [Accessed May 5 2014]. http://maxfarrar.org.uk/docs/CarnivalHistoryWYAS.pdf 2001.
Farrar, Guy., Smith, T. and Farrar, Max. *Celebrate! Fifty Years of the Leeds West Indian Carnival*. Huddersfield: D & M Heritage Publishers, 2017.
France, A. Interview with Max Farrar. Caribbean Carnival Symposium. Leeds Beckett University. Leeds, Nov. 1, 2014.
Hall, Tony. 'The J'Ouvert Popular Theatre Process: From the Street to the Stage.' In *Carnival: Culture in Action – The Trinidad Experience*, edited by Milla Cozart Riggio, 162–67. London and New York: Routledge, 2004.
———. Interview with Emily Marshall. Nov. 2. West Yorkshire Playhouse, Leeds, West Yorkshire, 2006.
Hamilton, D. Untitled Presentation at 'Staging Mas' Seminar, Leeds Beckett University, Leeds, Nov. 2006.
Hill, Errol. *The Trinidad Carnival: Mandate for a National Theatre*. Austin: University of Texas Press, 1972.
Khelewan, Vernon. *Trinidad Guardian*, February 1, 2015.
Kempadoo-Miller, R. Presentation on RJC Dance. Caribbean Carnival Symposium. Leeds Beckett University. Leeds, Nov. 1, 2014.
Liverpool, Hollis U. 'Origins of Rituals and Customs in the Trinidad Carnival: African or European?' *The Drama Review: Special Issue on Trinidad and Tobago Carnival* 2, no. 3, edited by Milla C. Riggio (Autumn, 1998): 24–37.

Marshall, E., and Hunte, C. Interviews with Participants. West Yorkshire Playhouse, Leeds, West Yorkshire, Oct. 30– Nov. 3, 2006.

Mauldin, B. *Carnival!* London: Thames and Hudson, 2004.

Perkins, A. K. 'Carne Vale (Goodbye to Flesh?): Caribbean Carnival, Notions of the Flesh and Christian Ambivalence about the Body.' *Sexuality & Culture*. (2011): 361–74

Powers, M. '"Leave Me Alone": Trinidad's Women find a Rallying Cry for This Year's Carnival.' *The Washington Post*, Feb. 26, 2017.

Prescod, C. Presentation at 'Staging Mas' Seminar, Leeds Beckett University, Leeds, Nov. 2006.

Riggio, Milla Cozart, Angela Marino and Paolo Vignolo, eds. *Festive Devils of the Americas*. Chicago, IL: Seagull Books, dist. by University of Chicago Press, 2015.

Riggio, Milla Cozart. 'The Carnival Story – Then and Now.' In *Carnival: Culture in Action – The Trinidad Experience*, edited by Milla Cozart Riggio, 13–30. London and New York: Routledge, 2004.

Riggio, Milla Cozart, and Rawle Gibbons. 'Pay the Devil, Jab Jab: Festive Devils in Trinidad Carnival.' In *Festive Devils of the Americas*, edited by Milla Cozart Riggio, Angela Marino and Paolo Vignolo, 189–220. Chicago, IL: Seagull Books, dist by University of Chicago Press, 2015.

Schechner, Richard. 'Carnival Theory After Bakhtin.' In *Carnival: Culture in Action – The Trinidad Experience*, edited by Milla Cozart Riggio, 2–12. London and New York: Routledge, 2004.

Turner, Victor. *On The Edge of the Bush: Anthropology and Experience*. Tucson, AZ: The University of Arizona Press, 1985.

Walcott, D. Nobel Lecture: 'The Antilles: Fragments of Epic Memory.' In *Literature 1991–1995,* S. Allen. Singapore: World Scientific Publishing, 1997.

Wood, D. *Trinidad in Transition: The Years After Slavery*. London: Oxford University Press, 1968.

Wuest, R. 'The Robber in Trinidad Carnival.' *Caribbean Quarterly* 36, no. 3/4, Konnu and Carnival – Caribbean Festival Arts (Dec 1990): 42–53.

CHAPTER 10
Rudder:
International Chantuelle as In-zile

Louis Regis

In 2015 the University of the West Indies (UWI), the premier tertiary institute in the Anglophone Caribbean, ceremoniously conferred the doctorate Honoris Causa on calypsonian David Michael Rudder. Some nationals have questioned UWI's award privately, alleging that Rudder has not been relevant since the late 1990s and that his permanent residence in Canada should have disqualified him automatically from being awarded the highly prestigious regional honour. Others have wondered publicly if the award was a privileging of the Western performance aesthetic over the African-based West Indian, and if Rudder was awarded because of what is perceived (by some) as his middle class status. While this questioning has largely taken the form of muttered dissatisfaction, the fact that it can arise is sufficient to warrant a preliminary investigation into the reasons the self-styled *International Chantuelle* is now regarded by some of his countrymen as an exile in his homeland, an inzile, to borrow a term from James Aboud, the self-styled lagahoo poet.[1]

David Rudder was born 6th May 1953 to working class parents in the cross-roads community of Belmont, where the traditional carnival visual and performing arts, nurtured to some extent by Orisa palais, Rada yard and Spiritual Shouter Baptist church, reached full flowering in the calypso and mas tents and in the several local steelband yards. In his teens Rudder, who was baptized first as an Anglican, then as Roman Catholic and thirdly as Spiritual Baptist in three separate ceremonies, served as apprentice to master coppersmith and masman Ken Morris. In the early 1970s he was also a founding member of the singing group *In-Larks*, and subsequently of *Thoughts for Tomorrow*, which recorded a 45 rpm whose sides were 'Mother Earth,' a tribute to fallen national freedom fighter Guy Harewood, and 'Haiti.' Rudder also served as a chorister at Kitchener's Revue during the carnival season and as backup vocalist at recording sessions; he developed his creative talent by composing jingles and honed his entrepreneurial skills by producing and distributing the singles 'Dougla Woman' (1978), and 'I Reggae Music' (1979) on his Bad Bull label.

In 1981 a natural progression brought him to Charlie's Roots, a band of remarkable musicians, led by composer/arranger Pelham Goddard. At first Rudder substituted for lead singer Tambu but his talents as singer/songwriter won him an honourable place in *The Multinational Force,* the band within *Roots.* He wrote or co-wrote 'Jungle Fever' (1981) and followed this with 'The River' (1983), 'Callaloo' (1984), and 'In a Calabash' (1985), the last three of which were themes for Peter Minshall's masquerade (mas) bands. Rudder auditioned unsuccessfully for a place in the 1985 national calypso monarch semifinals but 'Calabash,' the unsuccessful audition piece, copped third place in the Road March competition, thanks largely to its exposure on the fete circuit. Earnings from the 1985 season generated the capital with which Rudder produced *The Hammer* on his Lypsoland label. In 1986 he made a spectacular debut as a solo act with the tandem of 'Bahia Gyal' and 'The Hammer,' winning The Young Kings, the National Calypso Monarch and the Road March titles, three of the four major titles at stake that year.

Ruddermania was the term used to describe the frenzy that Rudder seemed to generate with every appearance. Calypso's newest superstar was featured in all national newspapers and tabloids as well as the *Gleaner* of Jamaica and the *Nation* of Barbados; he was the subject of major articles in the *Guardian* and *Sunday Observer* of London, the *Boston Globe, New York Times* and *Village Voice, Newsweek, Ebony* and *Cosmopolitan.* In 1996 Rudder was named National Goodwill ambassador by the directors of the United Nations Development Programme (UNDP). This honour, added to the numerous accolades, international contracts, and frequent international performances, justify his calling himself *International Chantuelle,* as he titles his 1999 album.

The substantive 'chantuelle' indicates that he is grounded in the tradition of high kaiso as he signifies in the phrase 'I am the seed of The Growling Tiger' in his 1987 hit song 'Calypso Music.' The descriptor 'international' indicates that his genius is not constrained by the physical and psychological boundaries which delimit and delineate the nation-state of Trinidad and Tobago and its people. In addition to indicating Rudder's extra-regional reach, the term 'international' connotes the timeless, a point made by Rudder himself in an interview with Gershwin Stephen (*TnT Mirror* January 10, 1989).

Polar differences in background, temperament, imagination and personality separate Sparrow, the first calypsonian to be honoured with the UWI's PhD honoris causa, from David Rudder, the third to be so honoured. Like Sparrow a biblical generation earlier, Rudder skyrocketed to stardom within a year of entering the calypso gayelle, but, unlike Sparrow, he did not have to negotiate a stormy past and the Damoclean sword of unbelonging; his personality allowed him to soar above the thunderstorms of criticism, picong and mépris[2] directed at him by traditionalists and by some of his new calypsonian peers, including some tentmates. Although, like Sparrow, his musical innovations define him as an avant garde experimenter who fuses the calypso form with Rhythm and Blues (R&B) and other genres that he favours, he is essentially far more traditionalist than he is given credit for. His themes are those covered by traditional calypsonians: national politics, crime, male-female relationships, international politics, cricket, calypso, carnival, steelband, endorsing the idea of One Caribbean, but his musical eclecticism enriches the musical variety of his treatment of these core calypso themes. The lyrical content of his songs is the product of deep thought informed by voluminous reading and by an extremely rare quality of genuine poetic imagination. These are the qualities that separate Rudder from his peers and, sadly, distance Rudder from his audiences.

This is not to say that Rudder lacks the capacity to rouse carnival revellers to frenzy for he has done precisely this time and again between 1986 and 1998 inclusive. He has demonstrated that he, like The Shadow and Blue Boy/SuperBlue among the contemporary kaisonians and Machel Montano and Bunji Garlin among the soca acts, can tap into that collective primal energy released during the carnival period. The mass ecstatic response to 'The Hammer' (1986), 'Bahia Gyul' (1986), 'Madness' (1987), 'Calypso Music' (1987), 'Haiti' (1988), 'The Engine Room' (1988), 'Rally round the West Indies' (1988), 'Panama' (1988), 'Bacchanal Lady' (1988), 'Nuff Respect' (1991), 'The Ganges and the Nile' (1999), and 'High Mas' (1998) is now part of the collective memory. The ecstatic response to this handful of songs, although welcome and well-deserved, occludes the fact that little attention has been paid to Rudder's artistic achievements as public poet even in the above named songs.

This essay offers a logocentric examination of *The Cricket Chronicles*, one of four theme-centred Rudder albums. *The Cricket Chronicles*, which was published to coincide with the staging of the International Cricket Council (ICC) World Cup of Cricket in the West Indies in 2007, is a compilation of thirteen songs on fourteen tracks (it offers a SoCa [sic] and a Rockaiso version of 'Lifted'); six of these songs were composed for the event while the other seven are re-makes.

Rudder divides the fourteen tracks into five 'Chapters'. Chapter 1, *This Is the Celebration*, comprises 'Lovely Day,' 'Caribbean Party,' 'Knock Dem Down,' 'It's a West Indian Thing (Bounce),' and 'Lifted (SoCa).' The first three tracks are celebrations of soca and calypso music. 'Lovely Day,' composed specifically for the album, echoes the love ballad of the same name by African-American soul singer Bill Withers, and it ironically recalls the phrase 'A lovely day for cricket', the first line of Relator's 'Gavaskar,' a highly popular derogation of the West Indies cricket team, which suffered an unexpected home Test series defeat to 'lowly' India in 1971. Rudder's 'Lovely Day' exudes positivity as the I-narrator exults that he is 'living in the livingness of life' and affirms this irrepressible attitude in the face of media-disseminated blues. 'Caribbean Party,' first performed in 1993, summons 'all the yuppies, the soldiers/ The dispossessed and the gangsters too' to 'this acre of ecstasy' where 'the rhythm destroys the demons' of doubt. 'Knock Dem Down,' first performed in 1992, echoes the Maestro calypso of the same name, which heralds the emergence of the fearsome four-pronged West Indian pace attack and singles out Michael Holding whose meteoric career between 1975 and 1987 coincides with the period of West Indian near absolute dominance. Rudder's 'Knock Dem Down,' however, is a tribute to the unstoppable cathartic power of soca music, expressed in the metaphors of militarism and militaristic rhetoric issuing from the propagandists of the first Gulf War of 1990–1991.

Tracks 4 and 5 'It's a West Indian thing (Bounce),' and 'Lifted (SoCa),' were both composed for *The Cricket Chronicles*. 'Bounce,' referencing inter alia the West Indian cricketer practice of saluting great strokes with a bumping exchange of one closed fist, celebrates cricket as a quintessentially Caribbean experience ('Nobody does it better, when we're on top of our game/ No fire can burn brighter than our Caribbean flame'). 'Lifted' challenges opposing players to demonstrate masculinity and commitment to country in the face of the sheer brutality of the West Indian game. 'Lifted' ends with a calypso style boasting of West Indian triumphs: a Mumbai massacre, a Rawalpindi rout, a slaughter in Sydney, a Kingston killer and so on. By opening a cricket-based album with three songs affirming the power of calypso-soca music, and linking these with two paeans to West Indian cricket, Rudder is signalling that the Anglophone Caribbean is best defined and expressed by its cricket and its music. *The Cricket Chronicles* is the best measure of this definition and expression.

Chapter 2, *The Glory Days*, comprises 'Here Comes the West Indies,' 'Legacy' and 'Rally round the West Indies.' 'Here Comes the West Indies,' title track of the 1994 album, declares the resurgence of the West Indies after their inspiring victories in 1993 on tour of Australia in both the Test series and in a tri-nation One Day International series which also involved Pakistan. Rudder co-opts the rhetorical boasting of the Caribbean badjohn/rude bwoy, although one can hear echoes of the rap/hip hop style of our North American cousins, testifying to the submarine unity of what Paul Gilroy theorises as the Black Atlantic whose foundation is its music. 'Legacy,' first recorded in 1996, is simultaneously a tribute to cricketing legends of yesteryear and a reminder to the current players of the glorious legacy bequeathed to them. 'Legacy' is a reflective piece, the insistent choric 'pound it in they brain' notwithstanding. Intended to inspirit the current generation of legatees, 'Legacy' has a quiet intensity and urgency unlike the rodomontade of 'Here Comes the West Indies.' 'Rally round the West Indies,' first performed in 1988, is an appeal to a West Indian public to support the team which was entering a period of decline after a glorious decade of near absolute dominance.

Chapter 3, *The Decline*, comprises the elegiac 'Smiling Eyes of Steel,' first appearing on the 2000 album *Zero*, and the ode 'Bankie's Son' first recorded on *Eclectica* in 2004. 'Steel' apostrophises the deceased all-rounder Malcolm Marshall, justifiably feared as a fast bowler but also proficient with the bat in the lower middle order. 'Bankie's Son' salutes that inspirational moment in Antigua in 2003 when the West Indies, needing to avoid a clean sweep at the hands of the mighty Australians, completed the largest successful run-chase in the history of Test cricket. Although the West Indies lost the series 1–3, the run chase, anchored by Omari Banks, son of famed Anguillan musician Bankie Banx, served (or should have served) as a salutary warning to all, including the Caribbean public, that West Indian warriorhood was still alive.

Chapter 4, *This Bloody Game*, features the rockaiso version of 'Lifted,' and 'Champions,' a philosophical statement on the importance of the West Indian cricket champions to the individual self-worth of the people they represent and the corporate psychological well-being of the region.

Chapter 5, *Epilogue*, comprises 'The Anthem' and 'Cricket (It's Over).' The first of these melds the melodies of 'Rally' and of 'High Mas,' Rudder's massively popular composition of 1998 which coopts the Gregorian chant in requesting that the merciful All-Father forgive those 'sinners' who cast their mortal burdens on the city in the ceremony of mass exorcism known as the Trinidad Carnival. 'The Anthem' was commissioned by the West Indian Cricket Board which, although faulted massively – and deservedly so – for its numerous giant missteps, still had the acuity to commission one of the region's leading song-writers to pen an anthem that could represent and inspirit the cricket-playing Caribbean region. On the other hand, 'Cricket (It's Over)' comments bleakly on the loneliness of the arena at the end of a game as 'the pitch that owned our souls/Now lies naked, cracked and scarred' and the members of the crowd 'tote or ride their feelings/right back to their yards.' The moment of communion is over and the congregants have dispersed to their private lives. Although the chorus states, 'It's over, until we meet to live and die again,' the dirge-like quality of the music conjures a sense of desolation and finality. In some ways it sounds as though Rudder is pronouncing the death knell of West Indian cricket, a feeling dramatically opposed to the irrepressible optimism of 'Lovely Day' when he gives himself up to the blessing of the day.

What emerges forcefully from *The Cricket Chronicles* is Rudder's belief that cricket is the major social cohesive in the sea-divided Anglophone Caribbean; what emerges just as forcefully is that cricket is the Anglophone Caribbean's secular religion, as well as the major site for the manifestation of the noblest qualities of the Caribbean personality.

'Rally round the West Indies,' the beginning of Rudder's song/sung engagement with cricket, previews his thoughts on the importance of the game to the region. Commenting on the decline of West Indian cricket, symbolized appropriately by Holding's withdrawal from the arena ('Way Down Under a warrior falls/Michael Holding falls in the heat of the battle'), 'Rally' reproves the archetypal supporter who shouts in anger, 'Michael shoulda left long time.' Such a comment issues far too readily from an ignorance which does not apprehend the larger socio-economic-political issues beyond the boundary of the playing field. This is the substance of the final all-important stanza:

> *Now they making restrictions and laws*
> *To spoil our beauty*
> *But in the end we shall prevail*
> *This is not just cricket*
> *This thing...goes beyond the boundary*
> *So is to you and me to make sure that they fail*
> *So we must take a side or be lost in the rubble*
> *In a divided world that don't need islands no more*
> *Are doomed forever to be at somebody's mercy*
> *Little keys can open up mighty doors.*

Referencing *Beyond a Boundary*, C.L.R. James's classic study of the origins of cricket and of the sociology of cricket in colonial Trinidad, Rudder declares that cricket transcends not only the physical limitations of the playing fields but is inextricably bound up with the very future of the cricket-loving Caribbean islands.

'Bounce' testifies to what seems to be Rudder's perception of the unifying potential of cricket to the region where a cricket ground is a 'meeting place of the clans'. This is emphasized in the invariable choruses:

> *It's a communion, feel the energy, the vibe*
> *A connection, it keeps us alive...this cricket*
> *Whether we're down or we're the best*
> *You wanna see my ticket*
> *Brother, it's beating in my chest*
> *And yours, and yours, and yours*
> *It's a West Indian thing.*

'Bounce' lists the names of the island states blessed by the gospel of cricket while 'Here Comes the West Indies' identifies each island 'posse' of diehard cricketing fans, singling out for special mention the eccentric Antiguan comic duo of Mayfield and Gravey as well as Macfingall, the Barbadian musician/calypsonian/comedian/schoolteacher whose region-wide travel and popularity with cricket fans throughout the region earn him the right to be called a Caribbean man.

'Bankie's Son' represents cricket as having the potential to inspire in other domains beyond the boundary of the cricket field. The opening lines of the song pose the question,

> *How do we reclaim the fire*
> *In these times of blight and bling*
> *When our very pride is playing hide and seek*
> *And chaos reigns over everything?*

While 'times of blight' seems to refer immediately to the unhealthy condition of West Indian cricket, a glance beyond the boundary indicates that the phrase can and must also refer to the economic downturn crippling the islands and negatively impacting the West Indian game. The related 'bling' refers immediately to the practice of West Indian cricketers sporting multiple chains and other accessories on the playing field, a malpractice deplored by Michael Holding on international television, but it also refers to the gross displays of ostentatious consumerism flaunted in the face of a growing mass poverty in the islands. Against this background the West Indian cricket defiance of Australia against all odds offers the hope that:

> *the genius man can build a clan*
> *That would step into the light*
> *And every mother and father, Caribbean leader*
> *Can turn round and start to make things right.*

Warriorhood, the central feature of Caribbean cricketing identity, is either present in or is the central theme of 'Rally,' 'Here Comes the West Indies,' 'It's a West Indian Thing (Bounce),' 'Legacy,' 'Steel,' 'Bankie's Son,' 'Champions,' and 'Lifted,' to present the songs in the chronological order of issue. 'Legacy,' first appearing on Rudder's 1996 album *Lyrics Man*, opens with a powerful affirmation of how Rudder perceives the cricket warrior/hero:

> *I thank God that in my life and time*
> *That I have known these men*
> *Confirming and reconfirming my Caribbean energy*
> *Striding to the centre*
> *With their arrogant beauty*
> *Every blur of red and flashing blade means so much to you and me.*

'Legacy' stresses the continuity of cricketing tradition and reaffirms the deep-seated hope that Rudder harbours for West Indian

(WI) cricket and, by necessary extension, for the future of the region:

> *And even as I speak a child is born in our islands*
> *His shoulders so broad they had to take him out by the way of Caesar*
> *A frightening thought to those bewildered knights*
> *Who stand in the way of our destiny*
> *Today they think it's hard*
> *Well tomorrow is harder.*

Here, the phrase 'those bewildered knights/ who stand in the way of our destiny' echoes that warning of 'Rally' about the unidentified cricket lords who, in the 1980s set about 'making restrictions and laws to spoil our beauty'; here, too, there is the optimism first voiced in 'Rally' that 'we shall prevail', a hope later realized to some extent in 'Bankie's Son.'

All of the immediately foregoing directs our attention to the significance of intertextuality which functions as the major operational principle in *The Cricket Chronicles*. The inter-referencing of songs elaborating the same themes and the continual echoing of theme, thought and in some cases phrase are structural elements of the collection's architecture. 'Smiling Eyes of Steel' and 'Champions' are emblematic of the Rudder meta/phorical design which manifests in *Chronicles*. These songs develop and elaborate the collection's major themes in a language that is self-consciously poetic.

Stanza 1 of 'Steel' is suffused with the religious overtones testifying to the link between spirituality and cricket which is also present in Earl Lovelace's 1996 novel *Salt*. In this novel Bango, who lives the gospel of healing of the nation from its terrible past, first appears to Myrtle, his future wife, looking in his cricket whites 'more like a young Shango priest than the cricketer he was' (136). In 'Steel' Rudder develops the cricket-spirituality link by implication:

> *One more brother of this life of cricket*
> *He has passed away*
> *One more disciple has left our yard, my people*
> *For a brighter day.*

The phrase 'brother of this life of cricket' suggests that Marshall was a member of the religious order dedicated to internationalizing the gospel of West Indian cricket; his passing is his leaving this life for 'a brighter day', the spiritual reward for his dedication.

Stanza 2 of 'Steel' represents cricket as the ultimate cohesive in the Anglophone Caribbean as the narrator marvels at cricket's wonderful power of attraction:

> *Who would have ever thought that a ball of leather*
> *Could move a people so*
> *Who could have ever dreamed that a piece of willow*
> *Could make emotions flow...and flow*
>
> *Farewell, mighty warrior*
> *Thanks for the memory*
> *Thanks for the joy*
> *Farewell, and godspeed, my brother*
> *Thanks for the rapture*
> *Thanks for the joy.*

C.L.R. James, the Afro-Saxon colonial, describes the ne'er-do-well Matthew Bondman as 'my first acquaintance with that genus Britannicus, a fine batsman, and the impact that he makes on all around him, non-cricketers and cricketers alike' (14). Rudder, who reads West Indian cricket as active resistance to the imperialistic tradition of Rule Britannia, has an entirely different frame of reference. In his choruses he locates Marshall in the romantic tradition of warrior hero and cricket hero:

> *Farewell, mighty warrior*
> *Thanks for the memory*
> *Thanks for the joy*
> *Farewell, mighty warrior*
> *Thanks for the memory*
> *Thanks for the joy*
> *Our joy, our joy, our joy.*

This figuring of Marshall as warrior echoes a similar representation of Michael Holding in 'Rally.' In the opening stanza of that song Rudder establishes a connection between the heroism of Tousasaint and Dessalines and the romance of the modern day cricketing heroes; this connection is reinforced by the fact that 'Rally' appears on the album *Haiti*. In 'Bankie's Son' the phrase 'a rebel's spark' references Rudder's description of Toussaint in 'Haiti' and that tradition of active resistance, the burning of the canefield that is traditionally the first sign that the enslaved have defied the depersonalization demanded by the plantation system and are reclaiming personhood.

Stanza 3 of 'Steel' exalts Marshall even higher than warrior:

You're descended from a line of kings
Men of speed and feel
With your smile that hides the pending thunder
Smiling eyes of steel...steel.

The references to royal descent and to the pending thunder immediately suggest that Rudder is linking Marshall imaginatively to Shango, Yoruba god of thunder, who is represented in most scholarly literature as a deification of an early Yoruba alafin who was conflated with Jakuta god of thunder. Afro-Caribbean religions, and specifically the Spiritual Shouter Baptist faith and Orisa worship, form part of Rudder's Black Atlantic and provide theme, ritual and rhythm for several of his calypsoes including 'The Hammer,' 'Bahia Gyal,' 'Erzulie' and 'Shango Electric.'

As if in re-affirmation of the poetic link between cricket and religion established in Stanza 1, 'Steel' reiterates the first stanza and ends with an attenuated 'farewell'. That final 'thanks for the memory, thanks for the joy' is the parting salute to a life which ennobled the region and inspirited its people.

'Champions,' composed for *Chronicles*, expands on the twin ideas of cricket as the unifier of the Caribbean and of the cricketers as the heroes of the Anglophone Caribbean:

There's a time in our lives
When a country forgets its woes and just lives and lives
Life, in its joy
And the oneness of which we dream is now ours to give

Chorus
Champions take our dreams, and make us all immortal
We dance, we cry, we scream, we see beyond the portal...of doom

2 Winners wield mighty wings
So we can all float above our everyday blue rhythms
Now we walk with kings
Through the ups and downs, but now all is so forgiven

Chorus

> *Champions take our dreams and make us all immortal*
> *We dance, we cry, we scream, we see and we are now immortal.*

In the Rudderian worldview the Anglophone or cricket-playing Caribbean is 'a country' and 'a people', as he sings in 'Steel.' In this worldview, the trans-island entity has been created by the fact that our cricketing champions have materalized our dreams of oneness and made us see beyond 'the portal of doom', a phrase which may represent the horror of the past and the 'everyday blue rhythms' of the present. Rudder sublimates the cricketing heroes into the source of the immortality enjoyed by all whom they represent and symbolically extends this idea into the future by the use of a chorus of children's voices that echo significant phrases and words. Then he restates stanza one before proceeding to the final stanza:

> *We are proud in our hearts*
> *Our heroes have brought us joy and we're so uplifted*
> *We walk in their path*
> *From the lonely streets to the halls of the great and gifted*
>
> *Champions take our dreams and make us all immortal*
> *We touch the face of God and we are now immortal*
> *Champions take our dreams and make us all immortal*
> *We dance, we cry, we scream, and we are now immortal.*

He ends by repeating the final exhortations to the public, 'Fly', 'Walk like a champion, Ah tell yuh walk like a champion, you are a champion.' Almost inevitably, this last reminds us of the passage in 'Legacy,' to wit,

> *And even as I speak*
> *a young man walks in our islands*
> *with a fire in his eyes and the cool of a champion's swagger.*

In this worldview the rapture of the cricket experience is continuously reborn on the playing field for the edification of the West Indian public.

Although West Indian cricket has been a theme for calypso for over 100 years (see Gordon Rohlehr's brilliant essay 'Calypso, Literature and West Indian Cricket'), there is nothing like Rudder's *The Cricket Chronicles* for imaginative engagement with the psychosocial dimension of the game. *The Cricket Chronicles*, an album featuring several song styles and a wide range from calypso to R&B, is an invaluable archive for those seeking to understand the complex relationships between music and society. By 2007 when *Chronicles* was published, however, Rudder was perceived by some as being out of touch with his primary audience. The metaphorical and even metaphysical quality of his poetry, his inward stretch, to borrow from Rex Nettleford (1992), leads him into creating new metaphors to describe the common reality; paradoxically this alienates him from those primary intended targets of his outward reach, those audiences who are not competent to do or comfortable with the imaginative work that he assigns us. As happens universally with creatives who are way ahead of their time, Rudder's paradigm-altering artistry challenges the unwritten codes and restrictive expectations of the popular art form in which he operates.

All things considered, however, the only explanation for the neglect of *The Cricket Chronicles* – and for most of Rudder's work – is the bizarre and incomprehensible mindset that separates the Trinidadian calypso year into two unequal parts. In the fevered carnival period, promoters of soca-driven inclusives colonize radio with dancehall soca spasms hectoring us to a mechanized frenzy, while the traditional calypso is becoming more lachrymose, or more stridently partisan, more didactic and preachy, less entertaining and less appealing; in the post-carnival calm, media managers and gatekeepers assume that the public does not want to hear calypso-soca and the nation as a whole, vocal on matters of far less importance, submits passively to this 'thinking'. Given this situation, therefore, Rudder runs the undeserved risk of being written off as irrelevant and reduced to the liminal position of in-zile, an exile in his homeland.

Notes
1. In footnote 55 to the essay 'Where Is Here?' (2007), Gordon Rohlehr writes: 'Inzile is a word coined (?) used by Trinidadian poet James Christopher Aboud, author of *Lagahoo Poems*, who spoke at the 25th Anniversary Conference on West Indian Literature (UWI, Trinidad, March 4, 2006) of his sense of being an exile within the country of his birth. 'I am an inzile, not an exile,' he said. (*Transgression, Transition, Transformation* 504).
2. Picong is an umbrella term for terms ranging from gentle banter to caustic satire. Richard Allsopp defines mépris as 'bad talk that is openly meant to cause harm' (379).

Works cited:
Allsopp, Richard, ed. *Dictionary of Caribbean English Usage*. Oxford: Oxford University Press, 1996.
Gilroy, Paul. *The Black Atlantic: Modernity and Double Consciousness*. Cambridge, MA: Harvard, 1993.
Gershwin Stephen. 'Rudder: No time tag on my music.' *TNT Mirror,* January 10, 1989, 29.
James, C.L.R. *Beyond a Boundary*. London: Stanley Paul, 1963.
Lovelace, Earl. *Salt*. London: Faber, 1996
Nettleford, Rex. *Inward Stretch, Outward Reach: A Voice from the Caribbean*. London: Macmillan, 1992.
Rohlehr, Gordon. 'Calypso, Literature and West Indian Cricket. In *Transgression, Transition, Transformation: Essays in Caribbean Culture*, 334–437. San Juan, Trinidad: Lexicon, 2007.
———. 'Where Is Here? What Jail Is This? Who Are We?' In *Transgression, Transition, Transformation: Essays in Caribbean Culture*, 457–507. San Juan, Trinidad: Lexicon, 2007.
Rudder, David. *The Brand New Lucky Diamond Horseshoe Club*. Lypsoland: CR038.
———. *Calypso Music*. Lypsoland: CR 06, 1987.
———. *The Cricket Chronicles*. Lypsoland: CT039, 2007.
———. *The Hammer*. Lypsoland: CR-05, 1986.
———. *Haiti*. Lypsoland ; CR-008, Barbados, 1988.
———. *International Chantuelle*. Lypsoland: CR 029, 1999.
Singh Valentino, 'Singing was my only vice.' *Sunday Guardian Magazine*, January 25, 1987. http://www.espncricinfo.com/ci/content/story/210445.html.

CHAPTER 11

The Current Calypso Music Scene in Trinidad and its Outlook: The Perspective of an International Follower of the Genre

Urs Berger

Every year the carnival season brings an explosion of musical activity in Trinidad and Tobago. Hundreds of calypsos are composed and performed in calypso tents, in anticipation of the competition to win the prestigious calypso monarch title on the night of the Dimanche Gras[1] show, on the Sunday before Ash Wednesday and the start of the Christian Lenten season. The subject matter for calypsos ranges from social commentary about previous year's events or topical life stories to simple party music. I have been a fan of calypso for more than 30 years and have observed marked changes in the availability of calypso recordings and the business practices over these years. This paper describes these observations. I have made these observations strictly as a fan. I am neither involved in the calypso business nor am I a calypso scholar. I grew up in Europe in Switzerland and was exposed to calypso music initially by listening to a radio show on Caribbean music in 1982. I subsequently grew into a fan of this music after a move to Baltimore, Maryland in the United States (US) for graduate studies, where I was again heavily influenced by a local radio show that played all the newest calypso tunes. I have amassed over these 30 years a sizable collection of several thousand items, and have a good overview of the development of this music.

History of calypso music recordings and their availability

An in-depth description of the history of calypso is beyond the scope of this article, and can be found in other resources (Rohlehr, Guilbault 21–38). Here, I will point out some major milestones for this unique music style. First, calypso is a relatively old genre of popular music whose recording history had already begun by 1912. Second, calypso is generally considered to be a major influence on the development of reggae music in Jamaica, whose international popularity has eclipsed that of calypso several times over (see O'Brien Chang 14). Third, for a short period in the 1950s, calypso was among the most popular musical genres around the world when the recording of 'Day-O' by Harry Belafonte led to the first million-selling album in history. Fourth, several songs based on calypso have become international hits, starting with 'Rum and Coca Cola' by Lord Invader in the '40s, 'Jean and Dinah' by Mighty Sparrow in the '50s, and Arrow's 'Hot, Hot, Hot' in the '80s, as well as 'Who Let The Dogs Out' by Anslem Douglas (in the cover version by the Baha Men) in the late '90s. Finally, apart from its influence on reggae, calypso has spawned several other popular music styles, including soca, rapso, chutney and ragga (Serwer).

As with any other genre of popular music, calypso has been available for most of the last century on analog shellac and vinyl discs, be it 78, 33, or 45 rpm discs in 12', 10' or 7' editions. Starting in the late 80s, Compact Discs (CDs) with calypso music have been issued, and more recently digital files have become available on online download sites. The production of vinyl discs of calypso music stopped around 2000. Throughout the years, there were several record labels that specialized in calypso in Trinidad and Tobago as well as the other major Trinidadian expatriate centres in New York, London and Toronto. Names for these record labels included SaGomes, Vitadisc, Balisier and Cook records in the '50s, RCA Victor, National and Telco in the '60s, Straker's, Charlie's, Camille, Village, Antillana and Semp in the '70s, and B's and JW in the '80s and '90s (see websites calypsography. com or discogs.com).

For the most part, calypso has been a singles-market, starting with the 78s in pre- and post-war times, the 7' singles that appeared in the mid-50s, the 33 and 45 rpm 12' singles that began in the '70s, and the more recent digital downloads of the yearly calypsos. Only the most successful calypsonians, including the Mighty Sparrow, Lord Melody and Lord Kitchener had yearly album-length releases starting in the late '50s. During the '60s, the songs of other calypsonians were sometimes compiled on Long Playing Phonograph Records (LPs), and every now and then, 'minor' singers also put out LP collections, such as Mighty Bomber or Young Killer. This began to change in the '70s, when more and more calypsonians started to release albums every year. The list of such calypsonians included Calypso Rose, Mighty Duke, Lord Shorty, Lord Nelson in Trinidad and Tobago, as well as Lord Short Shirt and Swallow in Antigua, and Arrow in Montserrat, among others.

Coincidentally with this popularity of calypso in the '70s, the musical accompaniment, which had primarily consisted of either traditional string bands or brass bands using traditional calypso rhythms, began to change. Arrangers like Ed Watson started to incorporate foreign rhythms like reggae, soul, and disco (Towne O'Neill). Lord Shorty experimented with the incorporation of traditional Indian beats into calypso, and the establishment of multi-track recording and the appearance of synthesizers further modernized the music (Towne O'Neill). By the end of the decade, a new hybrid was born in the form of soca (initially termed 'Sokah' by Lord Shorty), a more uptempo form that placed more emphasis on musicality and danceability than the calypso of old.

International Success of Calypso and Soca in the 1980s

By the start of the '80s, calypso was ready to conquer the world again, and the next decade turned out to be its most successful. The party hit 'Don't Stop The Carnival' by Swallow and then the international smash 'Hot, Hot, Hot' by Arrow in 1982 pushed calypso onto the international stage. This promoted the emergence of better distribution networks, which made it easier to find calypso in Europe. Also, a number of very talented musical arrangers, including Leston Paul, Frankie McIntosh and Pelham Goddard, pushed the musical development forward, and, together with the songwriting talents of Mighty Sparrow, Lord Kitchener, Mighty Duke, Chalkdust, Black Stalin, Calypso Rose, David Rudder, Merchant, Winsford Devines and Gregory Ballantyne, hit after hit was created. Most calypsonians now were able to release full-length or extended-play albums every year. The covers for these albums were mostly designed by the artiste Errol Dopwell, making them immediately identifiable for the distinct music genre that they represented. All this musical creativity, together with the increasing popularity of steelpan music, attracted more and more international visitors to join the yearly carnival celebrations in Trinidad and Tobago, and supported a thriving calypso records industry.

The 1990s – A Decade of Change

The success of calypso in the '80s continued for a few more years into the '90s, but then things began to change, as a result of several factors. First of all, the more uptempo soca style of calypso, which had existed side by side with the slower traditional calypso, came into its own. Soca hits like 'Free Up' by Tambu and 'Get Something and Wave' by Superblue were wildly successful, and a new generation of young artistes emerged that focused primarily on soca. Soca music also started to incorporate influences from other islands and new hybrids were created. Thus, dancehall dub style from Jamaica became very popular in Trinidad and Tobago and eventually mixed with soca in the ragga soca style. Indian chutney music made inroads and fused into chutney soca, and during Christmas season, the traditional string based music parang picked up the soca beat to form parang soca. Rapso, a mix of rap and calypso, and Bajan soca (a somewhat different interpretation of the soca beat, also referred to as the Bajan invasion) also started to become more popular ('Bajan' is shorthand for Barbadian, see Serwer). All these changes resulted in soca becoming the more dominant style for younger fans, and the older more laid-back calypso style was relegated back to the tents.

A second formative factor in the '90s was the switch from vinyl albums to compact discs as carrier of choice for the music. Initially, when CDs first appeared, most calypso artistes had stayed with vinyl to release their music, but now the public had switched to compact disc players to play music and expected to buy compact discs. The CD had about twice the capacity as a vinyl LP and this created a problem for a calypsonian who usually had two to four new songs available to record every year. Whereas a vinyl 12' was well suited to issue a couple of songs, a compact disc single with only two songs was not successful, probably because initially the pressing of CDs was relatively expensive, and in general, compact discs were sold at a premium price compared to vinyl. Record labels correctly assumed that fans were not willing to pay relatively high prices for CDs with few songs. In any case, a singles market for calypso, as it had existed for vinyl 7' or 12' singles, did not materialize. The obvious solution to this problem is, of course, to create collection CDs with the new songs, but this did not happen to an appreciable extent for calypso. Only one or two collection CDs appeared per year with the most successful songs and so in the '90s it became harder to collect the yearly calypsos.

A third event that shaped the calypso music industry in the '90s was that Eddy Grant, the internationally successful reggae artiste, signed up the cream of the crop of calypso artistes to his Ice Records label (Scaramuzzo). Superblue, Mighty Sparrow, Mighty Duke, Black Stalin, Calypso Rose, as well as Roaring Lion all recorded full-length albums for Ice Records starting in 1994. Eddy Grant's arrangements were creative and led to some exciting original music, particularly his two albums with the Roaring Lion. Ice Records was partnering with the internationally renowned reggae label Real Authentic Sound (RAS) records, and enjoyed excellent international distribution for several years. Eddy Grant also bought up the rights to most of the back catalog of calypso music, and he pushed for worldwide acceptance of calypso and soca (Scaramuzzo).

However, the excitement fizzled after two to three years, be it for lack of sales or other factors, and by 1997 only Rose and Duke were still affiliated with Grant. They released a few more albums over the next several years with Eddy Grant (Rose had another full length album in 1999, and Duke had albums in 1997, 1999 and 2003, and both appeared on a various artistes compilation in 1998). During this time when Ice Records had the biggest calypso stars under contract, the other major calypso labels produced fewer and fewer albums with new music and instead seemed to focus on reissuing the hits from their back catalog on CDs. By the end of the '90s, major stars like Black Stalin had to issue their music on small local labels that had no international distribution and were impossible to find outside Trinidad and Tobago.

The final factor causing changes in the calypso market was, of course, the digital revolution in the music industry and the emergence of the World Wide Web. Compact disc burning technology, mp3 file creation, cheap storage capacity and peer-to-peer file sharing networks all allowed calypso fans to easily rip their CDs and share them over the Internet. As it was now possible to make a perfect copy of a CD, rampant piracy developed, CD sales took a big hit, and record stores closed. Thus, by the end of the 90s, the calypso market, like the popular music business in general, was struggling with the loss of sales and distribution.

Calypso Music Releases on CD

The number of albums of new calypsos declined in the '90s, but the number of compilations and retrospectives (the latter popularly referred to in Trinidad and Tobago as retro, precisely because they reissued older music) skyrocketed. There was a whole series of Soca Gold CDs that collected the most successful songs from the '80s. There were retrospective compilations by Ice Records for the Mighty Sparrow,

Lord Kitchener, Lord Melody and Lord Invader that made available songs that were hard to find up to that point. Also, new labels emerged, such as Electro Sounds, which issued new soca as well as music from the '60s and '70s from more obscure calypsonians, or Rituals Records, which focused on new artistes in the rapso genre. Mighty Sparrow himself used the CD to release almost his whole catalog dating back to 1956 in 40 themed collection CDs. Other labels like JW/M&M Minor focused on collections for the yearly songs written for the steel band, while Carotte focused on live recordings of calypso. Finally, online record stores were appearing that made the ordering and buying of calypso music CDs much easier than before. No longer did you have to trek to Brooklyn to get the newest albums; you could just order them on your computer.

Thanks to all the CD reissues, an unparalleled amount of calypso music was accessible by the late '90s, but the changes caused by the digital revolutions soon led to the collapse of the calypso market after the turn of the millennium. Record stores closed, distribution networks folded and music labels disappeared. For a while, online websites, like eCaroh.com, or Musicrama.com, that sold calypso CDs soldiered on, but by the mid 2000s they folded as well. The technology company Apple finally developed a legal way to purchase music in the iTunes store, but they did not offer new calypso tracks (and still don't). Instead, the website Trinidadmusicstore.com opened around 2007, which allowed the download of some new calypsos. Artistes like Crazy, Sugar Aloes and King Luta participated and offered their music, but there were a lot of other calypsonians who did not. It is likely that they thought that the low price of 99 cents per song was not worth it, and that it would just lead to more piracy. After a few years, the Trinidadmusicstore changed its business model to a subscription basis (on the TrinidadTunes website), where with a monthly fee it was possible to listen to any track in the store before purchasing. This new approach, however, also did not last, and the TrinidadTunes website disappeared early in 2016.

Current Availability of New Calypso Songs

With the disappearance of national record store chains and the failure of online sites, it has become difficult to buy the yearly crop of calypsos. Only a few seasoned veterans like Chalkdust, Gypsy or Exposer still issue full-length albums with any regularity. Sometimes the new CDs are offered by the Trinidad-based Rhyners.com online, but mostly if you wish to purchase new calypsos in the US, you again have to go to Brooklyn and check whether Charlie's, Straker's, Hometown Music or JW Records has a copy.

A big caveat of buying new calypso albums, however, which has crystallized over the last decade, is that one rarely gets all new songs on a new album. It has become relatively common that on a new album that has eight to ten tracks, only about two or three songs are really new. The rest is more often than not recycled from previous albums, as has happened in 2017 with the albums by Gypsy, Chalkdust, and Exposer. This approach, which may be fine for the casual music-buying tourist, makes buying the new music unnecessarily expensive for the serious collector.

One can hear the new tunes on online radio from Trinidad and Tobago or look for them on YouTube, which has some of the new songs. In 2016 and 2017 clips of the Dimanche Gras and Kaisorama shows were uploaded to YouTube almost instantaneously. ITunes recently started to offer the back catalog of various soca and calypso labels, but not the new songs. Apart from it being a major effort for calypsonians to understand the requirements to sell their music on iTunes, it may simply not be very interesting financially for them to do so, considering the limited number of calypso fans and the big cut that iTunes takes. There is also a website called panonthenet.com that focuses on the yearly crop of pan songs; it offers the songs for listening but not for purchasing. Luckily, more and more video recordings of the calypso tent shows have become available on Digital Video Discs (DVDs), which are sold by the website sensay.com and others. This makes it still possible to keep up with the developments in calypso music.

Current Availability of the Back Catalog of Calypso Music and Copyright Issues

As mentioned earlier, the back catalogs for some labels like JW records, Charlie's Records, Rituals and others have finally become available in digital form on iTunes. All of Mighty Sparrow's 40 reissue CDs are also available as well as the pan CDs by Major&Minor and all the various releases by Rounder, Arhoolie and Cook Records that featured early calypsos. This makes accessible an unprecedented number of calypsos. However, a probably even larger amount of music has never been reissued and is waiting in limbo. In the early 90s, when he made a push to internationalize soca and calypso, Eddy Grant also bought up the rights for a lot of the calypso labels dating back to the mid-1930s (Scaramuzzo). He apparently planned to reissue all this music, but this has not yet happened. After he had reissued music from the Mighty Sparrow, Lord Kitchener, Lord Melody, Mighty Terror, Roaring Lion and additional compilations of other artists, the reissue programme stopped about 20 years ago. The reasons for this remain unclear; perhaps the original tapes were unsuitable or destroyed, or it would have been too expensive to master recordings from vinyl transfers. In the late '90s another label, Electro Sounds, tried to issue some of the artistes' works to which Grant owned the rights, but those releases disappeared after a while, which indicates that they did not have Grant's permission. Thus, the only way currently to hear some great calypso tracks from, for example, the '60s is to hunt down the original issues on eBay for exorbitant prices, or sometimes they can be found on YouTube (at wildly varying quality).

Some calypso fans have become fed up with the stalemate around calypso reissues and have taken matters in their own hands. Thus, an outfit called 'Radiophone Archives' is offering on iTunes the Lord Kitchener back catalog (Eldrige), and Irwin Chusid from 'Muriel's Treasure website' is selling compilations of calypsos on iTunes that he played on his radio show (murielstreasure.blogspot.com). These apparent infringements suggest that iTunes, or other online music download sites, are not taking copyright law very seriously, and that, as always, the onus falls on the calypsonians or the copyright holder to make any claims against infringements. Similar to iTunes, YouTube's offer makes YouTube a great resource for calypso fans and researchers, but it again tramples the rights of the artistes, and only benefits the uploaders (by making money on the ads) and YouTube. Unfortunately, calypso artists have been taken advantage of for a long time, starting with the suit that Lord Invader had to bring to get credit for and income from his chart-topping hit 'Rum and Coca Cola,' which had been plagiarized by popular entertainer Morey Amsterdam and popularized by the Andrews Sisters in the US (Burke). Calypsonians for the most part sold their rights to the songs to the labels at the time of recording, and the labels did not feel obligated to pay the them for subsequent sales. That is why the calypsonian Chalkdust finally stopped his collaboration with Straker's Records in the mid-2000s, after more than 30 years of releasing his albums on that label (Chalkdust, personal discussion Feb 2016).

Rampant CD piracy is still an issue for both soca and calypso artists in both Trinidad and Tobago and the US. In Trinidad, street vendors offer copied CDs or their own compilation mixes, without much impediment. I recently heard the prominent soca artiste Tony Prescott talk on Wack Radio (a radio station in San Fernando, Trinidad), about how he had been ridiculed by a pirate vendor outside a concert show. The pirate said he could sell many more CDs than Prescott, and nobody tried to stop him. In the US, the few remaining local record stores sometimes offer Disc Jockey (DJ) mixed CDs or they make their own compilations, all with questionable copyrights. All this seems to happen with the complete absence of law enforcement. Calypsonians are not in a position to hire lawyers and to enforce the laws, and they do not seem to get any help from their organizations. Therefore, it seems that they have resigned themselves to the current situation, and hope that they can make some money by selling CDs directly to the fans, either at shows or online on Facebook (for example, the calypsonian D'Juiceman did so before he passed away earlier in 2017) or on websites (Kurt Allen tried this on kurtallen.net for a while in 2016).

Current International Prospects of Calypso Music

Calypso music saw international success in the 1950s as well as the 1980s. Nowadays, though, there seems to be a debate every year about whether calypso music is dead or not. I have no doubt that calypso as an art form will survive, at least locally in the Caribbean, but it is questionable whether this music can again attract large international audiences. As the older generation of artistes passes on, the younger generation has not been able yet to successfully step in and carry the calypso mantle of heroes like Mighty Sparrow, Lord Kitchener, Lord Melody or Lord Invader. There is no shortage of talented young artistes around Trinidad, and the calypso art form is widely supported through instruction and competitions at primary schools. However, exceptional songwriters like the calypsonians of old are few and far between.

From my fan point of view, I would like to put forward the following suggestions that might be helpful in making this music successful on the international stage again. First, as an outsider it is difficult to find information about the new songs that have been issued. Nowadays, notwithstanding, it would be easy to create a central repository of information that interested fans could access. One approach could be that the artistes submit their information to a website, and then fans could get the information either via this website or a phone app. Second, an archive with information about calypso through the years would be very valuable. Fans could get information about previous songs of an artiste they like, and possibly information about where to buy the music.

Third, the quality of the musical arrangements of current calypso songs varies widely. To save money on recording costs, calypsonians nowadays record their songs in their home studios with limited instrumentation and at times inferior sound quality. To make an impression on the international stage, it would be helpful to have the assistance of professional musicians available for the recordings, potentially with a government supported studio. As a case in point, Calypso Rose recently received a French Grammy for her 2016 album on which she collaborated with the popular French-born arranger and musician Manu Chao (McCallister).

Fourth, calypsonians should realize that back-filling new albums with recycled old songs only hurts their reputation in the long run. It would be better if they could collaborate and issue their songs together on a CD. Fifth, it would be helpful if calypso music was no longer tied so strongly to carnival time, when several hundred songs are vying for the attention of the public in a short span of time between Christmas and Ash Wednesday. Since it is only required that a calypso has been composed after Ash Wednesday of the previous year to qualify for each carnival competition, perhaps it might be possible to release and play new calypsos more often during the fall so that songs can find a bigger audience.

Finally, there needs to be some sort of 'fair trade' calypso download website where fair payment to the artistes is emphasized and encouraged. Possibly, the maintenance of such a site could be supported by grants so that the calypsonians would receive as much payment for their work as possible. Such a site would need to be widely advertised and supported, particularly at the calypso tent shows, so that the visitors will know where they can get their calypsos.

In conclusion, Trinidadian calypso music is still alive and doing well locally but it will take a concerted effort to put it back on an international stage. The sweet sounds of Trinidad and Tobago should be heard once again around the world.

Note
1. Dimanche Gras (Fat Sunday), emerging from the French roots of Trinidad's carnival, is a competition that is held on Carnival Sunday. On this night, the calypso monarch as well as the King and Queen of the bands are ordinarily crowned.

Works Cited

Burke, Kevin. 'The Rum and Coca Cola Reader.' *Rumandcocacolareader.com*, http://www.rumandcocacolareader.com/RumAndCocaCola/main.html. Accessed March 2, 2017.

Eldrige, Michael. 'Ol' Time Calypso Come Back Again, Part 1.' *Yankeedollar*, https://yankeedollar.wordpress.com/2012/05/21/ol-time-calypso-come-back-again-part-1/. Accessed on March 29, 2017.

Guilbault, Jocelyn. *Governing Sound: The Cultural Politics of Trinidad's Carnival Music*. Chicago, IL: University of Chicago Press, 2007.

McCallister, Jared. 'CARIBBEAT: Trinidad and Tobago's Calypso Rose gets a French Toast in Paris for her award-winning latest album.' *NYDailyNews.com*, http://www.nydailynews.com/new-york/caribbeat-french-toast-calypso-rose-article-1.2970160. Accessed on April 22, 2017.

O'Brien Chang, Kevin, and Wayne Chen. *Reggae Routes: The Story of Jamaican Music*. Philadelphia, PA: Temple University Press, 1998.

Roehler, Gordon. *Calypso and Society in Pre-Independence Trinidad*. Port-of-Spain, Trinidad: Gordon Roehler, 1990: chapters 1–9.

Scaramuzzo, Gene. 'Hot Ice.' *The Beat Magazine* 12, no. 3 (1993): 30.

Serwer, Jesse. 'The Essential Guide To Soca.' *Redbullmusicacademy*, http://daily.redbullmusicacademy.com/2017/03/soca-guide. Accessed March 29, 2017.

Towne O'Neill, Connor. 'Ras Shorty I: The Soul Of Calypso.' *Redbullmusicacademy*, http://daily.redbullmusicacademy.com/2016/06/ras-shorty-i-the-soul-of-calypso. Accessed March 29, 2017.

Part IV: Challenging Cultural Assumptions – The Research X-Change

Research X-Change Introduction

Milla Cozart Riggio

In academic conferences, scholars typically share their research – through papers, panel discussions, plenary addresses, conversations – with other scholars, or sometimes the general public, often reinforced by artistic performances or exhibitions. In the *Turning Tides Conference*, Sunity Maharaj-Best and Milla Cozart Riggio introduced the Research X-Change to move proceedings beyond the ivory tower of academia and into the world where scholarly exchange could produce actual change. As the name suggests, the purpose of the Research X-Change was to bring together scholars and activists who had never met before, not to report on existing research but to initiate new shared ventures.

The Research X-Change generated eight 90-minute sessions: 'Artists Talk,' a conversation between Peter Minshall and Anida Yoeu Ali; 'Genders without Borders,' a workshop convened by Dr. Brunhild Kring to focus cross-culturally on Lesbian, Gay, Bisexual, Transgender and Queer (LGBTQ) issues; 'Memory Disorders: Culturally Influenced?' organized by Professor Sarah Raskin of Trinity College and her Trinidadian neuroscience student Consuelo Pedro; 'Public Archeology: Cultural Heritages and their Preservation,' proposed by Professor Martha Risser of Trinity College; 'Caribbean Conceptions of Blackness,' convened by Prof. Maurice Wade (Trinity College), which was merged with 'Racial Stereotypes in British and Trinidad Music,' proposed by NYU graduate student Julian Waddell; 'The Caribbean: A New Mediterranean and other Stereotypes,' convened by Profs. Gary Reger (Trinity College) and Gordon Rohlehr (UWI, Emeritus Professor); and 'Pan-Africanism and Pan-Asianism,' proposed by Prof. Jeffrey Bayliss (Trinity College specialist in Japanese history). Each Research X-Change workshop brought together varied pairings of artists, researchers, scholars, and activists from the United States and Trinidad and Tobago, meeting for the first time. Two of the eight sessions are represented elsewhere in this volume: Gary Reger's Part I essay and the 'Artists Talk' in Part V.

The two essays included in this section embody different aspects of what we hoped the Research X-Change could be. 'Genders without Borders' (Dr. Kring and Prof. Greenberg, with a statement by Dr. Gerard Hutchinson of UWI) reflects the complex interaction – the 'difficult conversation' – that occurs when doctors, scholars, and trained activists from different cultures must reconcile their disparate assumptions before they can begin a productive conversation about gender, in itself an invaluable guide to bridging cultural divides. 'Culture and Memory in the Caribbean' (Alea [Albada], Khan, Pedro and Raskin) illustrates how culturally-specific research can be generated through new encounters – creating change through ex-change.

CHAPTER 12

Gender Without Borders
Special Session: Research X-Change Workshop – LGBTQ Students and Communities

Brunhild Kring and Cheryl Greenberg

The format of a Research X-Change workshop is original and intriguing. Papers given at academic conferences typically are the culmination of the presenters' research and the endpoint of their scholarly work on a given topic. By contrast, contributors to a Research X-Change explore the beginnings of a research endeavour. Such a work group is open to people who have not previously collaborated and may be unfamiliar with each other. What unites them is the shared interest in a scholarly focus and the wish to take advantage of ad hoc opportunities for interdisciplinary discussion. The format of the Research X-Change workshop elicits an active stance, promotes a lively interchange, and inspires participants to articulate and refine their research questions. Under the best of circumstances, the exchange can generate future collaboration.

This ninety-minute session attracted participants from the United States (US) and Trinidad and Tobago of diverse academic and social backgrounds. It resulted in the kind of difficult but ultimately productive conversation that ensues when people with different assumptions attempt to converse in good faith with each other about a highly sensitive topic for the first time. This report attempts both to chronicle and define the nature of that conversation and, at the same time, to place it within the context of existing research into psychological and legal issues relating to gender variance phenomena in the Americas.

Sex and Gender

Topics pertaining to lesbian, gay, bisexual, transgender, queer (LGBTQ) issues, and sexuality in the widest sense of the word, often stimulate controversy. The terms gay, lesbian, bisexual and transgender are widely used and accepted. The meaning of the word *queer* is more ambiguous, and calls for an explanation of its history and context. *Queer* used to be a slang term for homosexuals applied with pejorative and abusive intent. However, in the 1980s, gender scholars began reclaiming the word as an affirmative umbrella term for gays, lesbians, bisexuals and other gender minorities. *Queer* is also used to describe unconventional erotic practices such as bondage, discipline, dominance and sadomasochism (BDSM). The 'Q' in LGTBQ additionally refers to those who are *questioning gender.*

Human sexual behaviour has been analysed and described through the lenses of different academic disciplines, ranging from biology, medicine, neuroscience, psychology, cultural and gender studies, history, anthropology, to the law and the arts. The American Psychological Association provides several glossaries explaining the differences between sex, gender, transgender, sexual orientation, and intersex conditions; the definition of these terms is based on consensus statements by leading biologists and sexologists and serves as an invaluable common frame of reference for any interdisciplinary and cross-cultural discussion. The following discussion is anchored in excerpts from topical pamphlets published by the American Psychological Association: 'Sex refers to biological status as male or female. It includes physical attributes such as sex chromosomes, gonads, sex hormones, internal reproductive structures, and external genitalia. Gender is a term that is often used to refer to ways that people act, interact, or feel about themselves, which are associated with boys/men and girls/women. While aspects of biological sex are the same across different cultures, aspects of gender may not be' (American Psychological Association, 2006b).

This thoughtfully worded, programmatic statement harks back to the classical research by John Money and Anke Ehrhardt. These sexologists endorsed the idea that sex and gender are separate categories. They further differentiated between gender role and gender identity. In summary, 'gender role is the public expression of gender identity, and gender identity is the private experience of gender role' (Money 4).

Contemporary developmental neuroscientists further elaborate on this observation. They confirm that the internal sexual structures and the external genitalia of the fetus differentiate into male or female under the influence of fetal hormones in the first trimester of pregnancy. By contrast, the sexual differentiation of the brain of the growing fetus occurs in the second half of the pregnancy (Friedman;

Swaab 17). Because of the time interval, physical sex and gender identity can be under the sway of contradictory stimuli. This twist of nature may set the stage for the discrepancy between anatomical sex and gender identity.

There is a constant need to update the glossary of gender variance and non-binary gender expressions as new social phenomena arise: in the clinical context of mental health treatment, we now distinguish *gender* as the outward presentation and behaviour related to maleness or femaleness, and *gender identity* as one's internal sense of being male or female. The term *transgender* denotes individuals whose gender identity does not match their birth gender. *Transsexuals* are persons who have or intend to transition medically with the help of heterotypical hormones and/or surgery. *Gender queer and gender fluid* denote individuals who describe themselves as being in between genders; they identify as neither a man nor a woman. They may identify as androgynous and consider gender to be on a spectrum. Finally, *cis-gendered* defines a person who feels concordant with their assigned gender on their birth certificate.

What is in a gender pronoun? An inquiry about preferred pronouns expresses respect for an individual's declared gender identity. The American Dialect Society anointed *they* as a singular, gender-neutral pronoun as their *2015 Word-of-the-Year* (American Dialect Society). The selection of *they* as a singular pronoun – e.g. someone left a book on the table; can they please pick it up? – recognizes its emergence in contemporary language as a rejection of the traditional binary of he and she.

Facebook, ever the social media trendsetter, undertook a diversity initiative in 2014 and devised an extensive list of gender identities for its subscribers ('Facebook Diversity'). Slate Magazine (Weber) condensed the fifty-six highly granular Facebook gender categories to seventeen basic options. The article provides definitions for the general reader: the new gender choices range from agender, androgyne, bigender, cisgender, female to male, male to female, gender fluid, non-conforming, non-binary, pangender, etc.

To make matters more complicated, even something as basic as a person's biological sex does not neatly fall into two binary categories of male and female. This statement is counterintuitive to most audiences, eliciting skepticism and disbelief. To imagine that anatomical sex exists on a continuum or may be a mosaic condition defies common sense. Money and Ehrhardt assert that a whole cascade of physiological and social factors has to develop in sync to render an organism one hundred percent male or female (Money 2).

About 0.05 per cent of babies are born with ambiguous genitalia, which doctors cannot easily classify as male or female. This is but one specific macroscopically visible example of degrees of intersex conditions giving rise to a considerable ambiguity and variation in the purely biological underpinnings of chromosomal, hormonal and anatomical sex (American Psychological Association 2008).

A chromosomal test is not sufficient to determine one's sex. 'A body's sex is simply too complex! There is no either/or. Rather there are shades of difference' (Fausto-Sterling 3). Fausto-Sterling's exasperated comments came in response to the ongoing and ultimately futile efforts of the International Olympic Committee to land on a failsafe test to determine which athletes may compete as men or as women. The public can follow the challenging task of defining someone as purely male or female in the popular press (Macur). Athletes have protested the requirement to parade in the nude in front of a committee inspecting their bodies as a demeaning procedure. Fausto-Sterling tries to help the public make sense of 'bodies that present themselves as neither entirely male nor entirely female' (Fausto-Sterling 3).

Sexual Orientation

Negative attitudes towards gay and lesbian people have a long history. Prejudice and antipathy may be motivated by irrational fear or moral disapproval, often enshrined in religious doctrine. Biological and social scientists in the second part of the twentieth century have taken an enlightened position and argued that the scientific evidence identifies same-sex attraction and sexual behaviour as falling within the scope of the normal range of human sexuality. 'Sexual orientation refers to an enduring pattern of emotional, romantic and/or sexual attraction to men, women or both sexes. Sexual orientation also refers to a person's sense of identity based on those attractions, related behaviours and membership in a community of others who share those attractions. Research over several decades has demonstrated that sexual orientation ranges along a continuum, from exclusive attraction to the other sex to exclusive attraction to the same sex' (American Psychological Association 2008).

In 1973, the Board of Directors of the American Psychiatric Association removed homosexuality from its Diagnostic and Statistical Manual of Mental Disorders (DSM). Therefore, same-sex attraction or sexual relationships are no longer considered sexually deviant, perverse or synonymous with a mental health disorder necessitating treatment. Most importantly, liberation movements by gay and lesbian political groups especially in the US have achieved progress in asserting the civil rights of sexual minorities, culminating in the addition of LGBTQ categories to anti-discrimination statutes in a number of states, and federal legalization of same-sex marriage in 2015.

Despite the normalization of same-sex attraction and the US Supreme Court's ruling in favour of marriage equality, the public continues to search for explanations for plausible causes of sexual orientation. 'There is no consensus among scientists about the exact reasons that an individual develops a heterosexual, bisexual, gay or lesbian orientation. Although much research has examined the possible genetic, hormonal, developmental, societal and cultural influences on sexual orientation, no findings have emerged that permit scientists to conclude that sexual orientation is determined by any particular factor or factors. Many think that both nature and nurture play complex roles; most people experience little or no sense of choice about their sexual orientation' (American Psychological Association 2008).

Being Queer in the Caribbean

To understand sexuality and explore the written and unwritten rules of sexual mores and behaviour in a culture as an outsider requires anthropological finesse. It is helpful to refer to Caribbean gender studies scholars with knowledge intrinsic to the culture, such as Kamala Kempadoo:

> Caribbean sexuality is both hypervisible and obscured. That is, it is celebrated in popular culture as an important ingredient in Caribbean social life and flaunted to attract tourists to the region, yet it is shrouded in double entendre, secrecy and shame (Kempadoo 1).

Kempadoo provides an overview of the available studies and so-called 'grey documents' (reports, conference papers and policy briefings) pertaining to 'trends in sexual practice' in the Caribbean. Her comments about same-sex relations highlight important cross-cultural conceptual differences. 'In many of these studies same-sex relations are not in the first instance claimed as identity but rather as activity, as people disclose information about their practice without identifying or viewing themselves as homosexual, queer, gay, lesbian, or transgender. The studies have also brought to the fore a commonality of bisexual behaviour. According to most of the research on Caribbean men-who-have-sex-with-men, many also have sex with women' (Kempadoo 5).

Men who have sex with men (MSM) is a classification created by epidemiologists at the height of the AIDS crisis in the 1990s (CDC HIV/AIDS Fact Sheet, September 2010). Taking a behavioural perspective rather than focusing on self-declared, identity-based categories, e.g. straight vs. gay or bisexual, allowed public health researchers to estimate disease risk more accurately. In her paper Kempadoo is not concerned with disease statistics; nor is she beholden to medical and legal taxonomy of European origin; the word *homosexuality* emerged publicly for the first time in Germany in 1869 (Fausto-Sterling 13). Kempadoo uses the term MSM to describe men who stretch the definition of heterosexuality to include same-sex interactions without resulting in a change of sexual identity.

Legal Issues in Trinidad and Tobago

In most of Latin America, homosexuality remains illegal. In Trinidad and Tobago, for example, Criminal Code Section 13 of the Sexual Offences Act prohibits it along with other acts like rape or sex with a minor. Section 16, on serious indecency, includes penalties for even consensual sex between two members of same sex. This may change – in February of 2017, activist Jason Jones filed a case in Trinidad courts to have Sections 13 and 16 overturned (Gay Rights Advocate Colin Robinson, personal communication).[1]

The level of enforcement, however, varies among Latin American and Caribbean nations. While the English-speaking nations generally have been the most resistant to overturning laws banning homosexuality, several, like Trinidad and Tobago, have rarely enforced them. It is not fully clear to researchers why these different levels of enforcement (and, presumably, commitment to homophobic views) exist, although in terms of homophobic discrimination and mistreatment, Latin America is – in the words of one social science researcher – a 'world laggard' (Corrales 1). Nevertheless, differences between Latin American nations are clearly real. A 2010 study of Trinidad and Tobago conducted by researchers at Vanderbilt University, for example, reported that only 15 per cent of citizens there supported legalizing gay marriage, compared with 58 per cent in Argentina or 23 per cent in Panama (Lodola and Corral 2).

Yet this does not necessarily reflect bigotry. A 2013 UNAIDS study found that 78 per cent believed it unacceptable to discriminate against people on the basis of their sexual orientation; 56 per cent reported they were 'accepting' or 'tolerant' of LGBTQ people (ILGA-LAC). For those interviewed, the issue of gay marriage seems to fall in the category of religion rather than civil rights.

(ILGA-LAC)

Figure 12.2: Support for Same-Sex Marriage in Latin America and the Caribbean 2010

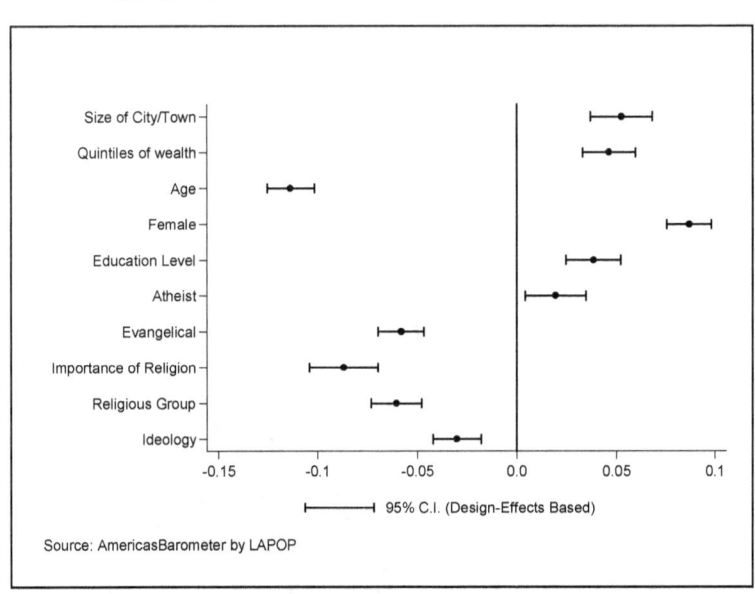

Broadly speaking, Latin American, like North American, views on LGBTQ issues are deeply affected by strength of religious ideology and rate of attendance at religious services. But, studies have also found other variables that have an impact on attitudes, including political ideology, socioeconomic status, age, level of education, and urbanism (Lodola and Corral 2–4). In figure 12.2 from 2010, individuals' attitudes toward gay marriage are measured by these different variables – the views of each are represented by the horizontal bars. Those bars to the right of the 0.0 line indicate a positive view of gay marriage; those to the left a negative view (sample size 28,217; Lodoba and Corral 5).

Yet these categories cannot tell the entire story, since Trinidad and Tobago's relative standing vis-á-vis its economic development produced a predicted approval rate of approximately 37 per cent, but an actual rate of only 15 per cent (Lodola and Corral 5). Clearly, as in the US, there is more investigation to be done. Perhaps, for example, the changing numbers between 2010 and 2013 represent real, measurable changes in attitude.

Some of these attitudinal changes may be due to citizen activism. There are locally-led organizations hard at work organizing on behalf of LGBTQ equality in Trinidad and Tobago. *CAISO: Sex and Gender*

Justice (formerly known as *The Coalition Advocating for Inclusion of Sexual Orientation [CAISO]*),[2] for example, was founded in 2009 in response to the unwillingness of the government to grant anti-discrimination protection to LGBTQ people. That same year, a study conducted by the University of the West Indies found that 80 per cent of the population believed sexual orientation to be a legitimate category for discrimination. The dramatic drop to 22 per cent who reported holding such views in 2013 (in the UNAID study) may well be thanks to CAISO's (and other organizations') efforts to hold public discussions alongside lobbying for anti-discrimination legislation (CAISO).

However, as participants in the Research X-Change pointed out, the political strategies of CAISO and other Trinidadian gay and lesbian activist organizations differ from those of US groups in that they are deliberately focused on local community building and political power to respond to local situations (www.caribbeanhomophobias.org).

Still, it is clear that distrust of LGBTQ people, if not outright hostility, remains a reality in Trinidad as much as elsewhere. On June 22, 2016, Selwyn Cudjoe wrote in his blog 'Gay and Straight Together' that while Trinidad and Tobago do not have the kind of openly anti-gay violence seen in Jamaica, he lamented 'how cruel we were and perhaps still are to those who are born or become gay or lesbian' in Trinidad. His 'guesstimate' that more than half of adults there are homophobic (aligning with the 2010 figures) 'causes us to wonder about the safety of gays and lesbians in our society' (Cudjoe).

Meanwhile, there are indications that a number of Trinidadian leaders, like some US black leaders, also view LGBTQ behaviours and identities as foreign to their cultural and historical norms, and therefore an imperialist force to be resisted. One goal of CAISO, therefore, is to reframe LGBTQ rights as an issue of human rights and civic responsibility within a Trinidadian context. Similarly, *Friends for Life*, another Trinidadian organization, develops therapeutic practices for psychologists and social workers to help LGBTQ clients based on local norms and cultural values rather than on standard Western theories that developed in very different social and cultural contexts. In other words, how attitudes toward homosexuality and gay marriage have evolved among Caribbean people (and by extension Caribbean-[US]Americans) remains as complex and mysterious as among US-born blacks. The importance of locally rooted activism remains as critical a factor in shaping political views as it does in native-born black communities in the US.

Difficult Conversations about Sex, Gender and Race

Since this Research X-Change workshop was organized to include participants with different political and ideological orientations, we entered into what in the realm of psychology we call a *difficult conversation*. We had tried to ensure that the workshop attracted a diverse group: US Americans and Trinidadians, whites and people of colour, clinicians, academics, and social activists. Generally, it is challenging to engage such a gathering and conduct a productive interdisciplinary and cross-cultural dialogue on a socially and politically controversial issue such as LGBTQ communities, particularly within one exchange of ninety minutes. Engaged in a polyphonic conversation, participants owned different aspects of the subject matter. The process of establishing a productive *difficult conversation* was, then, perhaps the most valuable outcome of this particular Research X-Change session.

One issue that came to the fore, largely thanks to the broad and open dialogue our convener fostered, was that Trinidadian social activists belonging to sexual minorities who are in the middle of a daily struggle for acceptance and emancipation do not approach these matters with mere academic detachment. They expressed their resentment of 'post-colonial know-it-all' representatives of the 'global North' who in the name of 'progress' and 'liberation' try to impose their cultural norms – once again – on their former colonial territories. Understandably, they are weary of outside intervention and question the underlying motivation of so-called 'allies' in the emancipatory struggle of LGBTQ people. In their experience, 'straight white folk' sometimes use gay and lesbian people for their own purposes as 'pocketbooks', e.g. accessories of 'hipness' or accoutrements of 'coolness', in an attempt to fend off any accusations of bigotry. They feel that straight people often overestimate the number of gays and lesbians and do not appreciate the loneliness and fatigue caused by always being in the minority. In addition, LGBTQ people in the US observe that most straight people there exaggerate how accepting their society really is. Therefore they do not recognize the daily challenges and threats faced by members of the LGBTQ community in the US. Additionally, the legalization of same-sex marriage notwithstanding, too many families in the US, as elsewhere, refuse to accept their gay, lesbian or queer children. The challenges facing LGBTQ people, then, are both intimate and social.

Derald W. Sue addresses cross-sectional discourses on race and gender in contemporary American society. He highlights daily microaggressions experienced by members of racial and sexual minorities (Sue 2010). Although his research in his 2015 book *Race Talk* focuses mainly on managing racial conversations, his suggestions also apply to similarly distressing exchanges about gender. He dissects ineffective interventions and outlines successful strategies for teachers, trainers and facilitators (230–44). Based on his studies, most participants hesitate to initiate or enter a charged dialogue. It offends our sense of politeness and propriety. Why push emotional hot buttons? Most people would prefer to do nothing, sidetrack or terminate the conversation, or appease the participants. Unfortunately, many people cannot help themselves and become defensive when the topic comes up. Sue argues against these interventions as non-starters.

Instead, he proposes that we begin by acknowledging our own identities and biases. Successful navigation of these conversations requires a degree of openness in dealing with potentially taboo topics, in order to transcend uncomfortable silences and tolerate differences in communication style. Our Research X-Change conversation began this way, which then opened up the space to discuss the specifics of LGBTQ issues facing Trinidadians and Tobagonians both at home and abroad that our report described.

GLAAD,[3] a US non-governmental media monitoring organization founded in 1985 by lesbian and gay people in the media, lists '10 Ways to be an Ally and a Friend' on its webpage (GLAAD). The first and foremost task, according to GLAAD, is listening and understanding. This dictum takes on particular poignancy when supporting LGBTQ rights in the so-called developing world. Attempts at advocacy can backfire and be perceived as cultural imperialism when undertaken without prior consultations with local groups. This is precisely why we sought to include local community members in our otherwise academic dialogue.

Difficult conversations may also be derailed because white people who belong to the majority culture are unaccustomed to being labeled by others and to have their good intentions challenged. They get easily overwhelmed and do not appreciate being made to feel guilty. In so-called diversity workshops, they often prefer to remain silent. People of colour also often hesitate to register their grievances about microaggressions they experience on a daily basis (Sue).

Managing such a conversation thus poses unique challenges. For a group immersed in a difficult conversation like ours the task was to facilitate a potentially heated exchange of ideas without allowing the conversation to deteriorate into an argument or hurt silence. Our group worked hard to balance honest and direct confrontation with sensitivity to the complex and sometimes conflicting emotional responses of all participants. The goal was to create a respectful atmosphere that allowed for the expression of diametrically opposed points of view among a diverse membership. For the group leader of such a conversation it is important to primarily control the process rather than the content of the dialogue (Sue 238).

We hope all the attendees of this Research X-Change meeting had a chance to articulate their stake in the topic. Even in situations where there may not be too many common denominators, carefully mediated difficult conversations allow all participants to hear each other's point of view, as we did, and acknowledge the different realities people experience. And this, in turn, strengthens our own research as well as our personal understanding.

Notes
1. Between the writing of this essay and putlicaton of this book, this situation changed, with *Jones v Attorney General*. In January 2018, the Honourable Mr Justice Davindra Rampersad of the High Court of Justice in Trinidad and Tobago deferred judgment after hearing arguments in this case. In a 60-page judgment on April 12, 2018, High Court Justice Rampersad declared the laws criminalizing same-sex relationships and intercourse to be unconstitutional. That is the situation as of late 2018. (see Oochong; see also Republic of Trinidad and Tobago. In the High Court of Justice Claim CV 2017-00720. http://webopac.ttlawcourts.org/LibraryJud/Judgments/HC/rampersad/2017/cv_17_00720DD12apr2018.pdf. Ed. note).
2. This Advocacy group, maturing in identity, changed its name between the time of the Conference, 2016, and the publication of this book in 2018. Information supplied by Colin Robinson. (Ed. Note).
3. GLAAD initially was an acronym for 'Gay and Lesbian Alliance Against Defamation,' but in March 2013 became the primary name to allow for greater inclusiveness.

Works Cited:
Achong, Derek. 'Judge sets April 12 for Decision in LGBT Lawsuit.' *Trinidad Guardian,* January 31, 2018.
American Dialect Society, 'Words of the Year.' *American Dialect Society News* January 8, 2016. http://www.americandialect.org/2015-word-of-the-year-is-singular-they.

American Psychological Association. 'Answers to Your Questions About Individuals With Intersex Conditions.' Washington, DC, 2006a. http://www.apa.org/topics/lgbt/intersex.pdf.

———. 'Answers to Your Questions About Transgender Individuals and Gender Identity.' Washington, DC, 2006b. www.apa.org/topics/lgbt/transgender.pdf.

———. 'Answers to Your Questions: For a Better Understanding of Sexual Orientation and Homosexuality.' Washington, DC, 2008. https://www.apa.org/topics/lgbt/orientation.pdf.

CAISO website: https://gspottt.wordpress.com.

CDC Fact Sheet: HIV and AIDS among Gay and Bisexual Men, Center for Disease Control and Prevention, September 2010. https://phpa.health.maryland.gov/OIDPCS/CSTIP/CSTIPDocuments/MSM_HIV.pdf.

Corrales, Javier. 'LGBT Rights in the Americas.' *Americas Quarterly* (Spring 2012); http://www.americasquarterly.org/node/3565.

Cudjoe, Selwyn. 'Gay and Straight Together.' June 22, 2016. http://www.trinicenter.com/Cudjoe/2016/2206.htm.

Facebook Diversity. February 13, 2014. https://www.facebook.com/photo.php?fbid=567587973337709.

Fausto-Sterling, Anne. *Sexing the Body. Gender Politics and the Construction of Sexuality.* New York, NY: Basic Books, 2000.

Friedman, Richard A. 'How Changeable is Gender?' *New York Times*, August 22, 2015. https://www.nytimes.com/2015/08/23/opinion/sunday/richard-a-friedman-how-changeable-is-gender.html?mcubz=1.

'Gay Rights Advocate Challenges TandT's Homosexuality Laws,' 2/23/17 *Daily Express* (Trinidad). January 23, 2017. http://www.trinidadexpress.com/20170223/news/gay-rights-advocate-challenges-tts-homosexuality-laws.

GLAAD. 'Be an Ally and a Friend.' 2007: https://www.glaad.org/resources/ally/2

ILGA-LAC. (Asociacion Internacional de Lesbianas, Gays, Bisexuales, Trans o Intersex para America Latina el Caribe). Website, http://www.ilga-lac.org/en/unaids-survey-finds-78-disagree-discriminating-gays-trinidad-tobago/

Kempadoo, Kamala. 'Caribbean Sexuality: Mapping the Field.' *Caribbean Review of Gender Studies. A Journal of Caribbean Perspectives on Gender and Feminism* 3 (2009): 1–24.

Lodola, Germán, and Margarita Corral. 'Support for Same Sex Marriage in Latin America.' *AmericasBarometer Insights* 44 (2010). http//www.vanderbilt.edu/lapop/insights/IO844.enrevised.pdf.

Macur, Juliet. 'What qualifies a Woman to Compete as a Woman? An Ugly Fight Resumes.' *New York Times,* August 4, 2017. https://www.nytimes.com/2017/08/04/sports/olympics/gender-dutee-chand-india.html?smprod=nytcore-ipadandsmid=nytcore-ipad-shareand_r=0).

Money, John and Anke A. Ehrhardt. *Man and Woman, Boy and Girl*. Baltimore, MD: Johns Hopkins University Press, 1972.

Republic of Trinidad and Tobago. 'In the High Court of Justice Claim CV 2017-00720.' http://webopac.ttlawcourts.org/LibraryJud/Judgments/HC/rampersad/2017/cv_17_00720DD12apr2018.pdf).

Sue, Derald Wing. *Microaggressions in Everyday Life. Race, Gender, and Sexual Orientation.* Hoboken, NJ: Wiley, 2010.

———. *Race Talk and the Conspiracy of Silence. Understanding and Facilitating Difficult Conversations on Race.* Hoboken, NJ: Wiley, 2015.

Swaab, Dick, F., and Alicia Garcia-Falgueras. 'Sexual differentiation of the Human Brain in Relation to Gender Identity and Sexual Orientation.' *Functional Neurolog:* Roma 24. no. 1 (Jan–Mar 2009): 17–28.

Diversity, 'Perversity' and Anger

Gerard Hutchinson

The idea of a difficult conversation is one worth repeatedly exploring especially in the context of diverse communities working to engage cultural change and evolution. Even within the practice of psychiatry there are fundamental differences in the approaches that might be needed in different cultures and which need to be constantly revised. In pockets of the Caribbean, psychiatry is still seen as complementary to spiritual and supernatural influence so the presence of spirit is always intimate in the processing of our experience.

The very concept of minorities predisposes to exclusion and some degree of patronizing whether the adjective is sexual or ethnic or anything else. This perception lies at the core of the problematic exchanges related to diversity. This is amplified when the interaction occurs between individuals who might seem to represent these majority and minority cultures or see themselves as doing so.

The LGBQT community in Trinidad and the Caribbean is struggling with this issue as the Caribbean comes to terms with the developmental demands of contemporary life and the need to reject many of the colonial perspectives that still inform current day thinking. 'Perversity' within diversity – where does one distinguish them? Can we reject the notion of 'perversity' altogether when childhood sexual abuse as one example remains such a pertinent developmental issue for everyone in the world.

This is where some anger comes from, because the need to accept diversity is not as profound in cultures where everyone sees themselves as diverse. Social class and entitlement become more significant as mediators of social interaction.

The belief that same-sex orientation is a 'perversity' remains embedded in the psyche of many Caribbean people, even still among some of those who openly reject it, so that the resultant conflict inevitably leads to psychological discomfort. Then on top of this there is the ambivalent relationship toward the North – progressive civilization and opportunity and even sexual freedom but also racial oppression, slavery and indentureship, colonialism and exclusion. The desire to internally explore these complex but critical uncertainties remains muted because the gaze remains outward rather than inward. Hence lies the importance of initiating the conversations and creating a climate (safe space) where people can speak freely and openly.

Mental health professionals may have gone past the etic vs emic debates about whether culture can cause mental distress or just flavour the way it presents, but culture certainly shapes the way one sees oneself. That self-visioning and perhaps articulating may not even be conscious but becomes more necessary when one person becomes set apart from an already set apart people. How does one enter the conversation and what does one seek to achieve? Is there a benefit from inclusion and can that inclusion be equitable and fair given the historical antecedents? Can we find comfort with the challenges or must we accept that feeling challenged is the path to self-discovery and tangible self-belief? How does one make sense of being the other – an object of history but yet encouraged to be a driver and architect of one's own destiny? When one is either celebrated as exotic, tolerated as different or rejected as perverse, how can one just be without any demands or any explanations? Questions without answers, we need still to talk and work with each other and never stop searching.

CHAPTER 13

Culture and Memory in the Caribbean[1]

Nicole Alea, Katija Khan, Consuelo Pedro and Sarah A. Raskin

The way that humans process information about the world would seem, at first consideration, to be universal. Events from one's life are remembered, for example, because the brain is wired to encode this information and store it, so that we can retrieve it sometime later. This process should perhaps not be contingent on a person's wider cultural context, but accumulating evidence suggests that it is. The relation between culture and cognition has been demonstrated for cognitive functions including memory, attention, processing speed, visual perception, problem-solving (e.g. Nisbett 2003), and the use of categorization and metamemory judgments (Park and Gutchess 2002). Differences in cognition by culture have most often been studied as a contrast between Western (individualistic) cultures and East Asian (collectivist) cultures. For example, Nisbett and Masuda (2003) have found that people in Eastern cultures, consistent with their collectivist value orientation, think beyond individual skills when solving problems across a variety of cognitive tasks (see also Masuda, Ellsworth, Mesquita, Leu, Tanida, and Van de Veerdonk 2008, for examples), and consider the broader context of a task. Westerners, however, with their more individualist value orientation and focus on independent successes, tend to have a greater reliance on the concrete rules and logic that are needed to solve cognitive tasks (Kitayama, Duffy, Kawamura, and Larsen 2003). Recent work, however, including the work conducted by the authors that is reviewed in this chapter, is extending beyond this East-West disctinction and beginning to look at less-often studied cultures (like the Caribbean), and more nuanced differences between cultures (e.g. in different types of memory), as well as the role of acculturation.

Knowing about cultural differences in cognition, however, extends beyond basic knowledge generation and has implications for clinical evaluations that use the *same* neuropsychological tests with *different* cultures. Cultural differences in performance on neuropsychological clinical measures seem to extend far beyond a need for language translation, as tests developed in one culture are often not validated in another prior to using the test to make clinical diagnoses (see Alea and Wang 2015 for a similar argument). For example, in dementia due to Alzheimer's disease, the most prevalent type of dementia (e.g. van der Flier and Scheltens 2005), memory impairment is a characteristic symptom (Jahn 2013), and a symptom that would seem to be culture free. However, in studies from the United States (US), there is evidence that some measures used to diagnose dementia of the Alzheimer's type might actually classify ethnic minorities more often as cognitively impaired when they are not. For example, although studies have reported higher rates of dementia in African American men over 65 (20.9 per cent) compared to white non-Hispanic men (11.6 per cent), the community-based screening measure was found to have a poor relationship to clinical diagnosis in Cuban men and African American women, which the authors speculated may be due to cultural bias in the measure they used (Demirovic, Prineas, Lowenstein, Bean, Duara, Sevush, and Szapocznik 2003). Fillenbaum and colleagues (2001) found similar results. They found that the most popular and widely-used cognitive screening instrument (i.e. the Mini Mental State Examination) wrongly classified six per cent of non-impaired whites, but 42 per cent of non-impaired African Americans. This work obviously implies that culture matters for cognition.

This link between culture and cognition extends beyond the society that one is born into because performance on cognitive measures seems to also be a function of the degree of acculturation, commonly conceptualized as multidimensional changes in values, practices and beliefs that take place with any intercultural contact, but most frequently studied in individuals living in regions other than where they were born (e.g. Schwartz, Unger, Zamboanga and Szapocznik 2010). For example, greater acculturation to a majority culture among African Americans, Asian Americans, and Latinas/os, for example, is associated with increased scores on measures of attention, memory, processing speed and problem solving (Arentoft, Byrd, Robbins, Monzones, Mirand, Rosario et al. 2012). As another example, this same study further found that for a group of adults fluent in English and self-identified as Latina/o and of Caribbean origin (Puerto Rico, Cuba, Dominican Republic), higher US acculturation scores were correlated with better performance on a variety of 'culture free' cognitive assessments, like memory, learning, problem solving and motor speed performance. However, even this link might not be straight forward. This same study found, for example, that those identifying as African but born in the Caribbean who immigrated to the US (i.e. African Caribbeans) had higher cognitive performance than Africans who were born in the US (i.e. African Americans), despite the fact that the Caribbean born Africans had lower acculturation to the dominant culture. This suggests that there may be other important factors that mediate the relation between cognition and culture, such as educational quality and access.

In this chapter, to narrow down the scope of work covered and to be congruent with the authors' expertise, we focus on the relation between culture and one particular cognitive domain: memory. Memory is a foundation of social communication and self-perception, impacting most every aspect of human experience (Zilmer, Spiers and Culbertson 2008). The processing of memories can be described using a three stage process: 1) registration or sensory memory, 2) short-term memory, and 3) long-term memory. Types of long-term memory can be classified into declarative or explicit memory and non-declarative or implicit memory. Declarative memory is explicit and can be accessed consciously. It is further divided into episodic (which is memory for personal life events, like a birthday or winning a race) and semantic (memory for information and facts, like knowing the capital of Trinidad and Tobago or how many legs a spider has) memory. Non-declarative memory comprises procedural memory (memory for actions and perceptual-motor skills, like riding a bike or playing the steelpan) and item-specific implicit memory (such as classically conditioned or primed responses, like jumping when a loud noise is heard). Long-term memory can also be classified by the temporal direction of the memory: it is either retrospective (memory for the past, which can include declarative, episodic, semantic and autobiographical memory) or prospective memory (remembering to do something in the future). Because we cannot possibly review the link between culture and every type of memory, in the current chapter, we focus our attention on the relationship between culture and (1) working memory (an aspect of short-term memory), (2) prospective memory (utilizing both working memory and long-term memory), and (3) autobiographical memory (an aspect of long-term, episodic memory). In each section below we first describe what the component of memory is and how it is frequently assessed in the literature, and then describe research on how culture might mitigate each type of memory. We also, as mentioned above, focus our attention to the work on culture and memory being done in the Caribbean, to move away from the predominantly East-West comparison, and particularly focus on research coming from Trinidad and Tobago.

Culture, Working Memory, and Digit Span

Working Memory and Digit Span

Baddeley and Hitch (1974) proposed the concept of working memory that refers to 'a limited capacity system allowing the temporary storage and manipulation of information necessary for such complex tasks as comprehension, learning and reasoning' (Baddeley 2000, 418). The working memory model comprises a control system called the central executive, which is assisted by two accompanying slave systems – the phonological loop (which controls language or speech-based, verbal and acoustic information) and the visuospatial sketchpad (which manipulates visual and spatial images). A fourth component, the episodic buffer, temporarily stores and integrates information from different modalities via a linkage with the long-term memory system. If you were asked to solve the multiplication problem 25 x 17 mentally, it would involve you using your working memory to temporarily maintain a mental representation of the problem while you solve it, concentrate and filter out any potentially distracting stimuli, and then access from long-term memory the necessary multiplication facts and operations to successfully solve the problem.

The way that working memory is conceived of today dates back to the concept of memory span, which can be traced to the late nineteenth century where Oliver Holmes (1871) and Ebbinghaus (1885) recognized that there seemed to be a limit or fixed capacity for the number of verbal items (usually digits) a person could correctly repeat. Jacobs (1886), Galton (1887) and Bolton (1892) later made the association between memory span and cognitive performance when they observed that memory span seemed to be shorter in persons with lower intelligence quotient (IQ). Digit span tests were included in intelligence tests for children (e.g. Stanford-Binet) on a wide scale in the early 1900s and were later included in Wechsler's Intelligence scales and Memory scales (1939, 1945). Factor analysis showed that in addition to previous findings of digit span being related to verbal and performance IQ, it appeared to also load on a third factor of attention and concentration (also referred to as freedom from distractibility in some studies; Crawford, Allan, Stephen, Parker, and Besson 1989). In the third edition of the Wechsler Adult Intelligence Scale (WAIS-III), digit span was also considered to be a measure of working memory (Golden, Espe-Pfeifer, and Wachsler-Felder 2000). The digit span test is now one of the most commonly used neuropsychological instruments in the measurement of working memory (Ostrosky-Solis and Lozano 2006).

The digit span test comprises two components: a forwards and backwards task. The digit span forward (DSF) task involves a random sequence of numbers which is read out at the rate of one digit per second and the patient is asked to recall the digits in order immediately after. Digit span backward (DSB) is a variation of the task in which the person is required to recall the sequence of digits in reverse order. Sequences usually start with a string of two to three digits in DSF and two in DSB and when correctly recalled, the examiner states the next number sequence which is increased by one digit up to a string of nine in the DSF and eight in the DSB. A person's span is indicated by the number of digits correctly recalled. Studies have reported average DSF as seven plus or minus two (Miller 1956), or six plus or minus one (Spitz 1972). Studies report approximately 90 per cent of adults achieving a span of five to eight within a range of four digits. (Kaplan, Fein et al. 1991; Wechsler 1945). The number of digits recalled in DSB is usually fewer than on the DSF task, and the difference can range from, on average, half a digit difference to a two digit difference (Black and Strub 1978; Kaplan, et al. 1991; Mueller and Overcast 1976; Reynolds 1997).

In the WAIS-III version of the digit span task, the forwards and backwards scores were combined to produce an overall score. However, researchers have long asserted that these two scores should not be combined; that the two tasks correspond to different memory processes and should be considered separately (see Owen, Lee and Williams 2000; Reynolds 1997; Tulsky et al. 2003). The DSB is considered the more cognitively demanding task which involves an element of cognitive transformation not required in the forward task (Jensen 1980; Jensen and Figueroa 1975). DSF is thought to engage the phonological loop of Baddeley's working memory model while the backwards aspect of the task would implicate a greater involvement of the central executive system, visuospatial sketchpad and the episodic buffer (Baddeley 2000; 2002; Ostrosky-Solis and Lozano 2006); hence its greater cognitive demand (see Li and Lewandowsky 1993, 1995 for supporting evidence).

Cultural Differences in Working Memory

Khan (2010) sought to assess the difference in performance on the DSF and DSB, and identify the contribution of culture, but also age, gender, and education, on performance in the Caribbean context. An adult lifespan sample from England, and Trinidad and Tobago were matched for age, gender and education and administered the DSF and DSB. Performance on both the DSF and DSB fell within ranges reported in the literature (Lezak 2004) but while DSF performance was not significantly predicted by age, gender, education or culture, DSB scores were significantly predicted by education and culture. While age was significantly related to performance on each of the DSF and DSB measures in bivariate correlations, no significant differences between performance on the two tasks were observed because of age in the regression models. This is not a surprising finding and concurs with the literature which report a lack of age differences between the two digit span tasks, especially in younger adults (age effects, if present, become noticeable only in older populations after age 65; Carlesimo, Fadda, Lorusso, and Caltagirone 1994; Craik 1977; Jarvik 1988). Education was also a significant predictor of both DSF and DSB performance (but not the difference scores, DSF-DSB), in which shorter spans were found in the lower education group while the average and higher education group performed similarly. This reiterates findings that the relation between education and neuropsychological performance is not a linear one but rather exemplifies diminishing returns. Between zero and four years of education, differences in performance are greater than between persons with five to nine years of education, and differences are even less between persons with more than ten years of education (Ardila, Ostrosky-Solis, Rosselli and Gómez 2000; Ostrosky-Solis, Ardila, Rosselli, Lopez-Arango and Uriel-Mendoza 1998; Ostrosky-Solis and Lozano 2006).

Group differences between British and Caribbean participants were also found on the DSB in which Caribbeans performed worse than the British participants, but not for DSF scores where performance was similar for both groups. This finding is in contrast to that of Boone, Victor, Wen, Razani and Ponton (2007), who found that the minority groups, African Americans and Hispanics in the US, had significantly lower digit span scores than the majority white group. However, this may be explained by the failure of that study to compare DSF and DSB separately. Jensen and Figueroa (1975) also found differences in performance between whites and African Americans (adults and children) on both DSF and DSB and noted that the difference between ethnic groups was larger on the DSB task, a finding which is confirmed by the Khan (2010) study. In a study by Fasfous, Hidalgo-Ruzzante, Vilar-López, Catena-Martínez and Pérez-García (2013) conducted in Spain, significant group differences in DSB were also found, with Spanish participants outperforming Moroccans. However, the Moroccan participants were native Arabic, not Spanish, speakers and having to perform the DSB task in one's non-native language could have rendered the task more difficult than that performed by the Spanish participants (see also Hedden et al. 2002 for how a culture's language structure might relate to performance on the digit span tasks).

The mean difference between the forward and backward condition (DSF-DSB) in the Khan (2010) study was similar to those previously reported (Black and Strub 1978; Kaplan, Fein, Morris and Delis 1991; Reynolds 1997) and of the four factors, only culture was a significant predictor of this difference, with Caribbeans showing a larger DSF-DSB discrepancy than the British group. Within group, differences (DSF-DSB) were also greater among African American children than white American children, and while this discrepancy decreased with age from 5 to 12 years, it was less apparent in the African American group (Jensen and Figueroa 1975; Mayfield and Reynolds 1997). The failure of this discrepancy to diminish with age into adulthood across ethnicities is also confirmed in the Khan (2010) study. The differences in performance on the DSF versus DSB tasks in Caribbean persons may be explained by examining the nature of the task, as it could be reflecting underlying cultural differences in verbal versus visuospatial skills. For instance, some authors suggest DSF involves a more verbal (De Renzi and Nichelli 1975), and stronger attentional element while DSB incorporates a visuospatial component that invokes the working memory system (Baddeley 2000; Lezak, Howieson and Loring 2004; Rapport, Webster, and Dutra 1994). While education accounted for the greatest proportion of variance of all predicators in both tasks, and the effect of education was greater in the DSB than DSF, it did not mitigate the relationship between culture and DSB.

If the DSB was a contextual task, then interpreting the cultural differences in performance between Caribbean persons and those of British heritage would be simpler (see Khan and Venneri 2016 for an example). Instead, interpretations are less clear. As previously mentioned, Kitayama and colleagues (2003) have demonstrated that cultures perform better on culture-consonant tasks (i.e. individualistic cultures perform better on context free tasks and collectivistic cultures on context-dependent tasks), and as such, it could be posited that for a context free task, such as digit span, British persons would outperform Caribbeans, who might sway toward collectivism (Descartes 2011). This might explain a portion of the Khan (2010) results, as only culture explained the difference scores between the DSF and the DSB. However, this does not explain why culture differences emerged for only the more challenging digit span task (the DSB) in Khan (2010). It might be that education is driving the cultural differences on context-free tasks, like the DSB, when comparing Caribbean populations to generally more developed countries because education accounts for a greater proportion of variance on tasks with stronger working memory components (i.e., like the DSB; Murre, Janssen, Rouw and Meeter 2013). However, education, not age or gender, removes culture as a distinguishing variable on working memory tasks, like the digit span, and thus additional demographic (e.g. socioeconomic status) and psychosocial variables (e.g. motivation, personality) need to be explored in future work.

Culture, Prospective Memory and Episodic Future Thinking

Prospective Memory

Prospective memory (PM), remembering to remember and carry out a future action, is an important part of everyday life (Ellis and Freeman 2008; Rendell and Thompson 1999). For example, remembering to take out the trash or take medications at the correct time are both everyday PM tasks. For individuals with neurological disorders, including traumatic brain injury (TBI), schizophrenia and Parkinson's disease, PM deficits have been shown to impact daily functioning (Mathias and Mansfield 2005; Raskin 2009; Raskin et al. 2012; Raskin et al. 2014; Shum, Valentine and Cutmore 1999; Shum, Levin and Chan 2011; Shum et al. 2004). In addition, PM performance has been shown to be affected by external variables, such as social motives, degree of incentives offered, and personal importance of the task (Walter and Meier 2014). Thus, the possibility of a relationship between culture and PM performance seems worth exploring as it could have implications for clinical assessment and daily life.

In everyday life, successful PM performance depends on many factors, including the ability to pay attention, to maintain the intention in working memory, to call the intention to mind at the appropriate time and to recall the content of the intention (Groot, Wilson, Evans and Watson 2002). In addition, metacognitive abilities such as monitoring ongoing performance, evaluation of outcome, and awareness of PM limitations are required (Guynn 2003). In any one individual who demonstrates a PM deficit, more than one of these related underlying abilities may be impaired.

PM may require time-cued remembering (e.g. remembering to return a phone call at 3:00 p.m.; Levy and Loftus 1984; Wilkens and Baddeley 1988), or may be prompted by an event-cue (e.g. remembering to take a roast out of the oven in response to the oven timer; Einstein and McDaniel 1990; Harris and Wilkens 1982; Kvavilashvili 1992). McDaniel and Einstein's (2000) multiprocess theory posits that the strategic encoding, monitoring, and retrieval demands of a given PM task will likely vary by these characteristics of the target cue. Thus, in most studies, event-based tasks have been found to be easier for individuals to perform, most likely because time-based tasks require the person to perform more self-initiated monitoring and retrieval to bring the intention to mind and check a clock or watch (Glisky 1996; Park, Hertzog, Kidder, Morrell and Mayhorn 1997; Sellen, Louie, Harris and Wilkins 1997). PM is hypothesized to place more demands on self-initiated monitoring and retrieval processes as compared to retrospective memory (RM; e.g. McDaniel and Einstein 2000). In fact, PM is dissociable from RM at the neural (e.g. Simons, Scholvinck, Gilbert, Frith and Burgess 2006), cognitive (e.g. Salthouse, Berish and Siedlecki 2004), and functional (e.g. Woods et al. 2008) levels.

PM is presumed to encompass a variety of cognitive processes (e.g. Smith and Bayen 2004). This includes the formation of the intention, strategic monitoring during the retention interval, recognition of the external cue, and an effortful and controlled search for retrospective recall, otherwise referred to as self-initiated retrieval. Finally, the actual recall and execution of the intention occurs and the PM task is (or is not) completed successfully. Thus, all measures of PM have a delay between the encoding and retrieval of the prospective task; there must be no explicit prompt when the occasion to act occurs; and there must be a separate ongoing activity (e.g. Einstein and McDaniel 1990).

Imaging studies have suggested that PM depends on rostral prefrontal cortex (rPFC) functioning, and, in particular, Brodmann area 10 (Benoit et al. 2011). rPFC has been shown to be engaged during the delay period that occurs between the intention formation and the execution of the intention (Burgess, Gonen-Yaacovi, and Volle, 2011). Brain activation during PM tasks has been distinguished from activation in areas associated with vigilance, dual task performance, and working memory (West 2008). Not surprisingly, damage to prefrontal regions can significantly impair PM functioning (Burgess, Alderman, Volle, Benoit and Gilbert 2009; Crews, He and Hodge 2007; Okuda et al. 1998; Sowell, Delis, Stiles and Jernigan 2001), and PM impairments have been measured in neurological disorders that are presumed to include dysfunction of prefrontal structures (Carey et al. 2006; Raskin, Buckheit and Waxman 2012; Raskin et al. 2014; Raskin et al. 2011).

Future Thinking

A related cognitive task is episodic or semantic future thinking, that is, the imagination of possible events that could happen in the future, allowing one to foresee specific future events (e.g. Atance and O'Neill 2001). This has been most often studied in regards to episodic future thinking, that is imagining possible future personal events. It has been argued that this is a part of Tulving's notion of autonoetic consciousness, that is essential for an individual's awareness of the self and identity in time from the past to the future (Atance and O'Neill 2001) and has been argued to have strong social value (D'Argembeau and Van der Linden 2012). The Constructive Episodic Simulation Hypothesis states that the extraction of episodic details from one's past experiences is used and then recombination is employed to generate novel future scenarios (Schacter and Addis 2007). Studies with people who have semantic dementia indicate that semantic memory is also required for successful episodic future thinking (Duval et al. 2012).

Episodic future thinking has been shown to be mediated by the medial temporal lobe (Benoit et al., 2011; Palombo et al. 2015). Semantic retrieval, however, has been shown to be mediated instead by inferior frontal and lateral temporal gyri (LaCorte and Piolino 2016). In contrast to episodic future thinking, semantic future thinking was examined in one study (Palombo, Keane and Verfaiellie 2016). Participants were asked to select a smaller amount of money immediately or a larger amount in the future, but first were asked to imagine what they would buy with the money. Individuals with amnesia due to medial temporal lobe damage were less inclined to wait after the semantic future thinking exercise, but they were able to make more patient choices (i.e. waiting for a larger reward) when scaffolding was provided to support accurate time tagging.

Individuals with specific damage to the hippocampus have frequently demonstrated impairments in future episodic thinking (e.g. Hassabis et al. 2007) but not in all cases (Squire, van der Horst, McDuff, Frascino, Hopkins and Mauldin 2011) and not in group future thinking. Individuals with TBI (Rasmussen and Berntsen 2012), Alzheimer's disease (Addis, Sacchetti, Ally, Budson and Schacter 2009), and mild cognitive impairment (Gamboz et al. 2010) have demonstrated deficits in both autobiographical memory and episodic future thinking. Individuals with TBI, however, do not show an impairment in producing external semantic details when imagining the future, but were impaired only when imagining internal or episodic details (Rasmussen and Berntsen 2012).

There have been relatively few studies of the idea of collective future thought, despite a considerable literature on the cultural differences in collective memory, and the role it plays in creating group bonds (Szpunar and Szpunar 2015). Collective future thought essentially involves the idea of future thinking by or on behalf of a group, such as a family, community, or nation. Szpunar and Szpunar (2015) argue that this phenomenon is comprised of individual psychological processes as well as social and group processes. An example given is when a new technology is introduced and the collective group imagines the impact that technology will have on the community. These collective future thoughts would entail both specific details of the event and patterns that structure all similar events (e.g. when you go to a restaurant, there are certain details that will always remain constant, such as getting a menu, ordering, receiving a bill, etc. Szpunar and Szpunar 2015). People with a strong sense that their group will continue into the future (i.e. collective continuity) show greater social wellbeing and lower rates of feelings of alienation (Sani et al. 2008).

To our knowledge there are no published studies examining cultural differences in prospective memory, future thinking, or collective future thinking. The only work found was an unpublished study that compared Chinese students with Canadian Caucasian students on a computerized laboratory measure of event-based, time-based and activity-based prospective memory. The Chinese students performed significantly higher on all measures than the Canadian students (Chang 2009). The authors speculate that the differences may be due to greater motivation to comply with tasks and greater vigilance due to a desire to meet a social obligation in the Chinese students. However, it is not clear that the tasks used were, in fact, equivalent in difficulty given the need to use rather different prospective memory items due to the differences in the languages.

Cultural Differences in Prospective Memory and Future Thinking

Given the dearth of empirical work, Raskin (2009) conducted a preliminary study of cultural differences in both PM and future thought in Caribbean and European participant groups. PM was measured using the Memory for Intentions Test (MIST) (Raskin 2009). The MIST includes both time-based and event-based cues that are either two minutes or fifteen minutes in duration between encoding and performance. The time-based cues allow for self-initiated retrieval ('In fifteen minutes, tell me that it is time to take a break') and, unlike most laboratory tasks, the event-based cues are related to the events that need to be performed (i.e. 'When I hand you a red pen, sign your name on the paper'). The response of participants can either be an action or verbal response. Due to the MIST's ability to measure different attributes of PM, it also allows for six types of errors to be analysed if failure of a PM task were to occur.

To measure future thought, we had participants imagine events that could happen in the next year and that were autobiographical in nature. Instructions and scoring were taken from two other studies (i.e. Irish, Addis, Hodges and Piquet 2012; Rasmussen and Berntsen 2012). Participants were instructed to 'Imagine a future event in the next month. A specific event that happens on one particular day. Please describe it with as much detail as possible; what you do and feel; who you are with, where it happens and how it happens.' Future event productions were scored for the number of internal (central to the imagined event) and external details (superfluous to the main event). To measure collective future thought, participants were asked to imagine the impact of specific future events on the community as a whole (e.g. increased temperatures due to climate change).

We included individuals from the Caribbean and those of European descent, all living in the US. There were four groups in total: a group from the Caribbean, a group whose parents had immigrated from the Caribbean but who had been born in the US, a group of European descent from the United States, and for comparison, a group of European descent from the US with TBI.

In terms of performance of the healthy groups on the MIST, there was a significant effect on a group on the 24-hour measure, event-based performance, and time-based performance tasks. Those who had lived their childhoods in the Caribbean demonstrated superior performance on the 24-hour item compared to those born in the US. The 24-hour item is included as a more naturalistic task and differences have been observed in other groups; for example, older adults are superior to younger adults on the 24-hour task despite being impaired compared to younger adults on the tasks performed in the laboratory setting. There was no difference between the groups on the event-based tasks; however, those born in the Caribbean performed significantly lower on the time-based tasks than those born in the US. Paired comparisons revealed that those who were born in the US to parents from the Caribbean performed no differently than those born in the US of European descent on any measure. As would be expected, those with TBI performed significantly worse than all other groups on time-based PM, event-based PM, total score and the 24 hour measure. In terms of errors, those with TBI demonstrated significantly more prospective memory errors (forgetting to do the task at all), as would be expected based on their brain injury. However, intriguingly, those born in the Caribbean were more likely than the other healthy groups to produce errors of completing the correct task at the incorrect time (i.e. they were too late in their performance), and those of Caribbean descent born in the US were more likely to make task substitution errors (performing a different task from the test) than any other type of error. Thus, PM differences between individuals from the Caribbean and those non-Caribbean individuals born in the US seem to centre around time-based tasks. This is intriguing because it may relate to theories of differences in time perception based on culture (e.g. Sinha and Gardenfors 2014) or social setting (Moskowitz 2017).

In terms of future thinking, individuals born in the Caribbean were superior compared to all other groups at collective future thinking but not at episodic future thinking. Those born in the Caribbean performed significantly more poorly at episodic future thinking when compared to those of European descent, but not when compared to those who had been born in the US of Caribbean descent. This interaction demonstrated that those born in the Caribbean actually show superior performance at collective future thinking compared to their own episodic future thinking and the opposite is true of those of European descent. Interestingly, those with TBI were impaired at both episodic future thinking and collective future thinking when compared to all groups.

This pilot study shows that there are cultural differences in PM and future thinking, especially, perhaps collective future thinking. The finding of differences in time-based prospective memory may be due to differences in time-sense or in differences in the strictness with which time is interpreted (e.g. do they place less emphasis on the difference between 2:30pm and 3:00pm?) in different cultures. The differences in collective future thinking could lead to differences in group bonding and sense of group membership, or could be reflective of existing differences, such as a greater sense of national pride on small islands.

Culture and Autobiographical Memory

Autobiographical memory is often described as a specific type of episodic memory (Tulving 1972) that people have for events from their personal past (e.g. Barsalou 1998), such as their first year in secondary school, Sunday beach 'limes', or their wedding day. There is general consensus that autobiographical memories are not verbatim recordings of what might have occurred during an episode or life event, but are instead reconstructed mental representations (Conway and Pleydell-Pearce 2000). The representations for an autobiographical memory are often times cued by one's context (e.g. Berntsen 1998) and reconstructed so that the memory is in line with an individual's current goals (i.e., the goals of the working self; Conway and Pleydell-Pearce 2000). This means that one's context is likely to have, at least, a twofold effect on autobiographical remembering: context will relate to *what* is cued and thus remembered (Ross and Wang 2010), and context will affect *why* something is remembered in an effort to meet the goals of the working self (i.e. the function of autobiographical memory; e.g. Baddeley 1988; Bluck and Alea 2002; Neisser 1978). There is perhaps no broader contextual press upon autobiographical remembering than that of cultural context (Alea and Wang 2015; Wang and Ross 2007). However, because all of the literature on culture and autobiographical memory cannot be reviewed below, we focus the current section of this chapter on work that has examined how the Caribbean cultural context might relate to what is remembered and why it is remembered.

What is Remembered in the Caribbean

One of the most well replicated effects about what is remembered about life is that there is a disproportionate number of memories recalled between the ages of 10 and 30 years-old, compared to other life periods; there is essentially a *reminiscence bump* in autobiographical recall (e.g. Rubin, Rahhal, and Poon 1998; Rubin, Wetzler, and Nebes 1986). Although there are a number of theoretical accounts for the reminiscence bump (e.g. life story account Glück and Bluck 2007), the most culturally-relevant is the life-script account (Berntsen and Rubin 2004). This account proposes that cultures have events that occur for most people at particular ages, such as secondary school entry in pre-teen years, marriage in one's late 20s, having children in one's early '30s, etc. These culturally-scripted life events, compared to other types of events, (1) tend to occur in the teenage and young adulthood years, (2) are more easily accessible from memory, and (3) tend to be about positive life experiences. That is, cultures tend not to have expectations about the age timing of negative life events (e.g. divorce might be culturally expected but the age of divorce is usually not). Thus, according to the life script account, the reminiscence bump should be disproportionately comprised of memories that are about positive culturally-scripted life events. Many studies across a variety of cultures find supporting evidence (e.g. Turkey: Erdoğan, Baran, Avlar, Tas and Tekcan 2008; Denmark: Rubin, Berntsen and Hutson 2009; Netherlands: Janssen and Rubin 2011), but not necessarily the one conducted in the Caribbean.

Alea and colleagues (Alea, Ali and Marcano 2014) had a sample of Trinidadian adults report memories in response to cue words (Rubin 1980) and then state how old they were when the event occurred. The valence of the memory was also reported. The memories were then coded by the researchers as being culturally-scripted life events (e.g. graduating primary school at 11 to 12 years-old). Two additional types of memories were coded for: unusual events (e.g. one-time events like losing one's mother at a young age) and ordinary events (e.g. repeated events typical in Trinidadian culture, like going to the beach or to a Carnival fete). It was found that Trinidadians did not have one extended reminiscence bump from 10 to 30 years-old, as is typical, but instead had two distinct reminiscence bumps and that these two bumps were there for both positive *and* negative experiences, and comprised of different types of events.

The first reminiscence bump was between 6 and 15 years-old, and was disproportionately comprised of *ordinary* positive (e.g. fetes) and negative (e.g. doctor visit) events. The second reminiscence bump was in the mid-twenties and disproportionately included *unusual* positive (e.g. last chemotherapy treatment before remission) and negative (e.g. being robbed at gunpoint) events. Two reminiscence bumps actually may be typical in cultures that lean towards collectivism (e.g. Turkey, Demiray, Gülgöz and Bluck 2009), like Trinidad might (Hofstede 2001), as older generations remember not only their own life events (e.g. their own doctor visits) but also, because of the strong social ties in collectivist cultures (Markus and Kitayama 1991), the life events of their kin (e.g. their children's doctor visits; see Demiray et al. 2009 for a similar explanation). The Trinidadian study is also not the first to show that reminiscence bump memories can be somewhat ordinary (e.g. Conway and Haque 1999; Jansari and Parkin 1996), but can also include distinctive or unusual life experiences (Demiray et al. 2009).

The finding from the Trinidadian reminiscence bump study (Alea et al. 2014) that was most at odds with the larger literature is that positive culturally-scripted life events were actually rare. Instead, culturally-scripted *negative* life events emerged in the first reminiscence bump, meaning that Trinidadians seem to have expectations about negative life experiences that are culturally bound, and expected to occur in the range of 6 to 15 years-old. But, what were the Trinidadians remembering? These culturally-scripted memories seemed to be about a particular event during this time, which was being interpreted negatively: taking standardized exams in school, which is an integral part of the education system between these ages in Trinidad and Tobago. For example, secondary school placement standardized exams in the Caribbean region involve a 'high stakes selection process' (De Lisle 2012, 112) for 'prestige schools,' and create anxiety for many students (Payne, 1988), and even potential mental health issues (i.e., depression) for students who place in lower-track schools (Lipps, Lowe, Halliday, Morris-Patterson, Clarke and Wilson 2010). To further increase anxiety in students, at least in Trinidad and Tobago, the results of secondary school placement are published in local newspapers for the nation to observe. Thus, it seems that the socio-educational system in Trinidad and Tobago is perhaps creating a scenario whereby when adults look back on their life, they disproportionately remember negative life-scripted events, whereas other cultures may focus on positive life experiences during this time.

Why an Event is Remembered in the Caribbean

Attempting to understand why life events are recalled involves adopting a functional approach to autobiographical remembering (e.g. Baddeley 1988; Bluck and Alea 2002; Pillemer 1992). This approach moves beyond trying to examine how memory works or what is remembered about life's events, and suggests that researchers explore *why* people remember autobiographical events (e.g. Bluck 2003; Bruce 1989; Neisser 1978). That is, when someone remembers an event from their life, it must be serving some purpose or function for a person, and that function likely aligns with their current goals (Conway and Pleydell-Pearce 2000). A number of functions of autobiographical memory have been suggested in the literature (see, for example, Cohen 1998; Harris, Rasmussen and Berntsen 2014; Hyman and Faries 1992; Pillemer 1992); however, the most widely-used model proposes that autobiographical memory serves three main, broad functions: self, social, and directive (see Bluck and Alea 2002 for a review).

The *self function* of autobiographical memory means that people remember life's events to better understand who they are (e.g. Baddeley 1988; Neisser 1988). Autobiographical events are reflected upon in order to speculate about who one is now and who one would like to become (e.g. Conway and Pleydell-Pearce 2000), to essentially consider whether one has stayed the same or changed over time (i.e., self-continuity; e.g. Barclay 1996; Bluck and Alea 2008). The *social function* of autobiographical memory involves remembering life's events and perhaps sharing those memories with others, for example, for social-bonding reasons (e.g. see Alea and Bluck 2003 for other social functions). That is, remembering autobiographical events allows people to initiate new relationships by sharing memories with people as a way to introduce oneself to others, as a form of conversation (Pasupathi, Lucas and Coombs 2002; Webster 1993). Remembering events shared with loved ones can also be a way to help sustain long-time intimate relationships because thinking about these events helps to keep bonds strong (e.g. Alea and Bluck 2007; Neisser 1978). The *directive* function of autobiographical memory involves using remembered life events to help solve current-day problems (Webster 1993) and to guide current-day behaviour (e.g. Baddeley 1988). Autobiographical events are also used to plan for future experiences (e.g. Baddeley 1988; Pillemer 2003). As one would expect, the Caribbean culture, when compared to other cultures, seems to press upon people to use autobiographical memory to different extents for self, social, and directive functions.

Cultural values, traditions, and daily demands within the Caribbean region seem to create differences in why autobiographical events are remembered (Alea, Ali and Arneaud, in press). A series of studies from Alea and colleagues (Alea 2015; Alea, Arneaud and Ali 2013; Alea and Bluck 2013; Alea, Bluck and Ali 2015) have been conducted in Trinidad and Tobago using the Thinking About Life Experiences Scale (TALE; Bluck and Alea 2011; Bluck, Alea, Habermas and Rubin 2005) as an assessment of how often people reflect on or share autobiographical events for self, social, and directive functions. In general, it seems that Trinidadians use the past in the present least often for social bonding and most often to direct their behaviour (Alea 2015). This pattern for the social function holds when comparing Trinidadians to Americans (Alea Bluck & Ali 2015). Trinidadians are less likely than Americans to use autobiographical memory to initiate and sustain social bonds. Interestingly, Asian societies (e.g. Japan, Maki, Kawasaki, Demiray and Janseen 2015) are also less likely than Americans to rely on the past for social bonding. It is not that Trinidadians devalue social ties and relationships and, in fact, Trinidadians at all ages have good relational wellbeing (Alea, Ali and Arneaud 2012). Instead it is probably that Trinidadians are using other cultural mechanisms to foster relationships (Alea, Bluck and Ali 2015). Collectivist-oriented values (Markus and Kitayama 1991; Hofstede 2001) in Trinidad and Tobago, close geographical proximity to kin (e.g. extended families living together, St. Bernard 2003), and perhaps especially the Trinidadian 'lime' (Erikson 1990) are probably all functioning to keep people close to one another in Trinidad and Tobago. Thus, remembering life's events is less needed to bond people together.

The collectivist-oriented values of Trinidad and Tobago compared to countries like the US (Hofstede 2001) have also been proposed as the reason why *the self function* of autobiographical memory seems to be used less often among Trinidadians compared to US Americans, particularly for Trinidadians who think about the past often (Alea Bluck and Ali 2015). The self in countries that value collectivism is not conceptualized as being independent from others, but is instead construed in relation to others (Markus and Kitayama 1991). This relational self-construal thus does not align well with using memories to define oneself, or to explore whether one has changed or stayed the same over time. Research has shown that in other collectivist countries, like China, for example, a relational self, rather than an independent self, is socialized early in life by the way that mothers talk to their children about life's events (e.g. Kulkofsky, Wang, and Koh 2009). This same socialization practice may be occurring in Caribbean countries where personal life experiences are only made relevant to the self when others are considered.

Using autobiographical memory to direct behaviour, make decisions, and plan for the future, however, seems to be relatively common in Trinidad and Tobago. Compared to US Americans, Trinidadians who think about the past often are more likely to use the past for the directive function of autobiographical memory (Alea Bluck and Ali 2015). Further, using autobiographical memory in this way predicts better psychological well-being among Trinidadians, but this relation is not there for US Americans (Alea and Bluck 2013). Thus, there seems to be something important about the directive function of autobiographical memory in the Trinidadian culture. One suggestion that has been put forward is that, compared to living in the US or other WEIRD societies (Western, Educated, Industrial, Rich, Democratic; Henrich, Heine, and Norenzayan 2010), living in Trinidad and Tobago or even on other islands in the Caribbean is just more difficult on a day-to-day basis. For example, crime is of great concern (Deoseran 2004) and poverty is still a major social problem (Granvorka 2015). Thus, decision-making by quickly relying on life experiences may be more heavily valued and necessary in countries with socioeconomic challenges, like Trinidad and Tobago (Alea, Bluck and Ali 2015), and thus when memory is used in this way, wellbeing is higher.

In sum, the press of culture on autobiographical memory seems to relate to both what is remembered about life and why autobiographical events are remembered. Although the mechanics of remembering autobiographical events may be the same for humans regardless of where they reside in the world (Rubin, Schrauf, Gulgoz, and Naka 2007), there may be unique socio-educational practices, regional and local values, and daily demands associated with living in the Caribbean region that create differences in how life's events are remembered and used in daily life among Caribbean people.

Summary: Culture and Memory for the Distant Past, in the Present, and for the Future

Taken together, the three lines of research about memory for the distant personal past (autobiographical memory), memory in the short-term (working memory), and remembering to do something in the future (prospective memory) highlight that, although some memory mechanisms may be universal (e.g. Rubin et al. 2007), the behavioural and performance outcomes seem to vary by cultural context. As the work reviewed in the current chapter highlighted, for example, individuals from the Caribbean are *sometimes* performing more poorly than individuals from European-based cultural backgrounds on measures of working memory (Khan 2010) and prospective memory (Raskin 2009), and their autobiographical memories tend towards being more negative (Alea et al. 2014). Summarizing across these lines of research it seems that the 'sometimes' cultural differences between Caribbean individuals and those from European descent might occur when: the task is particularly challenging and is more closely tied to education (e.g. DSB), when the task requires remembering to manage one's time well, and when the task might have a high individualistic-value orientation. There are also times, however, when individuals from the Caribbean are performing better than those born outside of the region, for example, on tasks that require thinking about a collective future and work that links using the personal past with wellbeing outcomes. Thus, the pattern is complex.

The challenge, however, is to interpret the meaning of these cultural differences in a context, like the Caribbean, and many other places in the world, that although they might sway one way or another, are neither clearly Eastern nor Western in their way of thinking and functioning in daily life. Memory researchers need to move away from the East-West dichotomy as the predominant distinction between cultures (Alea and Wang 2015) if we really want to understand the meaning and reason for cultural differences in memory processes. Research in the future will need to consider broader value orientations that represent the world's cultures well (not just WEIRD societies), the social and geographical makeup of communities (e.g. geographical proximity of extended family networks), the proximal psychological mechanisms influenced by culture that might account for behavioural outcomes in memory performance (e.g. personality, motivation, time orientation), and the role of cultural differences for societal indicators of a country's development (e.g. like education). The current work also highlights the importance of delineating subgroups within cultures (e.g. Caribbeans born in the Caribbean but living abroad and those born to Caribbean parents but never having lived in the region) and the role of acculturation. Research on acculturation seems particularly timely given the heightened levels of immigration that are occurring throughout the world.

Interpreting what cultural differences in memory processes mean for the actual lives of individuals residing in or from, for example, non-European and North American regions of the world, like the Caribbean, needs to be a priority. For example, although the current chapter provided evidence for cultural differences in each distinct type of memory process, these memory processes inevitably interact in an individual's daily life. Thus, more work is needed to examine, for example, how working memory might impact both prospective memory and autobiographical encoding of information. Both cross-cultural and longitudinal studies will be needed (e.g. Hatano 2005) to further establish and elucidate the complex relationship between culture and cognition. Finding this link may likely require moving beyond behavioural indicators of memory performance, and continuing to explore the underlying brain regions that demonstrate cultural differences in cognitive processing (e.g. Park and Gutchess 2002). However, to really understand cultural differences in memory processes, we also need to continue to ask questions about why, or what function a memory process is serving individuals in their daily life in their larger cultural milieu, and the implications for individuals in clinical settings. The answer to these questions will have consequences for the way that memory-related daily tasks, such as management of memory loss with age, medication adherence, eyewitness testimony, and educational and vocational training, are managed by individuals themselves, but also clinicians and governments in Caribbean societies.

Notes
1. Authors contributed equally and are listed in alphabetical order.

Works Cited:

Addis, D., D. Sacchetti, B. Ally, B. Budson, and D. Schacter. 'Episodic Simulation of Future Events is Impaired in Mild Alzheimer's Disease.' *Neuropsychologia* 47, 2, (2009) 660–671.

Alea, N. '"Bring Back de Ole Time Days": Why Trinidadians Remember.' In *Ageing in the Caribbean*, edited by J. Rawlins and N. Alea. Greenacres, FL: Lifegate Publishing, 2015.

Alea, N., S. Ali, and M.J. Arneaud. 'Over the Hill and Still "Liming": Psychological Well-Being in Young, Middle-Aged, and Older Adult Trinidadians.' *Journal of the Department of Behavioral Sciences* 2 (2012): 63–89.

———. 'What I Value and Why I Remember: Values and the Functions of Memory in a Trinidadian Lifespan Sample.' *International Journal of Reminiscence and Life Review* (in press).

———. 'The Bumps in Trinidadian Life: Reminiscence Bumps for Positive and Negative Life Events.' *Applied Cognitive Psychology* 28 (2014): 174–184. doi: 10.1002/acp.2975.

———. 'The Quality of Self, Social, and Directive Memories: Are There Adult Age Group Differences?' *International Journal of Behavioral Development* 37 (2013): 395–406. doi: 10.1177/0165025413484244.

Alea, N., and S. Bluck. 'Why Are You Telling Me That? A Conceptual Model of the Social Function of Autobiographical Memory.' *Memory*, 11 (2003): 165–78. doi:10.1080/741938207.

———. 'I'll Keep You in Mind: The Intimacy Function of Autobiographical Memory.' *Applied Cognitive Psychology* 21 (2007): 1,091–111. doi:10.1002/acp.1316.

———. 'When Does Meaning Making Predict Well-Being? Examining Young And Older Adults In Two Cultures.' *Memory* 21, no. 1 (2013): 44–63. doi: 10.1080/09658211.2012. 704927.

Alea, N., S. Bluck, and S. Ali. 'Function in Context: Why American and Trinidadian Young and Older Adults Remember the Personal Past.' *Memory* 23 (2015): 55–68. doi: 10.1080/09658211. 2014.929704

Alea, N., and Q. Wang. 'Going Global: The Functions of Autobiographical Memory in Cultural Context.' *Memory*. 23, no. 1 (2015): 1–10. http://dx.doi.org/10.1080/09658211.2014.972416.

Ardila, A., F. Ostrosky-Solis, M. Rosselli, and C. Gómez. 'Age-Related Cognitive Decline During Normal Aging: The Complex Effect of Education.' *Archives of Clinical Neuropsychology* 15, no. 6 (2000): 495–513. doi:http://dx.doi.org/10.1016/S0887-6177(99)00040-2.

Arentoft, A., D. Byrd, R. Robbins, J. Monzones, C. Miranda, A. Rosario, K. Coulehan, A. Fuentes, K. Germano, E. D'Auila, J. Sheynin, F. Fraser, S. Morgello, and M. Mindt. 'Multidimensional Effects of Acculturation on English-Language Neuropsychological Test Performance Among HIV+ Caribbean Latinas/os.' *Journal of Clinical and Experimental Neuropsychology* (2012): 34.

Atance, C., and D. O'Neill. 'Episodic Future Thinking.' *Trends in Cognitive Science* 5 (2001): 219–24.

Baddeley, A. 'But What the Hell is it For?' In *Practical Aspects of Memory: Current Research and Issues,* edited by M.M. Gruneberg, P.E. Morris and R. N. Sykes, 3–18. Chichester: Wiley 1988.

———. 'The Episodic Buffer: A New Component of Working Memory?' *Trends in Cognitive Sciences* 4, no. 11 (2000): 417–23.

Barclay, C.R. 'Autobiographical Remembering: Narrative Constraints on Objectified Selves.' In *Remembering Our Past: Studies in Autobiographical Memory,* edited by D. C. Rubin, 94–125. New York: Cambridge University Press 1996. doi: 10.1017/cbo9780511527913. 004.

Barsalou, L.W. 'The Content and Organization of Autobiographical Memories.' In *Real Events Remembered: Ecological and Traditional Approaches to the Study of Memory,* edited by U. Newsier and E. Winograd, 193–243. Cambridge: Cambridge University Press, 1988. doi: 10.1017/CBO9780511664014.009.

Benoit, R., S. Gilbert, and P. Burgess. 'A Neural Mechanism Mediating the Impact of Episodic Prospection on Farsighted Decisions.' *Journal of Neuroscience* 31 (2011): 6,771–779.

Berntsen, D. 'Voluntary and Involuntary Access to Autobiographical Memory.' *Memory,* 6, no. 2 (1998): 113–41. doi: 10.1080/741942071.

Berntsen, D., and D.C. Rubin. 'Cultural Life Scripts Structure Recall from Autobiographical Memory.' *Memory and Cognition* 32 (2004): 427–42. doi: 10.3758/BF03195836

Black, F.W., and R.L. Strub. 'Digit Repetition Performance in Patients with Focal Brain Damage.' *Cortex* 14, no. 1 (1978): 12–21. doi:http://dx.doi.org/10.1016/S0010-9452(78)80003-3.

Bluck, S. 'Autobiographical Memory: Exploring its functions in Everyday Life.' *Memory,* 11 (2003): 113–23. doi: 10.1080/741938206.

Bluck, S., and N. Alea 'Exploring the Functions of Autobiographical Memory: Why Do I Remember the Autumn?' In *Critical Advances in Reminiscence Work: From Theory to Application,* edited by J.D. Webster and B.K. Haight, 61–75. New York, NY: Springer, 2002.

Bluck, S., and N. Alea. 'Remembering Being Me: The Self-Continuity Function of Autobiographical Memory in Younger and Older Adults.' In *Selfcontinuity: Individual and Collective Perspectives,* edited by F. Sani 55–70. New York, NY: Psychology Press 2008.

Bluck, S., and N. Alea. 'Crafting the TALE: Construction of a Measure to Assess the Functions of Autobiographical Remembering.' *Memory* 19, (2011): 470– 86. doi: 10.1080/ 09658211.2011.590500.

Bluck, S., N. Alea, T. Habermas, and D.C. Rubin. 'A Tale of Three Functions: the Self-Reported Uses of Autobiographical Memory.' *Social Cognition,* 23 (2005): 91–117. doi: 10.1521/ soco.23.1.91.59198.

Bolton, T.L. 'The Growth of Memory in School Children.' *American Journal of Psychology* 4 (1892): 362–80.

Boone, K.B., T. L. Victor, J. Wen, J. Razani, and M. Pontón. 'The Association Between Neuropsychological Scores and Ethnicity, Language, and Acculturation Variables in a Large Patient Population.' *Archives of Clinical Neuropsychology* 22, no. 3 (2007): 355–65. doi:http://dx.doi.org/10.1016/j.acn.2007.01.010.

Bruce, D. 'Functional Explanations of Memory.' In *Everyday Cognition in Adulthood and Late Life*, edited by L.W. Poon, D.C. Rubin, and B.A. Wilson, 44–58. Cambridge: Cambridge University Press, 1989.

Burgess, P.W., N. Alderman, E. Volle, R.G. Benoit and S.J. Gilbert. 'Mesulam's Frontal Lobe Mystery Re-examined.' *Restorative Neurology and Neuroscience* 27, no. 5 (2009): 493–506. doi: 10.3233/Rnn-2009-0511.

Burgess, P.W., G. Gonen-Yaacovi, and E. Volle. 'Functional Neuroimaging Studies of Prospective Memory: What Have We Learnt So Far?' *Neuropsychologia* 49, no. 8 (2011): 2,246–257. doi: 10.1016/j.neuropsychologia.2011.02.014.

Carey, C.L., S.P. Woods, J.D. Rippeth, R.K. Heaton, I. Grant, and the HIV Neurobehavioral Research Center (HNRC) group. Prospective Memory in HIV-1 Infection. *Journal of Clinical and Experimental Neuropsychology* 28, no. 4 (2006): 536–48. http://doi.org/10.1080/13803390590949494.

Carlesimo, G.A., L. Fadda, S. Lorusso, and C. Caltagirone. 'Verbal and Spatial Memory Spans in Alzheimer's and Multi-infarct Dementia.' *Acta Neurologica Scandinavica* 89, no. 2 (1994): 132–38. doi:10.1111/j.1600-0404.1994.tb01648.x.

Chang, J. 'Adult Prospective Memory and Executive Function Performance: A Cross-Cultural Comparison of Chinese and Canadian College Students.' Master's Thesis. University of Victoria, Canada, 2009.

Cohen, G. 'The Effects of Aging on Autobiographical Memory.' In *Autobiographical Memory: Theoretical and Applied Perspectives*, edited by C.P. Thompson, D.J. Herrmann, D. Bruce, D.J. Read, D.G. Payne, and M.P. Toglia, 105–23. Hillsdale, NJ: Lawrence Erlbaum Associates, 1998.

Conway, M.A., and S. Haque. 'Overshadowing the Reminiscence Bump: Memories of a Struggle for Independence.' *Journal of Adult Development*, 6 (1999): 35–44. doi: 10.1023/A: 1021672208155.

Conway, M.A., and C.W. Pleydell-Pearce. 'The Construction of Autobiographical Memories in the Self-Memory System.' *Psychological Review*, 107 (2000): 261–88. doi: 10.1037/0033-295X.107.2.261

Craik, F.I.M. 'Age Differences in Human Memory.' In *Handbook of the Psychology of Aging*, edited by J.E. Birren & K.W. Schaie, 384–420. New York, NY: Van Nostrand Reinhold, 1977.

Crawford, J.R., K.M. Allan, D.W. Stephen, D.M. Parker, and J.A.O. Besson. 'The Wechsler Adult Intelligence Scale Revised (WAIS-R) – Factor Structure in a UK Sample.' *Personality and Individual Differences* 10, no. 11 (1989): 1,209–212.

Crews, F., J. He, and C. Hodge. 'Adolescent Cortical Development: A Critical Period of Vulnerability for Addiction.' *Pharmacology Biochemistry* and *Behavior* 86, no. 2 (2007): 189–99. doi: https://doi.org/10.1016/j.pbb.2006.12.001.

D' Argembeau, A., and M. Van der Linden. 'Predicting the Phenomenology of Episodic Future Thoughts.' *Conscousness and Cognition* 21 (2012): 1,198–206.

De Lisle, J. 'Secondary School Entrance Examinations in the Caribbean: Legacy, Policy, and Evidence Within an Era of Seamless Education.' *Caribbean Curriculum* 19 (2012): 109–43.

Demiray, B., S. Gülgöz, and S. Bluck. 'Examining the Life Story Account of the Reminiscence Bump: Why We Remember More from Young Adulthood.' *Memory* 17 (2009): 708–23. doi: 10.1080/09658210902939322.

Demirovic, J., R. Prineas, D. Loewenstein, B. Jean, R. Duara, S. Sevush, and J. Szapocznik, 'Prevalence of Dementia in Three Ethnic Groups: The South Florida Program on Aging and Health.' *Annals of Epidemiology* 13 no. 6 (2003): 472–78. doi: https://doi.org/10.1016/S1047-2797(02)00437-4.

Deosaran, R. 'A Portrait of Crime in the Caribbean: Realities and Challenges.' In *Caribbean Security in the Age of Terror: Challenge and Change*, edited by Ivelaw F. Griffith, 104–28. Kingston, Jamaica: Ian Randle Publishers, 2004.

De Renzi, E., and P. Nichelli. 'Verbal and Non-Verbal Short-Term Memory Impairment Following Hemispheric Damage.' *Cortex* 11, no. 4 (1975): 341–54. doi:http://dx.doi.org/10.1016/S0010-9452(75)80026-8.

Duval, C., B Desgranges, V. De La Sayette, S. Belliard, F. Eustache, and P. Piolino. 'What Happens to Personal Identity when Semantic Knowledge Degrades? A Study of the Self and Autobiographical Memory in Semantic Dementia.' *Neuropsychologia* 50 (2012): 254–65.

Ebbinghaus, H. *Memory: A Contribution to Experimental Psychology*. New York: Columbia University, Teachers College, 1885.

Einstein, G.O., and M.A. McDaniel. 'Normal Aging and Prospective Memory.' *Journal of Experimental Psychology: Learning, Memory, and Cognition* 16 (1990): 717–26.

Ellis, J, and J. Freeman, 'Ten Years On: Realizing Delayed Intentions.' In *Prospective Memory: Cognitive, Neuroscience, Developmental and Applied Perspectives*: edited by M. Kliegel, M. McDaniel and G. Einstein, 1–28. New York: Lawrence Erlbaum Associates, 2008.

Erdoğan, A., B. Baran, B. Avlar, Ç. Tas, and A.I. Tekcan, 'On the Persistence of Positive Events in Life Scripts.' *Applied Cognitive Psychology* 22, (2008): 95–111. doi: 10.1002/acp.1363.

Eriksen, T. H. 'Liming in Trinidad: The Art of Doing Nothing.' *Folk* 32 (1990): 23–43.

Fasfous, A.F., N Hidalgo-Ruzzante, R. Vilar-López, A. Catena-Martínez, and M. Pérez-García. 'Cultural Differences in Neuropsychological Abilities Required to Perform Intelligence Tasks.' *Archives of Clinical Neuropsychology* 28, no. 8 (2013): 784–90. doi:10.1093/arclin/act074.

Golden, C.J., P. Espe-Pfeifer, and J. Wachsler-Felder. 'Neuropsychological Interpretation of Objective Psychological Tests.' (2000): Retrieved from http://www.myilibrary.com?id=20727.

Gomboz, N., S. De Vito, M. Brandimonte, S. Pappalardo, F. Galeone, A. Iavarone, and S. Della Sala. 'Episodic Future Thinking in Amnesic Mild Cognitive Impairment.' *Neuropsychologia* 48 (2010): 2,091–97.

Glück, J., and S. Bluck. 'Looking Back Across the Life Span: A Life Story Account of the Reminiscence Bump.' *Memory and Cognition* 35 (2007): 1928–39. doi: 10.3758/BF03192926.

Granvorka, C.G. 'Poverty in the Caribbean.' In *Public Administration and Policy in the Caribbean,* edited by Indianna D. Minto-Coy and Evan Berman, 180, 443–62. New York, NY: Taylor and Francis Group, 2015.

Groot, Y.C.T., B.A. Wilson, J.J. Evans, and P. Watson. 'Prospective Memory Functioning in People With and Without Brain Injury.' *Journal of the International Neuropsychological Society* 8, no. 5 (2002): 645–54.

Gutchess, A H., A.J. Schwartz, and A. Boduroğlu. 'The Influence of Culture on Memory.' In *Foundations of Augmented Cognition. Directing the Future of Adaptive Systems: 6th International Conference, FAC 2011, Held as Part of HCI International 2011, Orlando, FL, USA, July 9–14, 2011. Proceedings,* edited by D.D. Schmorrow and C.M. Fidopiastis, 67–76. Berlin, Heidelberg: Springer Berlin Heidelberg 2011.

Gutchess, A.H., C. Yoon, T. Luo, F. Feinberg, T. Hedden, Q. Jing, and D.C. Park. 'Categorical Organization in Free Recall across Culture and Age.' *Gerontology,* 52, no. 5 (2006): 314–23.

Guynn, M.J. 'A Two-Process Model of Strategic Monitoring in Event-Based Prospective Memory: Activation/Retrieval Mode and Checking.' *International Journal of Psychology* 38 (2003): 245–56. doi:10.1080/00207590344000178.

Harris, C.B., A.S. Rasmussen, and D. Berntsen. 'The Functions of Autobiographical Memory: An Integrative Approach.' *Memory* 22, no. 5, (2014): 559–81. doi: 10.1080/09658211.2013.806555.

Harris, J. E., and A. J. Wilkins. 'Remembering to Do Things: A Theoretical Framework and an Illustrative Experiment.' *Human Learning* 1 (1982): 123–36.

Hassabis, D., D. Kumaran, and S. Vann. 'Patients with Hippocampal Amnesia Cannot Imagine New Experiences.' *Proceedings of the National Academy of Sciences* 104 (2007): 1,726–31.

Hatano, G. 'How Are Cultural-Historical Change and Individual Cognition Related?' *Mind, Culture and Activity* 12 (2005): 226–32.

Hedden, T., D.C. Park, R. Nisbett, L.-J. Ji, Q. Jing, and S. Jiao. 'Cultural Variation in Verbal Versus Spatial Neuropsychological Function Across the Life Span.' *Neuropsycholog,* 16, no. 1, (2002): 65–73. http://dx.doi.org/10.1037/0894-4105.16.1.65.

Henrich, J., S.J. Heine, and A. Norenzayan. 'The Weirdest People in the World?' *The Behavioral and Brain Sciences* 33, no. 2–3 (2010): 61–83. doi: 10.1017/S0140525X0999152X.

Hofstede, G. *Culture's Consequences: Comparing Values, Behaviors, Institutions, and Organizations Across Nations*, 2nd ed. Thousand Oaks, CA: Sage, 2001.
Holmes, O.W. *Mechanisms in Thought and Morals*. Boston: Osgood, 1871:
Hyman, I.E., and J.M Faries. 'The Functions of Autobiographical Memory.' In *Theoretical Perspectives on Autobiographical Memory*, edited by M.A. Conway, D.C. Rubin, H. Spinnler and W.A. Wagenaar, 207–21. Springer Netherlands, 1992. doi: 10.1007/978-94-015-7967-4_12.
Irish, M., D. Addis, J. Hodges, and O. Piguet. 'Considering the Role of Semantic Memory in Episodic Future Thinking: Evidence from Semantic Dementia.' *Brain* 135 (2012): 2,178–191.
Jacobs, J. 'The Need of a Society for Experimental Psychology.' *Mind*, 11, (1886): 49–54.
Jahn, H. 'Memory Loss in Alzheimer's Disease.' *Dialogues in Clinical Neuroscience*,15, no. 4, (2013): 445–54.
Jansari, A., and A.J. Parkin. 'Things That Go Bump in Your Life: Explaining The Reminiscence Bump in Autobiographical Memory.' *Psychology and Aging* 11 (1996): 85–91. doi: 10.1037/0882-7974.11.1.85.
Janssen, S.M.J., and D.C. Rubin. 'Age Effects in Cultural Life Scripts.'*Applied Cognitive Psychology* 25 (2011): 291–98. doi: 10.1002/acp.1690.
Jarvik, L.F. 'Aging of the Brain: How Can We Prevent It?' *The Gerontologist*, 28, no. 6 (1988): 739–47. doi:10.1093/geront/28.6.739.
Jensen, A.R. *Bias in Mental Testing*. New York: Free Press, 1980).
Jensen, A.R., and R.A. Figueroa. 'Forward and Backward Digit Span Interaction with Race and IQ: Predictions from Jensen's Theory.' *Journal of Educational Psychology* 67, no. 6, (1975): 882–93. doi:10.1037/0022-0663.67.6.882.
Kaplan, E., D. Fein, R. Morris, and D.C. Delis.'*WAIS-R as a Neuropsychological Instrument*.' San Antonio, TX: Psychological Corporation, 1991.
Khan, K. *Demographic and Ethnicity Effects on Neuropsychological Test Performance: Implications for Dementia Assessment in Caribbean Populations*. PhD Thesis, University of Hull, England, 2010.
Khan, K., and A. Venneri. 'Differential Effects of Culture and Education on Verbal Fluency: Implications for Neuropsychological Assessment.' *Manuscript Submitted for Publication*, 2017.
Kitayama, S., S. Duffy, T. Kawamura, and J.T. Larsen. 'Perceiving an Object and Its Context in Different Cultures: A Cultural Look at New Look.' *Psychological Science* 14, no. 3 (2003): 201–06. doi:10.1111/1467-9280.02432.
Kulkofsky, S., Q. Wang, and J.B.K. Koh. 'Functions of Memory Sharing and Mother-Child Reminiscing Behaviors: Individual and Cultural Variations.' *Journal of Cognition and Development* 10 (2009): 92–114. doi: 10.1080/15248370903041231.
Kvavilashvili, L. 'Remembering Intentions: A Critical Review of Existing Experimental Paradigms.' *Applied Cognitive Psychology* 6 (1992): 507–24. doi:10.1002/acp.2350060605.

La Corte, V., and P. Piolino. 'On The Role of Personal Semantic Memory and Temporal Distance in Episodic Future Thinking: The Tedift Model.' *Frontiers in Human Neuroscience* 10 (2016): 385.

Levy, R., and G. Loftus. 'Compliance and Memory.' In *Everyday Memory, Actions, and Absent-Mindedness,* edited by J.Harris and P. Morris 93–112. London, England: Academic Press, 1984.

Li, S.C., and S. Lewandowsky. 'Intralist Distractors and Recall Direction – Constraints on Models of Memory for Serial Order.' *Journal of Experimental Psychology-Learning Memory and Cognition* 19, no. 4 (1993): 895–908.

Li, S.C., and S. Lewandowsky. 'Forward and Backward Recall – Different Retrieval-Processes.' *Journal of Experimental Psychology-Learning Memory and Cognition* 21, no. 4 (1995): 837–47.

Lipps, G.E., G.A. Lowe, S. Halliday, A. Morris-Patterson, N. Clarke and R.N. Wilson. 'The Association of Academic Tracking to Depressive Symptoms Among Adolescents in Three Caribbean Countries.' *Child and Adolescent Psychiatry and Mental Health* 4, no. 1. (2010): 1. doi: 10.1186/1753-2000-4-16.

Lezak, M.D., D.B. Howieson, and D.W. Loring. *Neuropsychological Assessment.* 4th ed. New York: Oxford University Press, 2004.

Maki, Y., Y. Kawasaki, B. Demiray and S.M. Janseen. 'Autobiographical Memory Functions in Young Japanese Men and Women.' *Memory* 23, no. 1 (2015): 11–24. doi: 10.1080/ 09658211.2014.930153.

Markus, H.R., and S. Kitayama. 'Culture and The Self: Implications for Cognition, Emotion, and Motivation.' *Psychological Review* 98 (1991): 224–53. doi: 10.1037/0033-295X.98.2.224.

Masuda, T., P.C. Ellsworth, B. Mesquita, J. Leu, S. Tanida, and E. Van de Veerdonk. 'Placing the Face in Context: Cultural Differences in the Perception of Facial Emotion.' *J Pers Soc Psychol* 94 no. 3 (2008): 365–81. doi:10.1037/0022-3514.94.3.365.

Mayfield, J.W., and C.R. Reynolds. 'Black-white Differences in Memory Test Performance Among Children and Adolescents.' *Archives of Clinical Neuropsychology* 12, no. 2 (1997): 111–22. doi:http://dx.doi.org/10.1016/ S0887-6177(96)00016-9.

McDaniel, M., and G Einstein. 'Strategic and Automatic Processes in Prospective Memory Retrieval: A Multiprocess Framework.' *Applied Cognitive Psycholog,* 14 (2000): 127–44.

Miller, G. A. 'The Magical Number Seven, Plus or Minus Two: Some Limits on Our Capacity for Processing Information.' *Psychological Review* 63, no. 2 (1956): 81–97.

Moskowitz, G. 'Distortion in Time Perception as a Result of Concern about Appearing Biased.' *PLoS One* (2017): 12.

Mueller, J.H., and T.D. Overcast. 'Free Recall as a Function of Test Anxiety, Concreteness, and Instructions.' *Bulletin of the Psychonomic Society,* 8, no. 3 (1976): 194–96. http://dx.doi.org/10.3758/BF03335123.

Muangpaisan, W., S. Intalapaporn, and P. Assantachai. 'Digit Span aand Verbal Fluency Tests in Patients with Mild Cognitive Impairment and Normal Subjects in Thai-Community.' *J Med Assoc Thai* 93 no.2 (2010): 224–30.

Neisser, U. 'Memory: What are the Important Questions?' In *Practical Aspects of Memory*, edited by M.M. Gruneberg, P. Morris, and R.H. Sykes, 3–24. New York: Academic Press, 1978.

Neisser, U. 'Five Kinds of Self-knowledge.' *Philosophical Psychology* 1, no. 1, (1988): 35–59. doi: 10.1080/09515088808572924.

Nisbett, R.E. *The Geography of Thought: How Asians and Westerners Think Differently, and Why.* New York, NY: Free Press, 2003.

Nisbett, R.E., and T. Masuda. 'Culture and Point of View.' *Proceedings of the National Academy of Sciences of the United States of America* 100 (2003): 11,163–175. doi: 10.1073/pnas.1934527100.

Okuda, J., T. Fujii, A. Yamadori, R. Kawashima, T. Tsukiura, R. Fukatsu, et al. 'Participation of the Prefrontal Cortices in Prospective Memory: Evidence from a Pet Study in Humans.' *Neuroscience Letters* 253 (1998): 127–30.

Ostrosky-Solis, F., A. Ardila, M. Rosselli, G. Lopez-Arango, and V. Uriel-Mendoza. 'Neuropsychological Test Performance in Illiterate Subjects.' *Archives of Clinical Neuropsychology* 13, no. 7 (1998): 645–60. doi:http://dx.doi.org/10.1016/S0887-6177(97)00094-2.

Ostrosky-Solis, F., and A. Lozano. 'Digit Span: Effect of Education and Culture.' *International Journal of Psychology* 41, no. 5 (2006): 333–41. doi:Doi 10.1080/00207590500345724.

Owen, A.M., A.C.H. Lee, and E.J. Williams. 'Dissociating Aspects of Verbal Working Memory within the Human Frontal Lobe: Further Evidence for a "Process-Specific" Model of Lateral Frontal Organization.' *Psychobiology,* 28, no. 2 (2000): 146–55.

Palombo, D., M. Keane, and M. Verfaellie. 'The Medial Temporal Lobes are Critical for Reward-Based Decision Making Under Conditions that Promote Episodic Future Thinking.' *Hippocampus* 25 (2015): 345–53.

———. 'Using Future Thinking to Reduce Temporal Discounting: Under What Circumstances are the Medial Temporal Lobes Critical?' *Neuropsychologia* 89 (2016): 437–44.

Park, D.C., and A.H. Gutchess. 'Aging, Cognition, and Culture: A Neuroscientific Perspective.' *Neuroscience and Biobehavioral Reviews* 26 no.7 (2002): 859–67. doi: https://doi.org/10.1016/S0149-7634(02)00072-6.

Park, D.C., C. Hertzog, D.P. Kidder, R.W. Morrell, and C.B Mayhorn. 'Effect of Age on Event-Based and Time-Based Prospective Memory.' *Psychology and Aging,* 12, no. 2 (1997): 314–327. http://dx.doi.org/10.1037/0882-7974.12.2.314.

Pasupathi, M., S. Lucas, and A. Coombs. 'Conversational Functions of Autobiographical Remembering: Long-Married Couples Talk About Conflicts and Pleasant Topics.' *Discourse Processes* 34, no. 1 (2002): 63–192. doi: 10.1207/S15326950DP3402_3.

Payne, M.A. 'Adolescent Fears: Some Caribbean Findings.' *Journal of Youth and Adolescence* 17, no. 3 (1988): 255–66. doi: 10.1007/BF01538166.

Pillemer, D.B. 'Remembering Personal Circumstances: A Functional Analysis.' In *Affect And Accuracy In Recall: Studies of 'Flashbulb' Memories,* 4th ed., edited by E. Winograd and U. Neisser, 236–64. New York, NY: Cambridge University Press, 1992.

Pillemer, D. 'Directive Functions of Autobiographical Memory: The Guiding Power of the Specific Episode.' *Memory* 11, no. 2 (2003): 193–202. doi: 10.1080/741938208.

Rapport, L.J., J.S. Webster, and R.L. Dutra. 'Digit Span Performance and Unilateral Neglect.' *Neuropsychologia* 32, no. 5 (1994): 517–25.

Raskin, S., J. Maye, A. Rogers, D. Correll, M. Zamroziewicz, and M. Kurtz. 'Prospective Memory in Schizophrenia: Relationship to Medication Management Skills, Neurocognition, and Symptoms in Individuals with Schizophrenia.' *Neuropsychology* 28 (2014): 359–65.

Raskin, S.A. and M.M. Sohlberg. 'Prospective Memory Intervention: A Review And Evaluation Of A Pilot Restorative Intervention.' *Brain Impairment,* 10(1), (2009): 76–86.

Raskin, S., C. Buckheit, and A. Waxman. 'Effect of Type of Cue, Type of Response, Time Delay and Two Different Ongoing Tasks on Prospective Memory Functioning after Acquired Brain Injury.' *Neuropsychological Rehabilitation* 22, no. 1 (2012): 40–64.

Raskin, S.A. 'Memory for Intentions Screening Test: Psychometric Properties and Clinical Evidence.' *Brain Impairment* 10, no. 1 (2009): 23–33.

Rasmussen, K., and D. Berntsen. 'Autobiographical Memory and Episodic Future Thinking After Moderate to Severe Traumatic Brain Injury.' *Journal of Neuropsychology* 8 (2012): 34–52.

Rendell, P.G., and D.M. Thomson. 'Aging and Prospective Memory: Differences Between Naturalistic and Laboratory Tasks.' *The Journals of Gerontology: Series B: Psychological Sciences and Social Sciences 54B*, no. 4 (1999): 256–69.

Reynolds, C.R. 'Forward and Backward Memory Span Should Not Be Combined for Clinical Analysis.' *Archives of Clinical Neuropsychology* 12, no. 1(1997): 29–40. doi:http://dx.doi.org/10.1016/S0887-6177(96)00015-7.

Ross, M. and Q. Wang. 'Why We Remember What We Remember: Culture and Autobiographical Memory.' *Perspectives on Psychological Science* 5, no. 4 (2010): 401–09. doi:10.1177/1745691610375555.

Rubin, J. '51 Properties of 125 Words: A Unit Analysis of Verbal Behavior.' *Journal of Verbal Learning and Verbal Behavior* 21 (1980): 21–38. doi: 10.1016/S0022-5371(80)90415-6.

Rubin, D.C., D. Berntsen, and M. Hutson. 'The Normative and The Personal Life: Individual Differences in Life Scripts and Life Story Events Among USA and Danish Undergrads.' *Memory* 17, no. 1 (2009): 54–68. doi: 10.1080/09658210802541442.

Rubin, D.C., T.A Rahhal, and L.W. Poon. 'Things Learned in Early Adulthood are Remembered Best.' *Memory and Cognitio* 26 (1998): 3–19. doi: 10.3758/BF03211366.

Rubin, D.C., R.W. Schrauf, S. Gulgoz, and M. Naka. 'Cross-Cultural Variability of Component Processes in Autobiographical Remembering: Japan, Turkey, and the USA.' *Memory* 15, no. 5 (2007): 536–47. doi: 10.1080/09658210701332679.

Rubin, D.C., S. E. Wetzler, and R.D. Nebes. 'Autobiographical Memory Across the Adult Lifespan.' In *Autobiographical Memory*, edited by D.C. Rubin, 202–21. Cambridge: Cambridge University Press, 1986. doi: 10.1017/CBO9780511558313.018.

Salthouse, T.A., D.E. Berish, and K.L. Siedlecki. 'Construct Validity and Age Sensitivity of Prospective Memory.' *Memory and Cognition* 32, no. 7 (2004): 1,133–148. doi: 10.3758/bf03196887.

Sani, F., M. Bowe, and M. Herrera. 'Perceived Collective Continuity and Social Well-Being: Exploring the Connections.' *European Journal of Social Psychology* 38, no. 2 (2008): 365–374. doi: 10.1002/ejsp.461.

Sani, F. *Self Continuity: Individual and Collective Perspectives*. New York, NY: Psychology Press, 2008.

Schacter, D., and D. Addis. 'The Cognitive Neuroscience of Constructive Memory: Remembering the Past and Imaging the Future.' *Philosophical Translations of the Royal Society of London: B Biological Science* 362 (2007): 773–86.

Schacter, D., D. Addis, D. Hassabis, V. Martin, R. Spreng, and K. Szpunar. 'The Future of Memory: Remembering, Imagining, and the Brain.' *Neuron* 76 (2012): 677–94.

Schwartz, S., J. Unger, B. Zamboanga, and J. Szapocznik. 'Rethinking the Concept of Acculturation.' *American Psychologist* 65 (2010): 237–51.

Sellen, A.J., G. Louie, J.E. Harris, and A.J. Wilkins. 'What Brings Intentions to Mind? An In Situ Study of Prospective Memory.' *Memory* 5 no. 4 (1997): 483–507. doi: 10.1080/741941433.

Shum, D., H. Levin, and R. Chan. 'Prospective Memory in Patients with Closed Head Injury: A Review.' *Neuropsychologia* 49 (2011): 2,156–165.

Shum, D., M. Valentine, and T. Cutmore. 'Performance of Individuals with Severe Long-Term Traumatic Brain Injury on Time-, Event-, and Activity-based Prospective Memory Tasks.' *Journal of Clinical and Experimental Neuropsychology* 21, no. 1 (1999): 49–58.

Simons, J. S., M.L. Schölvinck, S.J. Gilbert, C.D. Frith, and P.W. Burgess. 'Differential Components of Prospective Memory?: Evidence from fMRI.' *Neuropsychologia* 44, no. 8 (2006): 1,388–397. doi: https://doi.org/10.1016/j.neuropsychologia.2006.01.005.

Sinha, C. and P. Gardenfors. 'Time, Space, and Events in Language and Cognition: A Comparative View.' *Annals of the New York Academy of Sciences* 1,326 (2014): 72–81.

Smith, R. E., and U.J. Bayen. 'A Multinomial Model of Event-based Prospective Memory.' *Journal of Experimental Psychology: Learning, Memory, and Cognition* 30, no. 4 (2004): 756–777. http://dx.doi.org/10.1037/0278-7393.30.4.756.

Sowell, E., D. Delis, J. Stiles, and T. Jernigan. 'Improved Memory Functioning and Frontal Lobe Maturation Between Childhood and Adolescence: A Structural MRI Study.' *Journal of the International Neuropsychological Society* 7, no. 3 (2001): 312–322.

Squire, L., A. van der Horst, S. McDuff, J. Frascino, R. Hopkins, and K. Mauldin. 'Role of the Hippocampus in Remembering the Past and Imagining the Future.' *Proceedings of the National Academy of Sciences*, 107, (2011): 19,044–48.

St. Bernard, G. *Major Trends Affecting Families in Central America and The Caribbean.* Prepared for United Nations Division of Social Policy and Development, Department of Economic and Social Affairs Program on the Family.' May 23, 2003.

Szpunar, P., and K. Szpunar. 'Collective Future Thought: Concept, Function, and Implications for Collective Memory Studies.' *Memory Studies* 9 (2015): 376–89.

Tulsky, D. S., D.H. Saklofske, J. Zhu, S.T. David, H.S. Donald, K.H. Robert, and P. Aurelio. 'Revising a Standard: An Evaluation of the Origin and Development of the WAIS-III.' In *Clinical Interpretation of the WAIS-III and WMS-III* 43–92. San Diego, CA: Academic Press, 2003.

Tulving, E. 'Episodic and Semantic Memory.' *Organization of Memory. London: Academic* 381, no. 4 (1972): 382–404.

Van der Flier, W., and P. Scheltens. 'Epidemiology and Risk Factors of Dementia.' *Journal of Neurology, Neurosurgery, and Psychiatry* 76 (2005): v2–v7.

Walter, S., and B. Meier. 'How Important is Importance for Prospective Memory: A Review.' *Frontiers in Psychology* 5 (2014).

Wang, Q., and M. Ross. 'Culture and Memory.' In *Handbook of Cultural Psychology*, edited by S. Kitayama and D. Cohen, 645–67. New York, NY: Guilford Press, 2007.

Webster, J.D. 'Construction of Validation of the Reminiscence Functions Scale.' *The Journal of Gerontology* 48, no. 5 (1993): 256–62. doi: 10.1093/geronj/48.5.P256.

Wechsler, D. *The Measurement of Intelligence.* Baltimore, MD: Williams and Witkins 1939.

Wechsler, D.A. 'Standardised Memory Scale for Clinical Use.' *Journal of Psychology,* 19 (1945): 87–95.

West, R. 'The Cognitive Neuroscience of Prospective Memory.' In *Prospective Memory: Cognitive, Neuroscience, Developmental and Applied Perspectives*, edited by M. Kliegel, M.A. McDaniel, and G.O. Einstein, 261–82. New York, NY: Taylor and Francis Group/Lawrence Erlbaum Associates, 2008.

Wilkins, A.J., and Baddeley, A.D. 'Remembering to Recall in Everyday Life: An Approach to Absentmindedness.' In *Practical Aspects of Memory*, edited by M. Gruneberg and R. Sykes, 27–34. London: Academic Press, 1978.

Wilson, R.S., and A.W. Kaszniak. 'Longitudinal Changes:Progressive Idiopathic Dementia.' In *Handbook for Clinical Memory Assessment of Older Adults,* edited by L.W. Poon, T. Crook, K.L. Davis, C. Eisdorfer, B. J. Gurland, A.W. Kaszniak, and L. W. Thompson, 285–93. Washington, DC: American Psychological Association, 1986.

Woods, S.P., L. Moran, M. Dawson, C. Carey, and I. Grant, HNRC Group. 'Psychometric Characteristics of The Memory for Intentions Screening Test.' *Clinical Neuropsychology* 22 (2008): 864–78.

Part V: Culture in Action – The Artists Speak

CHAPTER 14

The Museum of the Old Colony

Pablo Delano[1]

In 1898, the United States (US) intervened in the long independence wars of Puerto Rico and Cuba, going to battle with Spain over its colonial possessions. Hijacking the struggle for national sovereignty in the Caribbean, the US army invaded and occupied Puerto Rico. As Spain lost its last colony, the US gained new imperial territory. The Stars and Stripes was pronounced Puerto Rico's flag.

US authorities renamed the island Porto Rico, while attempting to impose English as the official language, an initiative that never succeeded. Some celebrated 'Porto' Rico's annexation to the US. Others resisted, carrying on the fight for independence through uprisings and clandestine operations, through peaceful or violent struggle during the twentieth and twenty-first centuries. Oscar López Rivera, an independence activist and one of the longest-held political prisoners in the US, was only recently released at the end of the Obama Administration after serving 36 years in prison.

Under occupation, the new colony was controlled by America's burgeoning military power, its economy redirected, and its status justified through US official discourse and propaganda. With annexation, the US imposed on Puerto Rico capitalist expropriation, modernizing programmes, and a colonial logic of social hygiene and racial hierarchy. Thus, imperialist thought and white supremacy shaped official policy, social mobility, and everyday life in Puerto Rico's new colonial order.

Images and early photographs had helped to justify American intervention in the 'Spanish-American' War. This persisted through occupation and annexation as photography expanded its influence in popular culture. Photographers, writers and 'experts' were deployed to the new colony of Porto Rico, producing images and narratives that helped to define this newly acquired, 'primitive' territory and its people for North American audiences. These photographs often depicted lush tropical flora and fauna, or captured the pathetic state of impoverished 'Porto Ricans' who would soon reap the 'benefits' of living as colonial subjects.

Puerto Rico is officially defined as 'a non-incorporated territory of the United States'. During the mid-twentieth century, the US approved a new constitution, permitted local gubernatorial elections, and encouraged US investment in the island even as it poured millions into military bases that would serve as the 'gatekeepers of the Panama Canal'. To justify the maintenance of Puerto Rico as a modern-day colony, the stream of propagandistic images and discourses continued, echoed by local media on the island beholden to American interests.

Today, in the wake of the so-called 'Debt Crisis', Puerto Rico is suffering a withering economic collapse, a humanitarian crisis and a massive exodus of its population. The US Congress underscored the island's colonial status by refusing it bankruptcy protection. Meanwhile, Wall Street speculators and predatory hedge funds pick it clean. On July 30, 2016, President Obama signed into law a bill that imposed upon Puerto Rico a fiscal control board appointed by US legislators with powers beyond that of any democratically-elected local leader. This Junta, as it is called on the island, is forcing privatization and austerity measures with catastrophic results, endangering pensions and public services as creditors lean on island officials to make good on its $74 billion debt.

The devastation left by hurricanes Irma and María, which struck Puerto Rico on September 6 and 20, 2017, respectively, has only worsened the island's already dire situation. It has dramatically unveiled Puerto Rico's crumbling infrastructure and extreme poverty. The sluggish aid response from local and federal authorities has resulted in a slow pace of recovery, contributing to the already collapsing economy, and brain drain. It has also shed light on the unequal power dynamics, highlighting the fact that while Puerto Ricans may be US citizens they do not receive the same benefits as US citizens living in the mainland. If not full-fledged American citizens, Puerto Ricans must then be considered colonial subjects of the US.

The Museum of the Old Colony was conceived as a personal reflection on the legacy of the US occupation in Puerto Rico. It takes the form of a conceptual art installation that both evokes and satirizes historical and anthropological museums built to celebrate the so-called achievements of Empire and superiority of the white people. The Museum provokes visitors with a century of images in a colonial logic that persists today. Its title derives in part from a popular carbonated beverage sold in Puerto Rico. The soft drink 'Old Colony', long gone from mainland markets, continues to be produced and bottled in Puerto Rico.

The Museum of the Old Colony was exhibited for the first time at Alice Yard, Port of Spain, as part of the Turning Tides conference. It has since been updated and mounted at The National Gallery of Jamaica (a fragment), The Argentine Biennial of Documentary Photography, The King Juan Carlos of Spain Center (New York University), The Museum of Contemporary Art of Puerto Rico and the Hampshire College Art Gallery (Amherst, Massachusetts).

Notes
1. This text introduces visitors to The Museum of the Old Colony installation at the Museum of Contemporary Art in San Juan, Puerto Rico, December, 2017. It was edited at various points by Ana Dopico (Director, King Juan Carlos I of Spain Center, NYU) and Marianne Ramirez Aponte (Director and Curator, Museum of Contemporary Art of Puerto Rico).

A group of Newly Made Americans at Ponce, Porto Rico. Single image from the Installation The Museum of the Old Colony.

All photographs of the installation by Pablo Delano.

Installation Detail, The Museum of the Old Colony, Alice Yard, Port of Spain, Trinidad

Installation Detail, The Museum of the Old Colony, Alice Yard, Port of Spain, Trinidad

The Museum of the Old Colony' 251

Overall view of gallery installation, The Museum of the Old Colony, Alice Yard, Port of Spain, Trinidad

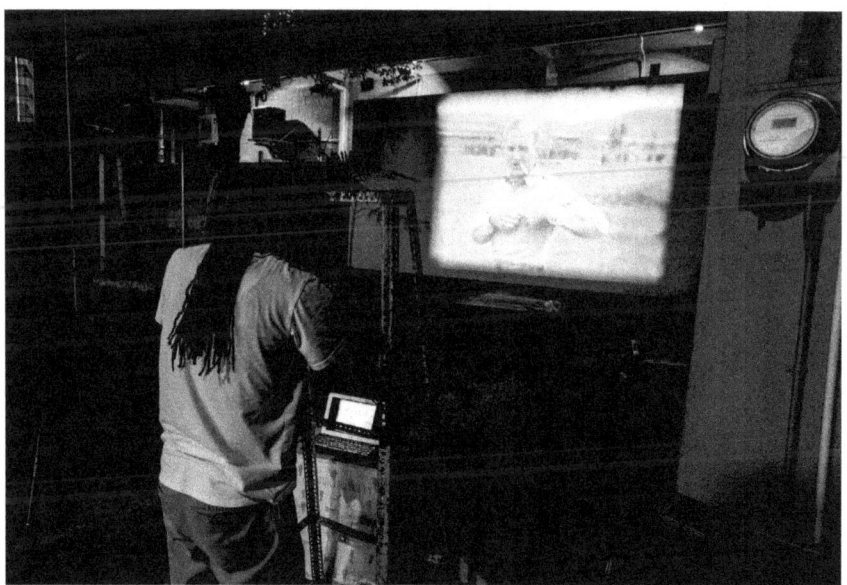

Projection, The Museum of the Old Colony, Alice Yard, Port of Spain, Trinidad

CHAPTER 15

A Proposal for 'performing Marcus and Amy'

Tony Hall

We are going to emancipate ourselves from mental slavery because whilst others might free the body, none but ourselves can free the mind.

Marcus Garvey speaking in Menelik Hall, Sydney, Nova Scotia, 1937

ESTRAGON: I'd rather he'd dance, it'd be more fun.

POZZO: Not necessarily.

EXTRAGON: Wouldn't it, Didi, be more fun?

VLADIMIR: I'd like well to hear him think.

ESTRAGON: Perhaps he could dance first and think afterwards, if it isn't too much to ask him.

VLADIMIR [to Pozzo]: Would that be possible?

POZZO: By all means, nothing simpler. It's the natural order. [He laughs briefly.]

From WAITING FOR GODOT (1953) by Samuel Beckett

In the nineteenth century the word 'emancipation' was used in European thought to indicate that someone had emancipated someone else. The freeing process was perceived to be entirely external, 'being led by the hand' to freedom. Someone or some group emancipated the enslaved Africans who were brought across the Atlantic Ocean in chains to the so-called 'new world'. Marcus Garvey, born Aug. 17, 1887, renowned Jamaican Africanist, turned this meaning of the word on its head in his 1937 speech in Sydney, Nova Scotia when he introduced the concepts of 'self-emancipation' and 'mental slavery' to the equation. In doing this, he possibly identified emancipation, in the historical context of the Caribbean, as a lifelong on-going process of personal liberation. Crucial to the concept of 'self-emancipation' is the notion of 'mental slavery', or personal identification, within the frame of one's own energy field, with the assumptions of 'natural servitude' and inborn inferiority that enabled the oppression of ancestors living in conditions of enslavement. Emancipation from physical enslavement is only the prelude to the kind of 'self-emancipation' or mental freedom that Garvey espoused.

This presentation will discuss what, in fact, Garvey was saying and what his pronouncement can mean in the twenty-first century Caribbean while also introducing the Marcus Garvey Theatre Project, **performing 'Marcus & Amy'.** This is a participatory theatre project, intended to engage participants, young and old, from Limon, Costa Rica, through to Blue Fields, Nicaragua, over to Kingston, Jamaica, to San Fernando, Trinidad and even further afield in a series of performance events in their various territories. Popular play-making explorations are proposed. In this way, **performing 'Marcus & Amy'** will use a performance model, based in Emancipation Performance Traditions developed in the Caribbean over many centuries of enslavement, to track the development and functioning, across the region, of Garvey's organization: the Universal Negro Improvement Association (UNIA), founded in Jamaica in 1914.

Finally, this proposal will touch on aspects of play and performance theories to present a rationale for the performance model as a popular research methodology based on self-emancipation as a life-organizing principle, theorizing emancipation as a daily renewal of liberation through personal play and a communal dance of action. Through this methodology, which utilizes a system of popular cultural archetypes, prototypes and stereotypes as guardians of or guides to human behaviour (a touch of Jungian analysis here; see, for instance, *Synchronicity* 140), **performing 'Marcus & Amy'** will re-visit some of the reasons for the rapid spread of Garveyism throughout the Grand Caribbean during his life time (1887–1940) and observe some of what has transpired on the ground, in this connection, since that time.

The Marcus Garvey Popular Theatre Project

1. Performing 'Marcus & Amy' – History & Background:

Marcus Garvey (August 17, 1887–June 10, 1940) was a black political leader, orator, publisher and entrepreneur born in St. Ann's Bay, Jamaica, British West Indies, who launched, with his first wife, Amy Ashwood Garvey (January 10, 1897–May 3, 1969) born in Port

Antonio, Jamaica, one of the largest mass movements of African people ever. Under the UNIA, founded in Jamaica in 1914, the Garveys created a movement dedicated to racial pride, economic self-sufficiency, and the formation of an independent black nation in Africa. Marcus Garvey was able to stir strong support for this endeavour among the poor urban black of New York City in 1916, soon after he arrived in Harlem.

Most black leaders in the United States (US) at the time regarded the self-educated Marcus Garvey as a 'buffoon' and 'imposter' especially after he announced The Empire of Africa and himself as President. Garvey was involved in fundraising to establish a steamship line, The Black Star Line (Delaware 1919), to usher African-Americans into their rightful place in the African global economy and to take the members of his UNIA back to Africa. In 1923, after infiltration by the Bureau of Investigation, he was accused, indicted and convicted of 'fragile mail fraudulent' practices in relation to these funds. As is to be expected, Garvey had many enemies among the white establishment and even the black leaders and the leadership of the National Association for the Advancement of Coloured People (NAACP) made it very clear that they did not support the Marcus Garvey Back-to-Africa movement. In 1927, after he was pardoned by then President of the US, Calvin Coolidge, and proclaimed an undesirable alien, he was deported back to Jamaica.

It is not widely known that Marcus Garvey's first foray into world affairs began in Spanish America, Limon, Costa Rica. In fact, Garvey's activities outside of the US as a whole are largely overlooked. The people up and down the Western Caribbean supported the Garvey project. He was one of them, though he only spent from 1910 to 1911 as a timekeeper in Limon at the United Fruit Company, with so many of his fellow Jamaican countrymen looking to better their lives. His short time there was formative in his social, political and economic education as a young journalist and activist. His presence as a minority in a Spanish American country fortified him with a foundational intelligence from which to project the UNIA beyond the confines of the US.

Garvey also turns up in accounts on African-American Theatre during the 1920s. He was responsible for amazing street parades in Harlem and stage pageants alongside other black activists of the time, most of whom disagreed with him, though they all, nonetheless, held the opinion that black drama was necessary to rehabilitate the stereotypical images of minstrelsy repeated over and over in the black musicals of the day.

It seems that Garvey's legacy, though further tarnished recently in the US by a made for television documentary (*Marcus Garvey – Look For Me in the Whirlwind* 2001), which Garvey's son Dr. Julius W. Garvey says is fraught with inaccuracies, fares in a different way in the Caribbean. Garvey, one of the first national heroes of Jamaica, also figures in the history of West Indian theatre, as one of the pioneers of this genre. It is reported that in the early 1930s, in Jamaica, he was chairman of an entertainment group that produced at least two of his plays, no doubt promoting his cause of entrepreneurship and self-sufficiency for people of African descent. Recent research also shows that it was mainly the far-flung Caribbean community, all through the Americas and into parts of Europe, which was really responsible for Garvey's widespread popularity and the prominence of his teachings and the Back to Africa movement.

The business of entrepreneurship and achieving total self-sufficiency for people of African descent, through economic means, are overlooked but remain significant aspects of Garvey's teachings. When we talk of applying Garvey's thought to practice, his position on economics is not where our interest is usually lodged. Beginning in Limon, Costa Rica, this Marcus Garvey Popular Theatre Project will explore the Garveys by focusing on the efficacies of applying Economic Garveyism.

2. Performing 'Marcus & Amy' – Sector Analysis:

The Marcus Garvey Popular Theatre Project wants to be a 'popular theatre' project, by which we mean, first, to find well-established and recognized 'local' group(s) (cultural or otherwise) through which a play ('a performance of some kind') can be created and executed. Through research on the ground this group will explore the significance of Marcus Garvey coming to and working in their community at the time he did; the significance of this foray to Garvey himself and to the eventual movement that he was to foster and, of course most importantly, to that community today. This group will have to seek out stories from the oldest inhabitants of the area, from researchers, scholars, other informants, ageing culture bearers, research old documents, seek out various media materials and other sources in search of 'the play'.

What is at the centre of this essence of the UNIA and Marcus Garvey that still walks the streets of Limon, still lives in Limon? It has disappeared elsewhere. Why does it persist there in Limon? Or has it disappeared elsewhere? We will find out. What is it that I felt the first time I encountered the Limon city centre and saw that 'turquoise building' – which has since burned down – looking back at me? What is the source of that single energy the people exude? What is the source of the memories, in spite of the stories of marginalization, at the hands of the larger Latin society in Limon, which they all recall and tell.

The issues of exploring where and who we are in the world are not normally encouraged openly in the Caribbean. This gross oversight, coming from the idea that ordinary people are only concerned with very basic survival, has led a significant part of most West Indian populations, both young and not so young, into a wilderness of deep despair and powerlessness.

Considerations of place and space (internal and external) are inextricably bound up with our social, political and economic survival. One of the only ways we can emerge from such a situation is through serious and focused reflection that can give rise to realistic creative action on every level. Community drama is one activity that can animate any group and facilitate an appropriate path to sensitivity and understanding.

Storytelling, one of the many skills that can be developed through a carefully orchestrated drama, play-making and performance process, is often a stepping-stone used to develop living skills in all participants. What happens most of the time is that living energy is stagnated, like pools of septic water, in situations that block its flow through the arteries of the senses. Sometimes these blockages lead to committing murder and different forms of anti-social activities. Telling stories, through the avenue of drama, play-making and performance, can free this blockage, can help isolate energies of fear, anger, shame, blame, revenge and neglect to provide spontaneous relief and begin a transformation of frustration and suffering into creative action and the blossoming of organic problem-solving intelligence.

3. Performing 'Marcus & Amy'
Description

Jouvay Popular Theatre Process (JPTP) is an approach to popular theatre, popular here meaning 'active and direct community participation' in the play-making and performance practice. Theorist Michael Etherton, argues that the words 'popular' and 'theatre' form a dialectic with each other. Popular means participation. Theatre means art (1982). Etherton says the more one participates in this activity, the better the art. But the more one participates, the deeper the politics also, so, the better the art, the more articulated the politics.

Through this stratagem, we can consolidate in our *selves* the full, creative, and imaginative energy of the emancipation traditions set down by our ancestors. In this way, JPTP can activate the liberating power of our emancipation ancestry and, through self-knowledge, lead to sophisticated personal and group action. JPTP, so named after the Jouvay ritual of 'a community awakening', which opens all major Caribbean carnival parades, is a mechanism for play-making and a dynamo for performance, which can evoke a poetic world through the ordinary person. Karmenlara Ely observes:

> [I]t developed out of complex intersections between Caribbean Carnival/festival roots, archives, memory and bodies. It is a vital, on the ground, response and a challenge to the inherited norms for performance practice in the Americas and West Indies. In the process, through its many phases, sonic spaces, fleshy wounds and rhythmic archives of everyday performance and play are excavated to bring alternative ways of remembering to the community.

JPTP, steeped in the emancipation performance traditions that developed during the periods of enslavement and indentureship in the Caribbean, emphasizes an exploration of the stereotypes, archetypes and/or prototypes of human behaviour and 'ritual actions' found in the traditional masquerade (mas), traditional religions (Orisa/Hindu/Christianity/ Islam/Animism), folklore and the popular imagination.

The characters discovered are viewed as warrior guides and/or guardians in everyday life through a process of 'spirit possession' derived from the rituals and the 'dance and fight' gayelle system of stick fighting (The Gatkha Calinda School), improvization (extempo, seen not just as calypso singing, but all of life as an extempo), and story-telling.

This JPTP then, adapted to suit the territory in which it is applied, becomes the basis for all play-making and performance-building. JPTP is nothing if it is not play and performance. It stems from the view that all of life is some sort of performance. That every action in which you engage creates or manifests a 'you' and that is a kind of performance. 'You' represents a performative entity. It is really the articulation of a form that we can see. Victor Turner, the renowned cultural anthropologist, who looked at theatre and ritual in depth and has led us to some understanding of the relationship of one to the other, says that 'performance' has nothing to do with 'form' (21, 22). But he also says that performance is the completion of an action.

From this perspective, performance is a living 'action' that dissolves form. Form is always dissolving to nothing, showing us 'action'. To completion. That is life and living. All of life and living is a transition, a transformation to nothing. To something else. To the constituent parts of the organism. That is what it means to be alive, living, to be transforming. So per-form-ance is going 'through' form, a manifestation, for want of a better word, of that transformation that is living. And then to death. A transition. The 'you' disappears. The constituent parts of the form remain in some form or other. The plays we make can be seen as 'live' rehearsals for the performances of life, of living.

The core activity of 'per-form-ance' is play. Play theorist, Johan Huizinga, (*Homo Ludens* 2, 8), sees play as not 'ordinary' or 'real' life, but as 'overlapping' elements 'of culture'. Even work can be play in some cultures. We in the masquerade, mas on these islands, know this very well. We 'play mas' all year round – an activity heightened at carnival time (Lloyd Best). A sophisticated mechanism by which we spontaneously assume different forms to live and survive. We have no idea what we see when we say we see something. A tree. A dog. We don't know what it is. We were told and we all agree to agree that that is a tree. A dog. You simply have to play the game or else we go crazy. We cannot communicate. Among a range of definitions, Huizinga states, 'play is free, is in fact freedom' (*Humo Luden*s 7, 8). So it is through performance and play that we have survived. And our real nation has always been the imagi-nation, to paraphrase Walcott, badly.

To return to and refute the nineteenth-century European definition of the word 'emancipation' as an entirely external freeing process, with 'Freedom' perceived as a concept:[1] once 'freedom' is seen as a concept or an idea, it is no longer 'Freedom'. That notion of 'freedom' someone can take from you or give to you is not true Freedom. Freedom wants to be free of all our concepts and ideas, even the idea of freedom itself. Garvey understood this when he introduced the notion of 'self-emancipation'. Indeed, such emancipation is not possible unless you are so gifted from birth as to be able to suspend thinking at will. Thinking is the activity of mental slavery. It doesn't matter the thought. Our self-consciousness binds us to a perpetual thinking of thoughts willy nilly. That is mental slavery. Nonetheless, in raising this very potent issue, Garvey possibly identified 'emancipation', in the historical context of the Caribbean and the Black Diaspora, as a lifelong on-going process of personal self-liberation from enslaving thoughts of scientific racism, which undermine Freedom. A process which, given the nature of 'thinking' and 'mental slavery', demands continuous personal observation and collective vigilance for each other. In putting forth these assumptions, Garvey arguably identifies 'emancipation' as the all-embracing organizing principle for the peoples of the Caribbean and the Black Diaspora.

The JPTP operates out of a probe into, and an on-gong 'awakening' to, this particular understanding of the structure and the shaping of the self imbedded in Garvey's teaching and in our understanding of the mechanisms of the traditional masquerade.

4. Performing 'Marcus & Amy'
Outputs

Using drama and play-making, performance events will be delivered. Initially a core group of actors/writers/improvisers, dancers (a choreographer), singers (maybe a choir master), musicians (a composer) will be located and this group will be prepared to deliver a performance or a series of performances. Once this gets going, different groups like youth, young or older adults, or others can be targeted for more specific Popular Theatre projects. JPTP workshops have already been initiated. In May, 2015, one was staged in Limon with adults and another in Puerto Viejo with primary school children. These were geared to identify and frame the core group that will produce the first plays and performances there.

The aims of this project will be: 1. To foster the development of original storytelling through drama, play-making and performance; 2. To provide an opportunity (in Limon/Cahuita, Costa Rica to begin with) for a play(s) using indigenous storytelling based on the legacy of Marcus and Amy and a vision of the Grand Caribbean to be performed in full productions (indoor and/or outdoor) for entertainment, personal and collective development.

The objectives broadly are: Firstly, to present the play(s) from the popular theatre process to promote the possibility of theatre practitioners (young and not so young) emerging to carry on such a process in their own communities. Secondly, to conduct drama workshops on the process of making and presenting plays and forms of indigenous storytelling for street, and stage; thereby involving the general public and specific groups in the creative process of play-making and performance. Thirdly, to prepare a script(s) and work process guidelines from this initiative; with the idea of connecting to similar initiatives throughout the region and, in the spirit of Marcus and Amy, with Caribbean people wherever they are in the world.

A local group will be given the opportunity to deepen its knowledge of this type of cultural work. This is the kind of project through which a local group can consciously present its community to itself using a performance process to help that community better appreciate, and thereby strategize further on how to consolidate, itself. From a play-making point of view the most important aspect of the project is for the participants/performers to discover, through the research, the popular cultural forms or strategies that the people have created over the years for their own survival.

The workings and functions of these forms/strategies can then be explored by participants/performers in the play-building phase to unearth (it is a form of archeology, according to Ely, 'excavation') the most effective 'habitable metaphor' or 'human dynamo' by which to give the play/performance a shape or structure, its inner working. In this way the energy of the play/performance should come from the discovered dynamic/dynamo which fuels the survival of the community.

The community tells itself what it already knows but it did not know what it knew all along. And finally out of the popular research will also come the best means through which the play/performance should be delivered back to the community. Who is the audience? Why? What is the nature of an 'audience' involvement/participation, the location or locations for all phases of the project, the date(s) and time(s) of days of the delivery, etc.?

5. Performing 'Marcus & Amy'
Performance Possibilities
   (a) Appearances – Any appearance by the Honourable Marcus Mosiah Garvey on a platform giving a speech will not only provide a lively and entertaining dramatic presentation but will also seek to put Garvey's West Indian legacy in perspective. His many varied views and positions on so many aspects of life and living on the islands have scarcely been really looked at widely, let alone reflected on. The kind of imaginative perspective that can be created from such an appearance can work on a number of levels for the general public. Appearances can also be made to schools where students can engage in discussions with Garvey, based

on research they would have done with their teachers. The actor playing the part will have in his repertoire different speeches of Garvey's. The work therefore can be amended appropriately for the specific selected or captured audiences. Emancipation Day celebrations and carnival day 'mas interventions' are only a few appropriate venues for Marcus and Amy Garvey appearances; both Amy Ashwood (January 10, 1897–May 3, 1969) and Amy Jacques Garvey (December 31, 1895–July 25, 1973, Garvey's second wife, born in Kingston, Jamaica) in their own vibrant and informed approaches to activism, were as much an inspiration to black men and women as was Marcus (see Addendum to this proposal for two 'appearances' that have happened by February 2018).

(b) A Theatre Piece – It is envisaged that as Popular Theatre, created and presented by the community (ordinary citizens or students), **performing 'Marcus & Amy'** will attempt to track the whereabouts of chapters of the UNIA still existent, or once alive and vibrant, in the entire Caribbean region. The project can serve as a catalyst for exploring and reflecting on Garvey's thought, through active performance values, in the regional community's consciousness, and even lead to the action of revitalizing UNIA chapters. Participants are encouraged to find their own Garvey inside themselves; to perform their own Marcus & Amy – probably though not necessarily the males Marcus and the females Amy. In this way Marcus & Amy become 'essences of character masks' (mas), which the participants explore and try on for size, play with, for living, for negotiating survival in this rehearsal for the on-going and changing performance of living and life.

Starting in Limon, Costa Rica, which is where Garvey started, a play created and presented by the community following the process outlined above will explore and reflect on the significance and effect of Garvey's continued presence and thought on the present day lives of the people. This initial phase of The Marcus Garvey Popular Theatre Project in Limon is supported by the chapter of the UNIA still operating there and will be conducted in English and Spanish. The Popular Theatre Process developed in this first phase will influence how the other phases in other parts of the region evolve. There are many options. For instance a bi-lingual core can come out of the Costa Rican phase, a small core of facilitators/actors/musicians who can travel all through the region, through both continental and island Caribbean, working with groups to help them create and present their own plays about Garvey and the UNIA in their locations.

Another is, of course, for a single dramatist/facilitator/playmaker, using the methodology developed in Limon, to simply move from location to location animating interested communities, connected or not to a Garvey and/or UNIA past, to explore the themes in question as they pertain to Garvey's thought and Economic Garveyism.

(c) Touring Play Productions and Drama Workshops – The project will deliver modules of drama units geared to generating storytelling skills to engender lasting life skills. The modules will be presented in such a way as to enable constant evaluation of their effectiveness. These drama units will form the platform on which the more sophisticated work of play and theatre making will be built. Thus, the activity in itself becomes an evaluation of what is happening on the ground. In addition, structured evaluations, by independent expert personnel, not directly involved in the project, will be carried out over fixed periods of time.

6. Performing 'Marcus & Amy'
Conclusion

The main impact of this project is intended to be on-going creative work in the area of drama, play-making and storytelling with a considered personal and communal developmental bias. This will be reflected in the many community and public events that come out of the duration of the project. It is also hoped that the activity from this project will not only generate artistic, creative and independent energies but that these will give rise to related career opportunities and income generating activities.

Marcus and Amy Garvey (both Amys) are present in all of us, always, all the time, not only those of us who share in the Garveys' Afro-descended history but in anyone who wishes to emancipate themselves from the tyranny of self-enslaving thought. In a speech in tribute to

Marcus, just before she died, Amy Ashwood said that Marcus was born connected to the universe and was never disconnected. Most of us have allowed all sorts of schemes to disconnect us, sometimes through no direct fault of our own. We are all born connected. There are many ways and means through play and performance in which we can allow ourselves to realize our connection to the energy of the universe.

Notes
1. Freedom, capitalized, will denote the sense of Freedom as a human condition, whereas 'freedom' indicates more common usage of the term, often distinguished from Freedom (true freedom). (Ed. note).

Works Cited:
Best, Lloyd. *Making Mas with Possibility.* Tunapuna, Trinidad and Tobago: Trinidad and Tobago Institute of the West Indies, 1999.
Blaisdell, Bob., ed. *Selected Writings and Speeches of Marcus Garvey.* Mineola, NY: Dover Thrift Editions, Dover Publications, 2005.
Ely, Karmenlara. 'Jouvay Popular Theatre Process: Introductory Note.' Presented at the Infinite Record: Archive, Memory, Performance Conference, Massachusetts Institute of Technology, Boston, MA, November 14, 2014.
Etherton, Michael. *The Development of African Drama.* London, UK: Hutchinson University Library for Africa, 1982.
Garvey, Amy Jacques. *Garvey and Garveyism.* Reprint edition. Baltimore, MD: Black Classic Press, 2014.
Garvey, Marcus. 'Mr. Marcus Garvey's Speech in Menelik Hall, Sydney, Nova Scotia, 1937.' http://jouvayinstitute.blogspot.com/2015/11/we-are-going-to-emancipate-ourselves.html.
Grant, Colin. *Negro with a Hat: The Rise and Fall of Marcus Garvey*, 1st ed Oxford, UK: Oxford University Press, 2010.
Hall, Tony. 'JPTP: The Essay (Part One).' Jouvay Institute, 2011. http://jouvayinstitute.blogspot.com/2011/01/jouvay-popular-theatre-process-jptp_18.html?q=jptp.
Hall, Tony. 'JPTP: The Essay (Part Two).' Jouvay Institute, 2011. http://jouvayinstitute.blogspot.com/2011/01/jouvay-popular-theatre-process-jptp.html?q=JPTP.
Huizinga, Johan. *Homo Ludens: A Study of the Play Element in Culture.* Boston, MA: The Beacon Press, 1950.
Jung, C.G. *Synchronicity. An Acausal Connecting Principle.* Princeton, NJ: Princeton University Press, 1960.
Lamming, George, ed. *Enterprise of the Indies* with Afterword by Lloyd Best. Tunapuna, Trinidad and Tobago: The Trinidad and Tobago Institute of the West Indies, 1999.

Martin, Tony. *Amy Ashwood Garvey: Pan-Africanist, Feminist and Mrs. Marcus Garvey No. 1 or a Tale of Two Amies.* Dover, MA: Majority Press, 2007.

Nelson, Stanley, dir. *MARCUS GARVEY: Look For Me in the Whirlwind.* Documentary: Firelight Media, 2000. http://www.pbs.org/wgbh/amex/garvey/filmmore/https://www.youtube.com/watch?v=TzEaafDy05U.

Turner, Victor. *The Anthropology of Performance.* New York: PAJ Publications, 1987.

Walcott, Derek. *Star Apple Kingdom.* New York: Farrar, Strauss & Giroux, 1980.

ADDENDUM: Since this project was conceptualized in Costa Rica in 2014 and presented at the Turning Tides Conference in 2016, there have been two manifestations of Marcus & Amy.

I. Performing 'Marcus & Amy': A Mas Intervention (2016)

(Marcus & Amy Garvey visited Trinidad in 2016 during the carnival season. The visit was hosted by The Marcus Garvey Popular Theatre Project under the auspices of Lordstreet Theatre Company.) http://jouvayinstitute.blogspot.com/2016/02/performing-marcus-amy-mas-intervention.html

February 4th, 2016 – Adam Smith Square, Port of Spain
National Carnival Commission of Trinidad and Tobago Carnival Celebrations 2016, Amy Garvey (portrayed by Penelope Spencer) and Marcus Garvey (portrayed by Michael Cherrie) won 1st and 2nd places respectively in the conventional Masquerade Category: Modern History for Senior individuals.

Photograph by Abigail Hadeed.

'Marcus and Amy' in Hartford, Connecticut

December 2, 2017: Dedication of Trinity College downtown facility on Constitution Plaza

Dario A. Euraque

Before the *Turning Tides* Conference celebrated the historic connections between peoples from the Grand Caribbean, the Trinity-in-Trinidad Program had become the venue for new cultural connections renewing old ties. These began first in 2014, when Trinity Professors Dario A. Euraque (historian) and Pablo Delano (photographer) began leading Trinity students in Trinidad to travel and study Caribbean Coast Rica, in particular the port city of Limon where in the 1910s Marcus Garvey (1887–1940) initiated a movement dedicated to black racial pride and economic self-sufficiency known as Pan Africanism and also established the Universal Negro Improvement Association and African Communities League (UNIA-ACL). Euraque and Delano engaged Tony Hall to join them in Limon, Costa Rica with the idea that playwright Hall could work with the life and times of Garvey in the Spanish-speaking Caribbean, a very different world from Jamaica and Trinidad and Tobago, birth places of Garvey and Hall.

In this context of contemporary post-colonial intersections across the Caribbean, Tony Hall conceived of the Marcus Garvey Popular Theatre Project. The Marcus Garvey Popular Theatre Project, thus, began as a theatre project to 'explore and reflect on the significance and effect of Garvey's continued presence and thought on the present day lives of the people [and] to recreate the UNIA in the Caribbean and beyond' (see Proposal above). From Limon, it travelled back to Trinidad and Tobago and was performed in Port of Spain in 2016, as what Tony Hall has called a 'mas intervention' in carnival celebrations of that year in Trinidad, as the intervention pictured in I above.

In the late summer of 2017, with funding provided from the Office of President Joanne Berger-Sweeney, Professors Delano and Euraque, Co-Directors of Trinity's Center for Caribbean Studies, proposed another incarnation of the Marcus Garvey Popular Theatre Project, in Hartford, Connecticut, far from Trinidad and Caribbean Costa Rica, and yet linked by long historic ties that stretched back to British and Spanish colonialism in the seventeenth and eighteenth centuries (see Cateau in this volume). Why not a 'State Visit to Hartford by Marcus and Amy Garvey'?

The Tides were Turning once more, now far beyond the Grand Caribbean, over the Atlantic Ocean and into the Connecticut River....

Between early fall and December of 2017 Delano and Euraque, anchored in the Center for Caribbean Studies, led a team of Trinity College faculty, students, administrators, Hartford City Officials, and residents, particularly from the city's West Indian community, to coordinate the space for the Garvey 'State Visit' to Connecticut. The venue was 10 Constitution Plaza, in downtown Hartford, where Hall's project inaugurated this space as Trinity College's downtown campus, the first of other Center for Caribbean Studies projects programmed for that location. A ceremonial welcome took place on the steps of 10 Constitution Plaza with City of Hartford officials and a representative of the State of Connecticut Governor's Office; President Berger-Sweeney greeted the Garveys. December 2 was declared Marcus Garvey Day in a proclamation from Hartford's Mayor Luke Bronin, and a citation from the Governor's office was read. Portraying Marcus Garvey and his wife were actors Michael Cherrie and Penelope Spencer. In addition to what was, in essence, a Trinidad mas presentation, Dermoth Brown, longtime Hartford-area resident and founder of the International Foundation for the Exoneration of Marcus Mosiah Garvey Connecticut, spoke about his motivation to start that organization. A festive meal of Jamaican food and discussion followed inside Constitution Plaza among 200 attendees (see illustration).

A parallel exhibit about the history of West Indians in Hartford was featured at Trinity College's Mather Art Gallery, 300 Summit Street, from November 15 through December 15, 2017. Titled *A Home Away From Home*, the exhibition was curated and written by Fiona Vernal, a Jamaican migrant to Hartford, Associate Professor of history and Africana studies at the University of Connecticut and a member of the Advisory Board of Trinity's Center for Caribbean Studies.

Marcus Garvey Day, December 2, 2017, Hartford, Connecticut.

All photographs by Pablo Delano.

CHAPTER 16

Inside the People TV, Our Images, Our Stories, Money in The Bank

Christopher Laird

Inside the People TV and *Money in the Bank* are the two pillars upon which the structure of this presentation is hung.[1] *Inside The People TV* comes from a scene in the southern Caribbean's first television soap opera or drama series: *Who The C.A.P. Fits...*

In this scene the mother is astounded to see her son on television where ordinary people do not often appear.

VSF#2 – Who The C.A.P. Fits... *(1977)*

She is not making reference to some socialist medium owned by the people – quite the contrary. She is using 'People' in the way we might use it if we took our child to our employer's home and he put his feet on their furniture and we told them, 'Take you foot off the People chair,' i.e. belonging to the ruling elite, those who have power over us, from the plantation house to the gated community. Our television, with its more than 95 per cent foreign content and what local content there is with its standard English did not seem to belong to or speak to and for the general population.

For *Money in the Bank*, I would like to introduce you to Theophilus Phillip, known as the Mighty Spoiler. A mischievous, but tragic figure,

Spoiler sang of a surreal world where magistrates charged themselves for contempt of court, where women learnt to talk backwards, where his sister had her brain switched with that of a cat, where putting an aerial in a roti could enable you to tune into radio Calcutta,[2] where he lived in a village where everyone had lost their memory and where the only way he could stop his shadow mocking him was to put his head on a train line. Of course he is best known for his calypso 'Bed Bug,' where he wished to come back after death as a bedbug so he 'could bite them young ladies, partner, like a hotdog or a hamburger'.

Though still a name that conjures amusement when mentioned today, Spoiler was not a clown. Few realize that in his time he was the man to beat for Calypso King, winning the crown three times between 1948 and 1955. But it is one of his less well known compositions I want to reference today: 'Money In The Bank.'

> *My cousin died many years in Toco*
> *And she leave a lot of money for Spoilo*
> *My cousin died many years in Toco*
> *And she leave a lot of money for Spoilo*
> *Now people saying that I lousy*
> *Saying that the Spoiler don't spend his money*
> *But if they put the world in a pitch-oil tin*
> *I cannot even pay a cent to see the thing spin*
> *Just because I have meh money in the bank since the age*
>   *of nine*
> *And Them big-shots put theirs on mine*
> *I have to wait again just a couple years*
> *In order to get out mine they have to take off theirs.*

Spoiler was our muse, the anarchy, the impishness, his surreal take on the world that seemed like nonsense but resonated deeply somewhere inside what we knew but could not articulate. The pitchoil tin is an everyday object, part of working class lives used for pitchoil (kerosene), biscuits, cooking oil, carrying water, as a planter, and as the percussion instrument for Jab Molassi and Blue devils at carnival where the tin is hit with a stick: 'Pay The Devil – Jab Jab.' Juxtaposing such a common household utensil with the planet created an archetypal dissonant Spoiler image.

As a side bar: In Banyan's second soap opera series *Morral*, in 1978, we inserted a pitchoil tin in every episode where its very commonality made it invisible.

VSF#5 – *from* Morral *(1978)*

Inside the People TV is also the title of the mural painted by Lari Richardson for Banyan between 1984 and the present in which are depicted those who have inspired us and those who have participated in our major productions.

VSF#1 – Inside The People TV *mural by Lari Richardson 1984–2004*

In the centre of the mural are three television screens cut from mirrors. If you look into them you will see directly 'inside the people TV', which is built from images of ourselves.

VSF#95 – *Detail of centre of* Inside the People TV *mural*

Spoiler speaks of an inheritance, a legacy, which he cannot access because of the ignore-ance and greed of 'them big shots', the ruling elite gatekeepers of our media and our culture.

Television began in much of the Caribbean on Independence day, replacing the British administration with a neo-colonial presence of the United States (US) in our bedrooms and living rooms. Now, the Caribbean is the region in the world most penetrated by foreign television images.

Back in the mid-1980s Dr Ewart Skinner did seminal work on the impact of US television in the Caribbean. Aggrey Brown and Roderick Sanatan of the Caribbean Institute for Mass Communication (CARIMAC) in *Talking With Whom*, their 1987 media analysis of 12 Anglophone Caribbean countries, note a major concern with 'the extremely negative impact on regional development and self-definition exerted by the influx of foreign programming through new technologies.' Professor Rex Nettleford, in his forward to that study states: 'At stake in all this is the desired access by outside interests to the collective intellect and imagination of a region which is still in the process of decolonisation as part of its post-colonial formation.'

It is in this context that Banyan wanted to provide Caribbean people with access, provide an opportunity to see themselves and the world through their own eyes. We wanted the Caribbean, and indeed everyone, to 'see the world spin'.

First: What is Banyan?

Banyan is the Southern Caribbean's first independent television programme production unit, established 40 years ago. And in those 40 years we have produced over 400 television programmes.

VSF#14 – Christopher Laird in Banyan's archive vault (2015)

In our archive vault, one wall is packed with those programmes. Over 2000 tapes of raw footage that fed into the making of these programmes and other footage that has not even been made into programmes yet. Invaluable, priceless records of the cultural and social life of the region over the past 40 years – ever since the invention of the video cassette.

VSF#15 – Kali Worship in Trinidad (1991)

VSF#16 – Shouter Baptist – Crossing Over (1989)

VSF#17 – Merry Monarch by Peter Minshall (1987)

VSF#20 – Johnkunnu in Belize, Caribbean Eye- Community Celebrations (1991)

VSF#21 – Ramleela, Trinidad. A RameelaA Ramleela, Dow Village (1987)

All of this is safe now because it has been digitized. Over 2500 video files, over 1000 hours of video accompanied by 14,500 records in a linked database.

Some of the highlights of our productions feature the Southern Caribbean's first television Soap Opera, *Who The Cap Fits...*, its first made for television movie, *The Rig*, written and directed by Derek Walcott and the ground breaking cultural magazine, *Gayelle*, that ran for six years chronicling our creative and cultural lives:

VSF#25

There is also the award winning documentary *And The Dish Ran Away With The Spoon*, on the effect of US television on Caribbean Culture shown in 150 countries,

VSF#26

Caribbean Eye, the only television series on Caribbean culture made in and by the Caribbean, still in demand by institutions the world over.

VSF#27

Unable to convince local television to programme endogenous content, in 2004 Banyan started the Caribbean's first free to air television station that programmed 100 per cent Caribbean content for general audiences: *Gayelle: The Channel*.

VSF#28

Our region is often treated as if it is a basin of diasporas, amusing and interesting only in terms of diasporic retention, our languages often viewed as 'broken' versions of European languages and our cultural forms as bastardized versions of old world cultures remembered, instead of being extraordinary examples of cultural resistance which resulted in original art forms that have changed the world. The region has struggled against the concept of being someone's diaspora and towards the building of a Caribbean civilization in its own right. Novelist and social scientist Marion Patrick Jones at the First Conference of Caribbean Women Writers (1988) described:

> A struggle against Spanish colonialism, French settlerdom, British colonisation and American imperialism. A struggle as important now as it was at the beginning.
>
> A struggle that does not make us overseas Europeans; that does not make us overseas Indians for whom missions must come out to teach us the 'real Hinduism,' we have kept ours.
>
> We are not overseas Chinese, that we have proved, the Overseas Chinese school collapsed.
>
> We are not overseas Africans. We are nobody's diaspora.
>
> We have our own diaspora and that we are interested in.
>
> We are Trinidadians, born in the Caribbean, with roots in the Caribbean, with a culture we fabricated and we struggled for.

Banyan set out to show how we, as a people, had, through patience, determination and existential need, built a foundation for a Caribbean civilization. We assumed that, by documenting and mirroring our culture and society, a repository could be constructed, and so a resource would be created for a more Caribbean-centred perspective.

> *Well from time I wake in the morning*
> *I know I have meh money but is the getting*
> *Run down the road and credit a taxi*
> *I say that I am going and collect currency*
> *Reach in the bank, if you see the cashier*
> *From left to right she shaking she finger*
> *Go away Mr. Phillip, no sense you stop*
> *Your money about two feet six from the top*

Spoiler's Chaplinesque character epitomises the Caribbean attitude of 'if I don't laugh I will cry' but he doesn't give up.

> *I pull so much strings, I pull cable wire*
> *To see if they could move meh money from centre*
> *Stand up by the bank, sometimes for a fortnight*
> *Walking in the rain, drying in the sunlight*
> *One day the cashier send and she call me*
> *I say, well today Spoiler have some money*
> *But instead of money, she say Mr. Thorn*
> *Just put another thousand on top and gone.*

So we did our work. Documenting, exploring, creating dramas, telling stories up and down the Caribbean for 40 years. In the process we constantly analysed the region's media environment which was becoming even more alienating as satellite and then cable systems came into play, flooding us with even more US content. As Errol Sitahal asks in *And The Dish Ran Away With The Spoon*: 'What happens when you dream other people's dreams?'

As a people we have become adept at decoding the images in our media and reinterpreting them in terms of our own experience. But with Banyan, with its cameras in the communities, those filters can be discarded, and communication comes directly to the viewer for the first time in our history. The effect is phenomenal.

In 2004, the first year of transmission of our all Caribbean television channel *Gayelle: The Channel*, there were incessant complaints from viewers that: They were late to do household chores, collect the children from school or get to appointments because they were looking at Gayelle. Some said they had to leave the house walking backwards so that they would not miss what they were watching on Gayelle. In fact, when we went off air late at night, people kept their sets on in case something happened on the screen. In the first few months of operation we stopped programming on weekends, put a camera pointing at the street and a crawling graphic on the screen which said: 'Why don't you turn off your television and do something with your family because that is what we at Gayelle are doing.' We were not heeded. People came down to the station and held placards up to the camera for their family and friends; they enacted dramas, played cricket and football in front of the camera. Even though we had had television for 40 years before Gayelle, the very presence of a channel which gave access to people, spoke their language, told their stories was intensely emotional and liberating.

Inside the People TV

How did we reach there?

As you know, in the region we live in at least two parallel worlds, on the one hand, the intimate world of the family and folk traditions where we comfortably use our first language, a Trinidad English creole; and on the other hand, the formal, jacket and tie world of the European languages of the establishment, whether that be colonial or neo-colonial or the ruling elite who, like Spoiler's 'big shots', cynically exercise their self-contempt by attempting to edit our heritage. Our television, established as it was, literally, on independence day, more as a symbol of development than as a tool for building new nations, operated almost exclusively in the formal realm.

As we journeyed into the People's TV, we were very aware, especially in the early years, that we were pioneering television programme production in the Anglophone Caribbean and we were conscious that we were in effect developing a Caribbean television aesthetic. We analysed our work. From that we developed principles that we applied and taught. All had to do essentially with the relationship between the on screen presenter and the viewer. Between the viewer and what he or she is observing through the screen.

This relationship nurtured a type of treatment on the screen that was more wonderment than exposition, more imaginings than images, more experience than description. The presenter was never the expert or commentator but was an explorer and inquisitor on behalf of the viewer; never insulting or underestimating the intelligence of the viewer by posing as friend or teacher but simply committed to getting answers to the questions the viewer wished to ask and exploring new worlds on his or her behalf. In short, make them spin in the pitchoil tin.

Sharing people, sharing stories, being inspired by the heroism of everyman. In effect we were subversives or guerrillas inside the people TV, sign language registers appropriate to context and situation.

VSF#31 – Gayelle presenters sneak into Trinidad & Tobago television (TTT) studio. (1985)

VSF#33 – Riot squad invades Gayelle public event. Drummit to Summit, April 2009

As we do in everyday life, we used different language registers according to the context and situation. The outcry from the establishment about departure from standard English on occasion led us to seek the views of people in Woodford square (the People's Parliament) of Port of Spain, Trinidad.

VSF#34 – 'If a person is to be on TV. He should be qualified enough to speak properly.' Gayelle *(1985)*

VSF#37 – 'I don't see anything wrong with the presenters speaking natural. In fact you do your best when you are natural.' Gayelle *(1985)*

VSF#38 – 'The language is no problem. All nations speaks in their own way. And I want to see myself on the TV just saying this.' Gayelle *(1985)*

We were developing a kaiso or calypso television, where comment is made through Metaphor, and to that we added Context and Immersion.

Metaphor we shared with the calypsonian who often used it to mask social or political comment. For example, in *And The Dish Ran Away With The Spoon*, the St. Lucian poet Kendel Hippolyte has a poem called *Watching Television*. We could have put him on a stool in a studio to read his poem. Instead we enlisted his sense of theatre to cast him as a madman or vagrant who, since they are common sights in our societies, tend to have the credibility of seers.

Watching television,
Watching television
Corn Flakes, cars, clothes
Children finally chose
Heaven was on the other side
of the white screen.
So all made a decision.
They left this hell
And walked right through
Into a commercial
About...Beans.

Eschewing the comfort of television studios and, courtesy of our tropical environment and way of life, where we live on the streets and the neighbour's life is as audible as ours, our studios are *plain aire*. This facilitated the use of Context to provide visual, nonverbal information on our subjects as well as Immersion, which put our presenters into the worlds of our informants. An example of our use of context may be our presenters looking for the poet Derek Walcott and utilizing the literal immersive image of the sea which plays such a role in Walcott's work.

VSF#41 – Tony Hall and Errol Sitahal meet Derek Walcott in And The Dish Ran Away With The Spoon *(1992).*

A feature on a Bélé feast in St. Lucia combines all three elements of Metaphor, Context and Immersion and comments on the place of the creole world in our lives.

Immersion: Presenter, Errol Sitahal, is pulled into the dance.

VSF#45 – Boots' explains the context to Tony Hall. And The Dish Ran Away With The Spoon *(1992).*

TONY: This is the Bélé. What is its significance?

KENNEDY 'BOOTS' SAMUEL: The Bélé is a real African survivor. It connects to our cultural heritage. It serves a social function in building community.

TONY: I notice they are singing in Creole.

BOOTS: That is our first language, the language of our soul. When our soul is participating, our love, our feelings, you get the language that means the most to us.

So what is Spoiler's response to the embargo of his heritage?

> *Is no sense to worry and go half-crazy*
> *More patience than Job, I thought take it easy*
> *Some have their cars to go Point Cumana*
> *But I am going to ride on my wooden scooter*
> *Some have their big fat turkey for Christmas*
> *But when the day comes I must eat a breakfast*
> *I done accustom, let me continue*
> *To live on vaseline and camphor ball stew*
> *Just because I have meh money in the bank since the age of nine*
> *And Them big-shots put theirs on mine*
> *I have to wait again just a couple years*
> *In order to get out mine they have to take off theirs*

Spoiler knows what he is singing about. If we have to eat 'vaseline and camphor-ball stew' to keep whole, we will do so. We will continue to thrive and create new forms despite the denial of our existence by our elite. After all, one of the region's greatest inventions, the steelband, was developed out of the banning of the drum by the colonial authorities.

In fact, while Spoiler was singing, the steelpan was being developed to enable chromatic or melodic progression on the instrument and with the help of Barbadian Lieutenant Nathaniel Griffith was being made into an orchestra, The Trinidad All Steel Percussion Orchestra (TASPO), which wowed the British public attending the Festival of Britain in 1951.

VSF#49 – Trinidad All Steel Percussion Orchestra (TASPO) performs in London 1951

Spoiler was one of the first calypsonians to record with a steelband.

The pioneering artist Jasper Johns said: 'Take an object and do something with it.' We took an empty oil drum and made the steelband and Spoiler takes the pitchoil tin and makes it a container for the 'world'. Some of the best art arises from a contemporaneous interpretation and reworking of the traditional.

For example, most of Peter Minshall's mas is inspired by traditional masquerade, such as his award winning king 'Satan in the Garden of Eden,' in his first band *Paradise Lost*, which was based on the traditional masquerade of the Bat.

> PETER MINSHALL: Let's go right back to the bat.
>
> > Somebody got a bat and studied it, and applied the detailing and architecture of the bat to a human being. So the piece of silk is attached all the way down the body on either side, and in the held palm of each hand are the manipulating canes that make the bat wings dance as the person dances The Bat.

VSF#51 – Bat masquerader, Port of Spain, Trinidad circa 1960

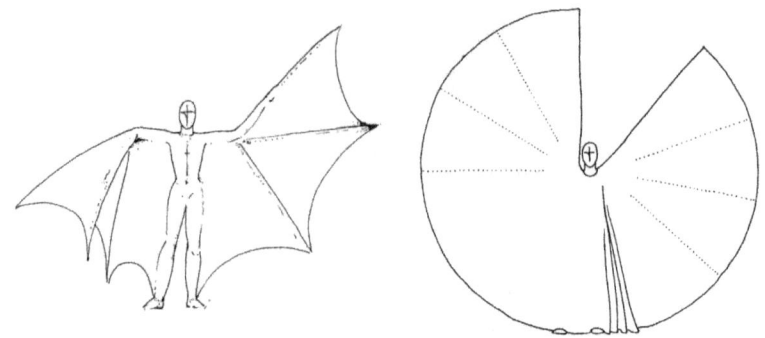

VSF#52 & 53 – Drawings for King costume for mas band Paradise Lost *by Peter Minshall 1976*

PETER MINSHALL: So I wanted to – perhaps subconsciously – take this to its next obvious logical step and I ended up by drawing a human figure who was – I think the best way to explain it, it was the Garden of Eden, so he was – the main stem of a leaf.

And from his ankles, right up the entire side of his body, going all the way up to his back, are lengths of cane that extend ten feet out on either side of him. So that the mas in fact is twenty feet wide. Very light aquatic netting attaches these extensions of cane, then there was halo around his head and the canes just continued up with one central pole right above his head so there was a circle of cane. (Interview with Peter Minshall by Christopher Laird in 2015 from film on *Paradise Lost*)

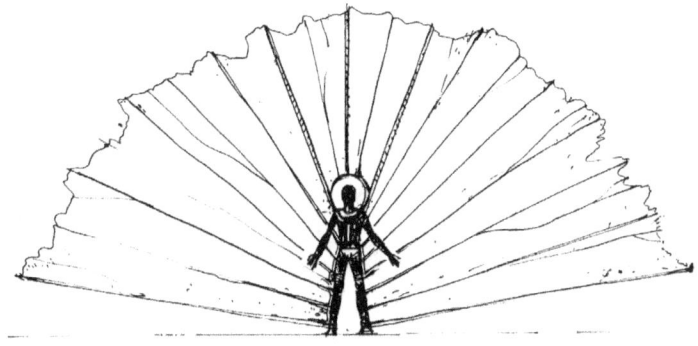

VSF#56 - *Drawings for King costume* Paradise Lost by Peter Minshall 1976

VSF#57 – *King of* Paradise Lost, *'Satan in the Garden of Eden'* by Peter Minshall 1976

If we do not have access to the traditional, to our legacy, as living memory fades, our culture is doomed to be, at best, a mediocre pastiche. But after 40 years of work and the last four years spent digitizing our archives and composing comprehensive metadata, we now have the world's largest digitized archive of Caribbean culture and society on video. Have a look at just an infinitely small sample of its content.

The digitized archive contains over 2500 video files, over 1000 hours of video accompanied by 14,500 records in a linked database. All accessible by a click.

Apart from those still with us who inhabit the archive, think of the giants who passed in the last 40 years, captured forever in the collection.

VSF#64 – Pat Bishop (1999)

VSF#66 – Lloyd Best (2002)

VSF#67 – Roaring Lion (Rafael de Leon a.k.a. Hubert Raphael Charles) (1990)

VSF#68 – Lord Kitchener (Aldwyn Roberts) (1988)

VSF#60 – Derek Walcott (1980)

VSF#70 – Boscoe Holder (2000)

VSF#71 – Louise Bennett (1984)

VSF#74 – Rex Nettleford (1989)

VSF#75 – Beryl McBurnie (1982)

VSF#80 – Dunstan St. Omer (1990)

VSF#81 – Martin Carter (1984)

VSF#82 – Rosa Guy (1990)

VSF#83 – Aimé Césaire (1988)

Think of the events captured:

VSF#84 – Caribbean Festival of the Arts (CARIFESTA) Cuba (1979)

VSF#85 – Caribbean Festival of the Arts (CARIFESTA) Barbados (1981)

VSF#86 – Caribbean Festival of the Arts (CARIFESTA) Trinidad & Tobago (1992)

Cultural and social science research is heavily invested in text, and video is often treated as a sideshow, an illustration of a text rather than as resource in its own right. This lack of appreciation of the power of video may be understandable with the region's lack of a comprehensive, well-documented and accessible video archive. But, now, with the Banyan digitized video collection, that has to change.

The Banyan Archive

Unprecedented Research Opportunites

I would like to sketch a few ways in which a video archive offers researchers unprecedented opportunities and in fact opens up whole fields of inquiry hitherto poorly served by text. An obvious example is Dance. Choreographers, practitioners and researchers have had, until now, to rely almost solely on the fading memories of an older generation, who are still with us, to reproduce, re-stage or study classical and traditional dances. Video is the only sure way to preserve dance. A similar point can be made about theatre. In fact, whole areas of anthropological research are suddenly facilitated by video in the analysing of festivals, religious practices, musical performance, oral culture, visual arts, and other aspects of our culture and heritage.

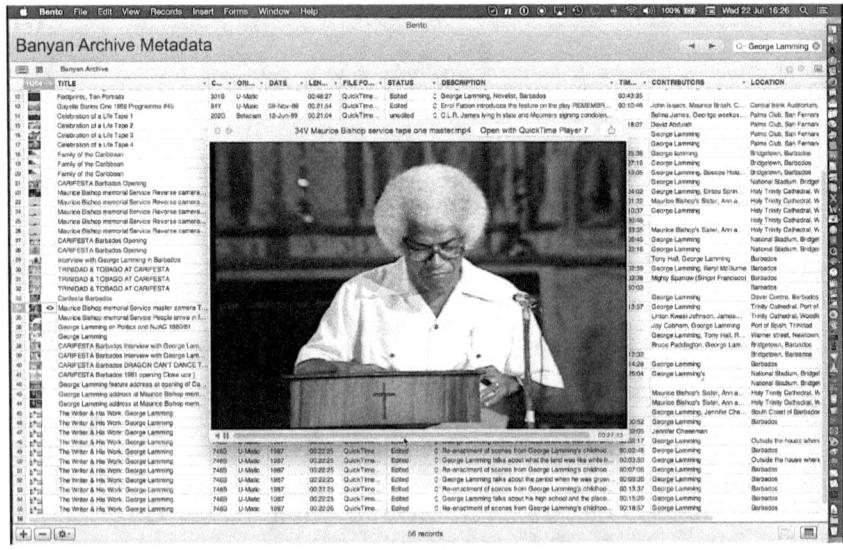

VSF#91 – Screen shot of Banyan Archive database close up (2015)

When your collection is the result of documentation by practitioners rooted in the culture, sensitive to its nuances and value, elements previously supported only by text suddenly come alive with added meaning and significance. Let me tell you a story: When I presented the completed digitized archive to the head librarian at the University of the West Indies in St. Augustine, Trinidad, I asked her to suggest a topic to search for in the database. George Lamming was suggested. Of the 56 records in the database that were identified we selected at random George Lamming's eulogy for Grenadian Prime Minister, Maurice Bishop, shortly after his murder in 1983. The occasion was a memorial service for Maurice held in the Holy Trinity Cathedral in Port of Spain, Trinidad. Now, one could say that all one needs to study the eulogy would be a transcript. But look at what would be missed. George Lamming's renowned facility as an orator, the sense of occasion, the emotion and purpose behind the delivery, the make up of the congregation – Maurice's mother and sister:

VSF#92 – *Congregation at memorial for Maurice Bishop – Maurice's Mother and Sister – Trinidad (1983)*

Activists from Europe, North America and the region: there you see, from the United Kingdom (UK), poet Linton Kwesi Johnston and Broadcaster and publisher Darcus Howe.

VSF#93 – Congregation at memorial for Maurice Bishop – Lynton Kwesi Johnson & Darcus Howe – Trinidad (1983)

VSF#94 – Birdsong Steel Orchestra playing at memorial for Maurice Bishop, Trinidad (1983)

But that is not all. When people see recordings of their own history and culture, with it is more than academic interest. A personal connection is made. For instance, the librarian asked me what steelband played at the service. The archive told us it was Birdsong. She said, 'Well you know, I was playing in the band.' And I was able to show her the band playing.

Then she said, 'My niece sang at the service.' I was able to show her niece singing.

VSF#95 – Wendy Pierre sings at memorial for Maurice Bishop, Trinidad (1983)

Then she said, 'Today is her birthday, I would love to give her a copy of that video.' No problem; personal connection.

Another thing video can do that other media cannot is show a practitioner commenting on his own work even while he is creating it. For example, distinguished water colourist, Jackie Hinkson, explaining his techniques and his decisions while actually painting:

VSF#96 – Donald Jackie Hinkson painting, Trinidad (2012)

When you have an archive covering 40 years and as large as the Banyan Collection, you have cross references within the archive itself. Not only can one see how people and events have changed over 40 years such as Derek Walcott:

VSF#97 – Derek Walcott (1980)

VSF#98 – Derek Walcott (1991)

Or C.L.R. James:

VSF#99 – C.L.R. James (1974)

VSF#100 – C.L.R. James (1980)

VSF#101 – C.L.R. James (1987)

But you also have early records of people in childhood who grew up to become significant figures in their field. For example, the internationally recognized Steelpan soloist Duvonne Stewart seen here arranging and conducting a major steelband, Renegades, for the 2015 Panorama competition:

VSF#102 – Duvonne Stewart (2015)

Was first interviewed at age eight in a panyard in Tobago in 1985.

VSF#103 – Duvonne Stewart (1985)

Or Soca mega star Machel Montano at age 11 at home with his family band:

VSF#104 – Machel Montano (1985)

And again last year with his award winning song for the Carnival.

VSF#105 – Machel Montano (2015)

The *Inside the People TV* mural is itself a document of memory, and the archive gives us, as Caribbean people, for the first time in our history, the opportunity to step back from the rush of NOW and look at our culture and society ever since the invention of the video cassette and add voices – some born more than 100 years ago – to our ever present inquiry into who we are and where we are headed.

For the first time we now have an accessible, vast and rich resource of visual/oral records of ourselves compiled by ourselves articulating our view of the world. We no longer have to rely solely on the odd Caribbean production or the mass of material generated outside the Caribbean about us and have to decode the stories of others to arrive at our truths. At long last the voices of the post-independence Caribbean can be heard among the video records of the world, demanding attention in their own right and inviting appreciation of the region's richness and stunning complexity.

This huge, unique and valuable resource, this memory of our cultural inheritance, this 'Money in the Bank,' remains largely inaccessible to the public, our students and researchers.

I leave Spoiler with the last words. From his calypso 'Lost Memories' about a village that had lost its memory. In his last verse he sings of Mr. Cornelius who, like Albert Camus' *Outsider*, is treated like a criminal because he did not cry at a funeral.

VSF#106 – The Mighty Spoiler (Theophilus Philip).

Mr. Cornelius had forgotten how to cry. Have we as a society become a Mr. Cornelius? Are we condemned to continue to forget how to remember?

> *Just because he lost his memory*
> *What an awful thing to stand up and see*
> *Put yourself in his position to imagine*
> *He forget to remember that he forget remembering*
>
> Lost Memories by Mighty Spoiler (Theophilus Philip)

Notes
1. Fifty per cent of this presentation consisted of video sequences. They are represented here by Video Still Frames (*VSF*). We have otherwise preserved the presentation format for this report. (Ed. note).
2. Calcutta is the name used for the Indian city of Kalkota. Both names are used in this book. In this case, Calcutta is taken from the calypso. (Ed. note).

CHAPTER 17

Artists Talk:
Peter Minshall and Anida Yoeu Ali

Moderated by Christopher Cozier

18th February 2016
Transcribed by Ronald Francis

'Artists Talk' brings together two performative artists, from different cultures, in conversation: Peter Minshall of Trinidad and Tobago and Anida Yoeu Ali of Cambodia and the United States (US). Introduced by Pablo Delano, guided by moderator Christopher Cozier and spurred by questions from the audience, the artists explore various parallels in their work. They reflect on the experience of performing art in public settings, vivified through the engagement and participation of the community, and sometimes, forces from a broader spiritual reality. The artists, both cognizant of their post-colonial social contexts and the transformative energy of art, speak frankly about the challenges of the process, the ephemeral nature of the performance pieces that they have created and personal experiences that have molded the work.

–Ronald Francis

Pablo Delano – Chair: It's an incredible honour for me to be here today with these three extraordinary artists. Mr. Peter Minshall is familiar to all of you. Mr. Peter Minshall whose *Dying Swan* melted my heart as I sat in cold, frigid Hartford Connecticut and turned on Facebook and saw this video which I watched over and over and over and over and over again. Mr. Minshall...has essentially invented a new art form here in Trinidad and Tobago. Anida Yoeu Ali is a...Cambodian-American artist whose work is performative and installation-oriented, and she is currently a visiting artist at Trinity College. [W]e also have, in Trinidad, an extraordinary contemporary artist whose work delves into Caribbean reality but also reaches far beyond to basically every continent,...Christopher Cozier to join the conversation. [W]e'll start by looking at a few examples of Mr. Minshall's work and Anida's work and Chris will moderate the conversation. I should say that Christopher Cozier is one of the co-founders, along with architect Sean Leonard and writer Nicholas Laughlin, of Alice Yard.

Anida: Hi everybody. Good afternoon. We can start with this image which is from a collaborative video piece, *Neang Neak*, which is a mythological creature, the serpent goddess coming out of Khmer myth, a deity who lands on earth and is essentially dealing with cultural simulation and shock. And so, this is a video retelling of a very codified, classical Khmer dance. I wanted to start with this because I think it related to a lot of your work, Mr. Minshall. This theme of collaborating [is pervasive] within my work; my media lab Studio Revolt is based between multiple cities. We actually call ourselves 'trans-nomadic' and 'sans studio', without a home essentially; my partner and I created in Cambodia, in the very context that we love, which is among the people and the everyday sights of Phnom Penh, Cambodia. So, these are just a series of public intervention pieces that deal with portraiture and coming to Cambodia and relocating the space where art happens, which for us is in the streets and at the mosque; places where people exist already, instead of locating it within a white cube space of art; bringing the art to the people and having the participants be the viewers of their own portraits. (*Referring to a slideshow*) These photos are encounters of me performing in the middle of the street before the police came to escort us away and this photo shows conversations with people over a 24-hour cycle, bringing the artist out into a public space and having seats be occupied by artists and everyday people, even through the monsoon rain. So, it's a question of identity and where art happens and where this place of creation can happen is a huge theme within my own praxis.

The Buddhist Bug is one of the most popular series in my work, and it is also one of my most ambitious projects that is rooted in performance, a hybrid creature that's both Muslim and Buddhist. The bug exists, again, in everyday spaces and challenges notions of otherness and foreignness. She is a fluid being, s/he. I prefer gender-fluid identity although language is very limited in talking about *the bug*. But here, the narrative plays out as the work takes shape. The work is a continuous ongoing work, kind of putting her in places that look at the Cambodian landscape in both the urban and the rural setting. Another facet of my work is with *Studio Revolt*, and our work with the deported community. These are young men usually and a few women who have been exiled to Cambodia as a result of policies set up against them in the US for things that they have done as teenagers. It is a more complicated series that we can get into if there is time. A lot of my work takes the female figure and makes her a sort of mythological heroine who performs with the wind, who performs in abandoned spaces, who creates these dances in rice fields. The use of material, textile and fabric, is very big in my work, which is also a parallel and a resonance with Minsh's work. *The Red Chador* is a new series with a new persona of the woman in a red, sequined chador who essentially is a Muslim walking around. Here, you see her. When she appeared in Paris, the motif was that 99 baguettes are about to be executed in the public realm. One French baguette per hour if certain demands are not met. In Fukoka, Japan, I take on motherhood and the issue of the working woman and their treatment as second class citizens in Japan. So again, the female body, the heroine is very huge in my work; taking these stories and making them mythological as well as the dominance of unconventional narratives; a resonance in my work.

Figure 17.1: Around Town 1 (The Buddhist Bug series), 2012, Phnom Penh, Cambodia

Artist: Anida Yoeu Ali; Photographer: Masahiro Sugano.

Peter: Let's do *Tan Tan and Saga Boy*. I have only recently been made acquainted with your work and the first thing I saw was, oh my goodness, it's the pumpkin caterpillar. I was immediately struck by the use of spirals. And, I was immediately struck by the fact that my friend Pablo Delano is the friend of this incredible artist because I was asked to write an introduction to a book that he did that was called *In Trinidad*; what I observed was that his work is very contemplative. Photography, I mean, it's a still, and I have only just learnt that your (Anida's) work has actual performance and movement, but when I saw [the] still of the bug, I thought well, if we were going to have a discussion, I'd like you to see the two human bugs that were made in Trinidad: *Tan Tan and Saga Boy*.

Figure 17.2. Tan Tan & Saga Boy, *from the masband Tantana, by Minshall; performed by Alyson Brown and Peter Samuel, Jr. Trinidad Carnival (1990).*

Photograph by Noel Norton. All Minshall images published by permission of Callaloo Company, arranged through Todd Gulick.

Alright! What was really exciting, for me, for us, for the Caribbean, is that there is one puppeteer and there is one puppet and the puppeteer's entire spirit informs the puppet – the puppeteer literally dances the puppet into being – right here in Trinidad – yes, they dance together as one! Alyson Brown as Tan Tan and Peter Samuel who plays Saga Boy, were invited to Kingston Jamaica to a performance in a carnival band. And Alyson returned to the hotel where we were housed about half-six in the afternoon [6:30pm]. It was just going into dark. I could tell that she was exhausted. (Alyson Brown speaking) 'Mr. Minshall, I went through the streets of Kingston and I could not take it off.' I mean, you're supposed to do that just for about 5 minutes and then take a rest. 'I danced the puppet for 4 hours. Mr. Minshall, I couldn't take it off because a sea of smiles kept opening in front of me.' And, I think that is as fine a way to describe art as any. So now, onto the latest:

Video of 'The Dying Swan'

Figure 17.3. The Dying Swan, by Minshall, performed by Jha-whan Thomas. Trinidad Carnival (2016).

Photograph by Shirley Bahadur.

Delano, Chair: I would ask the three artists to please take the stage now, and Chris [Cozier], as a Caribbean artist who is very familiar with Minshall's work, but also as an international artist, who can relate to what Anida's doing, if you can just give a spark to a conversation here.

Panelists take the stage.

Chris: I got the impression that, Peter, you wanted to say something to contextualize those two works.

Peter: No, I think things are going fine. (To Anida) Love your visuals. With my visuals. We now have the audience and everybody here has some kind of reference. (To an audience member) You want to say something?

Audience 1: The question has to do with your [Peter's] work about the serpent dancers and the images with the poles of power. Those images were entirely in black. For me, it was a flip on blackface minstrelsy where the energies of power are the white energies. I would like to know if you would speak a bit more to those characters at the bottom who were controlling the motion and the movement and the significance of that, as well as, how the hell did that get done?

Peter: You talking about the two puppets? Good question. It took 30 years. And, I wish Todd [Gulick] was here. The foremost puppet-making shop (in America) was run by a fellow called Curry who started off, as we all do, small, in New York, with Halloween costumes, who from very early on – when I met him later on, through Olympic connections – said, 'I've always loved your work.' And then he was influenced by it and we were all influenced by each other. *(To Anida)* I am so glad that I've seen your work for the first time. Anyway, Todd said something essential about the work that I do. I avoid the word 'costume'. I use the word 'mas'. It is our word. M A S, we make mas. I hate the word 'carnival'. It has such awful, cheap, nasty connotations. But you see *mas*, mas is deep and I have been seeing it since I was a child. In making mas, my job is to try to find ways and means for the expression of the human spirit; rephrase, to try to find ways and means for the expression of human energy, both spiritual and physical. And, it can happen with one or two, as you saw there, or it can happen with two thousand. I started off with a very simple puppet shape somewhere in the 1970s, and bit by bit, it developed. Because, it's the nature of the mas, it is about performance. As soon as you carry it up, try to get the aura of the person larger than life, you have to be very careful with the materials that you use. My earlier puppets were stick figures and that is why I found the connection. Then, I developed a spiral out of silk and fine, extruded fiberglass that gave the puppets body. I won't tell the whole story, but my colleague and partner for many years, Todd Gulick, it was he who pointed out, 'but Minshall, Curry makes puppets. You weren't out to make a puppet. You were out for the expression of human energy.'

And, what really thrills me is that the spine is just extended and becomes the spine of the puppet and – it's common sense really – the puppet has shoulders and your hands direct the hands of the puppet. And, the puppet's legs come off your shoulders, all properly hinged, go out there and come to your feet. So that when Alyson starts, (*singing and dancing*) 'ta ta ta ta ta ta', the whole of Alyson (*moving like a puppet*) – and I am so proud of who we are and who, more and more, we have been becoming. We can do things – it is our destiny. You see that ballet dancer? It was our destiny to take classical Africa and classical Europe and do *so* (*clasping his hands*) with it.

Chris: I wanted you to bring Anida into the conversation. I was thinking, with all the controversy that evolved around the ballet, you were saying that you're trying to find a solution to the white box and the spaces where art can happen. (*To Peter*) I kind of wonder if we are at a juncture, because I think that your work has negotiated that space quite a bit, where the [Queen's Park] savannah stage may be the 'white box' of our cultural landscape with its own kind of limitations. I think of that particularly because following your work over the years, one of the most spectacular experiences was when *Madame Hiroshima* moved through Washington and paraded around the Pentagon. It was spectacular to see this thing from Trinidad. And, it was followed by lots of police cars and security and so on. So, I want to talk a little about context, because I am interested in performative work. (*To Anida*) I'll let you jump in from there. This problem of context. (*To Peter*) And then, maybe Peter, you can follow on –

Peter: Yes. I like that whole thing about the 'white box'. And, I'll pick it up from him and throw this at you [Anida]. I did a band and I was asked by one of my younger people, 'Oh God, Minsh! Do something modern for the young people and dem.' And I, along with my friend Pat Bishop, had gone through the whole process of genuflecting on our knees when [Mark] Rothko's Reds were brought to the Tate [first installation 1961; *Red Mas* band 1998]. And, I looked at them and...I said, 'Okay. If Rothko could do a painting called *Red*, we're going to do mas called *Red,* which he [Chris] actually, in a critique, said, it was like a [red, bleeding] fissure [into the heart of the city] – the whole band was just red. Very simple. Very contemporary. And then, you get a little older and you suddenly realize that Rothko's *Red* is just really a red rectangle on a wall, whereas this was a living thing –

Anida: Moving through space –

Peter: And in the streets. And, not only that. The galleries of my little island are filled with art. I respect it. I love great painting. But, the galleries have wealthy ladies with handbags looking for stuff for their walls. There is something about the Trinidad carnival...I am trying to find the words today. Imagine a tree without breeze. What an awful thing? A tree, still. And, I thought, that's what happens when you take it out into the streets. A piece of carnival, a piece of mas, whether it's one person or two thousand, is something that is akin to nature. I really do feel that creativity runs throughout the universe, and as the artist, you're very lucky if you can string yourself into that. And the work that I call mas doesn't always work, like opera doesn't always work; my father taught me [that] if it is not working, tear it up and start again. The artist has to do that sometimes.

Anida: But also with performance. I feel like you have to get up on your feet. You have to embody your work; at least for me [because] I am not using other bodies but I am using my own body. That's when the work becomes alive and that's where it changes, and it must be experienced. It changes every single time you enact it and so it is very difficult to show documentation of a performance, let alone a still shot. These are just artifacts of a moment, of a continuous series of moments. But what's limited, what becomes commodified in what we call contemporary art, is that this resonance of the performative body in the still shot is not truly indicative of what the work means to me on a spiritual level. And, I think this is where I am connecting to your [Peter's] work too. I also feel the energy of the streets, of the rice fields, of the people that make my work. And, I always say this in a lot of my talks or when I am talking to people of a certain coded language called 'art-speak', ...that these are collaborative works. My work is nothing without the people of Cambodia participating in it in some capacity. You can't just talk about contemporary art in a place like Cambodia – you know it's very new there because of the language we're using. You can't just bring that idea and this 'white cube' aspect into a space that's been alive with art and culture and ritual for so many decades and centuries. And, you bring in this whole sort of 'white box' situation into a country and you're telling their artists this is what you need to do to make yourself an internationally-recognizable artist. When I entered that conversation, I just found it very problematic.

(Break in the recording)

Peter: Then, I saw that a *moko jumbie* was en pointe as a ballerina and I lived with it for 15 years but it was only just recently that some birds were coming into my outside studio and shitting over my work and in an effect to keep them out, I was putting some materials together and I said to him (*nudging colleague*), 'you know, this would make a nice ballet skirt.' Well, it would have been actually very Bollywood. And then, he went to search for the material and couldn't find it. (*To Anida*) One difference between us is that I never wear the work but the man who danced that...oh my God! The first thing I did when Jha-whan [dancer/actor] came into the studio, and he put the sticks on, I said, 'Jha-whan, if you could just blindfold yourself. Please don't think of it. Just do something that moko jumbies [have never done]. Just put those toes together and start doing it. The whole thing depends on that.' And he did it. It's quite amazing.

He actually studied the thing and has one stick and then, after the fact, you realize that, yes of course, Nijinsky was the only man of his time that went up on toe in *l'après-midi d'un faune*. And then, you suddenly realize that ballerinas are actually very sexy creatures, hooved animals. But, there is something else that I want to say and the best way I can say it is with [my friend Austin] Fido's help.

A 2015 letter to Minshall from his friend[Austin] Fido praising River [Mas Band 1983] is read

Peter: (*Reading his response to the letter*) *Minsh to Fido. January 6th, 2016. Your letter about the English academic's declaration that River was one of the great works of art of the twentieth century was, of course, deeply moving. It matters not a jot that it was somewhat inter-familial related because, as you tell it, there was not a jot of bias in the observation. My trial, Fido, my trouble and despair, is that I have always known that River, as played by 2000 natives of a small Caribbean island, in the carnival of 1983, was one of the most powerful statements made anywhere in all of the twentieth century on man and his environment. We must talk about River in depth, Fido, as soon as we see each other again, about God or the universe and its creative power, about chaos, faith, art, about what happens, about colour erupting out of the very earth in front of the Royal Gaol, the first stain of self-destruction. Just so, it came like a punishment out of nowhere. And then, the miraculous gale that suddenly swept down from the hills of Laventille to send River raging, confetti, people, rainbow water, the crab's bloodstained silks all pelting, ripping furiously across the [Queen's Park] Savannah stage, right there, in the middle of a blazing hot, bright, carnival Tuesday afternoon. That was mas! It was the highest mas. I did not do it Fido. I was not alone.* (*To Anida*) Ah! You're lucky – and you said it – you're lucky, if somehow [it works, it comes together]. You don't even know that it's happening. You don't even realize it. You don't analyse it. You do the work. I know the work of [Jackson] Pollock. (*Pretending to paint vigorously*) 'ta ta ta ta ta...I'm an artist ta ta ta ta'. (*Minshall is playing at being an 'artist', voicing and mocking the artist's sense of self-importance*). And this abstract expressionism is going on *wildly* in a studio and then you dry it off and hang it in the 'white box' and it looks like a piece of linoleum. Whereas *River*, in the out-of-doors, ...if you manage to get the threads of this tapestry correct, when two thousand people, native people of the Caribbean, all dressed in white, each with a squeezy bottle, start[ing] out by the Royal Gaol, this canvas [paints] itself. And then, when they hit the [Queen's Park] Savannah, there are power hoses of all the colours of the rainbow going thirty feet up into the air and the people are saying, 'wet me down!' And, the abstract expressionism is happening, a human, dancing, living canvas in front of your eyes and the confetti is being taken by the breeze from Laventille horizontally across the stage, and the audience is, some of it, getting soaked.

I had written a little story. *Mancrab* had fashioned an illusory rainbow of profit and luxury for all, and that's why all those rainbow colours get splashed among the people. And, *Washerwoman* was trying to protect the river from *Mancrab* building his factory on the banks of it, but *Mancrab* kills *Washerwoman* and throws his illusory rainbow of colour into the river, and the people, of course, with buckets and calabashes and anything that could fetch water, bathe themselves in *Mancrab*'s illusory rainbow colours and, in so doing, destroy themselves. And, it happened. They did it... right in front of your eyes. And, we, now, here, on the island and on the planet, live in the age of *Mancrab*. We are just beginning to realize that the rainbow is not the ill-advised highway, or the rapid rail, or the latest cellphone in the palm of your hand. The rainbow is you and you and you and you and you. The red needs to stand up next to the orange, next to the yellow, the green, the blue, and we need to get together. The rainbow is us the people. And, when you play *that* mas, you really will find the pot of gold. I really was going to do that band this year but I couldn't. Work was too hard and I was feeling a lot of pain. I think, out of the pain, came a *Dying Swan*. It's how it works. You don't plan it. If it comes, you accept it. You really do begin to realize that you have to be so humble. I duck the word genius. It's a very dangerous word. I duck it every time somebody throws it at me. I duck it.

Chris: Well, we have a question. Yes, go ahead.

Audience 2: Both of you enact your art, but you're [Anida] in the middle of your art and you are, Mr. Minshall, not on the outside, but directing, both of you, to 'this is what the story is. This is what I want this one figure to do.' I'd especially like to hear you talk about the teams that you have that you then have to pass this vision to, whether you're [Anida] in the middle of it, or you're [Peter] to the side of it. What if your team members, your other artists, get another vision because they're in the middle of the piece and the story goes awry? Then, it's not your story. Please comment on that.

Peter: That's a great question but it's what I just tried to say. My story was supposed to happen on the stage but on the day, one of the squeezy bottles got run over by a car at the bottom of the fence and some colour went up onto the people and that's what I meant. The people started squirting.

Audience 2: But, that wasn't your vision?

Peter: They were supposed to do the squirting on the stage! (*Audience laughing*) And please, something marvelous happened: the Cuban Biennial. I had a work that was called *The Dance of the Cloth* and I needed to find a place to do it. Finally found the beautiful Spanish courtyard, evidently, the most beautiful in Havana. And, *The Dance of the Cloth* is three men with canopies over their heads that are attached to the feet and they move.

Figure 17.4 The Dance of the Cloth, *by Minshall, concept illustration by Todd Gulick (2000).*

And there, in the courtyard was this damn, distracting statue of Christopher Columbus and I thought, 'Oh fuck!' And then, it hit me. He is there for a reason, Minshall. There are these three sails. It's the *Niña*, the *Pinta* and the *Santa María*. And, I had done a piece of work and it had had a crab. It was no longer a crab. It was three – a brown skin, a darker skin and a – three West Indian men – with these three cloths on them to [Albioni's] *Adagio* [recorded music accompanying the piece].

The Dance of the Cloth, *by Minshall, performed by Wendell Manwarren, Roger Roberts, and Dave Williams. Seventh Biennial of Havana, Cuba (2000).*

Photograph by Charlotte Elias.

works for me at times – 'Fuck!' – the wonder of it all. So I made a little speech to the gathered audience in Havana on the day. I said exactly what you're saying. You do it and then it goes into a space and the space and the people redo it, and then the rain falls and that does something else to it. Yes, things happen.

And that's exactly what I said just now. A raging breeze blew through – Madame Chaos saw the river and she came down. She planted she two foot and she lifted up her skirt and she called out 'Come chirren, leh we go.' And a big breeze blew through. I had nothing to do with it.

But that is what gave it its drama. That is what made it the work of art. That is why – don't get me wrong, I love great paintings, and they were called great masters because all they had was paint and brushes, and I have never stopped looking at Botticelli's *Venus Rising*. How did he pull this off? Because…a grown woman but she looking newly born. And, I'm going to be naughty now. But, when I look at the aged Rembrandt's self-portrait, I see the universe and the artist is truly present…you see that *Dying Swan* that joins a hundred years, the *Ballet Russe* to a Port of Spain, Trinidad carnival, …it was so much more interesting that it was a man doing it and doing it on stilts. Of course, we had to change some of the choreography because the stilts cannot dive. So, I said to him, 'Please…you're Orisha eh. So, right at the end there, Shango has to, like a hand of steel, hold your backbone.' And, the audience got it. 'And you have to die on the stilts.'

Chris: I was curious to hear about the idea of being truly present. Because the distinction that you (*to Audience 2*) made was between you [Peter] as an instigator of other bodies and you [Anida], your actual body. So, I kind of thought the notion [that] being truly present would be interesting to discuss.

Anida: Yea, also to answer your [Audience 2] question. For many performance artists, you have to let go. You have to let go because you allow those moments to play out. And, one example is the piece with the lady in the red dress in the rural rice field. That could not have happened without the spontaneity of the wind. In that moment, it wasn't planned to have that amount of wind on that day. But, the wind changed everything and made that piece what it's become, and if you look at all the different sculptural moments that happened with the red fabric, that moment when the Nāga, which is the mythological dragon, visits, it comes into being through the shape of the fabric. So again, I had to let go in order for the work to truly be birthed. And oftentimes, that's what you do especially when your body is the vessel for the moment. You can't redo it. You don't say 'go,' and then when someone comes into frame, 'that's not supposed to be.' You don't backtrack and do it again. You have to now work with whatever comes into being. I think that is why you cannot buy performance art. Performance art and performance must be experienced.

That live moment is even more important now in this world that we have all these different things that facilitate being a witness. Being not present with this live moment, that takes it away from what performance art is. What performance art is, for many of us, for myself, in terms of being present – *that* is my spirituality, *that* is my church. I may identify as both a Muslim and a Buddhist but I don't go to those temples to worship. My temple is art making in the context of this everyday setting. That's my temple.

Figure 17.6: Enter the Red Wind / Naga #1, 2012
A rice field outside Phnom Penh, Cambodia
Artist: Anida Yoeu Ali; Photographer: Vinh Dao.

Audience 3: Emily [Emily Zobel Marshall]. I am from Leeds and I had a question for both of you…the ballet and contemporary art, these could be viewed as elite art forms. And, I was wondering what people's reactions have been in Cambodia and in Trinidad to integrating those forms into a new setting.

Audience 4: Anida, about being present, being local, being in the space; there is something generative for the people that are there and for yourself. But, in a world that we claim to be globalized, there is something about not having access to your local. So, if I'm appreciative of your work but I can't get to Cambodia for that space, that performance, how do you feel about the fact that film or photography, in its limits, might be the only medium through which I can access or feel it. How do you feel about that relationship, the loss or the gain from the mediation?

Anida: Maybe, I'll take that question first from Davarian [Davarian Baldwin, Audience 4]. It's such a back and forth for me and unfortunately, I rely on documentation as the means to continue the narrative. At whatever point people are intersecting with the work, they have to ask specific questions and those questions lead to more questions in order for you to truly understand the work. So, you will never ever be able to experience the work in the way that it was performed in the moment. What you have is the resonance of that time and that moment and that period. And so, to take the work that's been created in Cambodia by the collaboration of Cambodians, to take it outside into the world to be shared, is to have these conversations, which is very important, I think, in order to make these connections that one could have never imagined, with Cambodia and the Caribbean, Cambodia and Trinidad. I am seeing so many similarities and parallels in post-colonial contexts with the resonance of recovering from trauma through the rebuilding with art and this revivalism. I would have never imagined having these kinds of conversations, but it's so important because it's relocating the voice of the periphery, re-centreing that, and making these more dominant conversations instead of always relying on the US and the Europeans. Because, that's what people imagine in Southeast Asia: that to be a truly recognizable, valued artist, you have to knock on doors and get the attention of the Americans and Europeans. But, had we had these types of conversations where we're relocating, decentreing these points, supposedly, where contemporary art is more valued, I think that's how we start to shift to making peripheries more central. So, it's very important for me to have those resonances.

Chris: I know Peter wants to jump in. The first question about elitism [is] a really important question in the context...talking about ballet and these forms being a contradiction almost. (...) But, it is funny because in the context of Trinidad, people were not questioning ballet in Peter's presentation in particular.

They were questioning whether it was *mas* or not. They were worried about Trinidadian form. It is ironic...a writer who is a friend always talks about how the relationship between these cultures is mediated by the relationship with the Euro-American narrative and so on. So, for someone of Peter's generation, ...yes, there's a kind of concern about canonical things: the ballet, you know. And in your own practice, you've (*to Peter*) deconstructed those things. You've...rumpled them up a bit, creolized them, so to speak...[and] I want to bring it into the other point – resonances, because I think there is something important about the problem of history in societies like ours, the process of history.

Anida: And who writes it?

Chris: (*Agreeing*) Internally and externally. But, I think in the context of carnival, there may be scant record of Peter's work but there are so many retellings in carnival as it exists. Whether you like the costumes or not, whether it's turned into a rigged show or not, there is a retelling of certain elements of your (*Peter*) work, which is a kind of ritualistic enactment of memory. So, I wanted to let both of [you] address the problem of tradition and the canon and, on the other side, this issue [of] resonance, history and record.

Peter: In 1980, I did a band called *Danse Macabre*. On the carnival Tuesday afternoon – the rest of the carnival was all sequins and prettified – there was this stampede of skulls and bones and burlap and shells and white fowl feathers, married to glossy, glowing, brown skin, arms and legs. It thundered across the savannah stage. Many years later – on the 8 of March 2013 – I was asked by UWI to give a talk about my life and work. Something electric happened to me and to the audience. At the end they lifted me so high up. My spirit soared. I got to a point where – I have to be surreal – where I actually saw *Danse Macabre*. I saw it, in my mind's eye, the living mas, thundering across the stage. And then my camera swiveled, and I saw MOMA (Museum of Modern Art, New York City), and all of a sudden I realized that **that** (*pointing to the savannah*) was a living work of art, whereas **this** (*pointing to the wall*) was still life. Do you understand what I'm saying?'

Laughter

Anida: *(Laughing)* How can we not?

Peter: And you're *(to Anida)* right. It happens in the moment. And yes, you need a resonance and memory. And you need photographs and you need things but it happens in the moment. And with reference to ballet...I've seen some great ballet. I don't think it's elitist. I went to London at the age of 21, in the early 60s and the first opera I saw – would you believe – *Götterdämmerung*. I mean, that's really throwing the boy into the deep end of the pool. I loved it. Now, there's good opera and there's bad opera. There's good ballet and there's bad ballet. And, there's good mas and there's *terrible* mas. And yes, I like stirring the pot, and she [Anida] obviously does, too. I mean, the lady in the red chador...stir the pot, darling!

Figure 17.7: The Day After *(The Red Chador series), 2016*
Seattle, Washington USA

Artist: Anida Yoeu Ali; Photographer: Masahiro Sugano.

Anida: She's going to Washington DC next. Hopefully, the curators get it through. I did want to say [something] about the question on elitism. You have to fully understand the history of Cambodia too. In the mid-1970s, as a result of Cold War politics, Cambodia went through a genocidal period of civil war in which 90 per cent of artists lost their lives. And that meant also a large majority of oral tradition was lost. Many art forms were lost as master artists were killed. There's been a huge recovery period from the 1980s onwards in preserving these forms. Music, art, dance have been pivotal in everyday life, and rituals were never disconnected from the people. So, that's been the basis of a lot of the work. So, now, we see these rituals play out in terms of weddings and birthdays. But, we also see it in major functions where dancers come to bless a stage, to bless the breaking of ground and to – whatever it is – the welcoming of a new baby. That dance, culture, music has always been a part of everyday culture and it's only with colonialism and that period of time that has separated art as an elitist form and given it a certain kind of [limited] access. It's only allowed for certain people. Post-war, in Cambodia, the people who maintained the art form were not the children of the elite and were not the elite. They were the children from the gutter. They were the ghetto kids. Those were the people that were given the art education because they couldn't afford general public education. So, the keepers of the culture were poor people in general who learned and relearned this craft, this work, overtime, and that includes the visual arts.

Currently, in contemporary Cambodia,...the keepers of the culture, in terms of fostering and cultivating this new contemporary art scene, [are] the poor kids who worked their butts off to try to acquire a different kind of knowledge to speak to their present time. I would have to say that includes me. You know, I came from nothing as a refugee. And now, of course, I have this knowledge and access, but it is not an easy road to pick as an artist, coming from nothing as a refugee, as a child of a war-torn nation, relearning the language, to working class, to middle class and then you drop down to artist class. Having that consciousness is also something that I am always aware of when I have the platform to speak about the work and to understand fully who I am speaking to and when I put on certain 'costumes' for certain people. I think we all know what we're talking about when we have to speak multiple languages to different audiences. But, the heart of my work – I do want my own people to acknowledge the work and have this intersection that allows for these conversations. That's why it has to take place on the streets of Cambodia, in the rice fields. Because, there is a farmer that comes through the space and can stop for a moment and ask me what is this orange worm, pumpkin worm, doing in the middle of my rice field. Can we talk about it? And then, I love it. You drop everything and you talk about it. You ask him, 'what do you think it's about?' And, I think that's the work of contemporary art. It's for us to question and provoke. It is not to provide the answer.

Chair: I wish we had another hour because it's been extraordinary to listen to the three of you. Thank you. We are out of time.

Applause

Notes

1. Deletions from the transcript almost always include only filler phrases that characterize oral speech (such as, 'you know') and do not – unless noted in the text – result in the loss of the actual conversation between the artists. (All notes are ed. note).
2. Ali's *The Red Chador: Beheadings* was a 12-hour durational performance at the Palais de Tokyo on April 20, 2015.
3. *Adoration of Hiroshima*, a protest mas in Washington, DC, 1985.
4. Cozier wrote: 'The presentation symbolized an incision into the superfluous gitter and biking parades that have taken over the streets in recent years. This red, bleeding fissure proclaimed that the mechanism called Carnival is still alive and hurting and as a people we still have a soul' (in Catalogue of art exhibition 'Caribe Insular Exclusión, Fragmentación y Paraíso', 1998, XXXI Bienal di Pontevedra, Galicia, Spain; reference provided by Todd Gulick).
5. The Queen's Park Savannah, known in Port of Spain as 'the Savannah', originally part of the St. Ann's Sugar Estate, is Port of Spain's largest common or green. Owned by the state with a perimeter of approximatly 3.5 kilometers (two miles), it occupies approximately 260 acres of largely grassy space in Port of Spain. Formerly the site of horse races, it is now the central location for carnival competitions and other major events.

Contributors

Alea (Albada), Nicole, PhD in Developmental Psychology, The University of Florida, was a Senior Lecturer in Psychology, in the Department of Behavioural Sciences UWI, and the Director of the Adult Development and Aging Lab in Trinidad and Tobago (ADALTT). Her research, which has been funded by Campus Research and Publication Fund awards, focuses on how and why adults from young adulthood to old age remember the personal past, and to what extent doing so relates to present-day psychological, social, and emotional well-being. Dr Albada has over 30 manuscripts published in international and regional journals and books, and is a frequent presenter at international conferences. She also has a co-edited book, *Ageing in the Caribbean*. She is a member of the American Psychological Association, the Gerontological Society of America, and the Society for Applied Research in Memory and Cognition. She is now a Lecturer in the Department of Psychological and Brain Sciences at the University of California, Santa Barbara.

Bauer, Janet, PhD in Anthropology, Stanford University, is a Professor in International Studies at Trinity College in Hartford, Connecticut, the former director of Trinity's Women, Gender and Sexuality Program, a member of Hartford's Commission on Refugee and Immigrant Affairs, and a visiting Fulbright Global Scholar. She teaches, conducts ethnographic research, and publishes on gender and mobility in Muslim societies (in the Middle East, Southeast Asia, Europe and the Americas). Currently she is working on a multi-sited research project on gender and race in Muslim Diasporas in Trinidad and Tobago, Canada, Germany and the United States.

Berger, Urs, PhD in Cell Biology, University of Basel, Switzerland, grew up in Switzerland and emigrated in his twenties to the United States where he studied neuroscience and cell biology. He had a career as neuroanatomist at various Harvard Teaching Hospitals, as well as in his own consulting and service business. He has published, or has contributed to, more than 50 basic science research papers, as well as two book chapters on kidney physiology. His main love, however, turned out to be calypso music, and he has devoted his time recently to the cataloging and archiving of this music. To that end, he completed a post-bac minor degree in Computer Science from Tufts University in Massachusetts. He is working on an online database for his extensive calypso records collection.

Cateau, Heather, PhD in History, The University of the West Indies, is a Senior Lecturer in Caribbean History at The UWI, St. Augustine Campus and the current Dean of the Faculty of Humanities and Education. She has held the positions of Head of the History Department and University Dean. Her research focus has led to a revisionary approach to plantation and enslavement systems in the Caribbean. Her publications include *Beyond Tradition, Reinterpreting the Caribbean Historical Experience* co-edited with Rita Pemberton, *The Caribbean in the Atlantic World* co-authored with John Campbell and *Capitalism and Slavery Fifty Years Later* co-edited with Selwyn Carrington. She has held Visiting Fellowships at the University of Iowa and the University of Cambridge. She is the current Vice President of the Association of Caribbean Historians.

Delano, Pablo, MFA, Yale University School of Art, is currently Professor of Fine Arts at Trinity College, Hartford, Connecticut. Delano was born and raised in San Juan, Puerto Rico. Solo exhibitions of his photographs have been held in galleries and museums throughout the United States, Latin America, Europe and the Caribbean. He has published several books of photography including *In Trinidad* (Ian Randle, 2008). Delano has taught art and photography at The International Center of Photography (NYC), The City University of New York, Montclair State University, Dartmouth College, and Brandeis University.

Euraque, Dario A, PhD in Latin American and Caribbean history, The University of Wisconsin (Madison), is Professor of History & International Studies at Trinity College, Hartford, Connecticut. His numerous articles and reviews have appeared in academic journals in the US, Europe, Latin America and the Caribbean. He authored:

Reinterpreting the 'Banana Republic': Region and State in Honduras, 1870s–1972 (University of North Carolina Press, 1996, Spanish editions, 1997; 2001); *Estado, Poder, Nacionalidad y Raza en la Historia de Honduras: Ensayos* (Ediciones Subirana, 1996); *Conversaciones Históricas con el Mestizaje en Honduras y su Identidad Nacional* (Centro Editorial, 2004); *Historiografía de Honduras* (Instituto Hondureño de Antropología e Historia, 2009); and *El golpe de Estado del 28 de junio del 2009, el Patrimonio Cultural y la Identidad Nacional de Honduras* (Centro Editorial, 2010). He is working on two biographies of Hondurans, a poet, Armando Mendez (1925–2003), and a banana cultivator and exporter, Rafael Lopez Padilla (1875–1963).

Francis, Ronald, BA in Spanish and Linguistics (hons), The University of the West Indies, is a PhD candidate in Linguistics and a Research Assistant at The UWI, St. Augustine Campus. His research interests are Creole phonology and morphology, literacy, language education and language policy in multilingual contexts.

Greenberg, Cheryl, PhD in American History, Columbia University, is a Professor at Trinity College, Connecticut. A scholar of African-American history and contemporary race relations, Greenberg has written and edited four books, with another in press. These and her many articles and anthology chapters focus on African American communities and their intersection with politics – particularly the Great Depression and New Deal, the civil rights movement, and Black-Jewish relations. Her current research, presented in part at the Trinidad conference, explores how and why different African American and Afro-Caribbean communities in the United States have shifted in their attitudes toward gay marriage. Cheryl has taught at Trinity College for 30 years, with brief stints away at the University of Helsinki in Finland, Nankai University in China, and Harvard University. She also teaches at Cheshire Correctional Institution, a maximum security prison in Connecticut.

Hall, Tony, BEd in Drama, University of Alberta and Advanced Diploma in Television Production, Northern Alberta Institute of Technology, Alberta, Canada, is a Trinidad playwright/screenwriter with Lordstreet Theatre Company. He formulated the Jouvay Popular Theatre Process to interrogate the role and function of the traditional masquerade (mas) characters trapped in emancipation traditions.

Recently known for 'mas interventions' into the Trinidad carnival, *Miss Miles* (Minshall Mas, 2014), *Performing Marcus & Amy* (2016), his other acclaimed works include, for the stage: *Jean & Dinah*...(1994), *Twilight Cafe* (2002), *Miss Miles the Woman of the World* (2011); for the street: *A Band on Drugs* (1990), *MUD!* (Norwegian Theatre Academy 2016); made for TV film: *And the Dish Ran Away with the Spoon* (Banyan/BBC 1994). Tony has lectured at California State University; Northridge; Prague Quadrennial; Indiana State University; University of Winchester, UK; Trinity College, Hartford, Connecticut and currently lectures in the Trinity-in-Trinidad Program.

Hutchinson, Gerard, Doctor of Medicine (DM) in Psychiatry, The University of the West Indies, is currently the Professor and Unit Lead in Psychiatry, at the School of Medicine, Faculty of Medical Sciences (FMS), UWI, St. Augustine Campus. He also serves currently as the coordinator of the DM Psychiatry programme, St. Augustine Campus and the Programme Director of the MSc Clinical Psychology programme. St. Augustine Campus. He functions as the Head of Psychiatry at the North Central Regional Health Authority. He received Masters degrees in Science and Philosophy from the University of London.

Kassim, Halima-Sa'adia, PhD in History, The University of the West Indies, is presently employed at the University Office of Planning, Regional Headquarters, UWI, St. Augustine Campus. She has published articles on the Muslim community related to education, gendered identities, cultural retention and negotiation in Trinidad and Tobago as well as on issues related to higher education administration and gender. She previously held the positions of Deputy Programme Manager for Gender and Development at the CARICOM Secretariat in Guyana, Head of Continuing Studies at Cipriani College of Labour and Cooperative Studies (CCLCS), and Special Advisor to the President of the Republic of Trinidad and Tobago. She has lectured in the Trinity-in-Trinidad Program in Trinidad.

Khan, Katija, PhD in Psychology, University of Hull, Yorkshire, England, is a Lecturer in Clinical Psychology in the Faculty of Medical Sciences at The University of the West Indies, St. Augustine Campus where she also coordinates the MSc Clinical Psychology Programme. She is the immediate Past President of the Trinidad and Tobago

Association of Psychologists. She worked previously at the University of Hull and University of Sheffield, England, where she was a part of the Translational Neuropsychology Group. Her research interests include the cultural effects on cognitive performance and the norming and validation of psychological tests for use with Caribbean populations.

Kring, Brunhild, MD in Psychiatry, Johann Wolfgang Goethe University, Frankfort/Main, Germany, is Associate Director, Counseling and Wellness Services, New York University (NYU) and Clinical Assistant Professor at the NYU School of Medicine, New York City. She graduated from the psychiatric residency training programme at Einstein College of Medicine. She dedicated her career to the psychotherapeutic and psychopharmacological treatment of patients in ambulatory clinics in New York City – always in conjunction with residency training and medical student supervision. At this point, she mainly works with young adults. She has a special interest in cross-cultural psychiatry and the psychological and sexual development of the emerging adult.

Laird, Christopher, Honorary Doctorate, The University of the West Indies (2009), has been a teacher, published the arts journal *Kairi* and run a theatre in Port of Spain, Trinidad and Tobago during the 1970s. He has produced over 300 documentaries, dramas and other video productions with Banyan Ltd. over the past 40 years, garnering a score of national, regional and international awards. He has overseen the establishment of what is arguably the world's largest collection of Caribbean culture on video in the Banyan Archive. In 2003 he founded, with Errol Fabien, the region's first all Caribbean free to air television station, Gayelle. He was the Chairman of the Board of the Trinidad & Tobago Film Company between 2011 and 2014.

Lovelace, Earl, Honorary Doctorate, The University of the West Indies (2002) and Trinidad and Tobago Chaconia Gold medalist (1988), was born in Toco, Trinidad and has spent most of his life on the islands of Trinidad and Tobago from which he draws creative inspiration for his work. An author of international acclaim, best known among his works are the classic *The Dragon Can't Dance* (1979), *The Wine of Astonishment* (1982), and *Salt* (1996), for which he won the Commonwealth Writers' Prize in 1997. His latest novel, *Is Just a Movie* (2012), was awarded the Caribbean Writers' Prize as well as the Bocas Literary Prize. He lives in Port of Spain, Trinidad, where he continues to write creatively and to participate in the cultural life of the island.

Maharaj-Best, Sunity is the Managing Director of the Lloyd Best Institute of the West Indies. The former editor of the *Trinidad and Tobago Review*, she is a widely acclaimed journalist and media consultant and also runs her own multi-media production company.

Marshall, Emily Zobel, PhD in Cultural Studies, Leeds Beckett University, is a Senior Lecturer in Postcolonial Literature at the School of Cultural Studies at Leeds Beckett University. She teaches courses on African American, Caribbean, African and Black British literature. Her research specialties are Caribbean literature, Caribbean carnival cultures, trickster studies and folklore and she has published widely in these fields. Her book, *Anansi's Journey: A Story of Jamaican Cultural Resistance* (2012) was published by the University of the West Indies Press and she is currently researching her forthcoming book, *American Tricksters: Trauma, Tradition and Brer Rabbit*, to be published by Rowman and Littlefield.

Misrahi-Barak, Judith, PhD in Anglophone Literatures, University of Burgundy, Dijon, France, is Associate Professor at University Paul Valéry Montpellier 3, France, where she teaches English and post-colonial literatures. She has published articles on Caribbean and Indo- and Sino-Caribbean writers, and the Diaspora (*Atlantic Studies, Commonwealth, The Journal of Postcolonial Writing, Moving Worlds, The Journal of the Short Story in English, The Journal of Haitian Studies, The Journal of Transnational American Studies, Black Studies Papers, International Journal of Francophone Studies, Interculturel Francophonies*...), as well as book chapters in edited collections, most recently *Tracing the New Indian Diaspora* (Om Dwivedi, ed. Rodopi, 2014). She is General editor of the series *PoCoPages* (Collection 'Horizons anglophones,' Pulm, Montpellier). More recent interests include Dalit literatures. She co-edited *Dalit Literatures in India* (Joshil K. Abraham, co-ed., Routledge, 2015) and was Co-Investigator on the AHRC Research Network series on 'Writing, Analysing, Translating Dalit Literature' (2014–16).

Morgan, Paula, PhD in Literature, The University of the West Indies, St. Augustine Campus, is Professor of West Indian Literature and

Culture in the Department of Literary, Cultural and Communications Studies at The UWI, St. Augustine Campus. She has published numerous articles on domestic violence, the interface of ethnic and gender relations, the construction of Caribbean masculinities, and pedagogical approaches to literary and popular discourses. She has written, edited and/or collaborated on numerous book length publications including *The Arc of Memory in the Aftermath of Trauma* (Editor, Interdisciplinary Press, 2015); *The Terror and The Time: Banal Violence and Trauma in Caribbean Discourse* (UWI Press, 2014); *The Culture of Violence: A Trinidad and Tobago Case Study*, edited with Valerie Youssef; an online Journal collection *In a Fine Castle: Childhood in Caribbean Imagi/Nations.* 2010) and *Writing Rage: Unmasking Violence in Caribbean Discourse* – coauthored with Valerie Youssef (UWI Press, 2006).

Neptune, H. Reuben (Harvey), PhD in History, New York University, is an Associate Professor of History at Temple University. Neptune grew up in Trinidad and was trained in the Department of History at NYU, where he specialized in the fields of Latin America and the African Diaspora. He is the author of several articles (published in journals including *The American Historical Review, Small Axe,* and *Radical History Review)* and one seminal book *Caliban and the Yankees: Trinidad and the U.S. Occupation* (2007). Interested generally in the cultural politics of imperial- and nation-building, he is currently at work on a book entitled: *The Scandal of 'Consensus': Post-Colonial History Writing in the Cold War U.S.,* which reconsiders the politics of US historiography during the early Cold War years.

Pedro, Consuelo, Doctor of Physical Therapy (DPT) candidate, New York University (NYU), is a national of Trinidad and Tobago who has always been interested in the role and effects of culture on cognition, rehabilitation and healthcare. In Dr Sarah Raskin's Cognitive Neuroscience Laboratory at Trinity College (Hartford, Connecticut), Pedro researched prospective memory and electrophysiology, studying acquired brain injury and exploring cognitive rehabilitation. These experiences led her to a DPT programme in the Steinhardt School of Culture, Education and Human Development at NYU, Class of 2020. The interdisciplinary conversation involving culture and memory plays a central but less documented role in the physical therapy rehabilitation outcomes that are central to her study.

Raskin, Sarah A, PhD in Neuropsychology, John Hopkins University, is a Board Certified Clinical Neuropsychologist and Professor of Psychology and Neuroscience at Trinity College in Hartford, Connecticut. She has published numerous articles investigating neuropsychological functions and cognitive rehabilitation for a variety of disorders, including brain injury. She co-authored the Memory for Intentions Test (MIST) published by Psychological Assessment Resources. She is co-author with Catherine Mateer of *Neuropsychological Management of Mild Traumatic Brain Injury*, published by Oxford University Press (2000) and is the editor of *Neuroplasticity and Rehabilitation,* published by Guilford Press (2011).

Reger, Gary, PhD in History, the University of Wisconsin (Madison), is a Professor at Trinity College in Hartford, Connecticut. With an MA in Greek, his work on the ancient Greek and Roman economy began with *Regionalism and Change in the Economy of Independent Delos* and continues with a project, based on case studies, surveying Greco-Roman economic history, for which he received a National Endowment of the Humanities Fellowship grant for 2017–2018. His other main interest is the history of human interaction with deserts broadly conceived across time and space. He has published essays on the southwestern deserts in *Boom California*, *Extrapolation*, and *Cultural History*.

Regis, Louis, PhD in Literature, The University of the West Indies, St. Augustine Campus, is a former Senior Lecturer in Literatures in English in the Department of Literary Cultural and Communication Studies at The UWI, St. Augustine Campus. He specializes in calypso research and West Indian literature, poetry and drama. His major publications are *Black Stalin Kaisonian* (Mona: Arawak, 2007), *The Political Calypso: True Opposition in Trinidad and Tobago 1962–1987* (Mona, Jamaica: UWI Press and Gainesville, FL: University Press of Florida, 1999) and *Race, Ethnicity and Nationalism in the Trinidad and Tobago Calypso 1970–1998* (Arawak: Kingston, Jamaica, 2017).

Riggio, Milla Cozart, PhD in English literature, Harvard University, is the James J. Goodwin Professor of English, Emerita, Trinity College, Hartford, Connecticut. Her research interests include English medieval drama, Shakespeare, Trinidad carnival, Ramleela in Trinidad, and the Garifuna throughout the Caribbean. She co-edited Pablo Delano's

In Trinidad (2008), and edited, among other books, a special edition of *TDR: The Drama Review* focusing on Trinidad carnival, (1998), *Teaching Shakespeare through Performance* (1999), *Carnival, Culture in Action – The Trinidad Experience (*2008), and most recently was lead editor on *Festival Devils of the Americas* (2015). Working with the National Carnival Commission of Trinidad and Tobago, she has co-ordinated three international carnival Conferences. She founded the Trinity-in-Trinidad Program. She also works as a professional dramaturg.

Index

Advocacy: of Indo-Muslim women, 90–99
African-Americans: and digit-span performance, 217; James and, 10
African enslavement: in Connecticut, 30–31; in Central America, 57–58
African Diaspora historiography: in Central America, 56–68
Africans: in Central America, 55–68
Afro-Caribbean novels, 76
Alea (Albada), Nicole, 327
Alexandria: comparison between New Orleans and, 43–44
Ali, Moulvi Ameer: influence on Indo-Muslim community, 91–92
Ali, Anida Yoeu, 307–326
American Civilization: by C.L.R. James and edited by Robert Hill, 2–19
American Mediterranean: concept, 40–41, 43–44, 49–50
American Psychological Association: study of human sexual behaviour, 196, 198–199
Aneesa: Muslim feminist, 111–114
Anjuman Sunnat-ul-Jamaat (ASJA), 97
Antoni: Robert: and carnival, 156
Archival work: in Bahadur's *Coolie Woman*, 79
Art: performance, 307–326
Autobiographical memory: culture and, 224–230; defining, 212
Ayoung-Chee, Anya: feminist activist, 152

Back catalogue: of calypso music, 185–187
Bakhtin, Mikhail: theory of the Carnivalesque, 146–148
Ballet: and carnival, 307, 311, 315, 324

Banyan: and Caribbean TV, 271–306
Banyan archives: and research opportunities, 296–306;
'Bankie's Son': analysis of, 172
Basic National Curriculum (BNC): in Central America, 57–59
Bauer, Janet: 327
Bélé ritual: and Caribbean TV, 283–284
Berger, Urs, 327–328
Beyond a Boundary: and cricket, 171
Black Jacobins: by C. L.R. James, 4
Black Star Line: Garvey and the, 254
Blue devils: in Trinidad and Tobago carnival, 154
Bonaparte, Elaine: and the experience of Caribbean female migrant workers, 134–137
Bonsal, Stephen: on Cuba, 46
'Bounce': analysis of, 171–172
British culture: and digit span performance, 216, 217
British Caribbean: links with Connecticut, 22– 34
Brown Girl Brownstones: Caribbean female migrant workers in, 126, 129–132; racism in; 130–133
Buddhist Bug: Anida Ali's, 308–309

Calinda: in carnival, 149
Calypso: history of, 179–183; David Rudder's contribution to, 164–177; and political satire, 151–153; Trinidad, 179–189, 269–270
Calypso Rose: French Grammy recipient, 186; music of, 182–183, 186; and sexual abuse in carnival, 151–152
Cambodia: Anida Ali and, 307–326
Canboulay: carnival practice, 149–150
Capitalism: and carnival 157–160

Caregiving: migrant workers and the emotional stress of, 137–139
Caribbean: autobiographical memory in the, 227–230; carnival, 147–162, 307–326; civilization, 277–278; defining the, xi, 36–37, 73–74; female migrant workers, 126–139; feminism, 104–105; Indian migration to the, 75–77; Mediterranean analogy, 36–50; migration to Central America, 63–67; migration to Connecticut, 32–34; television, 269–306
Caribbean Eye: Caribbean TV series, 276
Caribbean culture: and digit span performance, 216, 217
Carnival: and calypso, 165–177, 179–199; feminism in, 151–152; MAS vs, 312; in the Middle Ages, 146–149; power, performance and play in 145–162; roots of Caribbean, 148–150; as visual art, 285–288, 307–326
Carnival: by Robert Antoni, 156
Carnivalesque power: Trinidad carnival and the, 146–147, 285–288
Cateau, Heather, 328
Central America: African Diaspora studies in, 55–68
'Champions': analysis of, 175–176
Coalition Advocating for Inclusion of Sexual orientation (CAISO), 202–203
Cognition: and culture, 212–218
Compact discs: and calypso, 183–185
Cold War: and promotion of the USA, 4–5
Colonialism: studies in Central America, 57–59
Connecticut: enslavement in, 30–31; links with the British Caribbean, 22–34; "Marcus and Amy" performance in, 266–268; trade with the Caribbean, 24–30
Contestation for space: Indo-Muslim women, 93–95, 109–112

Coolie Woman: The Odyssey of Indenture: Bahadur, 77, 79–82
Costa Rica: Afro-descendant history and BNC of, 64–67; black population in, 57
Coughlin, Father: James and, 18
Creole feminism: potential of a, 116–118
Creolization/decreolization model, 115
Cricket: as unifying Caribbean force, 170–171, 176–177
Cricket Chronicles, The: analysis of Rudder's, 168–177
Cross-racial conflict: migrant domestic workers and, 130–133
Cuba: Bonsal on, 46
Culture: and cognition, 211–218; and memory, 211–231; and mental distress, 210–211

Dance of Cloth: Minshall's, 318–319
Danse Macabre: Minshall carnival band, 323–324
Darul Uloom Institute, 105, 106, 108, 109–114
Declarative memory: defining, 212
Delano, Pablo, 307, 328; Minshall on, 310
Dementia: and ethnicity, 212–213
Democracy in America: James and influence of, 13
Deprest, Florence: as civilizing influence, 41
De Tocqueville, Alexis: influence on James, 13
Digit span tests: and memory, 214–215
Dish Ran Away with the Spoon, The: Caribbean TV documentary, 275, 278, 282–283
Distilling industry: in Connecticut, 26
Diversity: and anger, 209
Domestic workers: Caribbean migrant, 128–130, 135–140
Durrell, Lawrence: and islomania, 36–37
Dying Swan: by Peter Minshall, 307, 311

Education: and digit span performance, 216–217
El Salvador: Afro-descendant history and BNC of, 60
Emancipation: defining concept of, 253–254
Emancipation performance: JPTP and, 256–259
Enslaved seamen, 31–32
Enslavement: carnival and, 148–150, in Connecticut, 30–31; maritime, 31–33
Entertainment industry: in the USA, 146–148
Ethnicity: in Central American BNC, 59–60; dementia and, 212
Etic vs emic debate: on culture and distress, 210
Euraque, Dario, 328
European liberalism: James and, 11–13

Facebook: list of gender identities, 197
Female migrant workers: Caribbean, 126–139; Latino, 128–129
Feminism: Caribbean, 104–105; in carnival, 151–152; defining, 95–96, 117–118; in the Indo-Muslim community in T&T, 88–100; Islamic, 104–120
Fernea, Elizabeth: and Islamic feminism, 106
First World: concept of USA as, 4–5
Fitna: concept of the female, 90, 93, 96, 99
France, Arthur: and the Leeds carnival, 157
Francis, Ronald, 329
Free individuality: concept, 7, 8–9, 12
Future thinking: defining, 220–222; differences between prospective memory and, 222–224

Gangster-detective fictional figure: in US popular culture, 15–18
Garifuna, 57, 61–62
Garvey, Marcus: background, 252, 253–254; in Central America, 66–67, 254, 255–257

Gayelle: Caribbean TV magazine programme, 275, 276–277, 278–282
Guatemala: Afro-descendant history and BNC of, 61; slave population in, 57
Gedney Clarke Family, 33
Gender: defining, 196, 197–198; and Sex, 195–206
Gender ideology: in the Indo-Muslim community, 90–93
Grand Caribbean: defining the, xii
Grant, Eddy: and calypso music, 182–183, 186
Greenberg, Cheryl, 329
GLAAD: advocacy for LGBTQ rights, 205–206
Guterl, Mathew Pratt: and the American Mediterranean, 43–44
Gutierrez-Rodriguez, Encarnacion: on Latino migrant domestic workers in Western Europe, 128–129

Hacienda san Jeronimo: slave population in, 57
Haiti: US occupation of, 5
Hakk, Tony: and J'Ouvert, 155–156
Haleema: Muslim feminist, 110–114
Hall, Tony, 329–330
Harrison Bundey Troupe: political activism of, 153
Hawthorne, Captain Nathaniel: and the Connecticut-Caribbean trade, 32
Hayden, Horace: Caribbean links, 33
Health tourism: Mediterranean and, 45–46
Heritage Islam: and feminism, 115, 117
Hippolyte, Kendel: and Caribbean TV, 282
Historiography: revised Central American colonial, 55
Homosexuality: defining, 200
Honduras: Afro-descendant history and BNC of, 61–62; black population in, 57
Hosein, Gabrielle: and female sexuality in carnival, 161

Huizinga, Johann: and theatre, 258
Humboldt, Alexander von: and the Caribbean-Mediterranean analogy, 36
Hutchinson, Gerard, 330

Ice Records: and calypso, 183
Identity: art and, 308; culture and, 210
In Trinidad: by Pablo Delano, 310
Indian culture: reconstruction of, 89–100
Indian Diaspora: creation of an, 76–85, 88–100
Indian indentured labourers: migration of, 75–77; Muslim population and, 89
Indigenous studies: in BNCs, 58–59, 61–68
Individualism: in the USA, 7, 11–12
Indo-Muslim: community in Trinidad and Tobago, 88–99; women and religion in the, 88– 89, 90–93, 94
Indo-Caribbean literature: emergence of, 76–85
Information: human processing of, 211–212
Inside the People TV, 269, 271
Intergenerational upward mobility: among Caribbean migrant families, 139
Islam: and Muslims in T&T, 89
Islamic Academy, 115
Islamic feminism: in T&T, 105–120
Islamic Heritage: and feminism, 105–120
Islamic Resource Society, 115
Itinerant feminism: defining, 104–105, 118–120

James, C.L.R: and cricket, 171; and the USA, 2-4, 6
Jouvay Popular Theatre Process (JPTP): background of the, 256–259
J'Ouvert: in carnival, 154–155

Kala pani: and Indian-Caribbean migration, 75–78, 82, 84–85

Kassim, Halima: Muslim activist, 98, 330
Kempadoo-Miller, Rhian: and the Leeds carnival, 157
Khan, Katija, 330
Kincaid, Jamaica: and Caribbean female migrant workers, 127; 132–134
Kring, Brunhild, 331

La Costa: black population in, 57
Ladies Organization: and Islamic feminism, 109–112
Laird, Christopher, 331
Lamming, George: and the USA, 5
Language: and gender, 197; and Caribbean TV, 281–282
Latin America and the Caribbean (LAC): historical perspective of the USA, 1–3; and LGBTQ issues, 200
"Leave me Alone": and sexual abuse in carnival, 151–152
Leeds West Indian carnival: commercialization of, 157–160; 146, 150; political activism in the, 152
Leffingwell, Joshua: Caribbean links, 33
'Legacy': analysis of, 173
Legislation: and sexuality, 200–203
Lesbian, Gay, Bisexual, Transgender, Queer (LGBTQ): issues in T&T, 201–203, 210–211; and Research X-Change, 204–206
Liberal freedom: character of, 8, 11–13
Liverpool, Hollis Urban: on Caribbean carnival, 148–149
Long-term memory: defining, 212
Lovelace, Earl, 331–32
Lowenthal, David: and islands, 36–37
Lucy: Caribbean female migrant workers in, 127, 132–134, 139
'Lyrics man': analysis of, 172

Madame Hiroshima: Minshall's, 313–314
Maharaj-Best, Sunity, 332

Mancrab: Minshall's, 317
Marcus and Amy: performance of, 254–263
Marcus Garvey Popular Theatre Project, 254–263
Maritime enslavement, 30–33
Marshall, Emily, 332
Marshall, Paule: and Caribbean female migrant workers, 126, 129–130
Mas: significance of, 312
Mediterranean: Caribbean analogy, 36–50; geography of the, 38; slavery in the, 45; tourism in the, 45–47
Melville, Herman: James and, 8–9, 16–17
Memory: Caribbean TV as, 277–278, 285–288, 296–306; and culture in the Caribbean, 211–231
Men who have sex with men (MSM), 200
Mental distress: culture and, 210–211
Mental slavery: Garvey and the concept of, 253
Mestizaje. *See* Miscegenation.
Middle Ages: carnival in the, 146–149;
Middle East: Islamic practice in the, 104–107
Mighty Spoiler: music of, 269–271, 278, 283–286
Migration: Caribbean-Costa Rican, 64–67; Caribbean female workers and, 126–139; Caribbean-Panama, 63–64, 66; between Connecticut and the Caribbean, 32–34; identity and, 89–90; Indian, 75–77
Minorities: and exclusion, 209
Minshall, Peter: artists talk, 307–326; interview on Gayelle, 285–288;
Miscegenation: in Nicaragua, 62–63; in Panama, 66; in Spanish colonialism, 59–60, 66
Misrahi-Barak, Judith, 332
Mohammed, Farida, 97
Mohammed, Rose, 94–95, 98, 109

Mohammed, Zenobia, 94
Mohammed, Zoonnahar, 94
Moko Jumbie: as ballet, 315
'Money in the Bank': Mighty Spoiler, 269, 270
Morgan, Paula, 332
Mosques: sexism in, 88–99
Mother-daughter conflict: among Caribbean migrant families, 130–131, 139–140
Muhammad, Prophet: daughters of, teachings, 89
Museum of the Old Colony: of Puerto Rico, 247–249
Muslim feminism: defining, 105–106, 117, 118
Muslim population: in T&T, 88–99

Nabbie, Sarah: Muslim activist, 98
National Association for the Advancement of Coloured People (NAACP): and Garvey, 254
National Commission on the Status of Women, 94
National Muslim Women's Organization, 115
Neang Neak: Anida Ali's, 307
Neptune, H. Reuben, 333
New Deal: era, 7
New Orleans: comparison between Alexandria and, 43–44
New World: vs First World, 4, 6
Nicaragua: Afro-descendant history and BNC of, 62–63
'Notes on American Civilization': by C.L.R. James, 2

Orhni: symbolism of modesty of Indian women, 90–91

Panama: Afro-descendant history and BNC of, 63–64
Pedro, Consuelo, 333
Phillip, Theophilus. *See* Mighty Spoiler.
Phillips, Wendell: James and, 8
Piracy: of calypso and soca music, 187
Play: in Caribbean carnival, 152–156

Political activism: relating to sexuality, 202–203
Political satire: calypso and, 152–153
Popular arts: in the USA, 13–16
Prospective memory: culture and, 218–220; defining, 212; differences between future thinking and, 222–224
Puerto Rico: US occupation of, 247–249
Purdah: in the Muslim community, 90–91, 94–95, 96, 99

Queer: in the Caribbean, 199–200; defining, 195–197
Qu'ran: and equality of sexes in worship, 93–94

Racism: in *Brown Girl Brownstones*, 130–133, domestic migrant workers and, 136
'Rally Round the West Indies': analysis of, 171–172, 173
Raskin, Sarah A., 334
Reclus, Élisée: and the Caribbean-Mediterranean analogy, 40
Red Chador: Anida Ali's, 309, 320, 324–325
Red: Minshall's, 314
Reger, Gary, 334
Regis, Louis, 334
Religion: and sexual orientation, 201–203
Religious spaces: Indo Muslim women in the, 83–99
Reminiscence bump study; T&T, 225–227
Research X-Change, 193–195, 204–206
Resistance: Caribbean carnival as, 147–150; cricket as, 174
Revival of the Umma (ROU), 115–116
Rig, The: Caribbean TV programme, 275
Riggio, Milla Cozart, 334
River: 1983 T&T carnival band, 316–317
Rudder, David Michael: calypsonian, 165–177; and UWI Honoris Causa award, 165

Salima: Muslim activist, 116
Schechner, Richard; and Caribbean carnival, 147–148
Segregation: of men and women in worship, 90–91, 93, 111–113
Self-emancipation: Garvey and concept of, 153–154
Sensory memory: defining, 212
Sex: defining, 186; and gender, 195–206; and travel, 48
Sexual behavior: study of human, 196–197, 200
Sexual Offences Act: T&T, 200
Sexual orientation: defining, 198–200, 209–210
Sexuality: in carnival, 151–152, 160–161; and colour in popular literature, 46–47; and Indo-Muslim women, 90
Shias: in T&T, 88–89; and sexual separation, 93
Short-term memory: defining, 212
Sisters Association: and Islamic feminism, 109–112
Sitahal, Errol: and Caribbean TV, 283
Skin mas: in carnival, 160–161
Slavery: in the Caribbean, 47. *See also* Enslavement
'Smiling Eyes of Steel': analysis of, 173–175
Smith, Captain John: and the Connecticut-Caribbean trade, 32
Smith, Venture: enslaved seaman, 31–32
Soca: emergence of, 182–184
Sparrow: and award of the UWI PhD *honoris causa*, 167
St Augustine Campus (UWI): and Trinity College, 22–34
Star system: in US entertainment, 17–19
Strachen, Ian: and Caribbean tourism, 48
Studio Revolt: Anida Ali and, 309
Sunnah: in T&T Indo-Muslim community, 91
Sunnis: in T&T, 88–89

Swinging Bridge, The: Espinet, 77–79, 82–85

Tablighi movement: and worship practice of Indo-Muslim women, 94–95
Tackveeyatul Islamia Association (TIA): empowerment of Muslim women, 91, 92–93
Tan Tan and Saga Boy: Minshall's, 310–311
Television: identity and Caribbean, 269–306; as memory, 277–278, 285–288
Third World: concept of, 1, 5
Three Worlds' concept: USA and the, 1, 3, 4
Totalitarianism: James and US, 10–11, and entertainment in the US, 17–19
Tourism: island connection, 37; sex and, 45–47
Trade: between USA and the Caribbean, 23–24
Transgender: defining, 197
Transsexuals: defining, 197
Travel: and sex, 48–50
Trinbagonian Muslim women: activism through Islam, 105–106, 108
Trinidad and Tobago (T&T): autobiographical memory in, 227–230; Islamic feminism in, 105–120; Muslim population in, 88–89; performance of "Marcus and Amy" in, 265; reminiscence bump study, 225–227; sexuality and legal issues in, 200–203; US occupation of, 5
Trinidad carnival, 146–162, 307–326; commercialization of, 157–158
Trinity College: Caribbean connections, 22, 34
'Trumpism': *American Civilization* and, 4
Turner, Frederick Jackson: James and, 9
Turner, Victor: on J'Ouvert, 154; on carnival and power, 147; and performance in theatre, 257–258

UNAIDS Study: on sexuality, 201–203
United Nations Educational, Scientific and Cultural organization (UNESCO): research on African diaspora curriculum in Central America, 56–60
United States of America (USA): in American Civilization, 2–19; Garvey and the, 254, 255; LAC's historical perspective of the, 1–3; occupation of Puerto Rico, 247–249
Universal Negro Improvement Association (UNIA): in Central America, 66–67; Garvey and the, 253, 254
University of Connecticut: and the UWI, 22, 34
University of the West Indies (UWI): and University of Connecticut, 22, 34
Upward mobility: Caribbean domestic migrant workers and, 130
US Television: Caribbean culture and the impact of,

Vannini, Margarita: and Afro-descent presence in Nicaraguan history, 63
Visual art: carnival as, 285–288, 307–326

Walcott Derek: and the USA 5–6; and carnival, 156; and Caribbean TV, 275, 283
Warriorhood: in Caribbean cricket, 172, 174–175
Washerwoman: Minshall's, 317
Wechsler Adult Intelligence Scale (WAIS–111): and digit span, 215
West Indian Theatre: Garvey and, 255
White box: art and the concept of the, 313–314, 315
Whitman, Walt: James and, 8
Who the C.A.P. Fits: Caribbean soap opera, 269, 275–276

Williams, Dr Eric: and trade between US and the British Caribbean, 23–24, 28

Women: in Anida Ali's art, 309; and carnival, 151–152, 160–161; James and, 10–11; religion and Indo-Muslim, 88–89, 90–93; migration and Caribbean, 126–139

Workers: Caribbean female migrant, 126–139

Working memory: and culture, 216–218; defining, 212; and digit span, 214–218

YouTube: and calypso music, 186

www.ingramcontent.com/pod-product-compliance
Lightning Source LLC
Chambersburg PA
CBHW050835230426
43667CB00012B/2007